UNGRAMMATI

CW01429283

Linguistic Literary Criticism from
The Battle of Maldon to Muriel Spark

G M E Burchett-Vass

MAPLE
PUBLISHERS

Ungrammaticalities: Linguistic Literary Criticism from *The Battle of Maldon* to Muriel Spark

Author: G M E Burchett-Vass

Copyright © G M E Burchett-Vass (2023)

The right of G M E Burchett-Vass to be identified as author of this work has been asserted by the author in accordance with section 77 and 78 of the Copyright, Designs and Patents Act 1988.

First Published in 2023

ISBN 978-1-915996-82-4 (Paperback)
      978-1-915996-83-1 (eBook)

Book cover design and Book layout by:

Maple Publishers
www.maplepublishers.com

Published by:

Maple Publishers
Fairbourne Drive, Atterbury,
Milton Keynes,
MK10 9RG, UK
www.maplepublishers.com

A CIP catalogue record for this title is available from the British Library.

Foreword

In a retelling of Ovid by Nicole Ward Jouve, *Narcissus and Echo*, Narcissus becomes Miranda, a writer equally celebrated for her works and her beauty. She graciously presides over a quasi-academic conference about her own poems and plays, where her reader-admirers compete for her attention. They offer an unqualified devotion, and their eyes become the multi-ocular lake in which she admires herself; their exclusively laudatory criticism is the multiplied echo of her self-esteem.

The narrative is focalised by the increasingly unhappy central character Heloise – who, feeling her love rejected, actually dares to deliver a more analytic paper. The complex experience of reading's challenges and reaching a critical understanding is truncated in Jouve's wry fable into a meeting of a perfectionist author-as-monster and her cult of adulatory followers.

The true complexity of how narratives are delivered, and how readers bring their own literary experience to the text, is the continuous subject of *Ungrammaticalities*. G. M. E. Burchett-Vass always keeps actual writers at a distance, and the attention is where it should be, on what appears on the page - verbally, visually, or both. Narratives, we are firmly told, just cannot be studied independently of the forms they take.

Each of the discussions gathered here could serve as a model of critical writing to any students who seek to achieve real literary competence - and could equally be a model to a large proportion of academics. What is inculcated, by many examples, are the rewards of acquiring stylistic tools for understanding narrative, with no side-tracks into biographical material, no over-sold contextual exposition or merely personal re-invention. This is criticism by a completely convincing reader, who writes a precise and decisive prose, and gives her readers helpful and selective exposition of major critical positions. A wide range of texts are persuasively discussed. These essays and chapters never prompt that sinking moment when an informed reader suddenly distrusts the critic they are reading. All readers here will think, yes, you really have read this. Well-chosen examples are discussed with such acuity that when a more general remark about the works of the writer under scrutiny is made, it is accepted as an informed view worth thinking about as a further enrichment of our reader experience.

The writer has chosen Michael Riffaterre's critical term 'Ungrammaticalities' as her main title – it has a special sense, which she explains in the expert summary of intertextuality that precedes her discussion of a group of very literary poems by the poet-academic John Heath-Stubbs. Maybe 'Ungrammaticalities' makes the collection sound more stern than it is: the essays offered here expound with a lively wit the things we might have been half aware of, or should have noticed, when we slap-dashed through the text ourselves. The pole star here is stylistics-based reading, while the attractive magnetic north is Muriel Spark. There is an implicit case for the importance of Spark's fiction, the reader being convinced of why Spark's novels and shorter fictions should be read, and how.

Perhaps the most read and applauded essay in this collection (when posted online) shows the author's readerly enjoyment of Gothic fictions and insight into their writerly delivery, when we are offered an account of the subtle horror Shirley Jackson's *A Visit* just as lucid as those we get of Spark's acerbic fictions (which themselves so coolly accommodate the supernatural).

Balancing the fictional minds in novels and short stories is a forceful discussion of the presence of well realised fictional minds in the medium the critic firmly calls comics, otherwise 'graphic novels'. The main exemplifying text is Rachael Ball's *The Inflatable Woman* (2015). The argument defends the medium, and opens out to the reader the ever-expanding field of its legitimate scholarly analysis. This is quite a shift from a writer (Spark) who could tartly require her readers to read the emotion 'between the lines'. The emotion is in the drawn lines of every panel discussed: the pathos of Rachael Ball's avatar Iris Pink-Percy, her fear about her cancer diagnosis, her hopes: in short, her fully-realised fictional consciousness.

This is a collection of critical essays of unfailing interest, and it is quite arresting to notice that some of the essays were non-obligate, that is, not written for a formal academic submission, but written simply as an expression of enjoyment and discovery. Those web-posted essays are somewhat less formally academic, but what a marvellous thing – good criticism written to share informed enjoyment. But as the writer of this Foreword, I will stop here, lest like 'Andreas K***' in Jouve's fable, I dissolve into quotations.

Dr R J Booth,
University of London. October 2023
('Narcissus and Echo' can be read in
Ovid Metamorphosed ed. Philip Terry [Vintage, 2001].)

Table of Contents

Preface

I first read Geoffrey Leech and Mick Short's *Style in Fiction* when I was working as an English teacher on New Zealand's south island, and it is no exaggeration to say that this marvellous book completely changed the way in which I read and was the stepping stone to fourteen or fifteen years of research, of which this book is the culmination. The book's initial section, *Style and the Form/Content Dichotomy*, is the document which was submitted for a Master's Degree at the University of Auckland, and which owes much to Leech and Short's work. This section is also available as a separate publication under the same title from Lambert Academic Publishing (2011).

The second section comprises work completed towards a PhD at the University of East Anglia, which I eventually abandoned. My subject was repetition in the novels and short stories of Muriel Spark, hence the focus in this book's second section is on Spark's idiosyncratic use of repetition, the nature of truth, and – connected to the latter – the *Verfremdungseffekt* of her pared-down style which aims to eliminate the creation of sympathy in the reader. I still think there is a valuable thesis to be written on this subject, but it will not be me who writes it.

In 2015 I became a postgraduate student for the third time at the University of Nottingham, where I completed their MA in Literary Linguistics, and the third section of the book is a compilation of essays and exercises completed during the course of this degree. The book's final section is less academic in tone because it mostly comprises a selection of the more popular blog posts published over the years on www.auntymuriel.com. The blog has been a repository for my writing for over a decade (at the time of writing), and the decision to publish my work in book form came about as a result of the realisation that when I can no longer finance the blog, the work will be lost, and I'd really rather that didn't happen.

After spending so many years in libraries, my enthusiasm for writing has exhausted itself and whether this is a hiatus or a now-permanent state of affairs is yet to be seen. The remainder of this preface is devoted to notes and disclaimers about the book to follow; the book's cobbled-together nature makes these observations necessary.

I take my title from a term coined by Michael Riffaterre, referring to a marker which functions as a site of significance for the (ideal) reader who can both identify and interpret it. This is explained further in the essay on intertextuality in the poetry of John Heath-Stubbs.

The referencing systems used change after the first section: I switch from MHRA to Harvard, because those systems were stipulated as a requirement by the universities of Auckland (MHRA) and UEA and Nottingham (Harvard). Harvard is the more popular referencing system in these days of electronic texts and publications, because the footnoting system of MHRA necessitates much flicking back and forth online which is less than ideal. I have not used MHRA since 2007; nevertheless, I baulked at the amount of work required to rewrite *Style and the Form/Content Dichotomy* with Harvard referencing, and have contented myself with leaving it as it is and confessing to my own indolence in this preface.

I ought to mention also the inward tussles I experienced over whether to use *s* or *z* in words such as realise, *-ize*, specialise, *-ize*, and, most importantly, focalise, *-ize*. My preference is for *s* every time, but almost all the sources I consulted spell *focalize* with a *z*, so I reached the rather unsatisfactory compromise of throwing in the towel and using a *z* for *focalize*, *focalizer*, *focalization* (et cetera), and an *s* for everything else.

Some references are missing or incomplete in the long essay on Spark's use of repetition in *The Bachelors*, *The Ballad of Peckham Rye*, and *A Member of the Family*; I have done my best to locate these references but have been unsuccessful, for which I apologise.

Finally, the index is my own work. I felt strongly that the book would benefit from having an index but couldn't afford to employ someone to do this for me, so I had a go myself. I apologise in advance for its shortcomings being, as it is, a first attempt at indexing.

I hope the book is both interesting and useful to its readers, and with that, I leave you to it.

G Mildred E Burchett-Vass

April 2024

Stylistics and the Form/ Content Dichotomy: 2005-2007

Introduction

i) What is stylistics?

Modern stylistics has existed in one form or another since Charles Bally coined the term *stylistique* in 1909, but its roots arguably lie 'in the *elocutio* of Aristotelian rhetorical studies'.[1] In spite of its longevity, however, stylistics as a discipline continues to resist definition, owing perhaps to its restless absorption of the newest linguistic models and theories, and its chameleonic adaptation to the prevailing linguistic *Zeitgeist*. A corollary of this particular characteristic is that stylistics has collected many different names along the way: literary stylistics, literary linguistics, linguistic stylistics, linguistic criticism, the new stylistics, practical stylistics, and so forth. At its most basic level, stylistics is the study of literary style, and its proponents base their analyses of literary texts in predominantly, although not necessarily exclusively, linguistic analysis. Paul Simpson, a practitioner in this field, writes that 'what…sets stylistics apart from other types of critical practice is its emphasis, first and foremost, on the *language* of the text…what captures the essence of the stylistic method is the *primacy* which it assigns to language'.[2]

In recent years two disciplines closely related to stylistics have grown rapidly: first that of cognitive linguistics, 'where language, thought, and conceptualization are seen to be *embodied*',[3] a field of inquiry with which I am not concerned in this thesis, and second, that of critical linguistics. The scope of critical linguistics extends far beyond texts perceived as literary, and its motivating principle is 'to explore the value systems and sets of beliefs which reside in texts; to explore, in other words, *ideology* in language'.[4] It is perhaps this attention to 'the social function of linguistic structures in literature'[5] which has prompted David Robey to write that 'stylistics has…begun to converge with aspects of Marxist criticism',[6] a statement that is more properly true of critical linguistics. However, the two disciplines of stylistics and critical

---

1   K. Green, 'Literary Theory and Stylistics', *Encyclopedia of Language & Linguistics* (2006), p. 261. Green notes that '*elocutio* dealt with the appropriateness of the expression and the relevance of its stylistic choices.'

2   P. Simpson, *Language, Ideology and Point of View* (1993), p. 3.

3   K. Green, 'Literary Theory and Stylistics', *Encyclopedia of Language & Linguistics* (2006), p. 265.

4   P. Simpson, *Language, Ideology and Point of View* (1993), p. 5.

5   D. Robey, 'Modern Linguistics and the Language of Literature', *Modern Literary Theory: A Comparative Introduction* (1986), p. 70.

6   Ibid., p. 71.

linguistics do often overlap – in the study of transitivity, for example, to which I shall return in chapter three.

To fully grasp the aims and objectives of stylistics, it is useful to have some idea of what was perceived as deficient in the pre-existing critical *status quo*. The twentieth century witnessed a great deal of critical activity and the emergence of numerous critical approaches ranging from Russian Formalism to deconstruction and semiotics to psychoanalytic theory. And yet for all this activity, when critic Ian Watt was asked in 1960 to write a paper on the style of Henry James, he described himself as 'virtually helpless...as far as any fully developed and acceptable technique of explicating prose is concerned'.[7] The 'acceptable technique' was still conspicuous by its absence in 1964 when Richard Ohmann wrote 'the most serviceable studies of style continue to proceed from the critic's naked intuition, fortified against the winds of ignorance only by literary sophistication and the tattered garments of traditional grammar'.[8] And more recently still, Michael Toolan has written that

> reading and writing about complex texts are skills, and...literary linguistics can be an invaluable crutch or catalyst.... There remain many graduate teachers of English...who lack the procedures – and procedural confidence – even to get started on their own communicable assessment of a Stevens poem or a Heaney sonnet.[9]

There are now some excellent stylistics textbooks available, such as those by H. G. Widdowson, Rob Pope, and Paul Simpson,[10] not to mention Geoffrey Leech and Mick Short's seminal *Style in Fiction*, designed to help both teachers and students of literature negotiate the arguably uncharted terrain of literary style. Katie Wales, the author of *A Dictionary of Stylistics*, notes that stylistics 'also helps students to be more independent in their judgments,

---

7   I. Watt, 'The First Paragraph of "The Ambassadors": An Explication', *Essays in Criticism* (1960), p. 253.

8   R. Ohmann, 'Generative Grammars and the Concept of Literary Style' (1964), *Linguistics and Literary Style* (1970), D. C. Freeman (editor), p. 262. Ohmann wrote in an earlier article that the study of style had necessarily been inclined 'to rely *only* on those impressionistic, metaphorical judgments which have too often substituted for analysis: dignified, grand, plain, decorative, placid, exuberant, restrained, hard, and the whole tired assortment of epithets which name without explaining.' R. Ohmann, 'Prolegomena to the Analysis of Prose Style', *Style in Prose Fiction* (1958), H. C. Martin (editor), pp. 1-24.

9   M. Toolan, *The Stylistics of Fiction: A Literary-Linguistic Approach* (1990), pp. 42-43.

10   H. G. Widdowson, *Stylistics and the Teaching of Literature* (1975), R. Pope, *Textual Intervention: Critical and Creative Strategies for Literary Studies* (1995), and P. Simpson, *Stylistics: A Resource Book for Students* (2004). Stylistics textbooks have therefore been available since the mid-1970s at least, but Toolan wrote the words quoted above in 1990 (see footnote 9). Toolan's words are really about the fact that stylistics had *not* at that time been widely adopted in English departments.

by forming their own interpretations of literary texts based on close readings and to be more confident in articulating them'.[11] The confident articulation of literary judgments has been facilitated by the precise and rigorous vocabulary of linguistic analysis that has been imported into stylistic studies. Keith Green writes that:

> stylistics arose partly because of the need in literary criticism to work with a set of agreed-upon and defined terms for the analysis and description of a particular kind of language, the language of literature. Such a language…would be built upon modern linguistic analysis.[12]

Relatively speaking, linguistic terms have well-established and inflexible meanings; there is a large core terminology and set of concepts that most linguistic models draw on, but it is also the case that alternative theories and/or models tend to be accompanied by new technical terms.[13] Nevertheless, it is still true to say that there is more agreement over the precise meaning of linguistic terms than there is over some of the terms routinely used in literary criticism – 'style' itself being a case in point, a term much-used and perhaps little understood.[14] And it is important that people who have essentially the same goal in view should understand one another. Vague and flabby terms simply add to the general confusion.

---

11   K. Wales, 'Stylistics', *Encyclopedia of Language & Linguistics* (2006), p. 214.

12   K. Green, 'Literary Theory and Stylistics', *Encyclopedia of Language & Linguistics* (2006), p. 261.

13   I am indebted to Jim Miller for this information.

14   Ohmann has defined style as 'a characteristic use of language' ('Generative Grammars and the Concept of Literary Style' (1964), p. 262), but critical essays on 'style' seem to be wide-ranging in their discussion, taking in everything from the social conditions surrounding the production of the work to the minutiae of the author's psychology. In his essay 'On the Style of Vanity Fair' (reprinted in *Style in Prose Fiction* (1958), Harold C. Martin (editor), pp. 87-113), G. Armour Craig focuses his discussion on the distance Thackeray establishes between the novel's narratorial voice and its characters; the reader is left to infer that which the narrator pretends not to know and does not tell. To be fair, Craig's essay does not pretend to be about *Thackeray's* style; the title makes reference to the style of this particular *novel*. Even so, what is under discussion here is surely a matter of technique – Craig's essay would be helpful in a discussion centred on narrative point of view, but it tells us very little about Thackeray's 'characteristic use of language'. An essay by Albrecht Strauss reprinted in the same volume ('On Smollett's Language: A Paragraph in *Ferdinand Count Fathom*', pp. 25-54) appears more promising. While Strauss' essay is arguably nearer the mark, one is still left with a list of techniques – use of formulaic method, stock phrases and eighteenth-century periphrasis, recurrence of animal imagery, and so on – all of which would enable a reader to produce a Smollettian parody, but, as Strauss himself notes, does not 'account for the robustness and verve of style which most readers of Smollett will rightly consider to be peculiarly his' (pp. 49-50). Strauss suggests that Smollett's voice is so difficult to isolate because 'the *persona* of the detached narrator' is largely absent. Strauss also links his observations to genre: he notes that in Smollett, what fails in pathos succeeds brilliantly in farcical comedy. Between them, Craig and Strauss discuss literary techniques, literary genre and narratorial point of view in their essays on 'style', but it could be argued that neither critic manages to identify the 'characteristic use of language' of the authors in question.

Hence the discipline of stylistics has grown considerably in response to the various demands of students, teachers, and critics: a demand in the first instance for a workable technique of literary analysis applicable in particular to prose texts. Stylistics furnishes the student of literature with a starting point. A preliminary linguistic analysis based, for example, on the checklist provided by Leech and Short in chapter three of their *Style in Fiction*[15] provides a way of collecting data to be analysed.

My final point in this brief survey is that in grounding the analysis in the text itself, stylistics avoids the pitfall of bending the text to fit the theory. In a spectacular swing away from the text-centred theories that dominated the first half of the twentieth century, critical approaches to literature from roughly the 1960s onwards grew increasingly alienated from the text, prompting Wolfgang Iser to write in 1974:

> all too often literary critics tend to produce their theories on the basis of an esthetics that is predominantly abstract, derived from and conditioned by philosophy rather than by literature – with the regrettable result that they reduce texts to the proportions of their theories, instead of adapting their theories to fit in with the texts.[16]

By way of contrast, Keith Green notes that 'stylistics in its anglicized form has tended to eschew the philosophical complexities and self-reflexive obsessions of literary theory.'[17] For some, stylistics answers the need to return to the words on the page, with the advantage of having discarded the inhibiting notion of 'literariness' championed by the Russian Formalists and having also shed the somewhat whimsical concept of verbal iconicity advocated by the Anglo-American New Critics.

There are, it would seem, many benefits to be reaped from a close working partnership between the two separate disciplines of linguistics and literary criticism. Critics gain a methodology and a vocabulary with which to formulate

---

15   G. Leech and M. Short, *Style in Fiction* (1981), chapter three, pp. 75-82.

16   W. Iser, *The Implied Reader* (1974), introduction, p. xi. To quote from personal experience, I recently consulted a collection of critical essays in the hope that someone would be able to shed some light on the text of Franz Kafka's *The Trial* (*Twentieth Century Interpretations of 'The Trial': A Collection of Critical Essays* (1976), J. Rolleston, editor). Instead I found that each critic interpreted the story according to his or her favoured theory. It did not escape my attention how easily Kafka's text could be bent around any particular reading applied to it: a circumstance which may reveal how slippery the text is, and how difficult it is to pin any one interpretation to Joseph K's ordeal. The most interesting reading by far was a semiotic investigation of Kafka's text (T. M. Kavanagh, 'Kafka's "The Trial": The Semiotics of the Absurd', ibid., pp. 86-93), which pinpoints K's inability to decipher the codes and signs.

17   K. Green, 'Literary Theory and Stylistics', *Encyclopedia of Language & Linguistics* (2006), p. 262.

and support their literary hypotheses, and linguists acquire a fertile testing ground – literary texts – on which to try out their latest theories: 'linguistic models offer a "way in" to a text, while the text itself allows for a challenging application for those models'.[18] But in spite of the mutual advantages to be gained from such a partnership, there exists a long and well-documented history of antagonism between linguists and literary critics, with, it appears, much blinkered obstinacy and wilful misunderstanding on both sides of the fence.[19]

Literary hackles were early raised by the strident and aggressive war-cries of linguists who made far-reaching claims for their subject,[20] and linguists were in their turn infuriated by the critics' ignorance of basic linguistic concepts, their lack of familiarity with the range of published material, and their assumption that linguists were simply mentally ill-equipped to deal with literary texts. It is the fate of the stylistician to have been caught in the No Man's Land between the two camps, linguistic and critical. A more detailed understanding of the peculiar position occupied by the stylistician can be partially achieved by a brief consideration of some of the objections raised against stylistics and a look at how – or if – these objections have been countered.

One criticism of stylistics frequently voiced is that there is little, if any, difference between a textual analysis purporting to be linguistic and the literary critic's activity of close reading. For the linguists at least this is not considered a problem. In 1966 Fowler wrote that 'modern descriptive linguistics is a natural companion to modern criticism because both are text-centred: both involve analysis, close reading, and both set a premium on accuracy and usefulness of description'.[21] But some critics apparently do not want such a companion and feel affronted by those linguists who presume to encroach upon their territory – hankering after 'literary forbidden fruit', as Helen Vendler puts it.[22] In 'The Limitations of Stylistics', Peter Barry comments upon Fowler's essay

18   P. Simpson, *Language, Ideology and Point of View* (1993), p. 4.

19   This antagonism is incisively documented in chapter one of M. Toolan's *The Stylistics of Fiction: A Literary-Linguistic Approach* (1990), pp. 1-27.

20   R. Fowler quotes both Harold Whitehall and Roman Jakobson in his essay 'The New Stylistics', *Style and Structure in Literature* (1975), R. Fowler (editor) pp. 1-18. Whitehall wrote 'as no science can go beyond mathematics, no criticism can go beyond its linguistics', and Jakobson is quoted as follows: 'poetics deals with problems of verbal structure.... Since linguistics is the global science of verbal structure, poetics may be regarded as an integral part of linguistics' (p. 1).

21   R. Fowler, 'Linguistics, Stylistics; Criticism?', *Lingua*, 16 (1966), pp. 157-158.

22   H. H. Vendler, book review of *Essays on Style and Language: Linguistic and Critical Approaches to Literary Styles* (1966), R. Fowler (editor), *Essays in Criticism*, XVI (1966), p. 457.

'Language and the Reader: Shakespeare's Sonnet 73'[23] as follows: 'nothing in this interpretation of the poem's imagery would be beyond the scope of conventional close-reading – indeed, it seems precisely the kind of observation which close-reading fosters'.[24] Barry also observes that presenting an insight 'in linguistic dress…does not convert it into something intrinsically linguistic'.[25] The frustration felt by the literary critics would be entirely understandable were it not for the fact that there is an important difference between a stylistic analysis and a close reading, as explained by Short:

> there is some considerable overlap between stylistic analysis and the more detailed forms of practical criticism.[26] The difference is, in part, one of degree rather than kind. Practical critics use evidence from the text, and therefore sometimes the language of the text, to support what they say. But the evidence tends to be much more selective than that which a stylistician would want to bring to bear. In that sense, stylistics is the *logical extension* of practical criticism. In order to avoid as much as possible the dangers of partiality, stylisticians…try to make their descriptions and analyses as *detailed*, as *systematic* and as *thorough* as possible.[27]

This summary of the stylistician's analytical approach may be somewhat idealistic, but Short's words do at least highlight the distance between a comprehensive stylistic analysis and close reading – the difference is in the levels of selectivity and partiality. But whether or not a stylistician can really lay claim to a complete absence of selectivity in her analyses brings me to the second criticism often levelled at stylistics as a discipline – that its claim to objectivity is spurious.

In *Exploring the Language of Poems, Plays and Prose*, Short writes that 'an enduring problem in literary criticism is that critics sometimes come to partial conclusions by concentrating on some aspects of a text to the exclusion of others'.[28] But, critics argue, the same is true of stylisticians. If stylistics is to lay claim to a scientific objectivity, then each and every stylistic analysis of a text should be utterly exhaustive – otherwise the stylistician, like the critic,

---

23   R. Fowler, 'Language and the Reader: Shakespeare's Sonnet 73', *Style and Structure in Literature* (1975), pp. 79-122.

24   P. Barry, 'The Limitations of Stylistics', *Essays in Criticism*, XXXVIII (1988), p. 182.

25   Ibid., p. 181.

26   'The more detailed forms of practical criticism' would presumably exclude the practical criticism of I. A. Richards, which ultimately privileges reader response over exhaustive textual analysis.

27   M. Short, *Exploring the Language of Poems, Plays and Prose* (1996), p. 6.

28   Ibid., p. 356.

lays herself open to the charge of focusing only on those areas of the text which actively support her original hypothesis. But can there be such a thing as a truly exhaustive description of a literary text? Such a description, even of a short poem, would be of considerable length;[29] exhaustive descriptions have been attempted in the past, only to be vilified for their tedium and their ultimate failure to shed any new light on the text in question.[30] Any reasonably exhaustive analysis of a poem is bound to throw up a great deal of information which is of little or no interest to a literary critic[31] – and an exhaustive analysis of a novel would take years, possibly decades, to complete, and is therefore quite impractical. So one must concede that the stylistician is indeed selective when it comes to choosing areas of a text on which to focus. Opponents of stylistics have not failed to point this out and stylisticians themselves have not attempted to deny this: 'any attempt to write a complete grammar of the poem would be gratuitous and would obscure the object of the analysis, for "one doesn't want to know every syntactic fact about a poem; one wants to know the significant ones".'[32]

But in fact stylisticians do not make their claim to objectivity on the basis of whether or not their analyses are exhaustive. The stylistician's objectivity is allegedly centred in her methods and the uses to which the data gathered is put. She revolves around linguistic data and literary hypothesis in a circular movement first described by linguist-critic Leo Spitzer, and summarised here by Katie Wales:

> [Spitzer's] concept of the *philological circle*...is characteristic of the stylistician's procedure still today: constantly and delicately moving between hypothesis, linguistic analysis of data, and critical explanation and aesthetic response, with a revised hypothesis if necessary.[33]

The deficiency of practical criticism as it stands is that the movement from intuition to text is not balanced by any movement back towards the

---

29   M.A.K. Halliday recognises that 'the only ultimately valid unit for textual analysis is the whole text', but he also acknowledges the difficulties inherent in this conclusion: 'it takes many hours of talking to describe exhaustively even the language of one sonnet'. M.A.K. Halliday, 'Descriptive Linguistics in Literary Studies' (1964), *Linguistics and Literary Style* (1970), D. C. Freeman (editor), p. 58.

30   An example of such an essay is D. Hymes' 'Phonological Aspects of Style: Some English Sonnets', *Style in Language* (1960), T. Sebeok (editor), pp. 109-131.

31   Mikhail Bakhtin argued that 'the linguistic analysis of a poetic work has no criteria for separating what is poetically significant from what is not'. M. Bakhtin, 'The Formal Method in Literary Scholarship' (1928), *The Bakhtin Reader* (1994), P. Morris (editor), p. 145.

32   R. Fowler, 'The New Stylistics', *Style and Structure in Literature* (1975), p. 6. Fowler quotes D. Freeman, 'The Strategy of Fusion: Dylan Thomas's Syntax', ibid., p. 21.

33   K. Wales, 'Stylistics', *Encyclopedia of Language & Linguistics* (2006), p. 215.

original hypothesis. The critic's first intuitive interpretation is allowed to stand unchallenged. It may even be the case that words and phrases that are unhelpful, or that actively contradict the critic's hypothesis, are simply ignored. Spitzer's method of constantly oscillating between text and interpretation should, in theory, remove all, or at least part, of the danger of selecting *only* those details which usefully support an initial arbitrary reading.

Other stylisticians have voiced their opinions in the objectivity debate. Short argues that if a stylistician formulates an interpretation of a literary text before conducting a linguistic analysis, she is not being any less objective:

> objectivity comes not from the order in which you do things, but in being systematic and careful in your argument, not overlooking unhelpful facts, and, in more general terms, constructing a clear and detailed relationship between your interpretative hypothesis on the one hand and your analysis on the other.[34]

As with the previous examples, it is the close relationship between linguistic data and literary interpretation that is highlighted. Simpson takes a different tack in playing down any original claim to objectivity that the stylistician may or may not have made. He describes what he believes to be a common misconception:

> the analyst stands by disinterestedly while the linguistic machine squeezes out of a text whatever meanings have been put there by the writer. Yet few stylisticians claim such objectivity. They prefer to recognise instead that all interpretations are in some sense context-bound and are contingent on the position of the analyst relative to the text.[35]

In recognising that interpretation and criticism do not take place in isolation – that these activities are communal rather than individual – Simpson brings stylistics into the realm of literary pragmatics, a field of inquiry that 'is concerned with the user's role in the societal production and consumption of texts'.[36]

To recap the arguments so far, then. The literary critics accuse the stylisticians of doing nothing more than producing close readings of literary texts and passing them off as linguistic analyses. The stylisticians reply that there is a certain amount of truth in this, but that their readings differ from those

---

34   M. Short, *Exploring the Language of Poems, Plays and Prose* (1996), p. 358.

35   P. Simpson, *Language, Ideology and Point of View* (1993), p. 3.

36   J. L. Mey, 'Literary Pragmatics', *Encyclopedia of Language & Linguistics* (2006), p. 256.

of the critics because a stylistic reading is supposedly more comprehensive, more meta-theoretical and more self-aware. But while stylisticians gather more extensive linguistic data, there is always an element of selectivity involved. So is stylistics therefore just a more technical version of practical criticism? Apparently not, because the stylistician's claim to objectivity derives from her working methods and meta-methods.

However – and here we come to the most serious charge levelled at stylistics and those who practise it – critics have claimed, with some justification, that these working methods are very far from being infallible; it has been suggested that the link between the linguistic data gathered and the interpretation finally offered is frequently tenuous, with the result that in the end a stylistic interpretation of a given text is equally as arbitrary in nature as the exegesis supplied by a literary critic relying solely on her critical perception and intuition. Stanley Fish is one such critic who has put forward this argument. In response to Ohmann's work on transformational grammar, Fish has written that 'a stylistician will interpose a formidable apparatus between his descriptive and interpretive acts, thus obscuring the absence of any connection between them'.[37] John Russell earlier voiced a similar concern: in what is a measured and tactful response to Ohmann's article 'Literature as Sentences', Russell comments on the effort involved in sifting through the linguistic apparatus necessary to Ohmann's way of proceeding. While conceding that Ohmann's work seems 'just what is needed in one way for alerting critics brought up under traditional grammar and rhetoric',[38] Russell notes that he is 'led to wonder, since meaning is the final goal of the analyst, whether the yield is worth the effort if so much that is intuitional must be worked over first',[39] and he concludes that 'a traditional rhetorical analysis… would take one further and faster toward the same goal'.[40] The charge, then, is that stylisticians inevitably produce the same or similar interpretations as

---

37 S. Fish, 'What Is Stylistics and Why Are They Saying Such Terrible Things About It?' (1972), *Approaches to Poetics* (1973), S. Chatman (editor), p. 114. Fish also notes on page 113 of the same article that 'a serious defect in the procedures of stylistics [is] the absence of any constraint on the way in which one moves from description to interpretation, with the result that any interpretation one puts forward is arbitrary.'

38 J. Russell, 'From Style to Meaning in "Araby": Comment and Rebuttal', *College English*, (1966), p. 170.

39 Ibid. I would like to add that though meaning may or may not be 'the final goal of the analyst', it is not the final goal of the teacher. The teacher is far more interested in imparting an understanding of *how* the text works, in order to enable the student to formulate readings of other literary texts independently of her teacher. This is an area perhaps where a stylistic approach is demonstrably more useful than a traditional analysis.

40 Ibid.

critics intuitively produce, but a stylistician needs more time to arrive at the same destination because she takes a lengthy detour down twisting linguistic byways. In addition, this detour is an unnecessary one, because the end result is the same: a critical reading based on intuition instead of empirical facts in spite of the stylistician's claims to the contrary.

How is one to answer this charge? There is certainly a grain of truth in the critics' claims. It is easy enough to find examples of linguistic readings of literary texts that either describe the grammatical structure of the text without contributing anything to a discussion of its meaning,[41] or there are those readings whose comments on the meaning of the text are only loosely linked to the accompanying linguistic analysis; I have already cited Barry's criticisms of Fowler's work as an example of the latter. However, it is equally possible to find instances of linguistic – or stylistic – readings that *do* make sensitive and perceptive comments on literary texts, and whose comments *are* grounded in linguistic analysis: for example, Fowler's discussion concerning point of view in Hemingway's 'The Killers',[42] and Leech and Short's astute and discerning textual interpretations in chapter three of *Style in Fiction*.[43] I would argue that one also has to ask what was expected at the outset – is stylistics supposed to provide the reader with a foolproof method of determining the 'meaning' of a literary work? The idea of the stylistician and the literary critic reaching the same destination contains an implicit assumption that there is a single 'meaning' to be found, which is unlikely to be the case. George Dillon writes with refreshing frankness on this subject:

> what sort of knowledge, then, can linguistic analysis provide the student of literature...? It cannot be a discovery procedure for finding interpretations, nor can it be a proof or validation of an interpretation... One engages in formal analysis to specify and articulate one's own response and perhaps to share it with others. It seems as though we are providing the grounds of our response, and from grounds to causes is but a short step, but in fact we may only be working out the consequences and ramifications of our response, according to rather loose and flexible canons governing how responses can be grounded in texts and with

---

41 For example, M.A.K. Halliday's analysis of 'Leda and the Swan' in 'Descriptive Linguistics in Literary Studies' (1964), *Linguistics and Literary Style* (1970), D. C. Freeman (editor); Halliday makes two separate points about the grammar of the poem, but he does not pursue these points any further with reference to literary effect, or the poem's meaning.

42 R. Fowler, *Linguistics and the Novel* (1977), pp. 48-55.

43 G. Leech and M. Short, *Style in Fiction* (1981), chapter 3, pp. 74-118. The texts studied are Joseph Conrad's *The Secret Sharer*, D. H. Lawrence's *Odour of Chrysanthemums*, and Henry James' *The Pupil*.

ample scope left for the ingenuity of the critic in formulating the poem's 'fashion of speaking'.[44]

With these words, Dillon sits contentedly in a comfortable middle-ground. Linguistic analysis does not claim to provide or validate the 'answers', nor does it dictate the method by which these answers should be derived. The claims of those who advocate a stylistic approach are arguably far more modest: that linguistic analysis provides both a way of engaging with the text and the means of articulating and supporting a critical response, a response which does not pretend to be definitive, but which *is* firmly based in the language of the text. It might be objected at this point that we are back to practical criticism again, but the advanced form of close reading offered by stylistic study is not the only tool available in the stylistician's kit.

The collected jumble of means and methods which make up the stylistician's tool-kit is another easy target for the invective of suspicious literary critics. The eclectic nature of this tool-kit reflects the eclectic nature of stylistics itself. In 1972 Fowler wrote that stylistics 'is a very diffuse and diverse set of interdisciplinary endeavours...no single descriptive practice is being recommended.'[45] This diffuseness of methods and approaches may be better understood when one considers the variety of activities in which stylisticians have traditionally been employed: pedagogy, pragmatic analysis, critical discourse, technical studies of poetic meter, attempts to classify and describe authorial style, forensic linguistics, and so on. But there is no denying that stylisticians make use of many theories, linguistic or otherwise; in 1964 Ohmann commented that 'the attempt to isolate the cues one attends to in identifying styles and in writing stylistic parody has sprawled out into an almost embarrassing profusion of critical methods',[46] and he proceeds to list twelve different methods of which he personally is aware.

The problem, as perceived by the detractors of stylistics, is precisely this practice of picking and choosing whichever method of analysis happens to be the most convenient or the most fashionable. Such a facility lends stylistics a disreputable air and denies it status as a methodology into the bargain. Stylisticians have also been vilified for advocating methods of analysis which have produced non-predictive rules: rules which produce the desired results for

---

44   G. L. Dillon, 'Whorfian Stylistics', *Journal of Literary Semantics*, (1982), p. 75.

45   R. Fowler, 'Style and the Concept of Deep Structure', *Journal of Literary Semantics*, (1972), p. 5.

46   R. Ohmann, 'Generative Grammars and the Concept of Literary Style' (1964), *Linguistics and Literary Style* (1970), D. C. Freeman (editor), p. 259.

one text but which cannot be applied with equal success to another.[47] What is in fact revealed here is the stylistician's commitment to theory-building. When an analytical method yields unsatisfactory results, the inadequacies of the theory are highlighted, thereby providing useful data for the ever-flexible stylistician. Inflexible approaches to the study of language seem doomed to failure, so perhaps stylisticians are wise to keep their tool-kit so well-stocked. They also draw on other related fields such as psycholinguistic theory, pragmatics and semantics, to name but a few. And of course, stylisticians do not discount the writings of critics – quite the opposite. Short has argued that these writings are themselves part of the stylistician's tool-kit:

> stylistic analysis is just as interested…in established interpretations as in new ones. This is because we are also profoundly interested in the rules and procedures which we, as readers, intuitively know and apply in order to understand what we read. Thus, stylisticians try to discover not just *what* a text means, but also *how* it comes to mean what it does.[48]

The question of a reader's intuition is an interesting one and it is a question to which I shall return in a later chapter. For the present, I wish to conclude this section of the introduction by addressing an issue central to stylistics, that of the supposed existence of a 'literary' language, a language that is different from 'ordinary' language.

The question of whether or not there is a special kind of literary[49] language is one that cannot be ignored, and it is undoubtedly one that has important ramifications for this thesis. Simpson points out that it is an axiom of modern stylistics that there is no distinction to be drawn between language in everyday use and the language one finds in works valued as literature.[50] If a category of language that is specifically literary does not exist, there is no reason why linguistic theories should not be applied to literary texts, and it is certainly

---

47 Fish, among others, found fault with the concept of transformational grammar, and in 1972 he wrote: 'It is possible…to salvage the game…by making it more sophisticated, by contextualising it. One could simply write a rule that allows for the different valuings of the same pattern by taking into account the features which surround it in context. But this would only lead to the bringing forward of further counterexamples and the continual and regressive rewriting of the rule. Eventually a point would be reached where a separate rule was required for each and every occurrence'. 'What Is Stylistics and Why Are They Saying Such Terrible Things About It?' (1972), *Approaches to Poetics* (1973), S. Chatman (editor), pp. 120-121.

48 M. Short, *Exploring the Language of Poems, Plays and Prose* (1996), p. 6.

49 While I acknowledge that there probably should be scare quotes around the words 'literary' and 'literature', I have not typed them because I feel that their constant appearance would be tedious for the reader; I prefer instead to state once and for all that I realise these are highly subjective terms.

50 P. Simpson, *Language, Ideology and Point of View* (1993), p. 3.

true that many linguists have not ventured into reading literary texts except as language data. Halliday writes that 'what the linguist does when faced with a literary text is the same as what he does when faced with any text that he is going to describe'.[51] The literary language debate also has significance for the second question posed in this thesis, whether form is inseparable from content. Arguably, one of the properties of literary language is its self-referential nature: the language calls attention to itself, and has no practical function beyond this. If there is no such thing as literary language, then *what* is said is perhaps more important than *how* it is said, which leads to the conclusion that any utterance contains a paraphrasable content which is independent of form. But there are several arguments to be weighed in the balance, and I shall begin with that of linguistic register.

The ability to recognise and reproduce different registers forms part of a language user's 'communicative competence'. Registers are distinctive varieties of language used in different situation types.[52] Halliday noticed that a single word or phrase is often enough to cue recognition of a register: for example, the word 'begat' is recognisable as biblical language, while 'indemnity' is a word one associates with insurance documents.[53] It can be seen, then, that there is an integral link between register and situation type – it is unlikely that one would use the phrase 'dearly beloved' outside of a church service, for example – but it takes only a moment's reflection to realise that this cannot apply to literary texts. Fowler notes that 'the literary text's

---

51 M. A. K. Halliday, 'Descriptive Linguistics in Literary Studies' (1964), *Linguistics and Literary Style* (1970), D. C. Freeman (editor), p. 67.

52 Bakhtin uses the term 'speech genres' for register in his essay 'The Problem of Speech Genres' (1952-1953). In her introduction to *The Bakhtin Reader* Pam Morris writes that 'the most interesting new area in this essay is the suggestion that the form of utterances is not a matter of free choice on the part of any individual speaker.... Bakhtin argues that speech genres impose an order and form on everyday speech in ways we are largely unaware of, but which can have a considerable effect upon our speech flexibility and ease'. P. Morris, *The Bakhtin Reader* (1994), p. 17. In other words, we do not have as much freedom as we suppose in the construction of our individual utterances.

53 Halliday also developed a method to help in the characterisation of register based on the field, tenor and mode of the text in question, where field, or domain, is the subject matter, tenor relates to the relationship between the participants and the formality of the situation, and mode concerns the type of channel –whether the text is written (a letter) or spoken (a radio play), for example – and the organisation of the text. Field, tenor and mode correspond approximately to Halliday's three categories of language function: ideational, interpersonal and textual respectively. Halliday makes what I think is an important contribution to the form/content debate here. He notes that ' "an early announcement is expected"…and "apologies for absence were received"…are not simply free variants of "we ought to hear soon" and "was sorry he couldn't make it".' (*The Linguistic Sciences and Language Teaching* (1964), p. 87, quoted in R. Fowler, *Linguistic Criticism* (1996), pp. 190-191.) If a different form triggers a different register, then the words spoken will surely be understood differently by the hearer/reader, in that the words of the message will be located in a different situation type. This, then, is one argument in favour of the inseparability of form and content.

language is not embedded in a real context of situation…but it creates its own situation, topic, and world for the reader to enter.'[54] The fictional situation is, after all, fictional, and the author's use of register is mimetic of language use in everyday reality. These arguments reflect the 'sovereign' nature of the text, to which I shall shortly return.

It is usually *not* the case that texts exhibit only one register. Such texts do exist, however, and these texts are described as 'monosemic', 'over-registrated', or 'hegemonic'; they are works in which 'there are no resonances or networks of multiple and expanding meaning',[55] for instance, legal documents and instruction manuals. In general, most texts are plural, or polysemic, in that they contain a number of registers. Mikhail Bakhtin's term for this phenomenon is 'heteroglossia', and literary texts in particular make use of many different registers. The following example is taken from Stevie Smith's *Novel on Yellow Paper*:

> Should I Marry a Foreigner?...You do not say, dear, if he is a man of colour. Even if it is only a faint tea rose – *don't*. I know what it will mean to you to GIVE HIM UP but funny things happen with colour, it often slips over, and sometimes darkens from year to year and it is so difficult to match up. *White* always looks well at weddings and will wash and wear and if you like to write to me again, enclosing a stamped addressed envelope, I will give you the name of a special soap I always use it myself and do not stretch or wring but hang to dry in a cool oven. My best wishes for your happiness, dear, I think it was very sweet of you to write.[56]

The registers included here are those of a written reply from an agony aunt in a magazine ('You do not say, dear', 'write to me again, enclosing a stamped addressed envelope'), an advertisement for soap powder ('will wash and wear'), and care instructions for a garment which one might find on the label ('do not stretch or wring but hang to dry in a cool oven'). However, the fact that a text is polysemic cannot be taken as an indication that its language is therefore literary; as previously stated, many texts not considered literary are heteroglossic nevertheless.[57]

---

54   R. Fowler, *Linguistic Criticism* (1996), p. 204.

55   R. Carter and W. Nash, 'Language and Literariness', *Prose Studies* (1983), p. 139.

56   S. Smith, *Novel on Yellow Paper* (1936), p. 35.

57   Fowler argues that when a text contains numerous registers, the point of association between the varieties has to be worked out, and therefore heteroglossia is intrinsically connected with defamiliarisation. R. Fowler, *Linguistic Criticism* (1996), p. 197.

One could ask whether literary language should itself be considered a register: however, there are problems with this suggestion. Taken out of context, literary language can appear decidedly un-literary. Terry Eagleton uses two examples to demonstrate this point. He writes that

> if you...murmur 'Thou still unravished bride of quietness,' then I am instantly aware that I am in the presence of the literary. I know this because the texture, rhythm and resonance of your words are in excess of their abstractable meaning.... Your language draws attention to itself, flaunts its material being.[58]

By way of contrast, Eagleton quotes the following from Knut Hamsun's novel *Hunger*: 'This is awfully squiggly handwriting!', and points out that

> the *context* tells me that it is literary; but the language itself has no inherent properties or qualities which might distinguish it from other kinds of discourse, and someone might well say this in a pub without being admired for their literary dexterity.[59]

It might be relatively easy to locate lines of poetry in a literary register, but as Eagleton demonstrates, this is more difficult with prose works, especially those that are more transparent than opaque.[60] An additional difficulty is that the existence of a literary register would be intrinsically linked to a definition of literature itself, and this definition has proved notoriously elusive. The existence of a canon of works considered to be literature is not sufficient as a criterion because the canon reveals far more about the society which compiled it than it does about those works which constitute it. Besides, as Ben Burton and Ronald Carter point out, 'canons are not immutable...tastes change and evaluations shift as part of a process of canon formation'.[61]

---

58   T. Eagleton, *Literary Theory: An Introduction* (1983), p. 2.

59   Ibid., p. 6.

60   G. Leech and M. Short, *Style in Fiction* (1981), p. 29: a text is 'opaque in the sense that the medium attracts attention in its own right; and indeed, the interpretation of sense may be frustrated and obstructed by abnormalities in the use of the lexical and grammatical features of medium.'

61   B. Burton and R. Carter, 'Literature and the Language of Literature', Encyclopedia of Language & Linguistics (2006), p. 267. Eagleton also recognises the truth of this argument: 'Anything can be literature, and anything which is regarded as unalterably and unquestionably literature – Shakespeare, for example – can cease to be literature.... Literature, in the sense of a set of works of assured and unalterable value, distinguished by certain shared inherent properties, does not exist.... Just as people may treat a work as philosophy in one century and as literature in the next, or vice versa, so they may change their minds about what writing they consider valuable. They may even change their minds about the grounds they use for judging what is valuable and what is not.' T. Eagleton, *Literary Theory: An Introduction* (1983), pp. 10-11.

Just as anything can be literature, Ronald Carter and Walter Nash have recognised that anything can be literary. In an article entitled 'Language and Literariness', Carter and Nash note that literary works make use of registers that are considered non-literary, but by implication this means that any word *can* be literary if it is employed in a literary text. Carter and Nash label this process as 'reregistration': a word or phrase connected with one register is transferred to a literary work, and once this happens the original register can no longer be seen to apply because the integral link between register and situation type has been broken. As Fowler puts it, 'the external register is therefore in the new text for some purpose other than its original function. Inevitably it becomes "estranged".'[62] Bakhtin analyses this shift in terms of the 'utterance'. He divides speech genres into primary (simple) and secondary (complex), novels being an instance of the latter. Bakhtin writes that 'primary genres are altered and assume a special character when they enter into complex ones. They lose their immediate relation to actual reality and to the real utterances of others.'[63] In the Stevie Smith passage quoted above, the mixture of registers from an advice column, a soap advertisement and a set of care instructions combine to give a humorous picture of a husband who is an accessory that must be made to 'match up'; he is likened to a garment that will stay as good as new year after year, but only with careful use.[64]

In addition to their concept of reregistration, Carter and Nash have also coined the term 'sovereignty'. They note that the literary text differs from other texts because it is 'not "used" for any practical purpose; it teaches its own use; it is sovereign in its own domain of language'.[65] Sovereignty 'denotes the self-supporting capacity of the text, its power to generate and develop a pattern of meaning, without reference to externals and without requiring of its readers any prior knowledge other than the common stock of experience'.[66] In addition, the reader is not *required* to do anything in a functional sense, as she would be if she were reading a recipe, for example. Carter and Nash also put forward 'displaced interaction' as a possible marker of a literary text: displaced interaction refers to the interaction of author and reader (Halliday's tenor, or

---

62   R. Fowler, *Linguistic Criticism* (1996), p. 205.

63   M. Bakhtin, 'The Problem of Speech Genres' (1952-1953), *The Bakhtin Reader* (1994), P. Morris (editor), p. 82.

64   Fish offers a similar argument to that proposed by Carter and Nash in his article 'How Ordinary is Ordinary Language?', *New Literary History* (1973).

65   R. Carter and W. Nash, 'Language and Literariness', *Prose Studies* (1983), p. 130.

66   Ibid.

interpersonal function), and it relates to the distance between addresser and addressee that the text is required to bridge.

It would be useful at this point to summarise and recap the arguments offered so far. There is considerable doubt over whether such a thing as a language use that is specifically literary actually exists; the reasons for doubting its existence include the lack of a definition of literature itself, and the fact that there is nothing inherently literary in much of the language which appears in a literary context. Literary language has doubtful status as a register because the lack of formal criteria make it difficult to identify, and in addition to this, literary texts make frequent use of non-literary registers, thus potentially redefining every language use as literary. This borrowing from other registers occurs in many types of language use, thus polysemy alone cannot be a possible marker of a literary text. Other possible markers include sovereignty, self-referentiality and displaced interaction: these are among the criteria listed by Burton and Carter, who argue for a functional view of literary language:

> literary language is not special or different, in that any formal feature termed 'literary' can be found in other discourses.

Yet, literary language *is* different from other language uses in that it functions differently. Some of the differences can be demarcated with reference to such criteria as medium dependence, reregistration, semantic density produced by the interaction of linguistic levels, displaced interaction, polysemy, and discourse patterning. What is prototypically literary will be a text that meets most of the above criteria.[67]

This 'prototypical' approach suits those who argue for a *cline* of literariness rather than an inflexible, problematic ruling about what is and is not literary language.[68] As far as this thesis is concerned, I feel that this approach serves to endorse the use of linguistic descriptions of language in literary texts, if the criteria listed by Burton and Carter are to be adequately explored and described. The argument that literary language *functions* differently is a consideration that will have to be incorporated into the form/content debate, to which I shall turn in the next section of this introduction.

---

67   B. Burton and R. Carter, 'Literature and the Language of Literature', *Encyclopedia of Language & Linguistics* (2006), p. 273.

68   Cf. Wittgenstein and polythetic categories of 'family resemblances'.

ii) Form = Content?

In embarking on this thesis I decided to set myself the project of answering to my own satisfaction the familiar question, whether form and content in literature are the same thing: is it possible to paraphrase a literary text? In carrying out my research into stylistic criticism and in preparing my own critical studies of style I have found this question a useful focus. I intend to argue that for given definitions of form and content, the two are indeed inseparable.

The belief that form and content are inseparable is a tenet of monism, whose advocates include Jan Mukařovský of the Prague School of poetics, New Critics such as John Crowe Ransom and Cleanth Brooks, and more recently, the novelist and critic David Lodge.[69] To the monist way of thinking, a change in the wording of an utterance provokes an alteration in the meaning, which is to say that it is impossible to paraphrase a literary text. Brooks published his essay 'The Heresy of Paraphrase'[70] at a time when critics were engaged in adjusting their focus away from authorial intention and from literature as socio-historical documentation, and were coming to rest their gaze instead on the language of the text, favouring close and attentive reading above historical and biographical research. Much water has flowed under the bridge since Brooks wrote *The Well-Wrought Urn*, and he was of course referring specifically to poetry instead of prose, but there is still much that is appealing in the idea that form and content are one and the same thing, particularly when one is confronted with a prose text that does not render itself easily to paraphrase. The monist position can be an extreme one, however; form and content are seen not only as inseparable but as indistinguishable. The excesses of monism can be checked by a degree of rationality. For example, the New Critics' somewhat immoderate concept of iconicity is one such excess, and Barry refers to this concept as the 'enactment fallacy':

> to the habit of exclusive concentration on the poem's verbal envelope the New Critics...added the doctrine of the organic fusion of form and content, making it obligatory to see formal details as intimately

---

69   David Lodge has since reassessed his position, however, and he notes in the afterword to the second edition of *Language in Fiction* (1984), p. 296, that he now considers himself an advocate of pluralism in the sense described by Leech and Short in *Style in Fiction* (1981), chapter one, pp. 29-34.

70   C. Brooks, 'The Heresy of Paraphrase', *The Well-Wrought Urn: Studies in the Structure of Poetry* (1947), pp. 192-214.

connected with content, since they had to enact meaning if they were not to be puritanically condemned as merely decorative.[71]

The notion of the verbal icon fell from favour once it was acknowledged that writers are in fact largely constrained by the language in which they write, and it is simply not possible for formal details to be always enacting content. There is obviously a difference, however, between the idea that form *enacts* content, and the supposition that form and content are inseparable: the two positions are not mutually exclusive, and it is possible for the former position to be untenable without greatly disturbing the equilibrium of the latter. The monist position can also be criticised for its emphasis on the concept of 'literariness', as originally devised by the Russian Formalists; if this concept can be placed on a rational footing by using the criteria outlined in the concluding paragraphs of the previous section of this introduction instead of relying on the subjective instincts of the critic, then once again the monist position is rendered more attractive.

In writing about the impossibility of paraphrasing a literary text Brooks was referring to poetry rather than prose, and the monist way of thinking is certainly more in accordance with poetic texts. One might ask why, considering that I intend to defend the view that form and content are inseparable, I have chosen to explore prose texts instead of poetry; my task would certainly have been easier had I chosen to write about the latter. Indeed, much of the critical discussion relating to form and content refers largely to poetry – and yet I have chosen prose. My reasons for doing so are quite simple. I do not see why the arguments traditionally put forward for suggesting that form and content are indivisible in poetry should not equally apply to prose, whether that prose be transparent or opaque. I dislike the implication that poetry is intrinsically more 'literary': the verbal patterning that exists between the various linguistic levels builds up wider resonances and deeper levels of meaning in both verse and prose. I believe that prose rhythms *can* be representational, although I accept that this is more generally a feature of poetic texts. In addition, I consider it misleading to suppose that language draws attention to itself only in poetic texts: consider, for example, the intricate prose style of Henry James in *The Ambassadors*, and how delicately the lines are poised. Indeed, in chapter one, I demonstrate that a passage from Mervyn Peake's *Gormenghast* [72] can easily be reconstructed as a poem, owing to the unusual density of parallel constructions

---

71   P. Barry, 'The Enactment Fallacy', *Essays in Criticism* (1980), p. 95.

72   Mervyn Peake, 1911-1968; although mostly known for his work as an artist and illustrator Peake is also the author of the *Gormenghast* trilogy, a work best described as a Gothic fantasy.

in a handful of lines. But my argument is not that some prose should be considered akin to poetry because it has poetic features: on the contrary, even the most sparse prose is the product of authorial decision and every authorial choice has to be weighed in the balance.

To return to the main argument of this section, it is important to clarify that which I wish it to be understood by my use of the terms 'form' and 'content', because these definitions are central to my argument. For my purposes, 'form' refers to the words on the page, how these words are arranged into sentences and paragraphs, the punctuation of a text, its layout, any additional considerations of graphology or orthography – in short, everything concerning the physical appearance of the text, and everything to which the reader has immediate access. More importantly, I also understand form to refer to *the whole text*, which as previously noted, is the only valid unit of study when dealing with literary texts. If 'content' is inseparable from form, then meaning resides in areas such as lexical choice at word level, and syntactic arrangement and punctuation at sentence level. On a textual level, meaning can be found in the arrangement and structuring of material, similar to the Russian notion of *syuzhet*, or the story as shaped and edited by the storyteller. To the definition of content must also be added the dimension of *context*, or the way in which literary language functions: the novel is a different kind of language event from an instruction manual.[73] However, I do not wish to claim outright that form is inseparable from content only in literary texts; nor do I wish to deny that it *is* possible to paraphrase some texts (the instruction manual again). I think it is safe to conclude that the further one travels along the cline of 'literariness' towards 'literature', the more it is true that form and content are the same thing; but this premise also holds true for non-literary texts that exhibit signs of literariness: some advertisements are very carefully constructed, and many jokes would not be funny – that is, would cease to be jokes – if they were stripped of their layers of verbal patterning. So, to recap, form = the *whole* text, and content = the whole text + *context* (literary language).

I would now like to take a closer look at the linguistic attempts to isolate the paraphrasable element of an utterance. These attempts were grounded in the theories of deep/surface structure and transformational grammar, and their

---

73   Bakhtin refers to the literary work as an 'utterance', regardless of the length of that work, and he asserts that 'thematic content, style, and compositional structure...are inseparably linked to the *whole* of the utterance and are equally determined by the specific nature of the particular sphere of communication'. M. Bakhtin, 'The Problem of Speech Genres' (1952-1953), *The Bakhtin Reader* (1994), P. Morris (editor), p. 81. Thus 'form' is the whole text and 'content' is the form plus its context.

success has been negligible. As far as my argument is concerned, the problem with these concepts is that they deal with utterances on a sentential level only; no account is taken of the ways in which sentences are punctuated, or how they work together within the text as a whole, with the inevitable result that many levels of meaning are ignored.

The deep structure of a sentence comprises two important components: proposition and modality. The proposition is the bare bones, the relationship between a noun and a predicate expressed in the simplest terms. Fowler describes the predicate as the 'semantic nucleus'[74] of a proposition; it is often realised as a verb or an adjective in the surface structure. The three basic types of predicate are *action, state* or *change of state*. If the predicate represents an event, or a state of being, the nouns of the proposition represent the corresponding participants or objects. These participants/objects are assigned different *roles* in the deep structure, namely, *agent, object, experiencers, patients, beneficiaries, instrument* and *location*. The modality component relates to point of view in fiction, and it expresses the writer's attitude towards both her subject, and her reader.

The deep structure undergoes a transformation via various rules of realization, and the result is the surface structure, 'an indirect expression of underlying semantic organization'.[75] So an utterance which is *ambiguous* has more than one possible deep structure expressed by one surface structure;[76] a *paraphrase*, on the other hand, is one of several alternative surface structures relating to a single deep structure. At first glance, it would seem that it is, after all, possible to change the form and retain the meaning, or, as Fowler puts it:

> sentences which are superficially dissimilar but 'mean the same' (are synonymous) are said to have the same deep structure. We can see that there is thus no one-to-one relationship between *meaning* and *form*; meaning is constant while form or surface structure diverges.[77]

However, there are at least three problems with this argument: neither the role of the reader nor the part punctuation has to play are properly accounted for, and the notion of meaning, or content, as it is understood here, is inadequate for the purposes of literary language.

---

74   R. Fowler, *Linguistics and the Novel* (1977), p. 13.

75   Ibid., p. 20.

76   An oft-quoted example of an ambiguous phrase is that of Hockett's telegram, which reads 'Ship sails today'. Is *ship* a noun (agent) or a verb (action, imperative)?

77   R. Fowler, *Linguistics and the Novel* (1977), p. 11.

The symbols on the page are the only tangible contact the reader has with the semantic meaning buried in the deep structure:

> our only access to the underlying meaning of texts is via the orders, forms and choices of words which we encounter on the surface, that is to say, we experience meaning only in the form given by the realization rules, the transformations, which the text employs. Meaning always comes to us processed by the form in which it is expressed.[78]

If the reader can only access the deep structure (content) via the surface structure (form), then surely, for the reader, *the form is the same as the meaning*. Having claimed that meaning and form do not enjoy a one-to-one relationship, Fowler states that 'a writer may transform his deep structures into surface structures which radically modify our apprehension of the propositional meaning of the text'.[79] It would seem, then, that the way in which the writer finally expresses the deep structure on paper can completely alter the way in which the fictional world is perceived by the reader:

> different surface structures make a radical difference to the impression the text makes on the reader: to his sense of the author's tone, of the rhythm of the text, of its affiliations with other texts; above all, to the reader's impression of the place of a text and of its author among the thought-patterns of a culture.[80]

Surely then, the only possible conclusion can be that meaning resides in the *surface* structure, and that form is therefore inseparable from content. This argument can be further supported by reference to the role of punctuation. Punctuation carries meaning: one only has to remove the punctuation of a text to see how vital it is to writing. And yet we often manage without it – text messages, for example, rarely carry punctuation, and it is a sad fact that many native English speakers live in woeful ignorance of the use and function of the apostrophe, and yet people still manage to communicate successfully. In literary texts, however, the absence or intentional misuse of punctuation is usually significant of something connected to the wider themes and purposes of the text; for example, in Daniel Keyes' short story 'Flowers for Algernon', Charlie Gordon's atrocious punctuation and spelling signify, within the novel discourse, his low intelligence:

---

78   R. Fowler, *Linguistics and the Novel* (1977), p. 22.

79   Ibid., p. 17.

80   Ibid., p. 11.

I had a test today. I think I faled it. and I think that may be now they wont use me. What happind is a nice young man was in the room and he had some white cards with ink spilled all over them. He sed Charlie what do you see on this card. I was very skared even tho I had my rabits foot in my pockit because when I was a kid I always faled tests in school and I spillled ink to.[81]

When Charlie's IQ is scientifically augmented, his punctuation and spelling are faultless. In addition to the argument above, it should also be remembered that punctuation and textual layout are vitally important to the fictional representation of speech and thought: this is an area to which I shall return in chapter two.

The third objection to the deep/surface structure theory is that it employs a definition of meaning, or content, that I consider to be severely impoverished; for example, a definition of meaning as Fowler intends the term to be used is 'cognitive or propositional meaning residing in deep structure'.[82] For the critic, this is simply too bald a definition to be of any use: ideas of propositional meaning, descriptive synonymy and truth conditions may satisfy the linguist, but the critic has need of a more detailed approach. And it seems that so much linguistic information has come to be included in the deep structure of an utterance, that the resulting structure hardly differs from its companion on the surface. In his article 'Style and the Concept of Deep Structure',[83] Fowler denies the existence of *optional* transformations[84] and argues that if transformations are to be meaning-preserving, everything must be accounted for in deep structure, including syntactic arrangements and lexical choices. Fowler preserves the deep/surface structure distinction, however, by maintaining that transformations do not contribute to meaning if they leave 'the paraphrasable content of a text untouched'.[85] But it is difficult to understand exactly what comprises this 'paraphrasable content' if deep structure is to include both the words that will appear in the final surface structure[86] *and* their syntactic arrangement.

---

81 D. Keyes, *Flowers for Algernon* (1966).

82 R. Fowler, *Linguistics and the Novel* (1977), p. 11.

83 R. Fowler, 'Style and the Concept of Deep Structure', *Journal of Literary Semantics* (1972).

84 If the phrase structure component represents obligatory transformations (the fixed element), transformational rules are optional (the variable component).

85 R. Fowler, 'Style and the Concept of Deep Structure', *Journal of Literary Semantics* (1972), p. 16.

86 I shall comment further on the ramifications of individual word meaning in chapter four.

In the same article, Fowler quotes extensively from the work of Ohmann, a staunch defender of transformational grammar. Fowler summarises Ohmann's conclusion as follows: 'the style of an author or a text can be expressed by a statement of the characteristic transformations which are employed, or of the characteristic combinations of different types of transformation'.[87] For Ohmann, the 'notion of style calls for different ways of expressing the same content'.[88] To summarise this argument as briefly as possible: in any human activity – and Ohmann uses the analogy of a game of tennis – there are fixed and variable components, that is, rules that must be obeyed, and the freedom of the individual to act within the boundaries of these rules. So, a tennis player must abide by the rules of the game, but she can choose the shots she wishes to play. Although the analogy does not correspond without difficulty to the activity of writing prose – it is possible, for example, to break grammatical rules for aesthetic effect without rendering a text incomprehensible to a reader – it holds well enough to support Ohmann's argument that

> the idea of style implies that words on a page might have been different, or differently arranged, without a corresponding difference in substance. Another writer would have said *it* another *way*. For the idea of style to apply, in short, writing must involve choices of verbal formulation.[89]

Given that the reader's only access to the underlying meaning is via the surface structure, and given that there are in all probability several choices of expression available to the author, any final authorial decision must therefore also articulate all possible variants that were eventually rejected. This conclusion lends support to Ohmann's proposal that in order to arrive at a description of an author's style which is not simply impressionistic and can be supported by valid linguistic data, it is necessary for the critic to explore those sentences which the author did *not* write, as a means to formulating a hypothesis, linked to the thematic and aesthetic qualities of the text, which can explain why the author chose to write as she did.

The next problem to be tackled is *how* to formulate these alternative constructions without straying from the original. Ohmann postulates that transformational rules can allow the critic or reader to do precisely this:

---

87   R. Fowler, 'Style and the Concept of Deep Structure', *Journal of Literary Semantics* (1972), p. 8.

88   R. Ohmann, 'Generative Grammars and the Concept of Literary Style' (1964), *Linguistics and Literary Style* (1970), D. C. Freeman (editor), p. 267.

89   Ibid., p. 264.

a transformation works changes on structure, but normally leaves *part* of the structure unchanged. And in any case, the new structure bears a precisely specifiable relationship to the old one, a relationship, incidentally, that speakers of the language will intuitively feel.[90]

Ohmann notes that 'some transformations import new content, others eliminate features of content, and no transformation leaves content absolutely unaltered'.[91] Although this statement appears to undermine his line of argument, Ohmann is careful to qualify what he means by content: 'the most useful sense of "content" – *cognitive* content – may be such that transformations do generally leave it unaltered'.[92]

Ohmann, like Fowler, uses only a limited definition of content, and it is arguably a definition that bears little relevance to literary texts. Although Ohmann confidently asserts that 'another writer would have said *it* another *way*', we are still unsure what *it* actually is. Leech and Short attempt an investigation into possible stylistic alternatives in chapter four of *Style in Fiction*, in which they provide a detailed analysis of a line from one of Katherine Mansfield's short stories (without the aid of transformational grammar!). Their conclusion is that the line written by Mansfield is superior to its alternative renderings on semantic, syntactic and phonological grounds – and they demonstrate effectively that in fact it is *not* possible to rewrite Mansfield's sentence. Ohmann's own attempts at critical analysis based on the methods dictated by transformational grammar have not met with universal acceptance. In his article 'Literature as Sentences',[93] Ohmann uses transformational grammar to analyse sentences from James Joyce's *Araby* and Conrad's *The Secret Sharer*. This article was met with various rebuttals, including an article entitled 'Linguistic Structure and Literary Meaning' by David Hirsch. Hirsch argues that the theory of deep structure is inadequately equipped to deal with literary language, and he demonstrates clearly the deficiencies of Ohmann's artificially generated sentences which supposedly form the core of Joyce's chosen sentence. Hirsch concludes as follows:

> the fact is that no other arrangement of Joyce's words (or substitutes for them) could possibly communicate the same content.... This is not to say that form and content can never be separated. It seems likely that

90 R. Ohmann, 'Generative Grammars and the Concept of Literary Style' (1964), *Linguistics and Literary Style* (1970), D. C. Freeman (editor), p. 266.

91 Ibid., p. 268.

92 Ibid.

93 R. Ohmann, 'Literature as Sentences', *College English* (1966).

in our everyday utterances we communicate meanings in one form that could as easily have been communicated in another. But the language of poetry is different. It communicates cognitive and emotive meanings in a special way.[94]

We are back, then, to the idea that literary language functions differently, and that as far as literary language is concerned, form and content are indivisible. Instead of attempting to formulate dubious paraphrases in an attempt to isolate and describe an author's style, it surely makes more sense to investigate the text in terms of medium dependence, reregistration, semantic density, displaced interaction, polysemy, and discourse patterning – the suggested criteria for identifying literary language. To the equation form = content, I would argue that we can now add another component: form = content = style.

iii) Texts and Theories

The remainder of this thesis is divided into four chapters on the subjects of foregrounding, speech and thought representation, point of view, and the role of the reader. I have referred to four narrative fictions: Mervyn Peake's *Gormenghast*, Emily Brontë's *Wuthering Heights*, Terry Pratchett's *Going Postal* and Charlotte Perkins Gilman's *The Yellow Wall-Paper*. The scope of the thesis moves gradually outward from the text to the narrator to the reader. Chapters two and three follow on naturally from one another in that the fictional representation of speech and thought is a subsection of fictional point of view. In chapter four, linguistic analysis alone is shown to be incapable of accounting for reader response.

Linguistic description can help the critic to explain clearly and objectively how textual elements are foregrounded: the problem, naturally, is how to identify these elements in a manner that is both consistent and ratifiable. *Gormenghast* is useful for two reasons: first, it is arguable that the entire text is foregrounded, and second, Peake's novel is opaque rather than transparent in that it solidly resists paraphrase. In making the attempt myself, some meanings had to be discarded and some senses lost.[95] *Wuthering Heights* is also considered in chapter one to provide the contrast of a relatively transparent text. Linguistic theories have already proved useful as far as the fictional representation of speech and thought is concerned. Brian McHale argues that Free Indirect

---

94   D. H. Hirsch, 'Linguistic Structure and Literary Meaning', *Journal of Literary Semantics* (1972), p. 88.

95   See Appendix C.

Discourse, like foregrounding, is one of the possible markers of a literary text.[96] The effects of speech representation are subtle and these effects are lost in paraphrase. Pratchett moralises freely through his use of Free Indirect Discourse, and *Going Postal* is both interesting and useful because its major protagonist is a seasoned criminal, yet he presents the reader with the most moral of arguments. One expects morality from an upright character such as Sam Vimes,[97] but not from Moist von Lipwig. Paul Simpson's transitivity and modality systems[98] provide easy and useful access to the study of point of view with the advantage that these systems force the student of literature to draw a conclusion based on textual evidence alone. Gilman's narrator is unreliable and the reader is eventually alienated from her. I return to *Wuthering Heights* in the final chapter when I discuss literary allusion as part of my investigation into how a reader makes sense of a text.

---

96   B. McHale, 'Free Indirect Discourse: A Survey of Recent Accounts', *Poetics and Theory of Literature* (1978).

97   Samuel Vimes is Commander of the City Watch of Ankh-Morpork and a character who appears regularly in the Discworld series.

98   See Appendices E and F.

Chapter 1: Foregrounding

i) The Background to Foregrounding

Jan Mukařovský, one of the founding members of the Prague Linguistic Circle, explores the concept of foregrounding (*aktualisace*) in an article entitled 'Standard Language and Poetic Language'.[1] Mukařovský is never in any doubt that there is a distinction to be made between 'standard' language and 'poetic' language, and he writes that 'the violation of the norm of the standard, its systematic violation, is what makes possible the poetic utilization of language; without this possibility there would be no poetry'.[2] We have already seen that the postulated existence of an exclusively literary language has since been thrown into question, but Mukařovský's work can be regarded in hindsight as a valuable precursor to the work on linguistic register. The identification of 'the norm of the standard' is likewise a contentious issue:[3] any attempt to classify language use according to some all-encompassing norm is bound to involve arbitrary decision-making and sweeping generalisations. However, the advent of the technological age and the rapidly growing role of computers in the gathering of linguistic data[4] means that is it becoming increasingly possible to establish the norms of a given *text*, as Rebecca Posner points out:

> computers...are being used mainly for the purpose of compiling concordances and frequency word lists [which] for students of style... provide the solid ground of the 'norm', on which the deviation of 'individual style' can stand out more clearly.[5]

Although computers have simplified the task of spotting deviation from the norms established within a given text, it remains problematical nevertheless to measure linguistic deviation within a text against any external standard: first, because a norm of standard language use is practically impossible to document

---

1   J. Mukařovský, 'Standard Language and Poetic Language' (1958), *Linguistics and Literary Style* (1970), D. C. Freeman (editor), pp. 40-56.

2   Ibid., p. 42.

3   Bernard Bloch is frequently quoted in relation to this issue, because Bloch asserts that the style of a particular text can be defined as 'the message carried by the frequency distributions and transitional probabilities of its linguistic features, especially as they differ from those of the same features in the language as a whole' (quoted in G. Leech and M. Short, *Style in Fiction* (1981), p. 43). Leech and Short point out that it is indeed possible to make some fairly reliable statements about the properties of language, but that the norm of 'the language as a whole' is not so easily identified as Bloch seems to imagine, and that 'without some clearcut notion...of what is meant by "the language as a whole", any sampling procedure is bound to involve subjective decisions' (p. 45).

4   In corpus-based analysis, for example.

5   R. Posner, 'The Use and Abuse of Stylistic Statistics', *Archivum Linguisticum* (1963), p. 126.

exhaustively,[6] and more importantly, because there are convincing arguments against the existence of a single standard language in the first place.

This dubious literary/non-literary distinction notwithstanding, Mukařovský recognised that foregrounding is possible in both poetic and standard language. In standard language foregrounding is subordinate to the function of communication. Conversely, in poetic language,

> foregrounding achieves maximum intensity to the extent of pushing communication into the background as the objective of expression and of being used for its own sake; it is not used in the services of communication, but in order to place in the foreground the act of expression, the act of speech itself.[7]

Mukařovský describes the relationship between poetic and standard language in terms of three positions on a language continuum. At one end of the scale there exists no distortion of the language, although Mukařovský is careful to note that this too represents a stylistic choice. At the mid-point of the scale, the language is distorted to a certain extent, but communication is still the dominant function of the text. At the far end of the scale, the language is distorted, and communication is now subordinated to aesthetic function.

Mukařovský complicates the notion of foregrounding by claiming that in poetry there are in fact two norms, that of standard language, and that of the aesthetic canon: Mukařovský argues that poetic language is not a special brand of the standard because it has at its disposal all forms of the given language in addition to its own lexicon, phraseology and grammatical forms.[8] Mukařovský concludes his article by noting that foregrounding contributes to richness of expression, and that it subsequently enriches the language. He notes that in

---

6   Maurice Gross makes some interesting observations on the failure of generative grammar to produce a workable grammar of the English language some twenty years after its initial inception; Gross suggests that generative grammar could have provided this description of the language as a whole that is currently lacking. He proposes various reasons for this failure, among them the fact that no room has been made for diachronic discussion, and that linguistic theory has been privileged over accumulation of data. M. Gross, 'On the Failure of Generative Grammar', *Language* (1979).

7   J. Mukařovský, 'Standard Language and Poetic Language' (1958), *Linguistics and Literary Style* (1970), D. C. Freeman (editor), pp. 43-44. Mukařovský takes the position that poetic foregrounding cannot create new means of communication; in the case of poetic neologisms, for example, their aesthetic function is endangered if they are created with communication in mind. Mukařovský's argument here takes in some of the unwanted extremes of monism, but there is in his words the germ of the idea that literary language functions differently.

8   The existence of an 'aesthetic canon' can be supported by reference to the fact that certain words and phrases are marked in the dictionary as belonging to a specifically literary register. The following notes can be found on page xxxi of the eighth edition of the *Concise Oxford Dictionary*: '9.3.6 *literary* indicates a word or use that is found chiefly in literature. 9.3.7 *poet.* (= poetic) indicates uses confined to poetry or other contexts with romantic connotations.'

standard language, foregrounding brings to the fore 'the essence of sentence meaning and the dynamic nature of sentence construction...the meaning of a sentence appears as the total of the gradually accumulated meanings of the individual words'.[9] Poetry, on the other hand, can foreground the relationship between the individual words and the subject matter of the sentence, and the semantic interrelationships of the words in the sentence – every word affects every other.[10]

In sum, Mukařovský's argument runs as follows. There is a distinction between standard and poetic language, and standard language provides the background against which poetic language can be thrown into relief, whereas poetic language employs its own established canon as well as borrowing from standard language. Foregrounding can occur in both standard and poetic language, but its function in literary texts is to highlight the expression itself, whereas in standard language foregrounding serves a communicative function.

Mukařovský's ideas have since been adapted and revised. The idea of a specifically literary language is no longer popular, and the precise way in which literary language functions has been more rigorously defined than it is in Mukařovský's three-point scale. It is also no longer fashionable to claim that literary texts do not communicate content, and that they exist purely as aesthetic objects; there is an element of truth in the claim that the function of foregrounding in literary texts is to highlight the expression, but we are perhaps less likely now to dismiss the idea that literary texts can communicate or that non-literary texts can have elements of literariness. Finally, the claim that standard language acts as background for literary language has to be re-evaluated: instances of foregrounding can only confidently be identified within the confines of the given text, because the only standard that can be established is that of the text. Any comparison to norms of language usage outside of the text will ultimately rest on subjective assumptions and inconclusive data. This final point can, I think, be cited in support of the claim that 'form' must relate to the whole text: the text, not the language as a whole, is the background

---

9   J. Mukařovský, 'Standard Language and Poetic Language' (1958), *Linguistics and Literary Style* (1970), D. C. Freeman (editor), p. 55.

10   Alex Rodgers' excellent and very thorough essay on W. H. Auden's poem 'O Where Are You Going?' constitutes an illuminating discussion on how this very process works: in working out the links between the words reader, rider, fearer, farer, horror and hearer – words that are placed in similar positions syntactically and which are also linked through phonological resemblance – the reader eventually arrives at a much deeper understanding of what is at first glance a strange and forbidding poem. A. Rodgers, '"O Where Are You Going?": A Suggested Experiment in Classroom Stylistics', *Language and Literature: An Introductory Reader in Stylistics* (1982), R. Carter (editor), pp. 123-161.

against which instances of foregrounding can be identified and from which they derive their meaning.

It should be noted that Mukařovský refers specifically to poetry in his article, but according to Leech and Short, foregrounding can also act as an aid to clarifying the distinction between transparent and opaque *prose* writing. The greater the number of foregrounded elements, the more opaque the text:

> the aesthetic theory of foregrounding or de-automatization enables us to see the references to TRANSPARENT and OPAQUE qualities of prose style...as more than vague metaphors...prose is opaque in the sense that the medium attracts attention in its own right; and indeed, the interpretation of sense may be frustrated and obstructed by abnormalities in the use of the lexical and grammatical features of medium...opacity can be equated with the extent to which the *reader* is required to be creative.[11]

The distinction between transparent and opaque will not always be a clear one, however; in reality, it is likely that texts will occupy positions on a sliding scale. Leech and Short begin their exploration of foregrounding and its implications by distinguishing between literary *relevance* (foregrounding), psychological *prominence* and statistical *deviance*. Deviance is defined as a 'purely statistical notion...the difference between the normal frequency of a feature, and its frequency in the text or corpus'.[12] Psychological prominence refers to those features which register in the mind of the reader.[13] Foregrounding is *not* the same thing as either prominence or deviation, because the foregrounded items must in some way be artistically relevant to other foregrounded items and finally to an interpretation of the text as a whole: 'we should be able to see a prominent feature of style as forming a significant relationship with other features of style, in an artistically coherent pattern of choice'.[14] A prominent feature may not have any literary function; prominence may be due to a writer's preference for short sentences, or monosyllabic words, for example. Therefore, 'the dividing line between foregrounding and

---

11   G. Leech and M. Short, *Style in Fiction* (1981), p. 29. See also introduction, p. 16, footnote 60.

12   Ibid., p. 48. The problem with this definition, of course, is the difficulty in establishing the 'normal frequency of a feature'.

13   This notion is inextricably linked to literary competence, and is different for every reader, depending on previous training, experience, and so on. See also chapter four of this thesis.

14   G. Leech and M. Short, *Style in Fiction* (1981), p. 50.

unmotivated prominence must be drawn in principle: where it is drawn in practice depends on a coherent literary interpretation of style'.[15]

Leech and Short also differentiate between *qualitative* foregrounding and *quantitative* foregrounding. Qualitative foregrounding is to be found in deviation from the language code itself, when the writer breaches some rule or convention; quantitative foregrounding is the deviation from some expected frequency. It should be noted here that an unusual or noticeable frequency does of course include examples of absence as well as presence: for instance, the absence of a rhyme in a line of poetry where there should have been one – thereby defeating reader expectancy – or the sudden shift away from a prominent pattern of parallel structures in a prose text. Of course, one form of foregrounding will eventually shade into the other: 'the quantitative foregrounding...of a prominent pattern of choices within the code shades into the qualitative foregrounding which changes the code itself'.[16] Is the lack of finite verbs in the Peake passage discussed in the following section an example of qualitative or quantitative foregrounding? It is more likely that it begins as one and ends as the other. One expects to see finite verbs in prose text, after all, and their initial absence will undoubtedly strike the reader as odd; as the passage progresses, however, their absence becomes the norm, and any finite verb introduced at this stage will itself be foregrounded as deviant from the code already established by the writer. I follow my discussion of the passage from *Gormenghast* with an exploration of a passage from a relatively more transparent text, Emily Brontë's *Wuthering Heights*.

ii) Semantic Density in Gormenghast

It is clear from the opening lines of *Gormenghast* that the reader is dealing with a unique text. It is a text that quickly establishes its own norms, and these norms can be briefly summarised as follows. Extra levels of meaning are created through a concentration of parallel structures, as detailed in Appendix B. Lexical items are linked through sound patterns, notably alliteration and pararhyme. Peake regularly breaks grammatical rules; for example, his text contains examples of the omission of expected items, and the use of grammatical ellipsis or deletion creates a sequence of fragmented sentences, particularly in the opening paragraphs. In addition, instances of nominalisation account in part for the noticeable lack of finite verbs. At word level, content words are shifted out of their more usual function, or they are employed in

---

15   G. Leech and M. Short, *Style in Fiction* (1981), p. 50. It will have been noticed that Leech and Short include the reader in their discussion of foregrounding, which Mukařovský does not.

16   G. Leech and M. Short, *Style in Fiction* (1981), p. 139.

a slightly unusual sense or in a sense that is tricky to place. Also prominent is Peake's idiosyncratic use of punctuation, the colon and semi-colon in particular. And yet I would argue that almost all the above constitute instances of foregrounding, because there is little here that cannot be justified in thematic terms. To alter the form of Peake's text is to lose something of its content.

In the following analysis, I have examined each of the seven paragraphs in question individually. Each paragraph is numbered and reproduced in full preceding its discussion for ease of reference, and the text in its entirety is reproduced in Appendix A. As noted above, Appendix B is an attempt to represent visually the parallel structures within the text; Appendix C is the result of my attempt to paraphrase these opening paragraphs as part of an investigation into whether the form could be altered without affecting the content. I would argue that the semantic density of this text renders futile any attempt at paraphrase.

Paragraph 1

> (1) Titus is seven. (2) His confines, Gormenghast. (3) Suckled on shadows; weaned, as it were, on webs of ritual: for his ears, echoes, for his eyes, a labyrinth of stone: and yet within his body something other – other than this umbrageous legacy. (4) For first and ever foremost he is *child*.[17]

This paragraph consists of four sentences numbered (1) to (4) above. The first and second sentences contain three words, the third, 34, and the fourth, eight. The opening and closing words of this paragraph are parallel in structure (proper noun/pronoun – copula verb *is* – adjective/enumerator):

Titus is seven S V C (subject –verb– subject complement)

he is *child* S V C

The omission of a determiner in the final phrase ('he is *child*', not 'he is a child') has a twofold effect. The parallelism thus created between this phrase and the phrase which opens the novel – 'Titus is seven' – links the two statements in the mind of the reader, thereby reaffirming Titus' status as a child. The word 'child', which usually functions as a noun, arguably functions here as an adjective, as does the enumerator, the cardinal number 'seven', the effect of which is that the word 'child', italicized in Peake's text for emphasis,

---

17   M. Peake, *Gormenghast* (1950) in *The Gormenghast Novels* (1995), p. 399. Subsequent references to this work are taken from the same page unless otherwise indicated.

describes Titus rather than simply telling the reader what he is, almost as if Titus is an embodiment of, or is representative of, every child in the world – an effect which becomes significant later in the extract. It is Titus' status as child which forms the basis of his rebellion against the oppressive atmosphere of the castle. Peake's use of parallel structures foregrounds this important information for the reader.

The first sentence also forms a parallel with the second, in that both consist of just three words. The second sentence is elliptical: 'His confines, Gormenghast.' The second word 'confines' could be interpreted in either an abstract or a concrete sense, depending upon whether the confines referred to are the actual stone boundaries of the castle or alternatively the restrictions and limitations in Titus' mind, in that Gormenghast is all he knows or all that he can conceive of. However, the third sentence would appear to reinforce the abstract interpretation of 'confines' in its description of Titus' upbringing and the way in which he interacts with and accesses the world available to him through his physical senses.

Peake's rich prose does not lend itself easily to paraphrase, not only because several differing but equally valid interpretations of a sentence or phrase are occasionally possible, but also because any paraphrase is likely to lose the 'poetic' qualities of the original text, finishing as merely a pale reproduction. I have noted in Appendix B the many parallel structures which contribute to the rhythm of Peake's text, and in Paragraph 1, as in the other paragraphs under analysis, there are many subtle phonological effects which one would also not wish to lose. Note the alliteration in '*S*uckled on shado*ws*; *w*eaned, as it *w*ere, on *w*ebs of ritual', and the echo in '*for his ears*, echoes, *for his eyes...*'. The italicized phrases echo each other, and the meaning of the text is thereby reinforced in its form. The word 'other' occurs twice, providing another echo in the passage, and the sound pattern of the word 'for' is repeated in the final phrase '*For* **first** and ever *fore*mo**st** he is *child*'.[18]

In writing my very literal paraphrase of this opening paragraph, I noticed that many deep structure verbs had been suppressed in their surface structure manifestations. The only verbs remaining are the copula 'is' – which, in

---

18   The characters in bold are an instance of pararhyme (**CVC**), another of Peake's sound patterns. (CVC: where C = consonant and V = vowel; the characters in bold are those on which the rhyme is founded.) However, the phrase in question here is very common in English. M. Short warns the student of literature against the dangers of 'over-milking' the significance of phonetic patterns. He notes on p. 116 of *Exploring the Language of Poems, Plays and Prose* (1996) that 'because English only has approximately 45 phonemes, there are bound to be a fair number of accidental alliterative and assonantal patterns in any text as a consequence of the chance distribution of sounds in groups of words. So we should not assume that all sound patterns will be significant in terms of interpretation.'

its insistence on Titus' state of being, perhaps serves to foreshadow Titus' rebellion – and 'suckled', 'weaned', both of which place Titus in the role of beneficiary instead of agent. Titus is not allowed to be active: he does not *hear* the echoes or *see* the maze of stone – they are provided by the castle for his ears and eyes.[19] Titus *is*, but he does not act.

Paragraph 2

(1) A ritual, more compelling than ever man devised, is fighting anchored darkness. (2) A ritual of the blood; of the jumping blood. (3) These quicks of sentience owe nothing to his forbears, but to those feckless hosts, a trillion deep, of the globe's childhood.

Sentence (1) consists of twelve words, and a subordinate clause is embedded within the main clause: 'more compelling than ever man devised'. This clause informs the reader that the ritual referred to in this paragraph is *not*, or is unlikely to be, one of the rituals observed at Gormenghast, all of which have been devised by Titus' ancestors. The present continuous verb form 'is fighting' locates the passage firmly in the immediate present; a battle is at this moment raging against the enemy, the 'anchored darkness'.[20] This enemy is fixed and immovable, 'anchored' in the liquid of Titus' blood, which by contrast moves and jumps.

The nine words of the fragmented second sentence tell us that this ritual is 'of the blood'; this phrase is paralleled in the words following the semi-colon, 'of the jumping blood'. The parallelism takes the form of the repetition and embellishment of a noun phrase; this repeated phrase 'of the blood', therefore,

---

19   Gunther Kress distinguishes between transactive and nontransactive structures as follows: 'events either appear in a transactive form…that is, portrayed as either arising directly as the result of some agent's action and with a direct effect on a goal (where both agent and goal may be either animate or inanimate), or in a nontransactive form, arising without such action, that is, as either a self-caused action or an action that happens in some unspecified way.' Clearly, the reader is presented here with the nontransactive form, the portrayal of events in the passive voice. G. Kress, 'Ideological Structures in Discourse', *Vol. 4: Handbook of Discourse Analysis, Discourse Analysis in Society* (1985), p. 34.

20   Peake's use of the present tense for the opening paragraphs of his novel lends the text a sense of immediacy; however, in the wider context of the novel, the use of the present tense also suggests and reinforces the idea of time standing still. Manlove notes that frequently within the structure of the novel's storyline 'time seems to be going both backwards and forwards, and the net effect is that the temporal sequence appears frozen'. C. N. Manlove, *Modern Fantasy: Five Studies* (1975), p. 226. Past, present and future are all one and the same. Change is the enemy of Gormenghast; changes take place over time; time does not move within the castle. As noted elsewhere in this thesis, tense should not always be taken as an indicator of chronological time. Ronald Carter has written that 'recent studies have contended that where a particular tense pattern dominates a text, what is communicated as a result is not so much a notion of time or chronology as a special modality'. R. Carter, 'Responses to Language in Poetry', *Literary Text and Language Study* (1982), R. Carter and D. Burton (editors), p. 32. In the case of Peake's novel, the present tense indicates not exactly the here and now, but the sense that what is described represents the general state of affairs, past, present and future.

is the pulse of the sentence, and the adjectival participle 'jumping' represents one of the 'quicks of sentience' mentioned in (3). This effect is reinforced by the rhythmical stress of the phrases:

/

of the blood

/   /

of the jumping blood

where the regular heavy stress on 'blood' is interrupted by an additional stress on the first syllable of 'jumping'.

The third sentence in Paragraph 2 is once again the longest, consisting as it does of 21 words, a coordinating construction ('but to') and a subordinate clause. There are some difficult words here: 'quick' is not listed as a noun,[21] but in Peake's text its *function* is clearly that of a collective noun. I have assumed that Peake meant the reader to understand the 'quicks of sentience' as referring to the jumps in Titus' blood mentioned in the previous sentence, if one is to assume that Peake has followed the rules, or guidelines, for the construction of a coherent text – namely, that the subject should not be randomly altered without giving the reader some indication of the change. My assumption is reinforced by the use of the determiner 'these' as an anaphoric reference: 'these quicks of sentience' refers back to 'the jumping blood' of the previous sentence. I have paraphrased 'quicks of sentience' as 'flashes of self-knowledge', to indicate Titus' growing awareness of himself as a child, rather than as the Earl of Gormenghast. By contrast, the word 'feckless' ('feeble, futile, ineffective, aimless, irresponsible'[22]) seems to undermine the force of these 'quicks'. The hosts are 'irresponsible' because in encouraging Titus to rebel, they are working *against* the castle.[23] Alternatively, the hosts are 'feeble' because Titus is as yet immature – or there is always the possibility that we are meant to understand both senses. Another tricky word to place is 'hosts'; but the phrase 'a trillion deep' would seem to suggest that 'hosts' should be interpreted in the sense of a large multitude.

---

21   *Shorter Oxford English Dictionary*, fifth edition, 2002.

22   Ibid.

23   C. N. Manlove, author of *Modern Fantasy: Five Studies* (1975), would most likely agree with this reading, his argument being that Peake became so involved with the world he created in Gormenghast, that he failed to provide Titus with a good enough reason for leaving it: 'so much does the castle of the Groans dominate [Peake's] imagination, that where other writers strive to get into their fantastic worlds, Peake struggles to get out' (p. 217)…'Throughout *Gormenghast* he shows his uneasiness in a continual search for some way of accounting for Titus' quest. He offers a confused variety of motives which still beg the question as to where they come from in the first place' (p. 233).

Paragraph 3

(1) The gift of the bright blood. (2) Of blood that laughs when the tenets mutter 'Weep'. (3) Of blood that mourns when the sere laws croak 'Rejoice!' (4) O little revolution in great shades!

In common with the preceding paragraphs, this paragraph consists of a series of fragmented sentences. It ends with an exclamative, and is perhaps the most 'poetic' of the paragraphs to be analysed. The second and third sentences in particular are poetic in that they are almost a mirror image of each other in their structure: *Of blood that* – verb phrase – *when the* – noun phrase – speech verb – imperative in direct speech. This whole paragraph presents the reader with six verbs in four lines, a relatively dense concentration of verbs, presented as forms of opposites and contrasts (laugh/mourn; weep/rejoice). This sudden proliferation of action verbs may be emblematic of Titus' growing state of defiance: the imperatives issued by the laws and tenets are disregarded and mocked by the rebellion in Titus' blood.[24] Titus' rebellion – referred to as a 'revolution' in (4) – is still 'little', opposed as it is to the 'great shades'. And how are we to understand 'shades'? Is Peake referring to the shadowy corners of Gormenghast castle, or to the ghosts of Titus' numerous ancestors – or both? And are we to understand 'revolution' as a rebellion, a change in the state of affairs, or as directionless turning in a circle? For Titus cannot escape Gormenghast – having left its boundaries, he is later compelled to return – albeit briefly – at the end of the trilogy. As the Countess prophesies at the end of the second novel, shortly before Titus leaves the castle: 'You will only tread a circle, Titus Groan. There's not a road, not a track, but it will lead you home. For everything comes to Gormenghast.'[25]

Paragraph 4

(1) Titus the seventy-seventh. (2) Heir to a crumbling summit: to a sea of nettles: to an empire of red rust: to rituals' footprints ankle-deep in stone.

This paragraph consists of only two sentences and the structure here is very similar to that of the first paragraph in that both begin with the proper noun 'Titus'. The first paragraph told us Titus' age, but now we are given

---

24 Manlove notes that Peake generally avoids the use of verbs – specifically action verbs - in connection with the castle itself: 'the power...comes from Peake's use of verbs: giving none to the castle, he frees its life from any link with the time-bound', *Modern Fantasy: Five Studies* (1975), p. 219. While this is an interesting point, I think it has to be noted that Manlove does not provide any quantitative data to support his assertion; without such data – which a stylistician would not, I think, have neglected to provide – his claim, although thematically plausible, is simply a hunch.

25 M. Peake, *Gormenghast* (1950) in *The Gormenghast Novels* (1995), p. 807.

his title: 'the seventy-seventh'. Leaving aside the obvious parallelism in the chosen enumerators (seven: seventy-seventh), the emphasis switches from Titus' status as a child to his status as the Earl of Gormenghast. The focus of the text has likewise shifted away from Titus' growing feelings of rebellion, and moved toward the castle itself – that which Titus has inherited from his ancestors, as opposed to that which he has been given by the other children of the world. The whole phrase forming the first fragmented sentence serves as a proper noun: it is an example of ellipsis – the phrase in its entirety should read 'Titus is the seventy-seventh Earl of Gormenghast'. The phrase reinforces Titus' role as Earl, immediately following two paragraphs which describe his rebellion as child. Titus is seven years old – but he is also the seventy-seventh Earl of Gormenghast.

There is a strongly marked parallelism in the second sentence:

Heir   to a...
to a...
to an...
to rituals' footprints

The images which follow in each of the succeeding phrases are those of decay and things overgrown. The image of the sea ('a sea of nettles'[26]) is recalled when the reader reaches the word 'footprints' a little later, but the footprints are not those in sand which are quickly erased by the sea – these footprints are 'ankle-deep in stone'. The rituals have left their mark indelibly on the castle.

This fourth paragraph is followed by the single word 'Gormenghast', the proper noun forming a paragraph all on its own. In this short extract, then, three paragraphs have begun with proper nouns, as follows:

Titus (is seven)
Titus the seventy-seventh
Gormenghast

The parallel structure exemplifies the power-hierarchy. Titus the seven-year old child is subject to Titus the seventy-seventh Earl of Gormenghast, and even the Earl himself is subject to the timeless power of the castle. The structure demonstrates where the power lies – with Gormenghast, a force so powerful that it is granted a paragraph all to itself.

---

26   Nettles are also plants on overgrown land.

Paragraph 6

> (1) Withdrawn and ruinous it broods in umbra: the immemorial masonry: the towers, the tracts. (2) Is all corroding? (3) No. (4) Through an avenue of spires a zephyr floats; a bird whistles; a freshet bears away from a choked river. (5) Deep in a fist of stone a doll's hand wriggles, warm rebellious on the frozen palm. (6) A shadow shifts its length. (7) A spider stirs…

This is the longest paragraph of the opening passage, consisting of seven sentences. The focus is still on the castle. The first sentence contains a combination of animistic and humanizing metaphors[27] to personify the castle, which is given a sulky and faintly malevolent personality (withdrawn/broods). The internal parallelism of (1) after the first colon is reinforced by the repeated *m*s in '*u*m*bra*' and '*imm*e*m*orial *m*asonry' and the (almost!) pararhyme in '*t*owers' and '*t*rac*ts*'. The answer to the question posed in (2) is seemingly anomalous because the question – 'Is all corroding?' – is ostensibly about the castle, but the answer is concerned with forces of nature (zephyr/bird/freshet) unconnected with the castle – until, that is, the reader comes to Titus once again, wriggling his 'doll's hand' within the 'fist of stone'. The question and answer imply the presence of a narrator and a narratee; Gormenghast itself is undoubtedly one of the characters of the trilogy, perhaps the most interesting character of them all. Peake's narrative voice is often situated within the consciousness of one of the characters, and more often than not the narration is given from the *castle's* point of view. Manlove comments that 'Gormenghast, considered both as place and society, is the most important character'.[28] In considering this short extract alone, it is interesting to note that the number of fragmented sentences rapidly diminishes once the subject turns from Titus to the castle. The castle is complete – hence the full sentences – but the immature Titus is not. Peake's syntax is in this respect iconic.

The themes of rebellion and escape are quickly picked up again after the interrogative of (2), and here we find a succession of action verbs: 'floats', 'whistles', 'bears away from'. The wind, the birds and the streams do not answer to Gormenghast: they are not subject to the castle's influence, unlike

---

27 Leech notes that these categories 'overlap, because humanity entails animacy'; the animistic metaphor 'attributes animate characteristics to the inanimate' and the humanizing or anthropomorphic metaphor 'attributes characteristics of humanity to what is not human'. 'Withdrawn' and 'broods' can at a stretch fit both categories, although 'ruinous' has a more dubious status. G. Leech, *A Linguistic Guide to English Poetry* (1969), p. 158.

28 C. N. Manlove, *Modern Fantasy: Five Studies* (1975), p. 217.

Titus, whom we meet again in (5). He is no longer Titus the seventy-seventh; he is no longer even a person, but a wriggling 'doll's hand', tiny and ineffectual against the 'fist of stone', the larger hand which holds him fast. But he is active – he 'wriggles' – and he is 'warm' and 'rebellious' where the castle is 'frozen'. But the castle is clearly not going to give in without a fight; (6) once again reinforces the images of stagnation and inactivity within the castle grounds: 'A shadow shifts its length.' The length of the shadow changes because time is passing – the shadows grow as the day wears on and the sun moves through the sky; what appears to be a verb of movement here ('shifts') actually is not at all – it is the *sun* that moves, not the shadow, nor whatever it is that is casting the shadow. Finally, the paragraph ends with a verb of movement after all – the spider 'stirs' – but with the image of the spider comes the association of cobwebs and dust. By the end of this paragraph it seems that the two adversaries are evenly matched. Titus is diminished in physical stature and located deep at the heart of the castle, but his eventual rebellion has been clearly marked in the text; Gormenghast is immeasurably huge, an inexorable power, but the freshet made its escape from the 'choked river', just as Titus will make his escape from the vast decaying mass of the castle. The final word is perhaps reserved for the castle: '*And darkness winds between the characters.*' How is one to paraphrase this? Leech and Short suggest that 'characters' could refer to the characters of the text – the letters of the alphabet.[29] But for the moment it would seem that the castle continues to exert its power over its occupants.

At the end of the opening passage, the reader has been introduced to the two adversaries: the enormous sprawling environs of the castle, with its weighty phrases and lexical items concerning stone and shadows, and the child Titus, with his action verbs and his tiny wriggle of rebellion. Peake foregrounds the theme of rebellion by a number of means. In the very first paragraph the omission of an expected article emphasises Titus' childlike status and subsequent phrases relating to Titus' various roles are placed in a series of parallel structures emblematic of the power hierarchy. At this stage, the power lies with the castle. Gormenghast is described in prepositional phrases separated by colons and semi-colons which give each phrase the weight of a sentence: 'to a crumbling summit: to a sea of nettles: to an empire of red rust'. The effect of this is to reinforce the castle's immense physical weight and its heavy influence on the lives of the inhabitants. Titus' immature status is embodied in the elliptical

---

29   Leech and Short provide an interesting analysis of a section of *Gormenghast* which immediately follows the one analysed here. This section opens with the words 'Who are the characters?', and Leech and Short note that '*characters* can mean either "letters, ciphers", or "people in the fiction" '. G. Leech and M. Short, *Style in Fiction* (1981), p. 140.

sentence structure associated with him but there is a sense of growing rebellion in the description of his 'jumping blood'; here the form arguably enacts the content. Peake's use of foregrounding therefore clearly signposts Titus' eventual rebellion at word, sentence and discourse levels.

iii) Foregrounding in *Wuthering Heights*

The opacity of the opening passage of *Gormenghast* requires the reader to actively construct meanings. I turn now to a comparatively transparent text, Brontë's *Wuthering Heights*. I hope to demonstrate that foregrounded items in this text also require the reader to be an active participant rather than a passive recipient. In the following analysis I have focused on anaphoric reference and parallel constructions, the impersonal pronoun coupled with the use of body parts as actor, and finally the use of parenthetical constructions.

The passage from *Wuthering Heights* I have chosen to explore is volume one, chapter three,[30] in which Lockwood passes the time before falling asleep reading the words Cathy has written; first those carved into the couch itself, which take the form of her given name followed by the three surnames she imagined herself to possess, and second, the words she has scrawled into the margins of those books which constitute her library.[31] These words recount the events of an 'awful Sunday' (p. 20), in which Cathy and Heathcliff are compelled to listen to Joseph's three-hour homily.

Lockwood's first dream is a re-enactment of Cathy's 'awful Sunday', in which Joseph is confused with the preacher Jabes Branderham and Lockwood himself takes the place of the child Cathy, forced to listen to a sermon consisting of *'four hundred and ninety* parts' (p. 23). At the commencement of the dream, Joseph and Lockwood are likened to pilgrims: Joseph carries a 'cudgel' which he refers to as a 'pilgrim's staff' (p. 23), and he admonishes Lockwood for

---

30 E. Brontë, *Wuthering Heights* (1847), Penguin Classics edition (1995), pp. 19-32. Subsequent references to this edition are marked in the main body of the text.

31 Critics have, of course, discussed Cathy's negative relationship with books. She makes herself ill on purpose in order to separate Edgar from his library, and from the passage discussed here the reader can see that even from a very early age she was ill-disposed towards literature. Instead of reading the books in her library, she defaces them with scribbled complaints about Hindley's ill-treatment of Heathcliff and with rude caricatures of Joseph. She hurls a volume into the dog-kennel, vowing that she hates 'a good book' (p. 21). Heathcliff follows suit, and his punishment is to be prohibited from eating meals with the family and from playing with Cathy. Heathcliff is later barred from pursuing his education any further, and books symbolise to a certain extent the social world that is represented by Thrushcross Grange and its inhabitants. One can add to these observations the fact that Lockwood piles 'the books up in a pyramid' against the hole in the window, in order to keep Cathy's child-ghost out (p. 25). It is significant also that Cathy's daughter wins Hareton over by encouraging him to read, thereby achieving what her mother could not – she accepts and sets out to improve the 'degraded' Hareton, where Cathy rejects the 'degraded' Heathcliff.

not having one. In parallel constructions separated by a semi-colon (pronoun + auxiliary verb + main verb), Brontë changes the main verb from 'going' to 'journeying':

> I was not going there;
> we were   journeying to hear... (p. 23)

Joseph, described as Lockwood's 'guide' (p. 23), was initially supposed to be showing him the way home, but Lockwood is now a pilgrim on a journey. In the paragraph which follows, the pilgrims become potentially condemned men: 'either Joseph, the preacher, or I...were to be publicly exposed and excommunicated' (p. 23). These events are reminiscent of the children's admonition at the hands – or tongue – of Joseph, and his assertion that 'owd Nick' (p. 22) would come to fetch them. Joseph's three-hour homily is magnified in Lockwood's dream to a sermon of prodigious length, each part of which deals with 'odd transgressions' (p. 23) or sins of which Lockwood was unaware; perhaps this reflects Cathy's mystification at Joseph's anger with the children for making themselves 'snug...in the arch of the dresser' (p. 21).

The Lockwood-Cathy/Jabes-Joseph confusion is made clear to the reader in the following section of Lockwood's narrative:

> Oh, how weary I grew. How I writhed, and yawned, and nodded, and revived! How I pinched and pricked myself, and rubbed my eyes, and stood up, and sat down again, and nudged Joseph to inform me if he would ever have done! (p. 23)

The pronoun 'he' could be understood to refer to either Jabes or Joseph himself, the previous reference to Jabes being sufficiently distant from this passage to render it possible that it is Joseph to whom Lockwood refers. Halliday and Hasan note that 'where the cohesive element is something like *he* or *one*, which coheres by direct reference to, or substitution for, another item, the presupposed element is typically a specific item in the immediately preceding sentence.'[32] It is significant, I think, that the last reference to 'he' which refers directly to Jabes Branderham is four sentences distant from the 'he' of Lockwood's complaint; 'Jabes' appears five sentences distant. It is plausible, therefore, that Joseph and Jabes could be confused in that ambiguous pronoun, and that this effect is intentional on the author's part. Joseph has taken the place of the preacher, and Lockwood, his head still full of Cathy's words, has taken the place of the recalcitrant child. The parallel constructions

---

32   M.A.K. Halliday and R. Hasan, *Cohesion in English* (1976), p. 15.

how weary I grew

How I…-ed, and…-ed, and…-ed, and …ed!

How I…-ed and …-ed…and…-ed…

and stood [verb –ed] …,

and sat [verb –ed]…,

and…! (p. 23)

mimic the fidgeting and complaining of a child.[33] These constructions – the use of 'how' to indicate the extent of an emotion or action and the use of 'and' as a conjunction to bind together a string of verbs, coupled with the use of exclamation marks to emphasise strong emotion and to provide the reader with an indication of the tone in which the text is designed to be read – are strongly reminiscent of Cathy's written style in her makeshift journal:

How little did I dream that Hindley would ever make me cry so!...

Poor Heathcliff!

Hindley…   won't let him sit with us,

nor eat with us any more;

and, he says,

he and I must not play together,

and threatens to turn him out of the house... (p. 22)

Lockwood's complaint, as Branderham is about to embark on the '*First of the Seventy First*' (p. 24), is the accusation of a child, that of being bored by an adult who has forced the child to sit still and listen, as Cathy is forced to groan and shiver her way through Joseph's homily. Jabes Branderham responds with the complaint that Lockwood 'didst…gapingly contort thy visage' (p. 24) – an adult's complaint that a child has been pulling faces, or yawning, instead of paying attention. Once again, the reader is given the impression that Lockwood has changed places with Cathy, and Joseph with Jabes Branderham.

Lockwood falls asleep for a second time, only to dream that he is visited by Cathy's child-ghost, a visitor he refuses to acknowledge as human; this refusal is made evident in his use of the impersonal pronoun to refer to the figure at the window, and his repeated use of body parts as actor in material processes.

---

33 Heathcliff also reprimands Lockwood on this score: 'your childish outcry has sent sleep to the devil for me' (p. 28).

The poor light obliges Lockwood to rely on his other senses. The child's face is distinguished only 'obscurely' (p. 25), and the focus throughout this second dream is on that which Lockwood can feel and hear. Lockwood uses the impersonal pronoun 'it' to refer to Cathy's voice, ' "Catherine Linton," it ['a most melancholy voice'] replied shiveringly', her wrist, 'I pulled its wrist on to the broken pane, and rubbed it to and fro', the creature, 'still it wailed', and Cathy's hand, or the grip of her hand, 'and maintained its tenacious gripe' (p. 25). Not once does Lockwood refer to 'she', or 'her', or even 'the child'. Cathy is an amalgamation of disassembled face, hand, wrist, fingers, and voice; she is kept distant from the world of the living by Lockwood's refusal to acknowledge her as anything other than a 'creature', and this effect is compounded when coupled with Lockwood's use of elegant variation to describe Cathy once Heathcliff appears on the scene. Cathy is, in turn, 'the little fiend', 'that minx', 'a changeling' and a 'wicked little soul' (p. 27); she is also linked with the witches of *Macbeth* in Lockwood's later reference to the 'brindled' cat 'Grimalkin' (p. 29). In Lockwood's eyes she is a malevolent sprite, in spite of Cathy's description of herself as a 'waif', homeless and helpless, and lost on the moors.

To recap, then: a calculated use of foregrounded anaphoric reference is in evidence once again, but the intention this time is not to confuse the characters in the reader's mind, but to place as much distance as possible between the disturbed sleeper and the wanderer on the moors. Lockwood's persistent use of the impersonal pronoun *it* to refer to Cathy's ghost, or parts of her ghostly body, has the double effect of distancing the ghost from the human beings – Lockwood and the reader – and of underlining Lockwood's callousness towards a child in obvious distress, a female child who has lost her way on the moors, and on a cold and wintry night, at that.[34]

Parenthetical constructions[35] are very much in evidence in both dream-sequences, and their role in each is to remind the reader that Lockwood is simply recounting his nightmares, and that the events described have not

---

34   There has been much discussion regarding the morality of Brontë's novel, and Q. D. Leavis was of the opinion that the book 'has a very firm moral effect. The technical means…for implying moral criticism without stating it, for making the reader do this work himself, is the technique of contrast and parallelism'. Q. D. Leavis, 'A Fresh Approach to Wuthering Heights', *Collected Essays Volume 1* (1969), p. 252. Leavis' argument is that the apparently cruel behaviour of one character is often offset by the brutal behaviour of another, and this parallelism constitutes part of Lockwood's role: 'Lockwood's horror of the household at Wuthering Heights is immediately offset by *our* horror at *him* when he then, in a real nightmare, brutally fights off the child begging…to be let in after losing the way on the moor' (ibid., p. 254).

35   By 'parenthetical constructions', I mean those clauses or sentences which are *not* part of Lockwood's dream narrative, and which represent an intrusion of Lockwood's voice into the dream-sequences.

actually taken place in the fictional 'waking' world. In his dream of Joseph and the preacher there are two such constructions, the second comprising two lengthy sentences (106 words in total). The first of these interruptions to Lockwood's narrative is as follows:

> Alas, for the effects of bad tea and bad temper! what else could it be that made me pass such a terrible night? I don't remember another that I can at all compare with it since I was capable of suffering.
>
> I began to dream... (p. 22)

The reader is notified, therefore, that the events to follow are imaginary. The second interruption is the longest, consisting as it does of a description of the chapel: 'I have passed it really in my walks...'; the adverb 'really' is also intended to act as an indication to the reader that Lockwood's walks are part of the 'real' world, whereas the particular journey he is currently relating is not. This description comes to an end with the words 'one penny from their own pockets' (p. 23). Although the digression is long, Lockwood's words do not destroy the gloomy mood of the passage, referring as he does to the 'embalming on the few corpses' lying in the swamp. The parenthesis is brought to an end when Lockwood brings us back to his narrative with the words, 'However, in my dream,' (p. 23) and the narrative continues until finally he is woken by the fir-tree's taps on the window. In his dream of Cathy's child-ghost, the reader is kept conscious of the fact that Lockwood is dreaming by the scattering of parenthetical phrases such as 'This time', 'I thought', 'when awake', 'the intense horror of nightmare came over me', and, most tellingly of all, 'why did I think of *Linton*? I had read *Earnshaw* twenty times for Linton', until finally we come to 'I discovered the yell was not ideal' (pp. 25-26). Brontë, through these parenthetical constructions, has gone to some trouble to distinguish between Lockwood's dream-world and the 'real' world of Wuthering Heights, and the reader is discouraged from confusing the two during Lockwood's narration of his nightmares. However, it is a different state of affairs once Lockwood is awake, and the effect is rendered more startling by these earlier attempts to convince the reader of the fictional nature of his dreams. Heathcliff, of course, is beside himself with anguish, believing as he does that Cathy's ghost has returned. Lockwood, too, seems to be convinced that his dream was real. He tells Heathcliff that the room is 'swarming with ghosts and goblins', and in reference to Cathy's ghost he asserts that 'If the little fiend had got in at the window, she probably would have strangled me!' (p. 27). In addition, let us not forget that the ghost identified herself as Catherine

Linton – a fact already remarked upon by Lockwood. After all, Cathy did not become Catherine Linton until she married Edgar, but Cathy's child-ghost clings to the name she bore when she died. As Catherine Linton, she is denied both the Heights and Heathcliff's presence.

By first convincing the reader that Lockwood's narrative is really only a dream, and then confounding the issue by having the characters behaving as if the aforementioned events had really taken place after all, coupled with the anomaly of the ghost's name, Brontë leaves the reader in some doubt as to whether Cathy's ghost did or did not come that night. In any case, the effect on Heathcliff is that which is important. John Hagan has commented as follows on this passage:

> when Lockwood arrives at Wuthering Heights and dreams of Catherine's ghost at the window, all of Heathcliff's anguished yearning is revived.... Heathcliff is convinced that his visitor has really seen the spectre he himself had hoped to see for all those eighteen years. Most significantly, it is on precisely this delusion that Emily Brontë arranges for the dénouement of the novel to hinge, for from this point onward Heathcliff can think of nothing but joining Catherine in death.[36]

It is certainly arguable that Heathcliff loses all lust for revenge once he hears Lockwood's tale of ghosts and goblins.

Lockwood's dream of Cathy's child-ghost is one of several episodes in the novel in which Brontë balances the supernatural with the plausible. We cannot know for sure whether or not Cathy's ghost did come to seek Heathcliff that night, nor can we be sure that the ghosts of Heathcliff and Cathy do not 'walk' at the end of the novel, despite the assertions of Lockwood and Nelly Dean to the contrary. Does Heathcliff really see Cathy herself shortly before his death, or is her appearance simply an hallucination, an effect of his self-imposed fast?

To sum up: foregrounded anaphoric reference indicates that the participants in Lockwood's first dream have changed places; certainly the Joseph-Jabes switch is made evident, and thus the Lockwood-Cathy switch can be inferred. The anaphoric 'he' is foregrounded because the reader will be forced to consider who 'he' is. McHale notes that a character, unlike the narrator, is not subject to the cohesive rules of the text and does not have to supply a referent.[37] It is unclear whether Lockwood is referring to Joseph or Jabes, but

---

36   J. Hagan, 'Control of Sympathy in "Wuthering Heights"', *Nineteenth-Century Fiction* (1967), p. 316.

37   B. McHale, 'Unspeakable Sentences, Unnatural Acts: Linguistics and Poetics Revisited', *Poetics Today* (1983), pp. 17-45.

I have argued that this is not a failure on Brontë's part but rather an intentional poetic effect allowing the switch between the characters to take place. The resulting confusion of Lockwood with Cathy explains how Cathy and not Lockwood comes to be accused of adultery. The foregrounded parenthetical constructions which represent Lockwood's intrusions into his own dream narrative support the carefully constructed fabric of the supernatural versus the plausible which is woven throughout Brontë's novel – a fabric which allows the more romantically inclined reader to believe that Cathy and Heathcliff do indeed walk the moors together once Heathcliff has joined Cathy in the quiet grave.

iv) Conclusions

In this chapter, we have seen many instances of foregrounding, both qualitative and quantitative: Peake's text in particular abounds in broken rules and unusual constructions which amount to examples of qualitative foregrounding, or breaches of the language code itself. The parallel constructions that constitute quantitative foregrounding, or deviation from an expected frequency, in *Gormenghast* contribute to the semantic density of the text: new meanings are created as the reader is required to interpret the links forged between the connected items.

We have also seen examples of prominence – sound patterns and parenthetical constructions – which are noticeable to the reader, but which lack thematic significance and therefore do not constitute an instance of foregrounding. We see how a collaboration between linguist and critic could prove useful: a linguistic description of a text can reveal what rules have been broken or what is unusual about a particular utterance; the critic can then use this information in the formulation of a coherent interpretation of a literary text, because it is only those examples of deviation and prominence that show thematic significance which can accurately be described as foregrounding. The theme of rebellion in *Gormenghast* is marked in foregrounded items such as parallel structures and elliptical sentences. Brontë's calculated use of anaphoric reference is important thematically because the character-switch between Lockwood and Cathy must be effected so that Cathy, and not Lockwood, can be seen to be charged with adultery: this point will be explored in more detail in chapter four.

Needless to say, foregrounding is lost in paraphrase, as I discovered in my attempt to paraphrase the opening paragraphs of *Gormenghast*. Foregrounding is not just textual decoration that can be discarded: foregrounded items support, reinforce, or even introduce the ideas or themes of a text, and as such constitute a vital component of content. To disregard foregrounded items, to exclude them from a paraphrase, to change the form in this way, necessarily entails a loss, or a change of content.

Chapter 2: Speech and Thought Representation in Fiction

i) Introductory

In this chapter I have explored how linguistic theories concerning spoken discourse have proved useful to the critic. I have focused in particular on the linguistic categorisations of the methods of representing speech and thought in fiction and how these categorisations can be usefully applied to various passages from a novel. Not only is the topic of fictional discourse an area where linguistic analysis has proved particularly useful, but it also provides several arguments in support of my hypothesis that form and content are inseparable in literary writing. These arguments relate to the subtle effects associated with each method on the speech and thought continuum, especially that of Free Indirect Discourse (FID); the lack of an 'original' utterance to which its written representation can be traced; and finally the important role punctuation has to play in the writer's attempts to represent spoken language.

The methods of representing speech and thought in written language have been carefully categorised following linguistic criteria, most notably by Leech and Short.[1] I have reproduced these categories in Appendix D, placing the options available to the author on a continuum with Pure Narrative (PN) on the far left and Free Direct Discourse (FDD) on the far right. In the fictional representation of speech, Free Direct Speech (FDS) represents the voice of the character without any interference from the narrator whatsoever – not even the inclusion of quotation marks and the reporting clause which characterise Direct Speech (DS); any movement toward the left on the continuum therefore represents an increasing degree of narratorial control. When we reach the Narrative Report of a Speech Act (NRSA), the character's actual words are lost altogether and the narrator provides only a summary of the sentiments expressed.

The fictional representation of speech and thought can serve many purposes in a prose work. Fictional dialogue, be it speech or thought, can advance plot or it can delineate and develop character; dialogue can also serve to 'describe setting or atmosphere, to present a moral argument or a discussion on cabbages and kings, or to perform any combination of these purposes.'[2] In addition, the dialogue of a novel can add to the illusion of reality created in fictional prose:

---

1   See G. Leech and M. Short, *Style in Fiction* (1981), chapter 10, pp. 318-351.

2   N. Page, *Speech in the English Novel* (1988), p. 55.

'language can copy reality. This is the case of fictional speech: here, the events being described as part of the mock reality are themselves linguistic, and so language is used to simulate, rather than simply to report, what is going on in the fictional world'.[3] It is important from the outset, however, to recognise that fictional speech does *not* resemble or imitate life: a glance at any transcript of real speech will reveal why this is so. Real speech is full of hesitations and pauses, stopgap noises, false starts, syntactic anomalies, interruptions, overlaps, and frequent transitions, all of which, if presented in written form, would render a text intolerable and unreadable.[4] In the past, critics have made the mistake of praising a novel's dialogue for its resemblance to real-life speech, but readers have since been alerted to the idealised nature of fictional dialogue.

Despite the differences between real and fictional discourse, there is no doubt that linguistic research has proved useful to critics in the analysis of fictional speech. Ronald Tanaka wrote an illuminating discussion on Edward Albee's *Who's Afraid of Virginia Woolf?*[5] based on the speech act theory of J. Austin as later refined by J. Searle.[6] Richard Ohmann, making use of the same theory in his article 'Literature as Act',[7] demonstrates how one character has to buy into the ideology of another in order to fulfil the felicity conditions[8] required for the successful completion of a speech act; viewed in this way, it becomes possible

---

3   G. Leech and M. Short, *Style in Fiction* (1981), p. 160.

4   Leech and Short comment on the differences between real speech and fictional speech in ibid., pp. 159-166.

5   R. Tanaka, 'Action and Meaning in Literary Theory', *Journal of Literary Semantics* (1972), pp. 41-56.

6   Speech act theory is the theory that people *do* things when they speak: promise, request, threaten, and so on; an extreme example is Ridcully's utterance, 'And I so rule', on page 322 of Terry Pratchett's *Going Postal*. Ridcully is the impartial adjudicator in the race to Genua, and his speech act makes the new ruling – no horses, no broomsticks – concrete and inviolable. These words are differentiated from Ridcully's other utterances by a marked formality of lexis and syntax. Much of the dialogue in Peake's *Gormenghast* novels is based on ritual, and each utterance is therefore a speech act similar to Ridcully's judicious ruling. Consider Sourdust's greeting to his master, Lord Groan: 'I, Sourdust, lord of the library, personal adviser to your lordship, nonagenarian, and student of the Groan lore, proffer to your lordship the salutations of a dark morning, robed as I am in rags, student as I am of the tomes, and nonagenarian as I happen to be in the matter of years' (M. Peake, *Titus Groan* (1946), in *The Gormenghast Novels* (1995), p. 48). All this just to say good morning! Sourdust can barely communicate outside of the wording pertaining to the Gormenghast lore, and the irony is of course that the significance of many of the daily rituals has been lost over the course of time, rendering the speech acts meaningless; the utterances of Sourdust and Lord Groan are empty – they no longer *do* anything.

7   R. Ohmann, 'Literature as Act', *Approaches to Poetics* (1972), pp. 81-107.

8   Katie Wales writes that 'in speech act theory felicity conditions refer to particular kinds of appropriateness valid for the successful functioning of speech acts, e.g. promising, ordering, threatening, requesting, etc. Utterances which do not satisfy various conditions are regarded as infelicitous, and, in a sense, as invalid speech acts'. K. Wales, *A Dictionary of Stylistics*, 2nd edition, 2001.

to identify and understand the assumptions and prevailing ideology behind a work of literature. Linguistic theories relating to spoken discourse have obviously proved especially useful to the critic writing about plays, as in the previous two examples; Short points out that 'drama is the literary genre which is most like naturally occurring conversation'.[9] But speech act theory is not the only linguistic theory to have proved itself useful and drama is not the only genre to benefit from the application of these theories. Critics have made use of Grice's maxims and his work on conversational implicature[10] in the analysis of prose texts.[11] Linguistic research relating to conversational management can be used to assess the balance of power between fictional conversational participants. The nature of a relationship between characters can be conveyed through forms of address and other linguistic indicators of politeness or formality. Linguistic categorisations of non-verbal communication can also usefully be applied to prose texts.[12] The main body of this chapter consists of a reading of Terry Pratchett's *Going Postal* based on some of the above theories and I hope to have demonstrated how useful they can be.

As mentioned previously, the topic of fictional discourse raises at least three arguments in support of the claim that form = content. The first of these arguments relates to the individual effects associated with each method of representing fictional discourse. It is important to bear in mind that here, as in all other areas of literary production, nothing is arbitrary:

> for no novelist can avoid continually exercising a choice between different modes of presentation...he must choose between dialogue and narrative or descriptive prose, or a combination of these in proportions which must be settled. If he decides to make use of dialogue, a further selection has to be made among the various ways of presenting speech.[13]

---

9   M. Short, *Exploring the Language of Poems, Plays and Prose* (1996), p. 168.

10 Extra meanings are created when Grice's maxims are deliberately flouted, and Grice refers to these meanings as conversational implicatures. Cf. footnote 42 in this chapter, but it should be noted that Grice insisted upon the difference between violating the maxims and flouting them. Violating a maxim may not necessarily yield an extra meaning; the creation of conversational implicatures is more likely if one simply flouts a maxim.

11 See, for example, G. Leech and M. Short, *Style in Fiction* (1981), chapter 9, pp. 294-304, in which the authors use Grice's maxims to investigate a passage from Ken Kesey's *One Flew Over the Cuckoo's Nest*.

12 David Graddol *et al.*, identify the following as functions of NVC (non-verbal communication): gesture, proxemics, body contact, posture and body orientation, facial expression and gaze. D. Graddol *et al.*, *Describing Language* (1994), chapter 6, pp. 146-189.

13 N. Page, *Speech in the English Novel* (1988), p. 23.

The critic must first recognise the decisions the author has made, and from there she can examine the author's choices – why this way and not that way? How does the representation of speech and thought function in the text as a whole? The author has, after all, deliberately chosen a certain position on the continuum because of its related effects; for example, DS lends a dramatic quality to the scene but often at the expense of narrative pace. The effects associated with each method of discourse representation are subtle and these overtones are inevitably lost in paraphrase. Of all the methods of speech representation, Free Indirect Discourse (FID) has attracted the most critical attention. This can possibly be attributed to the modern-day critic's preoccupation with point of view, in that FID can feasibly represent the voice of both the narrator and the character concerned at one and the same time. To digress just briefly, it is interesting to note the problems posed by the reading aloud of passages of FID from a novel. Does the performer read in her neutral narrator's voice, or in the voice of the character? Terry Pratchett's *Thud!* contains passages of FID in which the performer, Stephen Briggs, is forced to read in the voice of the character, a troll called Brick, because the text contains idiolectal elements that belong to Brick, but much of the text can also be attributed to the narrator.[14] This mingling of voices makes FID the perfect vehicle for irony, as any reader of Jane Austen can testify. In any case, the point remains that to alter the form of discourse representation is to change something of the content. Even the rendering of an utterance in Indirect Speech (IS) instead of DS necessitates several changes: the tense is back-shifted, proximal deictics are neutralised, and because the movement to the left on the continuum takes the reader further away from the character's voice, emotion markers are usually expunged.[15]

The relationship between DS and IS on the continuum brings me to the second argument in support of the claim that form = content. Ann Banfield, in an essay entitled 'Narrative Style and the Grammar of Direct and Indirect Speech', convincingly argues that DS and IS are not transformationally related as Richard Ohmann had earlier claimed.[16] This is helpful in that it removes the onus on the reader to see one form of speech as derived from, or prior to, another. Brian McHale upholds Banfield's assertion, although he does not

---

14   For example, the passages on pp. 152-153 and 186-187 of the same novel.

15   Compare, for example, the following IS rendering of a DS original: 'Miss Dearheart asked Moist what he wanted.' and the DS original: 'Well, what do you want, Mr. Clever?' T. Pratchett, *Going Postal*, p. 313.

16   Ohmann presents this argument in his paper 'Generative Grammars and the Concept of Literary Style' (1964), *Linguistics and Literary Style* (1970), D. C. Freeman (editor), pp. 258-278.

support her argument in its entirety.[17] McHale directs our attention to another important difference between real-life speech and fictional speech:

> the principle [*sic*] drawback of the traditional account…is the assumption built into it that the three types of represented/reported discourse are derived from one another, FID from ID, ID from DD…. Admittedly, this account does capture the average speaker's sense of how these types are related to each other, and his ability to convert one version into another; but in fiction this intuition is falsified, or, more to the point, it is fostered as part of novelistic illusionism. In the everyday production and use of represented/reported discourse, it is theoretically always possible to recover the 'original' direct utterance from the derived non-direct versions, or at least to think of it as being recoverable, 'basic' to the non-direct transforms. This is obviously not so in fiction, in which there is no direct 'original' prior to or behind an instance of ID or FID; the supposedly 'derived' utterances are not versions of anything, but themselves the 'originals' in that they give as much as the reader will ever learn of 'what was really said'.[18]

The relevance of this line of reasoning to the form/content debate is the idea that there is no unobserved content lurking behind the text in the form of an original utterance that has undergone a transformation. As McHale says, the form to which the reader has access – the words on the page – is the only form that has ever existed, and as such is the unique source of content.

The third and final point regarding form and content in the fictional representation of discourse is that concerning the use of punctuation. It is generally agreed that the English writing system is badly equipped to represent spoken language, and that writers must do the best they can with the tools available to them. Textual layout helps the reader understand who said what, the convention being that a new line is used when a different character begins speaking. Words heavily stressed by a speaker are italicised: ' "Have you gone *completely* mad?" said Miss Dearheart.'[19] A dash might lead the reader to infer an interruption:

> 'That was for essential maintenance – ' Mr Slant began.
>
> 'No, it was for repairs,' snapped Vetinari.[20]

---

17   B. McHale, 'Free Indirect Discourse: A Survey of Recent Accounts', *Poetics and Theory of Literature* (1978), pp. 235-287.

18   T. Pratchett, *Going Postal* (2004), p. 256.

19   Ibid., p. 245.

20   Ibid., p. 73.

An ellipsis might represent a momentary hesitation: ' "There's...hints, here and there, but really we need something more solid..." '.[21] Punctuation, always important, plays an even greater role in discourse representation. It is here, perhaps as nowhere else in written texts, that the author's choice of punctuation can guide the reader toward one particular interpretation.

The section that follows is the result of the application of some of the above theories to certain passages from Terry Pratchett's 2004 novel, *Going Postal*.

ii) Speech and Thought Representation in *Going Postal*

Terry Pratchett, the author of the hugely popular Discworld series, is a writer who, like many modern authors, makes extensive use of dialogue. Pratchett's dialogue serves both to advance plot and to delineate character, but there is more to it than this: through his use of FID, Pratchett is able to pass comment on both the characters he creates and the world they – and by allegorical extension, we – inhabit. Pratchett's use of FID enables the characters to comment both on themselves and on other characters, and the narrator can do the same. The allegorical nature of the text means that there is frequently a real-world counterpart to which the comments of the narrator/ character also apply. For modern-day readers, comments of a moral nature are generally more palatable when they come from the mouths of fictional characters rather than that of the narrator. The idea that literature exists to edify and instruct the reader is now old-fashioned, but this is what Pratchett manages to do nevertheless. The didactic purpose of the text is achieved through FID without alienating the reader: because his voice is inextricably intertwined with that of his characters, the narrator can moralise without appearing to do so.

Going Postal is the twenty-ninth title in the Discworld series. One of the themes of this novel is freedom: the character of Moist von Lipwig allows Pratchett to explore the nature and true extent of individual freedom when that individual is a member of a larger community. Moist is an extremely gifted con-man who has spent his life swindling for personal gain, and he is forced to come to terms with the effect his actions have had on others; his parole officer, a golem called Mr. Pump, acts as Moist's conscience, but the access the reader is granted to Moist's thoughts through numerous passages of DT and FID reveals a man capable of sympathizing with the plight of others and

---

21   T. Pratchett, *Going Postal* (2004), p. 68.

one who eventually shuns his old ways. Mr. Reacher Gilt,[22] an unscrupulous businessman and the real villain of the piece, represents in one sense the tyranny of the free market when it is not subject to government intervention, and in a more moralistic sense, the sin of avarice. Moist, despite his initial introduction to us as a fraud and a cheat, is the romantic hero who triumphs over the black-hearted malefactor: Gilt does not survive the events of the story, choosing instead to end his own life rather than to make amends as Moist did.

In this section of the chapter, I intend to discuss Pratchett's chosen methods of discourse presentation, the fictional depiction of the power-balance between characters in terms of conversational management and the use of speech adverbials, and finally, Pratchett's use of orthological and graphological deviation. The passages I have chosen to look at are as follows: Moist's first conversation with Miss Dearheart and Lord Vetinari's meeting with the financiers (pp. 66-78); Moist's conversation with Captain Carrot following the fire in the Post Office (pp. 242-244); the beginning of the race and Moist's conversation with Reacher Gilt (pp. 320-323); and the scene in the Great Hall at Unseen University in which the miscreants are publicly accused (pp. 331-342).[23]

A close examination of the passages in question reveals that the narrative is mostly a mixture of Direct Speech (DS), Pure Narrative (PN) or Narrative Report of Action (NRA),[24] Free Indirect Discourse (FID), and Direct Thought (DT).[25] There are some rare examples of Narrative Report of a Speech Act (NRSA):

---

22   The name is a pun on Robert Louis Stevenson's Long John Silver; Mr. Reacher Gilt has an eyepatch and a talkative parrot, like his piratical counterpart. The piracy as far as Gilt is concerned is not robbery on the open seas, but embezzlement on a grand scale. His parrot, instead of repeating 'pieces of eight', habitually cries 'twelve and a half per cent', an allusion to the percentage of people who would actually receive their money if everyone simultaneously decided to withdraw their savings from their bank accounts. The word 'gilt', with its reference to what is only a *superficial* covering of gold, is also a clue to the real nature of this particular character.

23   *Going Postal* is, of course, just one novel of an entire series set on the Discworld, and it should be borne in mind that Lord Vetinari, Captain Carrot and Mr. Slant are firmly established characters in the minds of Pratchett's readers through their appearances in earlier novels. The other characters featuring in these extracts, Moist von Lipwig and Reacher Gilt included, are new inventions. I have chosen these extracts in particular largely because they provide ample material for the effective illustration of the points I wish to make.

24   PN is the terminology of M. Toolan, *Narrative: A Critical Linguistic Introduction* (2001), p. 119, and NRA that of G. Leech and M. Short, *Style in Fiction* (1981), p. 324. I have decided to use Toolan's PN, to avoid any possible confusion between NRA and NRSA. Toolan also retains NRSA; see p. 139 of his book.

25   The absence of quotation marks means that the latter could be described as a form of Free Direct Thought (FDT), but the presence of reporting clauses suggests that these passages are in fact somewhere between DT and FDT on the speech/thought continuum. It is, in fact, fairly common practice amongst modern authors to omit the quotation marks around the representation of a character's *thoughts* in order to differentiate between this and the representation of a character's *speech*.

1. In a silence punctuated by chuckles from the crowd, Pony tried to explain, in so far as he now had any grip of what was going on. (p. 320)[26]

Rarer still are instances of Indirect Speech (IS): there are no examples in the passages studied.[27] DS is by far the most common representation of speech used in these passages, and in Pratchett's novels in general – as a result, it is relatively easy to rewrite many pages of any Pratchett narrative as a playscript – but there is another construction which appears with almost as much regularity as DS, and that is DT with an inversion of the reporting clause leading into a passage that could be a continuation of DT or could equally be classified as FID. For example,

2. (1) And what would you have done against a banshee? Moist had thought. (2) You suspect Gilt. (3) Well done. (4) But people like Gilt don't bother with the law. (5) They never break it, they just use people who do. (6) And you'll never find anything written down, anywhere. (p. 244)

The second person pronoun 'you' of (2) and the evaluative phrase in (3) attribute these sentences to Moist, whose words are addressed silently to Captain Carrot, but it is arguable that (4) to (6) could be classified as either a moralistic narratorial comment on 'people like Gilt' as part of the text's allegorical function, or these words could represent a continuation of Moist's DT – or perhaps both. Similarly, the 'you'll' of (6) could equally be addressed specifically to Captain Carrot, or, more generally, to the reader, a device which arguably has the effect of animating the reader by directly involving her in the text. A related technique is the considered placing of the reporting clause in (1), 'Moist had thought', which is placed *after* the reported clause; the effect of this delay is to plunge the reader into momentary uncertainty about whether the words are those of the narrator or of the character – the longer the reported clause, the greater the effect – although in the example quoted above it is reasonable to conclude that the words belong to Moist. The uncertainty is more marked in passages like the following:

3. There's no stink more sorrowful than the stink of wet, burnt paper, Moist thought. It means: the end. (p. 242)

---

26   T. Pratchett, *Going Postal* (2004). Subsequent page references to this novel are marked in the main body of the text. Examples and sentences are numbered for ease of reference.

27   In fact, I have been so far unsuccessful in my search for an example of IS in Pratchett's novel; it would appear that Pratchett does not make use of this form of speech representation at all.

In examples 2 and 3, the narrative arguably slips into FID following the reporting clause. Other examples are more easily classifiable:

4. (1) All *they* wanted to do was be delivered, he thought. (2) At a time like this, sitting on the sea bed for nine thousand years seemed quite attractive. (p. 242)

Even without the temporal deictic 'like this', the sentiments expressed and the contextual evidence[28] make it relatively easy to identify (2) as representing the voice of the character alone: there is no bivocality between character and narrator here, and note the ease with which (2) can be represented in DT: it is necessary only to alter the verb-form from the narratorial past tense to the present tense of the character ('seemed' to 'seems'), and to add a reporting clause:[29]

5. At a time like this, sitting on the sea bed for nine thousand years seems quite attractive, he thought.

This is FID sourced in character, meaning that the reader can attribute the utterance entirely to Moist. The specificity of the fictional situation, unlike example 2, renders pointless any attempt at an allegorical interpretation. An ironic narratorial voice is not needed here.

The amalgam of narrator/character voice in Pratchett's text is pervasive; some instances are difficult to spot and may be overlooked on a first reading:

6. 'We do a pamphlet,' said almost-certainly-Miss Dearheart, pulling open a drawer and flipping a thin booklet on to the desk. (p. 66)

This time, the voice of the character has invaded the *reporting* clause: Moist has just noticed that Miss Dearheart wears no rings on her fingers,[30] prompting him to conclude that she is not married, and therefore 'almost-certainly-Miss'. The reporting clause itself is embedded in what is clearly a

---

28 The golem Anghammarad, who perishes in the Post Office fire, actually spends nine thousand years sitting on the sea bed (see pp. 153-155 of *Going Postal*).

29 This new rendering of 4 into DT passes Toolan's 'framing or commutation test' on p. 132 of *Narrative: A Critical Linguistic Introduction* (2001). See footnote 35 below for more details.

30 This fact is once again reported via DT with inversion: 'No rings on her fingers, Moist noted.' The inversion is necessitated in this case by the verb 'noted'; if the reporting clause were to precede the reported clause, a subordinating conjunction 'that' would have to be added:

Moist noted no rings on her fingers. (indicates an unacceptable sentence)

Moist noted *that there were* no rings on her fingers.

PN clause, thus further burying the intrusion of Moist's voice.[31] The phrase in question could not belong to the narrator, because an omniscient narrator would presumably know whether or not one of her characters was married.

This technique of 'slipping' between the various voices of the text can be noted elsewhere:

> 7. (1) They had a werewolf with them. (2) Oh, probably most people would have thought it was just a handsome dog, but grow up in Uberwald with a grandfather who bred dogs and you learned to spot the signs. (p. 243) [32]

In (2), the use of the exclamatory 'Oh' more usually associated with spoken language, the second person pronoun and the reference to Moist's childhood places the utterance in the realm of FID: (2) could represent Moist's thoughts or the narrator's voice. An omniscient narrator would know about Moist's upbringing, just as she knows whether or not Miss Dearheart is married. Another example of slipping can be found on page 67:

> 8. On the Tump…the big tower…glittered with semaphore.

> It was good to see the lifeblood of trade and commerce and diplomacy pumping so steadily, especially when you employed clerks who were exceptionally good at decryption.

Although the sentiments expressed and the use of the second person pronoun suggests that we are looking at the scene through the eyes of Lord Vetinari, the surface narrative purports to be PN, just as in example 7.

---

31 In the following example from another Discworld novel, *The Fifth Elephant* (1999), the voice of the character is seen to invade and to take over the narratorial role when Sam Vimes visits an influential family of werewolves: '"Have seat!" the Baron barked. Vimes had been trying to avoid the word, but that was exactly how the man spoke – in short, sharp sentences, every one an exclamation.' T. Pratchett, *The Fifth Elephant* (1999), p. 250.

32 This passage raises another interesting point. If Moist grew up in Uberwald, he would presumably have an Uberwaldian accent, yet in Stephen Briggs' reading of the novel for the audiobook version, Moist's accent is neutral, the same voice as that of the narrator. The reason for this is presumably that an audiobook version of a novel read for the most part in a feigned foreign accent would be as wearisome for the listener as it would be for the performer. The principal is the same as that which dictates that narrators should not generally 'speak' in a dialect other than Standard English. Norman Page cites the example of Joseph from Emily Brontë's *Wuthering Heights*: 'Joseph remains…a minor character: one could hardly imagine him charged with the narration of any part of the story. [Brontë] seems to have been aware that small helpings of dialect are likely to satisfy the keenest appetite, and it is revealing that Ellen Dean…is a very superior kind of servant…a well-spoken woman with…little sign in her speech of her regional origins'. N. Page, *Speech in the English Novel* (1988), p. 71.

Pratchett combines FID with an interesting use of punctuation to produce a curious effect on page 68, in which Lord Vetinari is in conversation with his secretary, Drumknott:

> 9. 'There will be an opportunity,' said Vetinari. Being an absolute ruler today was not as simple...[a lengthy passage of what is arguably FID follows]...A thinking tyrant, it seemed to Vetinari, had a much harder job than a ruler raised to power by some idiot vote-yourself-rich system like democracy. At least *they* could tell the people he was their fault.
>
> '...we would not normally have started individual folders at this time,' Drumknott was agonizing.

Lord Vetinari's DS is followed by a passage of FID which slips into what is perhaps Indirect Thought (IT) with the phrase 'it seemed to Vetinari';[33] the most interesting point, however, is the ellipsis which introduces Drumknott's DS and the past progressive verb tense of the reporting clause: 'was agonizing'. Together, these two factors suggest that Lord Vetinari had ceased to listen to Drumknott, and that the intervening passage represents his thoughts while Drumknott is still speaking. Lord Vetinari pays attention to what Drumknott is saying only when his reverie has ended. This technique has the additional effect of imbuing the text with an element of immediacy, as if the reader is witnessing events as they take place – events which include a momentary insight into Lord Vetinari's thoughts.[34]

Pratchett uses FID to confuse the voices of narrator and *two* characters in the passage just before the beginning of the race between Post Office and Grand Trunk:

> 10. (1) 'Is this why you appear so confident?' snarled Gilt. (2) And it *was* a snarl, there and then, a little sign of a crack appearing.
>
> (3) A broomstick could travel fast enough to blow your ears off. (4) It wouldn't need too many towers to break down, and heavens knew they

---

33   The use of the verb 'seemed' certainly indicates that the text is written from Vetinari's point of view.

34   There are similar instances of this technique to be found elsewhere in Pratchett's work. For example, a passage of FID sourced mainly in the character of Ronnie Carney from *The Truth* is also interrupted in a similar fashion when Sacharissa enters Carney's office, as follows: 'Dibbler had the knack. He'd make up some story about some huge monster being seen in the lake in Hide Park and five readers would turn up swearing that they'd seen it, too. Ordinary, everyday people, such as you might buy a loaf off. How did he do it? Carney's desk was covered with his own failed attempts. You needed a special kind of imagi-

"Why, Sacharissa," he said, standing up as she crept into the room.' T. Pratchett, *The Truth* (2001), pp. 386-387. The fractured word ending in a dash just before Sacharissa's arrival suggests the breaking-off of a train of thought, similar to the termination of Lord Vetinari's reverie in the above example.

broke down all the time, for a broomstick to beat the clacks to Genua, especially since it could fly direct and wouldn't have to follow the big dog-leg the coach road and the Grand Trunk took. (5) The Trunk would have to be really unlucky, and the person flying the broom would be really frozen and probably really dead, but a broomstick could fly from Ankh-Morpork to Genua in a day. (6) That might just do it.

(7) Gilt's face was a mask of glee. (8) *Now* he knew what Moist intended.

(9) *Round and round she goes, and where she stops, nobody knows…*

(10) It was the heart of any scam or fiddle. (11) Keep the punter uncertain or, if he *is* certain, make him certain of the wrong thing. (p. 321)

The changes in this passage are rapid. Over eleven sentences, the narrative voice shifts between the narrator, Moist and Gilt. Sentences (3) to (6) are arguably FID, a mixture of an informative narrator's voice, and Gilt's anxious assessment of the change in his situation now that Moist has a broomstick. The PN of (7) is followed by a trickier utterance in (8): this is not Moist's voice, and although it looks like another instance of PN, this is unlikely on reflection. Gilt does *not* know what Moist intends, but nor does the reader – at this point, only the narrator knows for sure. So where to place (8) on the continuum? If PN, the narrator is lying to us, so the utterance must reflect Gilt's point of view. This is FID sourced in the character, as Toolan's test will verify.[35] Sentence (9) is a line chanted when performing a trick with a coin under three cups: the cups are rapidly switched and the audience has to guess the whereabouts of the coin. At this point, the narrative is still rendered in FID, but the intermingled voices are now those of the narrator and Moist. The choice of discourse representation in this short passage neatly encapsulates the fierce rivalry between the two men at this crucial stage of the story; Pratchett's use of FID enables the reader to witness the internal processes of both antagonists, thereby adding to the suspense and excitement of this most important scene.

The most important point which has emerged from a careful reading of the chosen passages is that Pratchett tends to favour a technique of rendering speech which subtly shifts from DS or DT into FID. Why should this be so?

---

35   As mentioned in footnote 29 above, Toolan's test is useful when the reader wishes to identify a passage of FID as sourced in the character or the 'abstract narrator'. The following is the test for passages of FID sourced in the character: '[insert text to be probed, with any pronouns referring to the putatively discoursing character converted to first person, and with tenses converted to the present tense of thinking/speaking], *the character remarks, to themselves or other characters*'. M. Toolan, *Narrative: A Critical Linguistic Introduction* (2001), p. 132. So: 'Now I know what Moist intends,' Gilt remarked to himself.

Firstly, this technique allows the narrator to stay close to chosen characters.[36] The reader is naturally inclined to trust the narrator, and the mingling of the narratorial voice with that of Moist von Lipwig encourages us to sympathise with this character, despite the fact that he is introduced to us as a hardened criminal. The access we are given to Gilt's voice, however, has the opposite effect: we are made privy to Gilt's machinations which only helps to build the reader's antipathy towards the wealthy banker. Secondly, and as previously stated, the reader is far more likely to tolerate any narratorial moralising which is disguised as the words of a character, especially when that character has been shown to be as fallible as the rest of us.

Having discussed FID at some length, I wish to turn now to another topic mentioned in the introduction to this chapter, that of the use of titles and other forms of address in depicting fictional power-play. I shall begin with one of Pratchett's most powerful characters.

Lord Vetinari is the Patrician of Ankh-Morpork. His title relates to his status as ruler of the city, and he is generally considered a despot. Lord Vetinari himself is known variously throughout the Discworld series as 'Vetinari', 'Lord Vetinari', 'my lord', 'sir', 'his lordship', 'the Patrician', 'Havelock', and 'Havelock, Lord Vetinari', amongst other forms of address and instances of elegant variation such as 'his master'. 'Vetinari' predominates in the main body of the text, the narratorial voice occasionally making use of Vetinari's title to emphasise his social status: for example, in the reporting clause following Vetinari's explanation concerning his lack of attendance at Reacher Gilt's infamous parties: ' "Affairs of state take up so much of my time," said Lord Vetinari brusquely.' The sudden, and therefore foregrounded, use of Vetinari's correct title provides a reason for his non-attendance. Gilt is rich, but not of the same social standing as Vetinari. Vetinari's title is not inherited, but is linked to his status as ruler of the city; nevertheless, Vetinari is the scion of an old and immensely wealthy aristocratic family, and his lineage is therefore impeccable. The adverb 'brusquely' indicates a desire on the part of the speaker to change the subject; it is also an indication that Vetinari considers Gilt's remark to be both inappropriate and somewhat impertinent. Vetinari himself addresses the other characters correctly at all times. His secretary Rufus Drumknott is addressed by his surname, and Vetinari's clerks are addressed as 'Clerk' + first name, for example, Clerk Brian, Clerk Harold, Clerk Alfred. Vetinari addresses

---

36 Those characters kept at a distance are treated so for a reason. The reader is not allowed to witness the internal monologues of Miss Dearheart, for example; as the object of Moist's affections, she must remain inscrutable to the reader. We must be kept guessing as to whether or not she will accept Moist's proposal; in this way, our interest in the budding romance is sustained.

other members of Ankh-Morpork society always by the correct title; social distinctions are in this way rigidly preserved by the Patrician, and as protector of the *status quo*, it is in his interests to do so. It is noteworthy that in a scene from an earlier Discworld novel, *Men at Arms*, Dr. Cruces, who has something unpleasant to confess, addresses Lord Vetinari as 'Havelock', an indication that he is anxious to begin the exchange on an equal footing. Lord Vetinari already knows what the man has to say, and he in his turn does not address him by his first name, but as 'Dr. Cruces'. Needless to say, the conversation very soon takes an unpleasant turn for Dr. Cruces and he is summarily dismissed.

On pages 66-78 of *Going Postal*, Lord Vetinari meets with a group of bankers and financiers, including Mr. Reacher Gilt and the lawyer, Mr. Slant. These money-men have conspired to purchase the Grand Trunk Company at a fraction of its value from those who originally patented the technology; Vetinari also suspects Gilt and the assembled company of using illegal means to ensure that any rival company is doomed to failure, those means including the murder of John Dearheart. Lord Vetinari's remarks are pointedly directed to or away from the conversational participants: for example, 'ignoring that face'; 'looking directly at him'; 'said to the lawyer'; 'his eyes on Reacher Gilt's face'. In this way, Vetinari is controlling who can and cannot respond to his line of questioning. He deliberately ignores Reacher Gilt at the outset and later implicates him in the murder of John Dearheart. Vetinari's gaze rests on Gilt while his spoken utterance is addressed to another man present:

> 'There is no proof that we had anything to do with the boy's murder,' snapped Horsefry.

> 'Ah, so you too have heard people saying he was murdered?' said Vetinari, his eyes on Reacher Gilt's face. (p. 72)

David Graddol *et al.* point out in chapter six of *Describing Language* that 'people are remarkably sensitive to what others are doing with their eyes – no other aspect of non-verbal behaviour, except direct physical encounters, is capable of arousing quite the same intensity and subtlety of reaction'.[37] In commenting upon eye-contact, the authors note that 'a...specific extension of the idea that mutual gaze can be threatening is the idea that the person who is first to break gaze is yielding dominance to the other and admitting inferiority'.[38] An interesting fictional representation of this kind of NVC occurs between Vetinari and Gilt on page 76 of the same extract: 'Their eyes

37   D. Graddol et al., *Describing Language* (1994), p. 159.
38   Ibid., p. 160.

met…. Gilt and Vetinari maintained smiles, maintained eye contact'. In the end, neither man backs down: both turn at the same time to look at Horsefry, who, characteristically, interrupts their conversation with an idiotic remark. The two men establish eye-contact once more, but this time their look is conspiratorial instead of confrontational: 'Gilt and Vetinari shared a look. It said: while I loathe you and every aspect of your personal philosophy to a depth unplumbable by any line, I'll credit you at least with not being Crispin Horsefry' (p. 76). Beyond this, Vetinari is a man who deliberately gives few kinesic signals; occasionally though, he raises one or both eyebrows to show surprise, feigned or otherwise, or to indicate that he thinks the preceding remark is a stupid one.[39]

Mr. Slant is the third of the four conversational participants; his utterances account for approximately 16% of the DS in this scene. Vetinari has the lion's share of the DS, 49%, with Gilt on 20% and Horsefry on 15%. Throughout his conversational exchange with Slant, Vetinari controls the turn-taking process by instigating a question-and-answer pattern.[40] Gilt is silent for the first part of the scene, and he joins the conversation in response to a directly confrontational question from Vetinari. Gilt's entry into the fray is delayed this long because the reader is waiting for it; the reader has been primed earlier on to expect a battle of wills between Gilt and Vetinari, and Pratchett allows the tension to build by initially denying Gilt a voice.

In summary then, Vetinari is shown to be the dominant conversational participant through a variety of means. His social standing is reinforced where necessary by the narratorial voice in order to highlight his relative importance as lord and ruler of the city, and Vetinari maintains the social *status quo* in his own use of forms of address. Vetinari is a master of NVC, directing his remarks to specific conversational participants and using eye contact as a means of implication, challenge and conspiracy. In scenes involving the Patrician, Vetinari is given the highest percentage of DS, and he controls the verbal responses of other characters through calculated use of adjacency pairs.

---

39 Cf. Mark Haddon, *The Curious Incident of the Dog in the Night-Time* (2004), p.19. The protagonist and narrator, Christopher, is an autistic boy who cannot read body language and has many basic everyday signals explained to him by his teacher, Siobhan: 'I find people confusing. This is for two main reasons. The first main reason is that people do a lot of talking without using any words. Siobhan says that if you raise one eyebrow it can mean lots of different things. It can mean "I want to do sex with you" and it can also mean "I think that what you just said was very stupid."'

40 Cf. the work of E. A. Schlegoff and H. Sacks on adjacency pairs. This work is referred to in D. Graddol *et al.*, *Describing Language* (1994), p. 204. 'Adjacency pair' is a term used 'to refer to conversational sequences in which an utterance by one speaker depends upon an utterance made by another'. K. Wales, *A Dictionary of Stylistics*, 2nd edition, 2001.

The power-play between Vetinari and his opponents is also evident in Pratchett's use of speech adverbials, metaphors and similes, or in other words, the words and phrases the narrator uses to indicate *how* a particular utterance was spoken. As Fowler remarks,

> these comments are more than 'stage directions' giving indications of the speech acts and behaviour of the speakers; cumulatively, they add an emotional colouring deriving from the narrator's analysis of the relationship between the characters.[41]

The delicate power-play between Vetinari and his opponents from the business world is depicted and carried through Pratchett's choice of adverbial phrases accompanying the characters' words. Adverbs connected to Lord Vetinari's spoken utterances in this scene are 'calmly', 'quietly', or, more simply, the verb 'stated' on its own. Only one other character is allowed the use of the adverb 'calmly' in this particular scene, and that is Reacher Gilt; the power balance is thus nicely captured in Pratchett's use of the same word for the two adversaries.[42] When Vetinari later openly refers to the 'misfortunes' of rival companies to the Grand Trunk, Mr. Slant replies 'stiffly'; the adverb is not only apt for a character who is a zombie, but the forced manner of Mr. Slant's reply indicates that he knows he is on dodgy ground. Crispin Horsefry is the unfortunate young man whose stupidity leads him to make an utter

---

41   R. Fowler, *Linguistic Criticism* (1996), p. 152.

42   It is evident here and elsewhere that the reader is being encouraged to compare these two men and their respective philosophies on the concept of freedom. Pratchett even supplies the reader with two similar scenes in which we see the master speaking to a servant: Lord Vetinari and Drumknott, and Reacher Gilt and his Igor. The Patrician's question – 'Who will tell the tyrant he is a tyrant?' (p. 78) – is mirrored in the second of these scenes by Gilt's question, 'Igor, would you say that I'm insane?' (p. 273). Perhaps the reader is being invited to question whether Reacher Gilt is Pratchett's idea of Lord Vetinari 'gone bad'. The parallels between the two men are clear, but the difference is that Igor eventually abandons Reacher Gilt, whereas Drumknott only replies to his master's line of questioning with the irrelevant observation that 'what the world really needs are filing boxes which are not so flimsy' (p. 78). Here, Drumknott breaches Grice's maxim of relation; presumably he wishes to avoid the question. These maxims are discussed in various texts, including Graddol et al., pp. 124-125, and Leech and Short, pp. 294-5. Drumknott violates, rather than flouts, Grice's maxim of relation in providing a totally irrelevant answer to Vetinari's question. The implication is that Drumknott breaches one maxim in order to avoid breaching another, the maxim of quality, which dictates that one should not lie. Presumably there is a sense in which Drumknott does indeed consider Vetinari to be a tyrant. It is worth mentioning that Pratchett also encourages the reader to compare the conduct of Gilt with that of Moist: Vetinari gives both men the opportunity for salvation, but Gilt refuses to take it. Grice's maxims can also be useful in examining the passage following the fire in the Post Office in which Moist is interviewed by Captain Carrot (pp. 242-244). Moist is lying, and both the reader and the Captain know it. As one would expect, many of Carrot's speech acts are questions, or requests for information. Moist hedges these questions by repeatedly breaking Grice's maxims of either quality or quantity, that is, his replies are either untruthful or scanty, in all except one instance. When Carrot asks Moist if he has received any threats, Moist replies, 'None at all' (p. 244). This is true – but of course, Gilt is far too clever to openly threaten his adversary.

fool of himself in this scene, dealing as he is with men whose intelligence far exceeds his own. The following phrases are connected with Horsefry: 'said a voice'; 'he muttered'; 'snapped Horsefry'; 'yapped a voice'; 'he burbled'; 'said Horsefry, as if this was a source of immense pride'. Twice Horsefry is represented as a disembodied voice, breaking an uncomfortable silence with a misguided remark. His anxious reactions to Vetinari's rather pointed comments are 'muttered' and 'snapped', the muttering revealing a desire to speak without quite being heard, and the snapping indicating a childish inability to control his outbursts. Unlike Reacher Gilt, Horsefry lacks the courage of his convictions, and he quickly backs down in the face of Vetinari's calmly delivered threat. Horsefry yaps like a small annoying dog, and burbles like an idiot or a child. He is directly condemned by the narratorial voice in the phrase 'as if this was a source of immense pride'.

When accusations of wrong-doing are publicly made during a scene towards the end of the book, Vetinari maintains his equanimity while his opponents crumble. The adverbs connected with the soon-to-be-condemned men can be arranged into four groups, as follows:

i)   raised voices: 'screamed' (x 2); 'shouted'

ii) difficulty speaking/breathing: 'faltered'; 'protested weakly'; 'gasped'

iii) protesting/pleading: 'was protesting'; 'protested weakly'; 'pleaded'

iv) involuntary exclamations: 'moaned'; 'burst out'[43]

Vetinari's utterances, on the other hand, are simply 'said', or 'stated'. Even when he demands silence in the midst of the hubbub, he does not speak loudly; once silence is established he continues speaking 'in the same calm tone' (p. 335), while by contrast the wrongdoers falter and splutter.

The metaphors and similes used in place of adverbs are useful indications of the power relations between the characters. Vetinari is connected with the following phrases: (1) 'The sentence came out fast and smooth, like a snake's tongue, and the swift flick on the end of it was...' (p. 71); (2) 'cold as the depths of the sea' (p. 75); (3) 'Lord Vetinari's voice came out of the throng like a knife' (p. 341). Example (1) connects Vetinari with a snake, more specifically with a snake's tongue. The sea-depths of (2) remind the reader not only of the coldness of this particular character, but also of his personal hidden depths, and the depth of the extent of his knowledge. In (3) he is linked to a weapon – a knife – a fitting image for this character: Vetinari is an accomplished assassin,

---

43   Examples taken from chapter 14 of *Going Postal*, pp. 331-350.

trained at the city's Assassins' Guild, and the present Provost of Assassins. Figurative language connected with the miscreants conveys appropriately their predicament: 'Greenyham tried, aware once more of the creaking of ice' (p. 336); 'The cracks were spreading, the ice was breaking up on every side' (p. 336); 'Not only had the ice broken up, but he was on the floe with the big hungry walrus' (p. 337). Greenyham is eventually reduced to silence by the threat of imprisonment. The extended metaphor depicting his unenviable situation is a new take on the cliché, itself a dead metaphor, 'to be on thin ice'; the breaking up of the ice also indicates the increasing isolation of Greenyham and his associates from Ankh-Morpork's more law-abiding citizenry.

It has, I think, been demonstrated how linguistic theories of conversational management can contribute to an examination of the power-balance between various fictional characters at sentence, discourse and paralinguistic levels. It has been shown how literature imitates the real world in the importance attached to forms of address and forms of NVC such as eye contact. Speech adverbials are of course specific to the written word; these words and phrases represent an attempt on the writer's part to convey the tone of an utterance. Linguists do have the tools necessary for representing on paper the exact manner in which an utterance was rendered – pitch, volume, pronunciation, et cetera – but highly specialised knowledge is required to read such scripts. The novelist simply hints at the manner of an utterance and leaves the rest to the imagination of the reader.

There are ways, however, in which the novelist can provide more than just a hint of the way in which the characters' lines are delivered. Pratchett makes extensive use of orthological and graphological deviation to represent his characters' idiolects, speech mannerisms, accents and even voices. Deviant pronunciations are rendered by the imaginative use of phonetic spellings. The upper-class accent of the curator of Ankh-Morpork's museum and art gallery is represented by orthological deviations such as the addition of an *h* before almost every word beginning with *w*: 'hwere' and 'hwho' for example. Word-endings *ly* and *y* are rendered as 'eah', so 'mystery' becomes 'mystereah' on page 50 of *Thud!*; watchman Nobby Nobbs cannot understand a word the curator says, and mistakes his pronunciation of 'mystery' for 'mister rear'. A vampire who has forsworn blood in an effort to fit in with human society attempts to disguise his (stereotypical) vampiric pronunciation of *w* as *v* by overdoing his *w*s: ' "I don't believe wwwe have had the pleasure," he said, extending a hand. It should not be possible to roll your double-yous, but John

Smith managed it'.[44] By way of contrast, a female human who wishes to be mistaken for a vampire affects a vampiric accent: ' "Vell, zat is good news!" said Mrs Winkings, leaning back'.[45] Just as the vampires have an accent which we might associate with their popular cinematic counterparts, the subservient Igors speak, as we might expect, with a pronounced lisp: ' "Oh, we Igorth are no thranger to marthterth of an enquiring mind, thur," said Igor gloomily'.[46]

The obvious example of use of graphological deviation to represent voice is that of Death, who always speaks in capital letters; on page 263 of *Interesting Times*, we are told that Death has a voice like 'a cemetery in midwinter'. When Death comes to collect Anghammarad on page 241 of Going Postal, he tells him 'YOU HAVE REACHED THE PLACE WHERE THERE ARE NO MORE ORDERS.' Some other examples of graphological deviation include the headline of 'The Times' on page 282 and the 'mystic' language of the golems on page 66 of the same novel. In *Thud!* we see troll graffiti on page 176, designed to look as though it has been carved in rock by a troll's forefinger, and a magical dwarfish symbol decorates the pages with increasing regularity as the Summoning Dark catches up with Vimes (see illustration). These latter examples represent instances of textual, rather than verbal, pragmatics but they do add a distinctive flavour to the text. One might speculate that the fantasy/allegory genre within which Pratchett writes grants him the freedom to stray from the traditional paths, but it is possible to find examples of this kind of experimentation in the work of other authors: in *Tristram Shandy*, for instance, Laurence Sterne presents the reader with two completely black pages to represent a period of mourning – a speech act with no words.[47]

iii) Conclusions

It was suggested in the introduction to this thesis that one of the ways in which linguistic study has an advantage over critical writing is in the rigour and specificity of its terminology. The linguistic categorisations of the rendering of

---

44   T. Pratchett, *Thud!* (2005), p. 19.

45   Ibid., p. 21.

46   T. Pratchett, *Going Postal* (2004), p. 273.

47   K. H. Basso has written an interesting essay on the function of silence in Western Apache culture, where to remain silent actually represents a conversational turn: ' "To Give up on Words": Silence in Western Apache Culture' (1970), P. P. Giglioli, *Language and Social Context* (1972), pp. 67-86.

fictional speech and thought have certainly proved useful to the critic, as has been stated.

We have seen that there are many linguistic theories useful to the critic in the analysis of speech representation: speech act theory, Grice's maxims, theories relating to conversational management, to name but a few. Fictional utterances make up an important part of the fictional world. However, it is important to remember that the fictional representation of speech is merely a representation, and an idealised representation at that. The ways in which we communicate are complex and not entirely understood.

I have argued for the usefulness of linguistic theories for examining narrative fiction, but I feel I should note that it is not the case that one needs to be aware of the existence of these theories in order to respond 'appropriately' to a text – for example, it is obvious that Vetinari is in control throughout his meeting with the financiers without the critic being aware of theories relating to conversational management – but linguistic theory could help the critic to explain exactly *why* she responds as she does. The precise way in which Vetinari controls the direction of the conversation can be partly explained by even a sketchy knowledge of adjacency pairs, for example, and the simple statistics relating to DS can support a critical intuition regarding who speaks most. As always with the use of statistics, though, it pays to be cautious: a garrulous character is not necessarily the one in control. Other factors must be weighed in the balance. Pragmatic analysis of utterances, that is, language use in context, must take into account contextual factors such as addresser-addressee relationship. This still holds in the fictional world, but such details will have been established as part of that world: Lord Vetinari's social and political status compared to that of Reacher Gilt, for example.

In this chapter I put forward three arguments relating to the form/content debate. I mentioned the differences in effect that exist between the various points on the speech/thought continuum, the lack of an original utterance to which any fictional discourse can be traced, and the effects associated with the use of various punctuation marks.

The subtlety of the effect associated with the use of FID is, I think, the strongest argument in support of the inseparability of form and content. Austen's *Emma* would be a very much inferior novel if the passages of FID prevalent throughout were to be neutralised by a different rendering in Indirect Thought, for example. FID, as well as being the perfect vehicle for irony, and, as we have seen here, moralising, is also an extremely useful concept for the study of point of view, in that the reader is led to question whose voice it is that she is hearing. In the case of speech adverbials, we saw how a simple trick such as using the same adverb for two evenly-matched adversaries can be enormously effective in contributing to a picture of the power-balance between characters. Finally, Pratchett's orthological experiments can give the reader a clearer idea of how an utterance is delivered, and his graphological decorations help the reader to form a mental image of his extraordinary Discworld. All of the above, I think, can be cited in support of the hypothesis that form and content are inseparable.

Chapter 3: Fictional Point of View

i) Introductory

In this chapter I provide an overview of recent developments in the stylistic approach to the study of fictional point of view. I have explored in turn the four basic linguistic categories relating to point of view: these are spatial, temporal, psychological and ideological. In discussing temporal point of view, I have made extensive reference to Gérard Genette's categorisations of fictional time. Linguistic methods can be useful to the critic because linguistic studies have provided criteria which allow for the positive identification of fictional point of view, notably Paul Simpson's models of transitivity and modality following the work of Boris Uspensky and Roger Fowler. I have also mentioned M.A.K. Halliday's work on transitivity and Stanley Fish's important objections to this work. The main body of the chapter consists of an extended analysis of transitivity and modality in Charlotte Perkins Gilman's short story *The Yellow Wall-Paper* following Simpson's frameworks. While the transitivity patterns of a text have much to communicate, a naïve reading may lead to a false conclusion. It is imperative therefore that transitivity data be considered both in context, and in relation to other data, in this case the modality of Gilman's text, which expresses the increasing estrangement of the narrator as she heads towards a mental breakdown. Any alteration of the form which ignores the textual patterns of transitivity and modality is inevitably to alter the way in which the reader responds to and interprets the text, thereby occasioning an alteration to the text's content.

In examining point of view, there are many different kinds of relationship to be explored: the relationships existing between author, reader, narrator, narratee, the fiction, and the relationships between characters within the fiction, to say nothing of implied authors, implied readers, and so on. These levels of discourse are often collapsible: in a first-person narrative, for example, the narrator is also a character within the fiction, and in some cases can represent a manifestation of the implied author or even the author herself;[1] a third-person narrator is often a merger of the implied author and the narrator, which creates an omniscient narrator. Alternatively, the levels can be extended: although not necessarily directly participating in the fiction, a third-person narrator can still take part as an intrusive narratorial voice, commenting on and judging the characters of the fictional world; thus the narrator develops a persona and

---

1   Charles Dickens' semi-autobiographical novel *David Copperfield* is often cited as an example of this 'collapsing' of discoursal levels.

a viewpoint of her own, a viewpoint which does not necessarily reflect the opinions of the author.[2]

As previously stated, the four basic linguistic categories relating to point of view, following the work of Simpson and Fowler, are spatial, temporal, psychological and ideological. Spatial and temporal categories explore the position adopted by the narrator:

> spatio-temporal point of view allows access to the 'fictional reality' which unfolds in the course of a story. The linguistic co-ordinates of space and time serve to anchor the fictional speaker in his or her fictional world, which, in turn, provides a window and vantage point for readers.[3]

Spatial viewpoint is indicated through deictic adverbs (here/there), demonstrative pronouns (this/that), deictic verbs (bring/take), and locative expressions, defined by Simpson as 'phrases which are governed by prepositions denoting place and direction and which function to identify the positioning of people and objects relative to the speaker and addressee'.[4]

Peake's *Gormenghast* trilogy provides a wealth of material for the study of point of view; Peake dips in and out of the consciousness of his characters, and is tricksy and playful even when in the role of third-person narrator, deliberately pretending to a limited knowledge of his own fictional world. For the moment, however, I wish to consider the use of spatial deixis in a passage from *Titus Groan*. The passage is too long to be quoted in full: I refer to the opening four paragraphs of the chapter entitled 'Tallow and Birdseed',[5] in which the reader is introduced to the massive Countess of Groan, resting in her room after having given birth to Titus.

The description of the Countess' room begins nine feet above the floor, with its focus on the candelabrum, 'Like a vast spider suspended by a metal

---

2   It has been noted that this is a favoured technique of George Eliot. For example, in *The Mill on the Floss* (1860), Eliot's narrator intervenes on Maggie's behalf at the moment when Maggie is tempted to elope with Stephen Guest: 'When Maggie first read this letter she felt as if her real temptation had only just begun. At the entrance of the chill dark cavern, we turn with unworn courage from the warm light: but how, when we have trodden far in the damp darkness, and have begun to be faint and weary – how, if there is a sudden opening above us, and we are invited back again to the life-nourishing day?' (Penguin edition, 1979, p. 647). The words of Eliot's narrator are clearly designed to exonerate Maggie in the reader's eyes; in the end, however, Eliot the author does not let Maggie fall, but drowns her in the final flood.

3   P. Simpson, *Language, Ideology and Point of View* (1993), p. 15.

4   Ibid., pp. 13-14. Simpson also refers to Uspensky's 'sequential survey' (p. 19), in which the narratorial viewpoint moves from character to character and from detail to detail, requiring the reader to piece all the information together.

5   M. Peake, *Titus Groan* (1946) in *The Gormenghast Novels* (1995), pp. 40-43.

chord [*sic*]'.[6] From this lofty position, the reader's gaze is led down the 'long stalactites of wax' that have dripped from the candelabrum to a 'cone of tallow' collecting on the corner of a 'rough table'.[7] The narratorial 'camera' then draws back to comment on the room's general appearance: 'The room was untidy to the extent of being a shambles'. The focus now zooms in again to examine the bed, 'at an angle, slanting away from the wall'; from here, the narrator comments upon the shadows cast by the guttering candles – the shadows of four birds and the enormous head of Gertrude, the Countess of Groan. From the Countess herself, the narratorial viewpoint takes in the birds which rest on her shoulders and arms, and finally we move upwards once more, to look at the ivy-choked window through which the birds penetrate the Countess' room. The reader is given more than just a detailed examination of the room's contents: the visual sweep downwards from ceiling to bed and up again to window gives us indeed a bird's eye view, an impression of flight around the room. The unkempt appearance of the room reflects the Countess' negligence of everything but her birds and her cats, an impression that is borne out by her curt dismissal of Nannie Slagg and the new-born Titus.

The second category is that of *temporal* point of view. Fowler writes that this can be broadly summarised as 'the impression which a reader gains of events moving rapidly or slowly, in a continuous chain or isolated segments'.[8] Once again, deixis is important: the deictic adverbs 'now' (proximal) and 'then' (distal) can ground a reader in the textual time frame; tense itself has a temporal-deictic function, but as Simpson points out, 'the relationship of tense deixis to actual time is complex',[9] as linguists have long acknowledged.[10]

Narrative time is not the same thing as real time: in narrative, cause does not necessarily have to precede effect, and so on. But texts *are* iconic in that the reader must read a narrative one sentence at a time and one page after another.

---

6   M. Peake, *Titus Groan* (1946) in *The Gormenghast Novels* (1995), p. 41. It is possible that 'chord' is a misspelling for 'cord' overlooked by the editor; Peake's spelling was apparently not one of his strengths. However, given Peake's idiosyncratic way with words, it is equally possible that the spelling of 'chord' was intentional and that the reader is invited to think of a spider suspended by a musical note.

7   One of the themes of Peake's trilogy is reinforced by spatial deixis in that the reader's eye view is drawn down one of the waxen towers described as 'stalactites', highlighting the length of time it has taken for these streams of wax to accumulate; this of course adds to the picture we have already formed of the castle as a place of timeless stasis and torpor.

8   R. Fowler, *Linguistic Criticism* (1996), p. 127.

9   P. Simpson, *Language, Ideology and Point of View* (1993), p. 15.

10   In a rejoinder to Peter Barry, Francis Austin notes that 'confusion of tense with time has been studiously avoided by linguists for years, centuries even'. F. Austin, 'Making Sense of Syntax: A Reply to Peter Barry', *English Studies* (1985) p. 167.

Leech and Short refer to the 'tyranny of succession': 'a reader…must decode in a fixed order'.[11] Reading in this sense is a linear activity, just as life is lived from one moment to the next. On the other hand, texts are *not* iconic because the author has the liberty to play around with the fictional representation of narrative time.

Gérard Genette has contributed a great deal to the study of the fictional representation of time, and his work is helpfully summarised in chapter three of Michael Toolan's *Narrative: A Critical Linguistic Introduction*. Toolan outlines Genette's classifications of the temporal options available to authors as follows.[12] The first category is that of *order*: the actual sequence of events compared to their textual representation. Genette refers to textual 'anachronies' of time, which can be classified as 'analepses' (flashbacks) and 'prolepses' (flashforwards). Most of the events of *Wuthering Heights* are told in flashback, of course, and examples of both techniques can be found in Peake's *Titus Groan*. The first eight chapters detail events immediately succeeding the birth of the heir of Gormenghast, but in the ninth chapter the reader is taken back to a period shortly before Titus' birth, when the loquacious Doctor Prunesquallor informs Nannie Slagg that he is shortly to deliver the Countess of a child. In chapter ten, the reader is thrust once again into the present for a brief summary of the events so far. Peake then embarks on a prolepsis for a single paragraph before continuing with the story and Nannie Slagg's quest for a wet nurse:

> For his first few years of life, Titus was to be left to the care of Nannie Slagg…. During the first half of this early period only two major ceremonies befell the child and of these Titus was happily unaware, namely the christening, which took place twelve days after his birth, and a ceremonial breakfast on his first birthday.[13]

Peake's manipulation of fictional time has also been commented upon elsewhere: Manlove refers to Peake's 'mode of narration, in which the order of events is frequently reversed'.[14] In this way, Peake's chosen form can be seen to highlight one of the major themes of the novel, that of timelessness and lack of change.

Genette's second category is that of duration, or the amount of text time granted to events in the story. A period of five seconds could be described in as

---

11   G. Leech and M. Short, *Style in Fiction* (1981), p. 211.

12   M. Toolan, *Narrative: A Critical Linguistic Introduction* (2001), pp. 42-3.

13   M. Peake, *Titus Groan* (1946) in *The Gormenghast Novels* (1995), p. 66.

14   C. N. Manlove, *Modern Fantasy: Five Studies* (1975), p. 226.

many pages, or a period of twenty years summarised in a sentence. There are various techniques available to the author for achieving such effects. An ellipsis gives no text space at all to an event, and at the other end of the continuum, an event can be stretched so that its duration is significantly elongated. Between these two points exist the descriptive pause, in which the text is of a descriptive nature and has no story duration, the summary, in which the time frame is compressed so that only the main features of a scene are in evidence, and the scene itself, in which the duration of the story event is more or less equal to its duration in the text. In order to explore further these techniques, I wish to consider another example from a different narrative text: the scene from Edith Wharton's *The Age of Innocence* in which the Newland Archers give a farewell dinner for the Countess Ellen Olenska. Madame Olenska is shortly to leave New York for Europe, and Newland, who has fallen in love with her, is frantic at the thought of her departure. Time is therefore an important factor in this scene, because Newland is aware that every passing moment brings them closer to the moment when they must part. He passes the evening in a daze, only dimly aware of what is going on around him. Chunks of time are summarily skipped, punctuated by moments of direct speech, when summary becomes scene as Newland focuses on what is being said around him. The rapid progression of the evening's events is marked in phrases such as the following: 'after an interval'; 'had been engaged for some time'; 'at this point'; 'they presently joined the ladies'; 'At length he saw that'; 'in a moment she would be gone'; and 'A moment later'.[15] And then she is gone.

Genette's third and final category is that of *frequency*, concerning the number of times an event is related: an event that happens many times – a journey to work, for example – might be related in the narrative only once, whereas a single event might be related many times, perhaps by different characters in order to provide a variety of viewpoints. This latter technique is a favourite among writers of detective fiction: it allows the author to explore the criminal act from the vantage point of each of the participants. Kate Atkinson uses this technique in *Case Histories: A Novel*, in which the circumstances surrounding the deaths of Laura, Olivia and Keith are retold from various perspectives as the reader follows private detective Jackson Brodie in making his enquiries.

A great deal has been written on the psychological and ideological categories of fictional point of view by linguists and literary critics alike.

---

15   E. Wharton, *The Age of Innocence*, Penguin Twentieth-Century Classics, 1996. Quotations are taken from pages 275-280.

There is some inevitable blurring between the psychological and ideological categories, but I shall attempt to deal with them separately.

Simpson defines the psychological point of view as 'the ways in which narrative events are mediated through the consciousness of the "teller" of the story'.[16] It is important to note that, even if the 'teller' of the story is not palpably in evidence, a narrator is *always* present, an intrusive voice – like the narrators of George Eliot and Henry Fielding – or an invisible presence.[17] The *fabula/syuzhet* distinction is perhaps nowhere more in evidence than in the author's choice of narratorial voice.[18]

Genette also made a contribution to this particular aspect of point of view with his work on focalization. He identifies three types: zero, internal and external. Uspensky identifies four planes of point of view,[19] and Fowler refined Uspensky's work with his narratorial Types A to D.[20] Simpson revised the Fowler-Uspensky categorisations, but he retains the broad distinction between first- and third-person narrator as a starting point. More recently, Toolan has adopted Simpson's work, with only one or two minor glosses.[21]

The choice of first- or third-person narrator forms the basis for Simpson's two Categories A and B. Category A is a first-person, homodiegetic narrator. Category B is a third-person, heterodiegetic narrator, and B is split again into two more categories, narratorial and reflector mode. The narratorial mode consists of a third-person narrator with varying degrees of omniscience, and the reflector mode constitutes a narrative written in the third person but situated within the consciousness of a participating character;[22] this character interacts with the events of the text at varying levels of distance, from active to passive involvement. It is not the case, of course, that the fictional point of

---

16   P. Simpson, *Language, Ideology and Point of View* (1993), p. 11.

17   Mieke Bal writes that 'as soon as there is language, there is a speaker who utters it; as soon as those linguistic utterances constitute a narrative text, there is a narrator, a narrating subject.' M. Bal, *Narratology: Introduction to the Theory of Narrative* (1997), p. 22.

18   The distinction between *fabula* and *syuzhet* is that between the story itself and the way in which the story is told. This distinction was first drawn by the Russian Formalists and later adopted by the French Structuralists as *l'histoire* and *discours*.

19   These planes are: i) ideological; ii) phraseological (which includes discussions of characters' names and the representation of their speech); iii) a) spatial, and b) temporal; iv) psychological, which corresponds to Genette's focalization. Uspensky's work is summarised in chapter nine of Fowler's *Linguistic Criticism*.

20   R. Fowler, *Linguistic Criticism* (1996), chapter nine.

21   M. Toolan, *Narrative: A Critical Linguistic Introduction* (2001), pp. 68-76.

22   J. K. Rowling's *Harry Potter* books are a good example of this category: the fiction is viewed predominantly, although not always, through Harry's eyes.

view exhibited in any one text is solely fixed in one category or another: point of view can shift between chapters, paragraphs, or even sentences.

Transitivity and modality are important factors in the identification of the ideology behind a text, and together with pragmatics these three concepts go a long way towards providing a comprehensive picture of a text's ideological point of view. As any practitioner of critical linguistics would be quick to point out, no text is completely neutral, and every text has its ideology.[23] Exponents of critical linguistics have taken up the idea of transitivity as detailed by Halliday in his influential article on Golding's *The Inheritors*.[24] Deirdre Burton makes use of the transitivity model to provide a feminist reading of Sylvia Plath's *The Bell Jar*, following the work of Halliday and Berry, a reading which effectively demonstrates the powerlessness of the female narrator, and her inability to take control of her surroundings.[25]

Halliday's work has not been without its critics, however: Stanley Fish launched an attack on Halliday's article in 'What Is Stylistics and Why Are They Saying Such Terrible Things About It?' Fish dismisses Halliday's conclusions as 'arbitrary', arguing that 'Halliday's interpretation precedes his gathering and evaluating of the data, and it, rather than any ability of the syntax to embody a conceptual orientation, is responsible for the way in which the data are read'.[26] Simpson acknowledges that Fish's objection is 'too serious to ignore',[27] but he demonstrates that although texts can exhibit similar patterns of transitivity – and Simpson uses Golding's *Pincher Martin* as an example to compare against *The Inheritors* – these texts must be interpreted differently. He notes that,

---

23   Fowler's celebrated mind style – a world view constituted by ideational structure – is based on Halliday's ideational function of language, and corresponds to Uspensky's ideological plane.

24   M. A. K. Halliday, 'Linguistic Function and Literary Style: An Inquiry into the Language of William Golding's "The Inheritors"', *Literary Style: A Symposium* (1971), S. Chatman (editor), pp. 330-368.

25   D. Burton, 'Through Glass Darkly: Through Dark Glasses', *Language and Literature: An Introductory Reader in Stylistics* (1982), R. Carter (editor), pp. 195-214. Simpson notes that the transitivity patterns of Plath's text would remain the same even if it were a *male* protagonist undergoing electric shock therapy, which undermines Burton's theory that the transitivity patterns reflect the ideology of a patriarchal society. However, I am tempted to suggest that if the protagonist had been male to begin with, the entire text would have been written differently. Perhaps a comparison with Ken Kesey's *One Flew Over the Cuckoo's Nest* (1962), in which a male protagonist undergoes a similar treatment, would reveal some differences in transitivity patterns. Unfortunately, I have no room for such an investigation here.

26   S. Fish, 'What Is Stylistics and Why Are They Saying Such Terrible Things About It?', *Approaches to Poetics* (1973), S. Chatman (editor), pp. 109-152.

27   P. Simpson, *Language, Ideology and Point of View* (1993), p. 111.

where the problem of interpretative positivism arises is where a *direct* connection is made between the world-view expounded by a text and its linguistic structure. Amongst other things, this step will commit an analyst to the untenable hypothesis that a particular linguistic feature, irrespective of its context of use, will always generate a particular meaning ... equating a language form directly with a particular mind-style is problematic, especially when the *same* linguistic feature is used by the *same* author to develop a completely *different* fictive world.[28]

Simpson acknowledges that it 'would be difficult, indeed, to exorcize interpretative positivism completely from stylistic analysis',[29] but he points out that the model of transitivity is just 'one means of analysing a text's meaning', and that 'it would be hard…to imagine what an exhaustive account of the meaning of a text would look like if it *ignored* patterns of transitivity.'[30] He concludes finally that 'a particular linguistic form may have a number of functions, depending on its context of use'.[31] Transitivity patterns should not therefore, be interpreted in isolation, but should be analysed in context and in conjunction with other data.

In the following section I conduct my own analysis of the transitivity patterns in Charlotte Perkins Gilman's *The Yellow Wall-Paper.*

ii) Transitivity in *The Yellow Wall-Paper* [32]

I shall begin by examining the text in terms of the transitivity model discussed above: this model is reproduced in Appendix D, and is explained in full in chapter four of Paul Simpson's book *Language, Ideology and Point of View* and in an article by the same author entitled 'The Transitivity Model'.[33] The model consists of four processes – material, verbalization, mental, and relational – which I shall examine in turn. Considerations of space have rendered it impossible that I comment in detail on the entire story; I have therefore restricted my observations to two extracts, one from the beginning of the story and one from near the end. I wish to emphasise the nature of the changes in the transitivity patterns that accompany the narrator's worsening

---

28 P. Simpson, *Language, Ideology and Point of View* (1993), p. 113.

29 Ibid.

30 Ibid., p. 116.

31 Ibid., p. 117.

32 C. P. Gilman, *The Yellow Wall-Paper* (1890), *The Yellow Wall-Paper and Other Stories* (1995), R. Shulman (editor), World's Classics edition, pp. 3-19. Page references are included in the main body of the text.

33 P. Simpson, 'The Transitivity Model', *Critical Studies in Mass Communication*, 5 (2), 1988, pp. 166-72.

mental condition and to this end, I have also provided some brief comments on the patterns that appear at the very end of the story. My conclusion is that the transitivity patterns considered in isolation would produce a misreading of Gilman's text.

Gilman's story is based on her personal experience with mental illness. Her nameless narrator is prescribed rest by her physician husband John, and she is not allowed to write in case it tires her. The narrator, deprived of stimulating company and activity, becomes obsessed with the pattern on the wall-paper in her room; this obsession eventually leads her into madness.

Extract 1 (page 4: sentences numbered for ease of reference)

(1) I get unreasonably angry with John sometimes. (2) I'm sure I never used to be so sensitive. (3) I think it is due to this nervous condition.

(4) But John says if I feel so, I shall neglect proper self-control; so I take pains to control myself – before him, at least, and that makes me very tired.[34]

(5) I don't like our room a bit. (6) I wanted one downstairs that opened on the piazza and had roses all over the window, and such pretty old-fashioned chintz hangings! (7) but John would not hear of it.

(8) He said there was only one window and not room for two beds, and no near room for him if he took another.

(9) He is very careful and loving, and hardly lets me stir without special direction.

(10) I have a schedule prescription for each hour in the day; he takes all care from me, and so I feel basely ungrateful not to value it more.

(11) He said we came here solely on my account, that I was to have perfect rest and all the air I could get. (12) 'Your exercise depends on your strength, my dear,' said he, 'and your food somewhat on your appetite; but air you can absorb all the time.' (13) So we took the nursery at the top of the house.

---

34   Compare this to: 'I did write for a while in spite of them; but it *does* exhaust me a good deal – having to be so sly about it, or else meet with heavy opposition' (pp. 3-4). It is the necessity of having to *conceal* her writing that tires the narrator, and not the act of writing itself; in (4) above, it is the pretence of putting on a brave face in front of her husband that makes her tired.

There are six material processes (processes of 'doing') in this passage, five of intention and one of supervention.[35] Sentences 7, 9 and 10 contain clauses in which John is the actor of a material – action – intention process; in sentence 13, both John and his wife are the actors of the same process, but the extent to which his wife is involved in this 'joint' decision is negligible, as will be demonstrated below.

In a story which is so obviously about female repression, it is not surprising that John should be seen as 'doing' things; he is the 'actor' and the 'sayer' in this passage, whereas the narrator, his wife, is the 'senser', the subject of mental processes. John is seen to overrule his wife on every occasion. The passage is structured roughly as follows:

I get unreasonably angry…/But John says…

I don't like our room a bit…/but John would not hear of it.

He said…

He…hardly lets me stir…

he takes all care from me…

He said…

said he…/So we…

The use of the conjunctions 'but' and 'so' is interesting: every time the narrator attempts to express herself, she is cut short by John's intervention – constructions beginning 'I think' or 'I said' are often followed by 'but John…'. The word 'so' indicates that a course of action is undertaken as a result of John's wishes: 'So we took the nursery'. Sentences 5 and 6 demonstrate quite clearly the narrator's desire to take a different room, so the decision to take the nursery is yet another example of her acquiescence to her husband's wishes – and the decision proves to be a fateful one.

The transitivity of sentence 4 shows the narrator as the actor of an intention and a supervention process: the action she undertakes is to *control* herself in front of her husband, the result of which (the supervention clause) is that she becomes very tired. In the clause 'I take pains to control myself', the actor and the goal are one and the same; the circumstances are 'before him, at least'. Thus even when the narrator is the actor of a material – action – intention

---

35   P. Simpson, *Language, Ideology and Point of View* (1993), p. 89: 'Action processes may…be… subdivided into *intention* processes (where the actor performs the act voluntarily) and *supervention* processes (where the process just happens)'.

process, the action undertaken is to control her actions, and to behave as her husband would wish her to behave.

When John is the actor of an intention process – sentences 7, 9 and 10 – his is a more forceful role. John is shown to be controlling and domineering. Sentence 9 is particularly telling: the narrator tells us that John is 'very careful and loving', but the phrase which follows would be more suited to a description of a jailer guarding his prisoner than a careful and loving husband. Indeed, a closer examination of the text reveals many references to prisons and captives. The narrator's enraptured description of the house contains references to 'hedges and walls and gates that lock, and lots of separate little houses for the gardeners and people' (p. 4). One is left with the impression of lots of little compartments and divisions, with the inhabitants slotted neatly into their correct cells. This impression is sustained in the narrator's description of the garden, 'full of box-bordered paths, and lined with long grape-covered arbors' (p. 4). Everything is sectioned off or covered over. The nursery itself is no better: 'the windows are barred for little children, and there are rings and things in the walls' (p. 5). One has only to remove the phrase 'for little children', and what is left could be a description of a torture chamber.[36] Later on, of course, the narrator is to imagine bars in the wallpaper as well: 'At night in any kind of light, in twilight, candlelight, lamplight, and worst of all by moonlight, it becomes bars! The outside pattern I mean...' (p. 13). Even the passages describing the narrator's view through the nursery's large windows read, in context, like a prisoner gazing longingly at the outside world.

There are four verbalization processes in this extract (processes of 'saying'), and all belong to John. His utterances are represented in both indirect and direct speech in sentences 4, 8, 11 and 12. In sentence 4 he cautions his wife to control herself;[37] in 8 he explains his reasons for not wishing to take the room downstairs; in 11 he reminds his wife of how much trouble he has been put to on her account – a remark surely designed to make her feel guilty of ingratitude and to persuade her to acquiesce to his wish to take the nursery;

---

36   This has been noted elsewhere. Loralee MacPike writes that 'the nursery's windows are barred, making the setting not only a retreat into childhood but a prison' ('Environment as Psychopathological Symbolism in "The Yellow Wallpaper" ' (1975), *The Captive Imagination: A Casebook on 'The Yellow Wallpaper'* (1992), p. 138), and Sandra Gilbert and Susan Gubar note that 'the "rings and things", although reminiscent of children's gymnastic equipment, are really the paraphernalia of confinement, like the gate at the head of the stairs, instruments that definitively indicate her imprisonment' (*The Madwoman in the Attic* (1984), p. 90).

37   Note the use of the generic present tense here ('says'); it suggests that this is an oft-repeated or habitual utterance on John's part.

and in 12 he takes control of his wife's exercise régime, diet, and even her breathing!

John's reasons for not wishing to take the room downstairs (8) can be compared to his wife's reasons for preferring it (6). John's wife likes the room because it is pleasing to the eye and because it opens onto the veranda, thus giving her access to light, space and the outside world. John complains that it is too small and not airy enough: these remarks are reasonable, it would seem, but his third objection is not so palatable – there is no other room close enough to enable him to keep his wife under surveillance. The principle of climax[38] is important here: the third reason is placed last, and is thereby given the most prominence in the sentence. Once again one is given the impression of a jailer guarding his prisoner.

There are a total of five mental processes (processes of 'sensing'), three of reaction and two of cognition, and they all belong to the narrator. The reaction processes are to be found in sentences 1, 5 and 10, and the cognition processes in sentences 3 and 6. These processes are discussed as follows.

(1) I get unreasonably angry with John sometimes.

The adverb 'unreasonably' is an interesting choice: *who* exactly thinks she is being unreasonable? The reader may consider her anger to be perfectly understandable, and one is led to suspect that this is in fact a filtered version of John's voice that we are hearing here: *his* point of view and *his* voice constantly interfere with those of his wife. This can be seen, perhaps, in the transmutation of her anger into a heightened sensitivity ('I'm sure I never used to be so sensitive'),[39] and then again into a 'nervous condition' (3). This last phrase in particular, along with 'temporary nervous depression' and 'slight hysterical tendency' (p. 3) have the ring of a language which is specifically male, a language of vague pseudo-medical terms used for illnesses or conditions traditionally considered to affect only women. A modern reader would possibly be inclined to identify the narrator's ailment as postpartum depression, but the narrator herself seems to be anxious to convey the opinion that her illness is caused by her husband's refusal to let her write. Her apparent

---

38 Leech and Short define the principle of climax as follows: 'in a sequence of interrelated tone units, the final position tends to be the major focus of information'. G. Leech and M. Short, *Style in Fiction* (1981), pp. 222-223.

39 It is worth pausing perhaps to consider what (unspecified) time frame the narrator has in mind. Was she less sensitive before she had the baby, or before she married John, or before they took up residency in the house, or two days ago, or some time in the distant past? The time at which this perceived change came about is surely important considering the nature of the narrator's distemper.

ingratitude referred to in 10, 'I feel basely ungrateful not to value it more', is then immediately qualified by her husband's comment in 11, 'He said we came here solely on my account'; we are led to infer that he effectively manipulates her feelings of guilt and even encourages her to take the blame for her illness. In 3, she attributes her anger to her 'nervous condition', but it has already been suggested that this idea has been planted in her head by her husband: a righteous anger is watered down to a 'nervous condition', and her use of her husband's phrase exemplifies the extent of his influence over her.

The relational processes (processes of 'being') concerning the characters' reactions to the downstairs room have already been discussed; the remaining processes in this category relate to the narrator's feelings about her illness and her husband (intensive: 2 and 9 respectively), and her possession of a schedule prepared for her by John (possessive). It has been shown that the narrator's assessment of her own condition is unreliable, tempered as it is by her husband's point of view, and that her assessment of him – 'very careful and loving' – is countered by the words that follow in which John is seen to restrict her movements as well as her thought processes. The fact that she possesses a carefully prepared 'schedule prescription' is simply further evidence of her husband's attempts to dominate her.

Extract 2 (page 15)

(1) I really have discovered something at last.

(2) Through watching so much at night, when it changes so, I have finally found out.

(3) The front pattern *does* move – and no wonder! (4) The woman behind shakes it!

(5) Sometimes I think there are a great many women behind, and sometimes only one, and she crawls around fast, and her crawling shakes it all over.

(6) Then in the very bright spots she keeps still, and in the very shady spots she just takes hold of the bars and shakes them hard.

(7) And she is all the time trying to climb through. (8) But nobody could climb through that pattern – it strangles so; I think that is why it has so many heads.

(9) They get through, and then the pattern strangles them off and turns them upside down, and makes their eyes white!

At this stage of the story, the narrator's mental condition has significantly deteriorated, and she has convinced herself that the convoluted pattern on the wall-paper in the nursery is holding a woman, or a number of women, prisoner. As a result, the transitivity patterns in this passage are markedly different from those of the first.

The number of material processes is significantly higher: 17 compared to six, three of which are supervention processes, and the remainder, processes of intention. It is still *not* the narrator who is the actor of the majority of these processes, however: the actors in this passage are the wall-paper (2), the pattern (9),[40] the woman in the paper (6), and the heads that break through the paper (9). Of course, what is immediately striking is that two of these actors are inanimate and the other two are non-existent. The way in which the world is perceived by the narrator is now markedly different from the reader's view of reality.

The other processes in this passage are two mental processes of cognition with the narrator as senser (5) and a relational – possessive process with the wall-paper as carrier (8). The narrator's grasp of reality is rapidly deteriorating. From the opening words of her narrative, the narrator presents herself as a highly imaginative person. In the early stages of the story, the narrator imagines the paper to be alive: 'This paper looks to me as if it *knew* what a vicious influence it had!' (p. 7), but when coupled with the following descriptions of the 'kindly wink' of the knobs of the bureau, and the chair regarded as a 'strong friend', the reader is led to interpret the rather unbalanced observation about the wall-paper as simply another example of this narrator's particular foible, a habit of treating everything as if it were alive. At this stage, then, the reader is not encouraged to take these remarks too seriously. The observation that: 'There is a recurrent spot where the pattern lolls like a broken neck and two bulbous eyes stare at you upside down' (p. 7) is likely to be understood as a game similar to that of seeing pictures in clouds, or faces in the knots of a tree's bark. But in extract two, events have taken a rather more sinister turn: the narrator now considers the upside-down eyes to be the eyes in the heads of all the women who have tried to escape from the paper prison, and who have

---

40   Both these examples arguably constitute an event process because the actor is inanimate, but this line of reasoning is problematic because the narrator believes these things to be animate.

been strangled in the attempt. The broken necks and bulbous staring eyes are now positively chilling.[41]

By the end of the story, events have taken another turn. The narrator now identifies herself with the woman, or women, trapped inside the wall-paper, and this is reflected in the number of material – action – intention processes with the narrator now finally as actor: for example, 'I peeled off all the paper I could reach'/ 'I wonder if they all come out of that wall-paper as I did'/ 'here I can creep smoothly on the floor'/ 'I kept on creeping just the same'/ 'I've got out'/ 'I've pulled off most of the paper...' (pp. 18-19). However, her actions are irrational at best. She has removed the wall-paper, in the belief that she will now be free; nevertheless, she expresses a desire to stay inside the house in a mental – reaction process: 'I don't want to go outside. I won't...' (p. 18). Now the narrator wishes simply to remain in the nursery, where she can 'creep'. It is difficult to know how this verb is to be understood: what *exactly* is she doing? Contextual evidence suggests that she is constantly moving in a circle around the room, with her shoulder pressed against the wall: this explains the marks on her clothes found by Jennie, and the 'streak that runs around the room', except behind the bed which is nailed down and the narrator cannot move it – she even bites off a piece of the bed's corner in her frustration. The narrator remarks that 'my shoulder just fits in that long smooch around the wall, so I cannot lose my way' (p. 18). The narrator has taken over the position of actor and she seems to have shaken herself free of John's influence, but at the expense of her sanity. Her actions relate to her destruction of the paper, her imagined escape from its confines, and her 'creeping': even when her husband faints at the sight of her, her reaction is to continue her 'creeping' and simply to climb over his inert body every time she completes a circuit of the room. In a clause expressing a relational – intensive process the narrator tells us that she has actually tied herself with a rope: 'I am securely fastened now by my well-hidden rope...' (p. 18), a rope that only a few sentences previously had been reserved for use on the woman trapped in the paper: 'I've got a rope up here that even Jennie did not find. If that woman does get out, and tries to get away, I can tie her!' (p. 18). The narrator also imagines that she will have to return to her position behind the pattern once night falls, and the reader can see how closely she now identifies herself with the prisoner in the paper.

---

41   Gilman's narrator imagines many inanimate things to be possessed of a life of their own. She personifies not only the wallpaper and items of furniture as we have seen, but also the paper's smell: 'I find it hovering in the dining-room, skulking in the parlor, hiding in the hall, lying in wait for me on the stairs' (p. 14), and the moonlight, 'I hate to see [the moonlight] sometimes, it creeps so slowly, and always comes in by one window or another' (p. 11).

To conclude: when the story commences, John's role is the dominant one. He is the 'doer' and 'sayer' of the material and verbalization processes. His wife's actions at this point are of acquiescence and self-control. She is also denied a voice with which to protest: only John speaks, and he also takes steps to prevent his wife from expressing herself in writing. The narrator has only her thoughts, being as she is the 'senser' of the mental processes, but even here John's influence is felt and his voice constantly interferes with hers. As the narrator's mental condition deteriorates, the transitivity patterns alter. The number of material processes almost triples, with a corresponding increase in the ratio of intention: supervention processes.[42] But the actors of these processes are largely inanimate or non-existent, reflecting the narrator's altered view of reality – a world-view that the reader can no longer share. It is only at the very end of the story that the narrator finally becomes the actor of the material – intention processes, but this reading is deceptive. She may be the actor, but her actions are irrational and cannot be read as any kind of empowerment. The narrator has, of course, invented her own madness and escaped her shackles by retreating into insanity. The apparent empowerment gleaned from a reading of transitivity patterns alone is therefore an illusion: Gilman's narrator may be free, but only because she is utterly lost.

iii) Modality in *The Yellow Wall-Paper*

Simpson devised his modal grammar with the aim of improving upon the system for identifying fictional point of view put forward by Fowler in *Linguistic Criticism*. Simpson found anomalies in Fowler's system having put it into practise in the classroom; it was discovered that certain points of view were not adequately represented and that the criteria for identifying point of view led to occasional contradictions. Following Simpson's modal grammar, I identified the fictional point of view in Gilman's story as Category A negative.[43] This category is characterised by the presence of epistemic and perception systems, or in other words, modal expressions of knowledge, belief

---

42 The figures are as follows:

	1st extract	2nd extract
Number of material processes	6	17
Ratio of intention: supervention processes	5:1	14:3

43 I have reproduced Simpson's system of modality in full in Appendix E. Gilman's story has a first-person narrator, placing the narrative in the A category; the negative shading provides a distancing effect creating a less co-operative narrator. Negative shading is characterised by the foregrounding of epistemic and perception systems, and words of estrangement.

and cognition or perception.[44] Of the modal expressions I identified in Gilman's narrative, over half – 56% – were epistemic or perceptive, 24% were boulomaic (expressions of desire) and 20% were deontic (expressions of obligation, duty and commitment).[45] Epistemic expressions can be identified through the presence of epistemic modal auxiliaries (relevant wording in bold), 'they **must have** had perseverance as well as hatred' (p. 8), modal adverbs, '**Perhaps** that is one reason I do not get well faster' (p. 3) and 'I'm getting really fond of the room in spite of the wallpaper. **Perhaps** *because* of the wallpaper' (p. 9), modal lexical verbs and perception adverbs. Modal lexical verbs (I think/I suppose/I believe) account for 44% of identified epistemic constructions in Gilman's story.[46] It is fitting, of course, that a narrative such as this, one that is almost wholly concerned with the mental state of its narrator, should contain so many constructions relating to cognitive processes. Simpson also notes that modal systems of the A negative category often feature 'comparative structures which have some basis in human perception'[47] such as looked/seemed/appeared.[48] These structures contribute to the sense of estrangement because the narrator is expressing her uncertainty about the nature of the world around her.

Evaluative adjectives constitute part of the perception system which is a subset of the epistemic system. Gilman's narrator makes considerable use of evaluative adjectives in the portrayal and description of herself and other characters, for example: 'mere ordinary people like John and myself' (p. 3). Many of these adjectives take on different connotations when placed in context, however. John, for example, is described as follows: 'John is practical in the extreme', 'a physician of high standing', 'He is very careful and loving' (pp. 3 and 4). These assessments seem positive at first glance, but when one digs beneath the surface certain tensions appear. Husband and wife are in fact shown to be mismatched from the very beginning. The opening of the narrative evinces a narrator with an overly-romanticised view of the world,

44   P. Simpson, *Language, Ideology and Point of View* (1993), p. 51.

45   Much of the deontic modality of this text belongs to John; he is seen to be continually reminding his wife of her 'duty' in utterances such as, 'He says...I must use my will and self-control and not let any silly fancies run away with me' (p. 10).

46   Examples are as follows: 'It was nursery first and then playroom and gymnasium, **I should judge**...' (p. 5); '**I suppose** when this was used as a playroom they had to take the nursery things out...' (p. 7); '**I verily believe she thinks** it is the writing which has made me sick!' (p. 8); 'I lie here on this great immovable bed – it is nailed down, I believe – and follow that pattern about by the hour' (p. 9); '**I think** that woman gets out in the daytime!' (p. 15). Relevant wording in bold.

47   P. Simpson, *Language, Ideology and Point of View* (1993), p. 58.

48   Again, examples from Gilman's text are as follows: 'This paper **looks to me** as if it knew what a vicious influence it had!' (p. 7); 'There was one chair that **always seemed like** a strong friend' (p. 7); 'He **seems** very queer sometimes, and even Jennie has an inexplicable look' (p. 13); 'He...said I **seemed** to be flourishing in spite of my wallpaper' (p. 14). Relevant wording in bold.

demonstrated in the way in which she describes the house: 'ancestral halls', a 'colonial mansion', an 'hereditary estate', a 'haunted house'. The character/narrator freely acknowledges that her vision is 'romantic', but she writes nevertheless: 'Still I will proudly declare that there is something queer about it. Else, why should it be let so cheaply? And why have stood so long untenanted?' (p. 3). The questions invite the reader to share the narrator's point of view.[49] The reader, no doubt, believes that she is about to read a ghost story, for how many hundreds of ghost stories have begun exactly like this? Immediately following this introduction, the reader learns that John laughs at the narrator, that he 'has no patience with faith, an intense horror of superstition, and he scoffs openly at any talk of things not to be felt and seen and put down in figures' (p. 3). This description has serious implications for the husband-wife relationship: not only will John laugh at her romantic sensibilities, he is unlikely to listen to her views regarding her illness. This is made evident when the narrator tentatively suggests that perhaps John's status as 'a physician of high standing' – on the surface, an attribute – is the reason she does not make progress towards recovery.

The distancing effect established through the modality of the text is enhanced by Gilman's use of names. The significantly nameless narrator refers to other people by name, as if the reader is already familiar with the characters of the story: 'Mary is so good with the baby. Such a dear baby!' (p. 6). Mary is presumably a maid, or a nurse, hired to provide the young mother with assistance. The baby, like the narrator, is nameless, but we are told that he is male: 'I *cannot* be with him, it makes me so nervous' (p. 6, emphasis in original). The baby plays no part in the narrative, however, except that of being lauded and then avoided by his mother. Other characters in the text include 'mother and Nellie and the children' (p. 8), about whom no information is provided, and 'Cousin Henry and Julia' (p. 7), who are described as 'those

---

49   Generic sentences also invite the reader to share the narrator's point of view, and there are two in Gilman's narrative that are worth commenting upon: 'John laughs at me, of course, but one expects that in marriage' (p. 3). The irony of this statement is unmistakable, and it arises from a mismatch of contrasting values between the narrator's words and the reader's beliefs. A writer can appeal to shared values, 'in spite of the differences in the standards of different ages, groups, and individuals' (G. Leech and M. Short, *Style in Fiction* (1981), p. 276), and I like to think – I hope! – that those values do not include the expectation that a marriage partner should be ignored and ridiculed. There is arguably a difference here between the values of the narrator and those of the author – Gilman's choice of theme and subject matter should make that evident – but the irony arises nevertheless in the gap between the values of narrator and reader. The second generic statement is as follows: 'I never saw so much expression in an inanimate thing before, and we all know how much expression they have!' (p. 7). This comment can be considered in the light of comments made previously regarding the narrator's tendency to personify inanimate objects. The ability of the reader to share the narrator's point of view obviously becomes progressively more difficult as the narrator sinks further and further into madness.

stimulating people'. The word 'stimulating' arguably constitutes an instance of Free Indirect Discourse in that it is unclear whose voice is represented here. If part of John's utterance, then the word clearly has negative connotations: John does not wish his wife to come into contact with anyone who might disturb her peace; if part of his wife's utterance, then the word is a positive one: she longs to visit Henry and Julia because she finds it 'discouraging not to have any advice and companionship about [her] work' (p. 7).

One character about whom we do know a little more is Jennie. The reader infers that Jennie is John's sister, and the narrator's descriptions of her are equally ambivalent: 'Such a dear girl as she is, and so careful of me! I must not let her find me writing' (p. 8), and 'She is a perfect and enthusiastic housekeeper, and hopes for no better profession' (p. 8). In the first example, Jennie's worth as 'a dear girl' is immediately qualified by her role as spy for her brother; the narrator diplomatically describes Jennie's snooping and interference as her being 'careful' of her patient. The phrase 'hopes for no better profession' seems to be a double-edged one: is Jennie being criticised for wishing to remain an old maid, waiting and spying on the young couple? Is the narrator resentful of Jennie because Jennie has proved herself efficient where the young wife is ineffectual? The deontic modality of the sentence beginning, 'I must not let her...', reveals the narrator's mistrust of her husband's sister. This mistrust stretches to John, and later as far as the narratee/reader: 'I have found out another funny thing, but I shan't tell it this time! It does not do to trust people too much' (p. 16). There are two other points to be made concerning names in this narrative. The following table details the ways in which the narrator and John refer to one another, in the order in which they appear in Gilman's narrative. The points of note are the patronising nature of John's endearments, and the final entry in the narrator's column – 'that man' – which indicates that she no longer recognises her husband.

Narrator of John	John of the narrator
one's own husband	my dear
a physician of high standing	dear
John (*predominates in the text*)	blessed little goose (*patronising*)
he	his darling (*centred on him and his needs*)
Dear John!	his comfort (*centred on him and his needs*)
dear John	little girl (*patronising*)
young man	darling
John dear	bless her little heart (*patronising, and ...*)

Narrator of John	John of the narrator
that man *(no longer recognises her own husband)*	she *(... talks to her in the third person, as one would to an animal or a child)*
	my darling *(before a reprimand)*
	my darling *(a persuasive tone)*

The second point centres around the narrator's comment in direct speech close to the end of her narrative: 'I've got out at last,' said I, 'in spite of you and Jane?...' (p. 19) Now, who is 'Jane'? Is this an editor's error for 'Jennie'? (And what is the purpose of the question mark?) Is it possible that Jane is the narrator? If so, she not only fails to recognise her husband, but she no longer knows herself. Elaine R. Hedges notes that 'there has been no previous reference to a 'Jane' in the story, and so one must speculate as to the reference. It could conceivably be a printer's error, since there are both a Julia and a Jennie in the story.... On the other hand, it could be that Gilman is referring here to the narrator herself, to the narrator's sense that she has gotten free of both her husband and her 'Jane' self: free, that is, of herself as defined by marriage and society'.[50]

By the time the narrator's judgments of the other characters alter, the reader has come to understand that the change is not in the other characters but is within the narrator herself. John and Jennie are understood to be more cautious with their patient, now that she has begun to behave so strangely. There are two discourses occurring simultaneously, as before: the reader interprets the story on two levels, firstly through the mind style of the narrator, and secondly via the fictional reality as perceived by John and Jennie, indicated through their speech and actions.[51] However, by the end of the story the reader identifies with John and Jennie more than she does with the narrator; this is an odd chain of events for a first-person narrative, in which the reader is usually led to identify and sympathise with the narrator, almost regardless of what that

---

50   E. R. Hedges, 'Afterword to "The Yellow Wall-Paper" ' (1973), *The Captive Imagination: A Casebook on 'The Yellow Wall-Paper'* (1992), footnote, p. 136).

51   It is not difficult to find examples of authors who have used a similar technique: for example, in Mark Haddon's *The Curious Incident of the Dog in the Night-Time* (2004), the narrator is Christopher, a fifteen-year-old boy who is both autistic and an extremely gifted mathematician. The reader, unlike the story's narrator, is more than capable of interpreting the speeches and body language of the other characters, faithfully recorded by Christopher in his notebook. There are therefore two discourses occurring simultaneously, as is the case in Gilman's *The Yellow Wall-Paper*, but the difference between the two narratives is that Christopher's perpetually puzzled interpretations of the world about him are finally contagious, which is obviously not the case with Gilman's narrator. By the time the reader arrives at the end of Christopher's narrative, she will have had occasion to question the behaviour of 'normal' human beings, and to find them wanting when compared to the logical and practical outlook of the story's autistic narrator.

narrator says and does. At this stage of the story, the narrator considers that 'John is so queer now' (p. 16), 'Jennie wanted to sleep with me – the sly thing!' (p. 17), and 'That was clever [of me], for really I wasn't alone a bit!' (p. 17). The narrator notes a change in John's behaviour; Jennie is described as 'sly'; the narrator comments that she herself has been very 'clever' in fooling Jennie into thinking that she would rather sleep alone. The reality is, of course, that she is alone – there is no woman behind the paper.

To sum up: the modality of Gilman's story falls into Simpson's A-negative category, and, not surprisingly for a short text, remains consistently within this category. The majority of the modal constructions in the story express the narrator's desires, thoughts and beliefs; expressions of obligation, duty and commitment – deontic modality – are reserved almost exclusively for John. The sense of estrangement that is characteristic of the A-negative category is a perfect vehicle for the fictional rendering of the psychological distance that separates the narrator from first her husband and finally the reader. This distancing effect is achieved through the use of verbs (looked/seemed/appeared), evaluative adjectives, names, and the narrator's final refusal to co-operate with the reader. These modal patterns read in conjunction with the transitivity patterns discussed in the previous section reveal that the only way in which the beleaguered wife can take control of her life is to invent a new reality for herself, a reality which is beyond the comprehension of the other characters in the story and, ultimately, the reader.

iv) Final Word

The linguistic categories of transitivity and modality have proved themselves to be of enormous use to the critical linguist whose aim it is to uncover the ideology behind any given text; however, I hope to have demonstrated that these concepts also have a place in literary criticism.

Previously, when linguists were engaged in advocating the deep/surface structure model, modality was part of the deep, not the surface, structure; in expressing as it does an attitude toward the subject matter, modality is an essential and indispensable component of meaning. In 'Freudianism: A Critical Sketch' Vološinov/Bakhtin writes 'all elements of the style of a poetic work are permeated with the author's evaluative attitude toward content and express his basic social position.'[52] Gilman's use of deontic modality in the portrayal of John's character, for example, expresses clearly the author's

---

52   V. Vološinov/ M. Bakhtin, 'Freudianism: A Critical Sketch', *The Bakhtin Reader* (1994), P. Morris (editor), p. 170.

contempt for the young physician's treatment of his wife. Transitivity likewise is about more than simple power relations. It expresses a world-view, as seen in Gilman's narrator's belief that inanimate objects are alive, for example; this is what allows those objects to be the actors in material – intention processes. If the transitivity patterns and modality of Gilman's story were to be lost in a paraphrase, one would be left with a very different story. I *think* therefore that these considerations can be added to the argument that form = content.

Furthermore, it has been seen once again how linguistic methods can be beneficial to the student of literature. The linguistic concept of deixis proves very useful in describing spatial and temporal point of view, and with regard to the latter I suspect that linguists probably have something to teach critics about grammatical tense and its relationship to time. But the most important point is that once again, as already seen in chapters one and two, it is *linguistic* criteria that are proving their worth in literary criticism, providing useful and practical models for the study of foregrounding, speech and thought representation, and fictional point of view.

Chapter 4: The Role of the Reader

i) Introductory

In this final chapter I wish to focus entirely on the reader and the reader's role in relation to the various levels of discourse existing in a text. The factors affecting the reader's understanding of the text can be roughly organised into three categories. First, the organisation of the text or its physical form, that is, the words and sentences on the page and the way in which these sentences are punctuated and arranged. I took a brief look at punctuation in chapter two and syntactic arrangement in chapter three; in this chapter I take a closer look at lexical choice. The second factor affecting a reader's understanding is her empirical knowledge of the world. Readers bring to the text vast stores of background knowledge which enable them to give shape and meaning to the words on the page. The final factor is that of education: readers are distinguished by their varying levels of literary competence. In order to answer the question of how a reader makes sense of a text, I shall be exploring the following four areas in turn: a) *individual word meaning*, in which I hope to demonstrate that a reader's understanding of lexical items constitutes far more than a simple dictionary definition; b) *schemata, frames and scripts* show how a reader applies her knowledge of the world to the texts she reads; c) *literary competence* adds the more specific dimension of the reader's knowledge of other texts, of which d) *literary allusion* is an even more specialised instance. Categories c) and d) carry important implications for the questions proposed in this thesis in that these categories show how linguistics alone is insufficient to achieve a full understanding of a literary text. The specialised knowledge of the critic comes into play where it is vital, for instance, to be able to accurately identify a literary allusion or to situate a text within a particular genre; I will be investigating these questions in more detail, pertaining to problematic allusions in Brontë's *Wuthering Heights* – allusions which arguably contain the key to a fuller understanding of the text. As for the question of form and content, I stand by my conviction that they are inseparable but I concede that once the reader is taken into account the definition of 'content' becomes more complicated; however, I feel that the arguments presented here add weight to the assertion that literary language functions differently rather than detracting from the proposition that form and content are one and the same.

Before addressing the question of how a reader makes sense of a text, I present a brief overview of the development of reader-response criticism and comment further on the roles of author and reader as respective producer and consumer of texts.

In 1959 Michael Riffaterre in 'Criteria for Style Analysis' suggested that since we cannot know the author's intentions, it is better to focus on the response of the reader.[1] Riffaterre recognised early on the displaced interaction that distinguishes the literary text from other types of text, and he writes that the author has a more difficult task than the speaker due to the absence of extra-linguistic means of expression: the author has limited graphological means at her disposal – for instance, the examples from Pratchett's work in chapter two – but these means are a poor substitute for the expressive capabilities of tone, gesture, volume, pitch, et cetera. The author, writes Riffaterre, is therefore more conscious of the message, and introduces unpredictable elements, or stylistic devices, into the work in order to ensure that the message is decoded as intended. These stylistic devices, according to Riffaterre, can be identified by the average reader (AR); however, Riffaterre reserves the right to correct that which the AR finds and he classifies typical AR errors as faults of omission or addition.

Stanley Fish also deplores the exclusion of the reader in literary history, but he parts company with Riffaterre in that he does not believe it possible to divide a text up into utterances that may or may not have a literary effect. Fish has made several important contributions to reader-response criticism through the formulation of his 'affective stylistics'. He argues that meaning cannot be extracted from a literary work, but is to be found in the reader's experience of reading it: the experience of an utterance *is* its meaning.[2] Fish's method involves 'an analysis of the developing responses of the reader in relation to the words as they succeed one another in time',[3] and this basic premise means that at times his arguments come dangerously close to the idea of form *enacting* content; nevertheless, the value of Fish's work should not be underestimated. Fish's method compels the critic to ask what a certain text or part of a text *does*, rather than what it *means*, a question that reflects Fish's focus on experience rather than extraction; in addition, Fish draws attention to the temporality of the reading experience, in that the reader responds to a temporal flow in a left to right direction, at least in texts written in English.[4] The effect of this reading

1   M. Riffaterre, 'Criteria for Style Analysis', *Word* (1959), pp. 154-174.

2   S. Fish, 'Literature in the Reader: Affective Stylistics', *New Literary History* (1970), p. 131.

3   Ibid., pp. 126-127.

4   The fact that a reader responds to a left to right temporal flow has some very interesting implications for graphic novels and comic books in particular; indeed, in *Tintin: The Complete Companion*, Michael Farr notes that 'when…Tintin bursts into the cabin to find Bobby Smiles already gone on page 18 of the colour edition, he logically rushes out to the right; in the black and white version he had dashed out to the left, disrupting the natural flow of left to right dictated by the reader's eye' (p. 36).

experience is lost in the activity of criticism, writes Fish, and he states that it is criticism, not reading, that loses sight of the text. The temporal model posited by Fish among others has at least one ramification for the form/content argument: if content is produced by the reader's experience of reading in a temporal framework, then some content is inevitably lost if the reader does decide what the text 'is about'; the clues, false trails and red herrings, are, for Fish, part of the meaning of the text in that they constitute part of the reading experience. Carole Berger writes in support of this argument in her article on Jane Austen's villains:

> although the spatial metaphor of recent decades has produced much useful criticism, it has obscured the fact that form also has a *temporal* dimension, manifest in the reader's sequential experience of a work. My analysis depends on the assumption that meaning is generated not only by the interpretation of a character's qualities and development in relation to the work as a whole, but also through the process of apprehending a character as we read.[5]

Berger adds a useful footnote: 'to the extent that the effects described depend on the reader's ignorance of future developments, they obviously apply only to a first reading. Subsequent readings yield different pleasures'.[6] One is only fooled by Willoughby and Frank Churchill once.

Another critic interested in reader response is Steven Mailloux, who provides a useful overview in 'Learning to Read: Interpretation and Reader-Response Criticism'. Mailloux summarises the work of various critics including Wolfgang Iser and Stephen Booth, and he adds to their arguments his own premise that

> every critical approach embodies a set of interpretive conventions used to make sense of literary texts. Such interpretive conventions are shared procedures for creating meaning, and they consist of interpretive assumptions manifested in specific critical moves.[7]

Indeed, in a separate article Mailloux demonstrates how critics have made sense of a 'maimed' text; the fact that they were able to do so at all indicates

---

5   C. Berger, 'The Rake and the Reader in Jane Austen's Novels', *Studies in English Literature, 1500-1900* (1975), p. 544.

6   Ibid., footnote.

7   S. Mailloux, 'Learning to Read: Interpretation and Reader-Response Criticism', *Studies in the Literary Imagination* (1979), p. 93.

how powerful these interpretive conventions can be.[8] According to Mailloux's reasoning, the reader/critic is a member of an interpretive community, and the 'history of literary criticism is a chronicle of the changes in…shared interpretive strategies'.[9] Furthermore, Mailloux neatly summarises the different roles assigned to the reader: she is *in* the text as narratee, or she dominates *over* the text as the creator of meaning, or she produces meaning by interacting *with* the text. The reader has also collected an assortment of epithets: she is implied, educated, ideal, informed, et cetera. The implied reader is a product of the displaced interaction between addresser and addressee, and she is defined by Leech and Short as follows:

> because the author can assume knowledge which any particular reader might not necessarily have, we have to conclude that the addressee in literary communication is not the reader, but…the IMPLIED READER; a hypothetical personage who shares with the author not just background knowledge but also a set of presuppositions, sympathies and standards of what is pleasant and unpleasant, good and bad, right and wrong.[10]

Bakhtin argues that the implied reader is instrumental in the very construction of the literary work in his *Problems of Dostoevsky's Poetics*: 'Every literary discourse more or less sharply senses its own listener, reader, critic, and reflects in itself their anticipated objections, evaluations, points of view.'[11] Authorial correspondence, drafts, and so on, reveal some authors' concern that the reader should resemble the implied reader as closely as possible. One authorial strategy with this aim in mind is to refer directly to the reader – Fielding's guiding hand in *Tom Jones* is an oft-quoted example. The reader shares a relationship not only with the author, but also with the narrator

---

8   S. Mailloux, '"The Red Badge of Courage" and Interpretive Conventions: Critical Response to a Maimed Text', *Studies in the Novel* (1978), pp. 48-63. A bowdlerised version of Stephen Crane's book was published by Appleton & Co. in 1895, and its critics fell into three camps: those who used existing interpretive conventions relating to that particular genre at that particular time and who arrived at a misreading; those who dismissed the text as incoherent; and finally those who, because of a greater sensitivity to those conventions, arrived at a reading which reflected more accurately the text in its completed state. Mailloux concludes that this critical activity demonstrates 'how traditional literary conventions function as interpretive conventions – shared strategies for making sense of texts' (p. 49). It is noteworthy that most critics fell into the first camp, and that they were those who simply ignored the conflicting evidence of the expurgated text, while the more sensitive critics in the third camp did not.

9   S. Mailloux, 'Learning to Read: Interpretation and Reader-Response Criticism', *Studies in the Literary Imagination* (1979), p. 93. Mailloux's article, written in 1979, reflects the contemporary reaction against the intentional and affective fallacies of Wimsatt and Beardsley.

10   G. Leech and M. Short, *Style in Fiction* (1981), p. 259.

11   M. Bakhtin, *Problems of Dostoevsky's Poetics*, reprinted in part in *The Bakhtin Reader* (1994), P. Morris (editor), p. 108.

and/or the characters; often the reader is called upon to judge the characters, and by extension, herself. The technique of encouraging self-judgment is an authorial means for educating the reader, assuming that the role of literature is to edify. Mailloux's reader is an active participant, not a passive observer, and Mailloux parts company from Fish and Riffaterre in his refusal to separate reader from critic:

> it is true that reader-response criticism claims to approximate closely the content of reading experiences that are always assumed to pre-exist the critical performance. But what in fact takes place is quite different: the critical performance fills those reading experiences with its own interpretive moves.[12]

Mailloux asserts that it is impossible to separate the two activities of reading and criticism and that one activity necessarily entails the other.

Meaning is created from an elaborate network of integration and cooperation between author, reader, and text. To ignore the reader would be to place the creation of meaning squarely at the point of production, that is, at the feet of the author. Alternatively, one could remove both author and reader from the equation, as American New Critics did,[13] and argue instead that meaning is inherent in the text itself. But to treat the text as aesthetic *object* instead of *discourse* is a viewpoint that is currently unfashionable amongst practitioners of stylistics. Fowler notes that if a text is treated as discourse, this represents a 'corrective to the...traditional claim in literary criticism that texts are objects

---

12   S. Mailloux, 'Learning to Read: Interpretation and Reader-Response Criticism', *Studies in the Literary Imagination* (1979), p. 107.

13   In their influential essay, 'The Intentional Fallacy' (1954), Wimsatt and Beardsley argue that authorial intention should not be the standard by which a literary work is measured, and that even if the author can and does give a straight answer as to intended meaning, this answer still has little to do with the actual work. Wimsatt and Beardsley do not go so far as to place the reader at the forefront of critical attention, however – indeed, their companion essay to the essay mentioned above, 'The Affective Fallacy' (1954), hotly denies such a position in its firm assertion of the supremacy of the text. Wimsatt and Beardsley appear anxious to prove that the exegesis of a poem cannot be arrived at via an examination of *emotions evoked* in the reader of that poem: 'the report of some readers...that a poem or story induces in them vivid images, intense feelings, or heightened consciousness, is neither anything which can be refuted nor anything which it is possible for the objective critic to take into account' (ibid., p. 32). This is true, but does not, I think, adequately address or explore the suggestion that the reader gives meaning to the text: the reader's *emotional* response to a literary work is only a small part of the equation. The authors are keen to argue that meaning resides *solely* in the text, concluding as they do that 'though cultures have changed and will change, poems remain and explain' (ibid., p. 39). This last conclusion seems to me to be overly-optimistic: it is hardly difficult to find instances of texts – certain passages in Shakespeare, for example – which make little sense to modern readers owing to changes in the code itself over the passage of time, and it is in these instances that a diachronic knowledge of the code is invaluable. See W. K. Wimsatt and M. C. Beardsley, *The Verbal Icon* (1954).

rather than interactions.... But "literary" texts...*do* speak: they participate in society's world-view and social structure'.[14] In stylistic analysis, the text has come to be regarded as a *message*, a communication which passes between author and reader, and bearing in mind the emphasis this kind of analysis places on the text as discourse in both its production and reception, it would seem to be an unpardonable omission to ignore the recipient of the 'text as message', the reader herself. As Wimsatt and Beardsley have noted, the *production* of a literary work may be private, but its *consumption* is public: 'the poem...is embodied in language, the peculiar possession of the public'.[15]

The history of the author has been a chequered one: she has been put on a pedestal, only to be later declared irrelevant and finally proclaimed dead. In a paper entitled 'Against Theory', Steven Knapp and Walter Benn Michaels have reinstated – or resuscitated! – the author, but only by simultaneously removing the need to consider authorial intention: 'once it is seen that the meaning of a text is simply identical to the author's intended meaning, the project of *grounding* meaning in intention becomes incoherent'.[16] Knapp and Michaels suggest that we should believe that the author meant what she wrote – a reasonable enough approach that brings us back to the guiding or manipulative author who steers the reader towards an intended meaning. All the work on pragmatics over the last twenty years indicates that texts guide readers and listeners in constructing an interpretation.[17] Iser bases his theory of reader-response criticism on the premise that the reader fills in the textual gaps left deliberately by this author-guide: the text (or the author through the text) provides instructions for the production of meaning[18] but these instructions are not exhaustively explicit, thus allowing the reader some interpretive freedom – indeed, the plurality of a text, its openness to a number of readings, is one of the possible hallmarks of a literary text – but the reader is not given *carte blanche* to create meaning at will. According to Iser, what the text contains is not meaning, but a set of directions for assembling that meaning;[19] my contention in proposing that form and content are inseparable is that a different set of directions leads to a different meaning.

14   R. Fowler, *Linguistic Criticism* (1996), p. 130.

15   W. K. Wimsatt and M. C. Beardsley, 'The Intentional Fallacy', *The Verbal Icon* (1954), p. 5.

16   S. Knapp and W. B. Michaels, 'Against Theory', *Critical Inquiry* (1982), p. 724.

17   I am indebted to Jim Miller for this point.

18   Jim Miller notes that this ties in with a concept or label from discourse analysis: procedurals. These are words and phrases like *anyway/however/on the other hand*, which signal to the reader and listener how to relate the interpretation of one chunk of text to the interpretation of another chunk.

19   Iser's arguments are helpfully summarised and discussed in S. Fish, 'Who's Afraid of Wolfgang Iser?', *Diacritics* (1981), pp. 2-13.

ii) How Does a Reader Make Sense of a Text?

a) Individual Word Meaning

...an investigation into the perceived meaning of the words *tourist* and *traveller.*

tourist...*n.* a person making a visit or tour as a holiday; a traveller, esp. abroad...

traveller...*n.* **1** a person who travels or is travelling. **2** a travelling salesman. **3** a Gypsy...[20]

Leech and Short invite their reader to compare two alternative translations of the opening passages of Franz Kafka's *The Trial.*[21] In the first translation by Willa and Edwin Muir, the man who has come to inform Joseph K. of his arrest is likened to, or linked with, a tourist, and in the second translation by Douglas Scott and Chris Waller, he has become a traveller. A small difference, perhaps, but I decided to conduct a small-scale survey, in order to discover for myself the possible associations of each of these words in the minds of various readers. The results were quite surprising, and from the data collected I was able to conclude that word meaning is exceptionally fragile and can alter considerably according to factors such as the age of the respondent, or even the time of year.[22]

A total of 37 people were surveyed from two different age groups, as follows:

Age group of respondents (in years):	Number of responses:
13 – 19	24
20 – 60	13

---

20   *The Concise Oxford Dictionary of Current English*, 8th edition (1990).

21   G. Leech and M. Short, *Style in Fiction* (1981), pp. 352-354.

22   An additional consideration, according to Vološinov/Bakhtin, is that of social status. In *Marxism and the Philosophy of Language*, it is asserted that 'various different classes will use one and the same language. As a result, differently oriented accents intersect in every ideological sign. Sign becomes an arena of the class struggle.' V. Vološinov/M. Bakhtin, *Marxism and the Philosophy of Language*, reprinted in part in *The Bakhtin Reader* (1994), P. Morris (editor), p. 55. Undoubtedly the gender of the reader also creates differences in the perceived meaning of words, but I cannot comment on this particular issue in relation to my survey because the respondents were not asked to identify themselves as male or female. I can, however, quote a personal instance in which I disagreed with a male reader over the interpretation of the phrase 'well-developed'. Angua from Terry Pratchett's Discworld series is described as such, and while I, a female reader, imagined the character to have large breasts, my male friend insisted that the phrase meant she was muscular. A great deal of other textual evidence supports my interpretation.

Each respondent was asked to write down the first words or phrases which came to mind on hearing the word *tourist*; the same exercise was performed with the word *traveller*. The responses were anonymous. To begin with I have summarised the most frequent responses to each word in turn before adding a few words of caution with regard to the overall interpretation of the survey's results; finally, I have written a general overview of the similarities and differences between the two words as recorded by the respondents surveyed. Words appearing in italics are those written by the respondents.

The word *tourist* produced surprisingly few references to *holiday*: only four were found. By far the greatest number of references – a total of 16 – were to vehicles in which a tourist might travel, and the increased volume of traffic as a result. Thirteen references were made to items a tourist might wear or carry, including five references to *camera*. Twelve references, 11 of which came from the 13 – 19 age group, were to people of *Asian* descent; 11 references were made to activities a tourist might undertake, such as *bungee jumping*; eight references were made to geographical features (for example, *waterfall*); six references were made to *travel* or *travelling* and six references were made to specific places tourists might visit (for example, *Germany, Amsterdam, Rotorua*); finally, there were four references apiece for *holiday* and *Barmy Army.*

The most frequent responses to the word *traveller* were as follows: a total of 21 respondents wrote the words *hitch-hiker, biker* or *backpacker*; 19 references were made to vehicles in which a traveller might travel; 12 references were made to *journeys* and eight references, seven of which came from the older age group, made mention of the traveller's occupation, for example *salesperson* or *business suit.*

In analysing these results, I found it important to bear in mind the following points.

1) The respondents were all either staff members or students at Cheviot Area School and they were all native speakers of English with the exception of two, one from each age group: one student from year 12 was bilingual and his first language was Maori; one staff member was a fluent English speaker but her first language was German.

2) An English woman – myself – asking a group of mostly New Zealanders for a response to these two words in particular inevitably drew some references to *Poms*!

3) The survey took place during the Lions' tour of New Zealand, hence the proliferation of references to the *Barmy Army, campervans, slow traffic*, et cetera; in addition to this, a recent news report had detailed the death of one woman in a road accident caused by a Lions supporter, which perhaps explains the references to *death* and *accidents*.

4) Some of those surveyed wrote paragraphs instead of individual words and phrases – possibly I had not issued clear instructions – and I may have misrepresented these responses.

5) I cannot judge the effect of asking for a response to these words in succession; possibly the results would have differed if I had left more time in between each request for a response. Having been asked for a response to the word *tourist*, the respondent would already be thinking within and around this particular topic, and the response to *traveller* may therefore be coloured by the previous response.[23] The respondents were always given the word *tourist* first, and there was some overlap of ideas with *traveller*, particularly among the 13 – 19 age group, who seemed to experience some difficulty in distinguishing between the two. There were frequent instances of repetition, which were duly noted.

6) In collating the results, I was aware that the responses would have been different had I surveyed a group of people from the UK, like myself, instead of from New Zealand. There would perhaps have been references to 'Germans' and 'towels' in response to *tourist*, and the response to *traveller* would almost certainly have included some very negative comments about nomadic groups commonly referred to as *travellers*.

I would like to begin this overview of perceived similarities and differences by noting those references which appeared in response to both words. Both lists contained many references to vehicles, so clearly the idea of travelling, or of making a journey (*travelling in other countries, overseas or travelling the world*), is connected to both words, although as we shall see later on, there were differences perceived in the type of travel undertaken and the method of journeying. Responses to *tourist* and *traveller* both incorporated ideas of equipment needed, notably *camera* for *tourist* and *water bottle* for *traveller*. Tourists and travellers alike were referred to as *visitors*, but only the responses to *traveller* allowed of visitors being either *foreign or fellow countrymen*. Both sets of responses made reference to *lots of people* and *lots of money*; references

---

23   This constitutes an instance of *priming*: 'preactivating a listener's attention…is known as "priming", the assumption being that if a word "primes" another (facilitates the processing of another), the two are likely to be closely connected.' J. Aitchison, *Words in the Mind* (2003), p. 25.

to *fun* and *excitement*, *Poms* and the *Barmy Army*, *carrying a backpack* and *accidents* also appeared frequently in response to both words. The words *tourist* and *traveller* themselves cropped up in definition of each other, as did the idea of *holidays*, but travellers were seen to travel for reasons other than being on holiday, an idea which was absent from the responses to *tourist*.

The differences between the responses to these two words can be briefly summarised as follows. Those surveyed did not consider themselves to be tourists if they were in New Zealand; the prevalent idea was that a traveller can travel abroad or at home, but a New Zealander is not a tourist in New Zealand (and perhaps we can assume that people from other nations would think similarly; I would find it difficult to think of myself as a tourist in England, even if I were doing the things tourists do, such as visiting the Tower of London and so on). A tourist, therefore, is someone who has come to your country from abroad; a traveller is usually someone who ventures forth to foreign parts. The overwhelming feeling gained from reading the resulting lists was that tourists invade, but travellers explore. The idea of *long-distance travel* was more prevalent in those responses to *traveller* than to *tourist*, and it was interesting to note that while both lists contained references to geographical features, there was a distinct difference between the kinds of features mentioned: *tourist* elicited the words *waterfall* and *countryside*, but *traveller* elicited *desert*: the traveller therefore, is connected with a harsh and adventurous terrain, whereas the tourist is placed in comfortable, easy surroundings. One response worth mentioning – although it is perhaps of limited significance, being only one response – is that the traveller *seeks*, while the tourist just *sees*. It was interesting to discover also that the traveller is defined by age where the tourist is defined by race; there were numerous references to *young person* for *traveller*, but nothing similar for *tourist*; the tourist was identified by where she had come from, for example, *Chinese*, *Pom*, *Asian* and *American*. It would not be misleading to say that respondents seemed to have a much clearer idea of what a tourist should look like – race, costume, objects carried, et cetera – but the traveller was not so clearly identifiable. Where the tourists were seen to come from specific places, the travellers were more generic – anybody could be a traveller. Travellers were seen to go *camping*, or to *do it on the cheap*; in comparison, tourists spent a lot of money. As previously mentioned, the traveller often had an occupation, such as *salesperson*, *gypsy*, or *fruit-picker*, but the tourist did not. The tourists undertook many activities (*sightseeing*, *bungee jumping*) but the travellers just travelled. The travellers got to know the country at grass-roots level, compared to the tourists who were just passing through. Finally, although this summary is by no means exhaustive, the idea of *tourist* incorporated the idea of planning – the tourist was an *idiot with a map* who carried *a suitcase instead of a rucksack* – and the traveller was linked with notions of spontaneity and exploration. The tourist had an agenda, a plan, whereas the travellers just upped and went whenever the urge took them.

It is quite clear then, even from this very inconclusive survey, that these two words are *not* interchangeable, and that they each carry a certain set of associations in the mind of the reader. To link Kafka's warder with a tourist is to set up a comparison which differs from linking him with a traveller. To cite a different example, one might respond to Shelley's famous poem very differently if the first line read 'I met a *tourist* from an antique land…'![24]

In conclusion, what has become clear is that readers do not store words in isolation, and that in discussing the meaning of a word it is probably more useful to take the holistic over the localist view.[25] Words are not stored in the mind in the same way they are stored in a dictionary: words are mentally linked to other words, and one word is capable of invoking a whole host of associations. Jean Aitchison discusses the importance of the *quality* of the links that form between words in *Words in the Mind*. She notes that 'the quality of the links in each case is probably more important than the exact location of the various pieces of information'.[26] Indeed, one of the words currently under discussion provides a very neat example of this point: the word *backpack* has become so closely linked with the word *traveller* that when the suffix *–er* is added to the word *backpack*, the new word formed – *backpacker* – is a synonym of *traveller*.

To all of the above must be added the important factor of *context*. It is quite probable that a reader will respond differently to the same word in different contexts, and of course, literary writing is arguably a context in itself. A word appearing in a poem derives its meaning from many sources other than its dictionary definition: it will gather associations from those words with which it is linked phonologically and syntactically within the poem itself; it will perhaps spark recollections in the reader's mind of its appearance in other poems which

---

24   P. B. Shelley, *Ozymandias* (1818).

25   In chapter five of *Meaning in Language* (2000), Alan Cruse describes the localist and holistic views of word meaning as follows: the localist view is that the meaning of a word can be finitely specified, in isolation from the meanings of other words in the language, whereas the holistic approach holds that the meaning of a word cannot be known without taking into account the meanings of all the other words in a language.

26   J. Aitchison, *Words in the Mind* (2003), p. 245.

will add yet another meaning dimension.[27] Within the confines of a single text, a word can gather associations and resonances that do not apply when that word appears elsewhere: for example, in Muriel Spark's *The Driver's Seat*, we learn at the beginning of chapter three that Lise 'will be found tomorrow morning dead from multiple stab-wounds, her wrists bound with a silk scarf and her ankles bound with a man's necktie, in the grounds of an empty villa'.[28] From this point onwards, the reader is exceptionally sensitive to the words 'silk scarf' and 'necktie' since these items have been implicated in Lise's murder, and the word 'villa' now takes on the additional meaning of 'scene of the crime'. The word 'villa' appearing in a holiday brochure is unlikely to have the same resonance: it would simply indicate a form of available accommodation.

b) Schemata: Frames and Scripts

Leech and Short provide a clear statement about the shared knowledge between author and reader:

> although the author of a novel is in the dark about his reader from many points of view, he can of course assume that he shares with his readers a common fund of knowledge and experience…quite a lot of general background knowledge of the world about us is needed to interpret even the simplest of sentences in a novel.[29]

Every day people are bombarded with vast quantities of information, and the way in which we cope with our experience of the world about us is to organise our observations into little packages, referred to as *schemata*. Fowler notes that schemata are mechanisms by which memory is facilitated and ordered: 'we store our ideas and experiences in terms of what is typical, what we take to be the usual attributes of an event or an idea'.[30] Schemata are organised into frames and scripts. *Frames* are clusters of typical features. Fowler gives the example of a child's birthday party: the features of this particular frame include jelly and ice cream, and blowing out the candles on a cake. *Scripts* are stories: they have a sequential ordering, either temporal

---

27   In addition, literary texts are rife with invented words – the many neologisms of Gerard Manley Hopkins, for instance – and yet the reader can still make sense of these words simply by drawing on what she knows of other words, and how the separate components of lexical items function in the grammar of her native language. The creation of new words is the subject of chapter 15 of Jean Aitchison's book, in which she discusses 'four types of word-formation process which are common in English: compounding, conversion, affixation and re-analysis.' J. Aitchison, *Words in the Mind* (2003), p. 186.

28   M. Spark, *The Driver's Seat* (1970), Penguin Modern Classics edition, p. 25.

29   G. Leech and M. Short, *Style in Fiction* (1981), p. 259.

30   R. Fowler, *Linguistic Criticism* (1996), p. 239.

or logical. At a wedding the groom should be in the church before the bride arrives, the best man has to make an embarrassing speech at the reception that follows, and so on. Schemata are packages of knowledge shared by members of a community, and this knowledge is acquired through a process of socialisation that begins at birth. Schemata help us to organise mentally our experience of living in the world, and they also help us to make sense of written texts. When faced with a text, 'readers will recognize, through cues, what kind of text it is, and deploy appropriate conventional schemata'.[31]

In the case of literary texts, schemata consist of knowledge of typical story-lines, frames for typical narrative situations and settings, and so on. Jean Aitchison provides a very nice example from literature:

> consider the conversation between Ackroyd and Boothroyd, two characters who visit a ruined abbey in Alan Bennett's play *A Day Out*:
>
> *Ackroyd*: They were Cistercian monks here...
>
> *Boothroyd*: It's an unnatural life, separating yourself off like that...There wouldn't be any kids, would there? And allus getting down on their knees. It's no sort of life...
>
> Here, the word monk...has triggered a whole situation, in which Boothroyd imagines silent corridors and monks praying.[32]

It is easy to see how a reader can apply her world knowledge to fictional texts in such instances, but how does the reader cope when the fictional world bears little or no resemblance to the world she inhabits? Distance between reader and text can manifest itself in various forms: texts can be difficult for the reader to access because they were written hundreds of years ago, or because they depict an alien culture. Stories written within the fantasy and science fiction genres are often set in a world other than the reader's own:

> most fictional texts create their fictional worlds through a relatively standard use of presupposition, schematic assumption and the like. But some texts...create special effects by assuming 'facts' that are so at odds with our normal assumptions that we cannot 'take them on', in the normal way.[33]

Leech and Short make the observation that readers can and do cope with such texts, provided they are consistent: 'CONSISTENCY is an important aid

---

31   R. Fowler, *Linguistic Criticism* (1996), p. 241.

32   J. Aitchison, *Words in the Mind* (2003), p. 72.

33   M. Short, *Exploring the Language of Poems, Plays and Prose* (1996), p. 234.

to credibility: an unfamiliar reality which obeys its own set of laws is more credible than one which does not'.[34] The world of Peake's *Gormenghast* is at first glance bewildering and disorientating, but the reader soon learns how to construct a version of this alternate reality. Our first glimpse into this strange world lights upon the curator Rottcodd in the Hall of the Bright Carvings, endlessly dusting the beautiful carvings that no one ever sees. We learn that while he knows it is 'the eighth day of the eighth month', he is 'uncertain about the year'.[35] The apparent futility of Rottcodd's existence and his peculiar indifference to the passage of time soon make perfect sense to us once we have immersed ourselves more fully in the eccentric world of Peake's enormous castle and the lives of its curious inhabitants.

But what of texts that are distanced from the reader temporally? Riffaterre argues for an analytical approach that combines synchrony and diachrony: he notes that the message survives as the author –or encoder – intended, but 'the decoders' linguistic frame of reference changes with the passing of time; the moment may even come when there is nothing left in common between the code to which the message refers and the code used by its readers'.[36] Before the reader can decode the message distant from her in time, it is necessary for her to acquire some specialised knowledge. Short writes that 'one important aspect of the work of English departments revolves around giving students the requisite schematic knowledge-base for responding sensitively to texts distant from them historically and/or culturally'.[37] It goes without saying that departments of linguistics can also offer a great deal of knowledge concerning the historical development of languages.

c) Literary Competence[38]

Linguistic competence is what enables the language user both to construct and to understand an infinite number of sentences in her native language, and it is this ability that generative grammar attempts to document. By contrast, *literary* competence 'is schematized knowledge possessed by those people who have had a literary education'.[39] Linguistic competence will undoubtedly vary from individual to individual, but the variation in literary competence will be much greater. Those who read English at university will probably

---

34   G. Leech and M. Short, *Style in Fiction* (1981), p. 158.

35   M. Peake, *Titus Groan* (1946) in *The Gormenghast Novels* (1995), p. 14.

36   M. Riffaterre, 'Criteria for Style Analysis', *Word* (1959), p. 159.

37   M. Short, *Exploring the Language of Poems, Plays and Prose* (1996), p. 234.

38   Cf. J. Culler, *Structuralist Poetics* (1975).

39   R. Fowler, *Linguistic Criticism* (1996), p. 241.

attain a far higher level of literary competence than those who leave full-time education at sixteen, for example. The extent of an individual's literary competence has a great deal of bearing on what sort of reader she is. To give a very simple example, the word *raven* may mean many different things to different readers. At one end of the scale, the reader may not recognise the word at all and for her, the marks on the page will have no significance – or *signified* – whatsoever. A reader a little further up the scale may know that the raven is a big, black bird; another reader may connect the word *raven* with stories about the Tower of London. Further still up the scale, the reader may make the connection with Edgar Allan Poe (or at least with that episode of *The Simpsons*!). The next reader might recognise the raven as a symbol or omen of death, which will colour her reading of the text. It is a simple example, but it is plain nevertheless that the reader who recognises the raven in the text as an ill omen will continue reading in a different frame of mind to the reader who thinks of the raven as just a type of crow.

Knowledge related to genre and other texts within that genre is also a feature of literary competence. It has already been noted that the reader of *The Yellow Wall-Paper* will, having read the opening paragraphs, be expecting to read a ghost story, once she has been informed of the house's cheap rent and lack of recent tenants. Readers of *Wuthering Heights* who are familiar with the novels of Sir Walter Scott will be expecting that Lockwood, a young man plunged into strange and sinister surroundings, should encounter a ghost during his enforced stay at the Heights, as indeed he does.[40]

To possess literary competence is to be familiar with literary schemata. The reader with literary competence is knowledgeable about various literary genres, which are stored in the head as frames: ghost stories should have creaking doors, guttering candles, and a fatally curious protagonist; westerns should have swinging saloon doors, pistol-duels at dawn, whisky and sawdust, and a drunken or dastardly sheriff. The reader with literary competence knows what the story should have in it, and roughly how the storyline should run. A more specialised form of literary competence is the ability in the reader to recognise literary allusion.

d) Literary Allusion

To refer in the wording of one text to the wording or storyline of another text, either directly or indirectly, is to bring to the original text all the associations connected with the other. Thus when Lockwood refers to the 'brindled' cat

---

40   I am indebted to Rose Lovell-Smith for this point.

'Grimalkin'[41] on the morning after his tortured night spent at the Heights, the reader familiar with *Macbeth* will no doubt recall the witches' chants of Act I scene (i), 'I come, Graymalkin!', and Act IV scene (i), 'Thrice the brinded cat hath mew'd'.[42] *Macbeth* is a play with more than its fair share of murder, ghosts, witchcraft and death, and the reader alert to these references will continue her reading of *Wuthering Heights* with all these associations in mind. The young Catherine has already taunted Joseph with her supposed dabbling in witchcraft; Cathy's ghost replaces that of Banquo's, and Heathcliff, like Macbeth, is arguably a murderer.[43] The notion of 'content' is complicated by the authorial use of allusion in that the borrowed phrases carry with them the baggage of the text alluded to – provided, of course, that the reader is able to detect and identify the reference in the first place.[44]

Allusion, literary or otherwise, has an even greater role to play in allegorical texts such as Pratchett's Discworld novels, and in this particular case the reader who misses the allusion will often miss the joke. A reader who is also a banker explained via the monthly electronic Discworld newsletter the reference, already mentioned in chapter two, to the repeated phrase 'twelve and a half per cent' uttered by Reacher Gilt's parrot. Other readers wrote in to shed light on the Discworld's clacks system:

> the Discworld's clacks system has...origins in a system devised by Claude Chappe which spanned 17th century France. It encountered opposition from peasants who thought that the 'clacking' noises were demonic and burned down the towers (think Borogravians in *Monstrous Regiment*).

> the clacks towers were actually based on...well, clacks towers!... From 1808-1814 during the Napoleonic war, it was used by the Admiralty as a semaphore station. This was operated by a shutter system and could help relay a message to or from Yarmouth in five minutes.[45]

---

41   E. Brontë, *Wuthering Heights* (1847), Penguin Classics edition (1995), p. 29.

42   W. Shakespeare, *Macbeth*, The Arden Shakespeare, ed. Kenneth Muir, pp. 4 and 105 respectively.

43   John Sutherland argues that Heathcliff is Hindley's murderer in an essay entitled 'Is Heathcliff a Murderer?' (1996) published in his book of the same name, pp. 53-58.

44   F. W. Bateson and B. Shakevitch write in their essay on Katherine Mansfield's *The Fly*: 'as flies to wanton boys are we to the gods, they kill us for their sport. If the victim did not show some spirit, the gods would lose their sport. (A half-consciousness of Gloucester's dictum is no doubt expected in the reader.)' The reader who does not pick up on this allusion will perhaps not form as complete a picture of the boss' character as will a reader who does recognise this reference from Shakespeare's *King Lear*. F. W. Bateson and B. Shakevitch, 'Katherine Mansfield's "The Fly": A Critical Exercise', *Essays in Criticism* (1962), pp. 50-51.

45   Readers' letters posted in *Discworld Monthly*, Issue 109, May 2006.

Another reader was sagacious enough to recognise the following literary reference:

> I was re-reading *Sourcery* recently and I noticed a remarkable similarity between the poetry by Creosote and several verses from Edward Fitzgerald's translation of the *Rubaiyat of Omar Khayyam*.... For example, the first verse of the *Rubaiyat* begins, 'Awake! for Morning in the Bowl of Night Has flung the Stone that puts the Stars to Flight.' and one of Creosote's poems begins, 'Get up! For morning in the cup of day, has dropped the spoon that scares the stars away.'[46]

Not being familiar with the *Rubaiyat* myself, this pleasant joke was completely lost on me until I read the above letter.

Much depends on the reader's ability in the first instance to accurately identify an allusion: the danger is that an incorrectly identified allusion may lead to a redundant reading of the text. In order to reach a full understanding of the significance of Lockwood's first dream in Brontë's *Wuthering Heights*, one has to recognise the biblical allusion in Branderham's sermon. In 1958, Ruth Adams published an article entitled 'Wuthering Heights: the Land East of Eden',[47] in which she identifies the source of the sermon as that of Genesis IV:24: 'If Cain shall be avenged sevenfold, truly Lamech seventy and sevenfold.' The biblical text Adams supplies refers the reader to the story of Cain, who, following the murder of his brother, moves to a land east of Eden, and whose mark serves as a warning to other men not to kill the slayer of Abel. Adams notes that the 'mark of Cain does not identify the condemned murderer. Rather it is protective'.[48] Cain's descendants likewise are not subject to retribution for their crimes and therefore, writes Adams, 'the race dwelling east of Eden can work its evils in the assurance that no conventional consequence of punishment will follow'.[49] This, Adams argues, is the world of Wuthering Heights and its inhabitants, and the function of Lockwood's first dream is to introduce the reader to this world:

> *Wuthering Heights*...is a book without conventional ethics or morality. Emily Brontë, aware of the adjustment such a pattern demanded of her readers, undertook to assist them from the very beginning. Thus, with Lockwood's dream of Banderham's [*sic*] sermon, she indicated that

---

46 Readers' letters posted in *Discworld Monthly*, issue 109, May 2006.

47 R. M. Adams, 'Wuthering Heights: the Land East of Eden', *Nineteenth-Century Fiction* (1958), pp. 58-62.

48 Ibid., p. 59.

49 Ibid.

readers were to travel east of Eden, in the company of those alienated from God and paradoxically protected by him against the punishing consequences of their deeds.[50]

There is much that is persuasive in this reading: Adams' explanation of the dream's function is coherent and credible. The two worlds of Wuthering Heights and Thrushcross Grange represent, for the reader, the entire reality of the text. Characters come and go – Heathcliff and Hindley both enjoy an absence of three years – but the reader never leaves the moors. The inhabitants of these two residences therefore appear to be a law unto themselves, distinct and separate from the world of justice and punishment which exists beyond, just as Cain lives free from retribution in the land of Nod.[51]

However, Adams' explication of the allusion makes no reference to the fact that Cain is kept alive *as a punishment*, a fact that would surely have some relevance to her reading. It is not entirely true that the inhabitants of Wuthering Heights – by whom I suppose Adams to mean Heathcliff and Hindley – commit crimes happily in the knowledge that no punishment will be forthcoming. Both men suffer cruelly following the deaths of their loved ones and the suffering of these two men is in turn visited upon those around them. Adams is wrong, I think, to compare the inhabitants of the land of Nod with those of Wuthering Heights and to subsequently neglect this aspect of Cain's story. The mark of Cain may be protective, but it is also what is keeping him alive to suffer.[52] Cain is made to wander the earth, a 'fugitive' and an outcast; never again is he to be allowed in the presence in the Lord.[53] His crops will never grow, forcing him to beg for food.[54] Adams could have compared the suffering of Cain to the suffering of Heathcliff, forced to endure eighteen years in a world without Cathy: 'The entire world is a dreadful collection of memoranda that she did exist, and that I have lost her!'[55] But why should Heathcliff be made to suffer as Cain did? At the time of Cathy's death his only crime is his elopement with

---

50   R. M. Adams, 'Wuthering Heights: the Land East of Eden', *Nineteenth-Century Fiction* (1958), p. 62.

51   Although this outer world does occasionally show its face from time to time: Heathcliff prevents Edgar from changing his will, and the lawyers can do nothing to help Hareton following Hindley's death, to cite just two examples.

52   *Genesis* IV:13-15: 'And Cain said unto the Lord, My punishment is greater than I can bear.'

53   To be excluded forever from the presence of God having once been welcomed into His presence is Mephostophilis' definition of hell in Marlowe's *Doctor Faustus*: 'Why, this is hell, nor am I out of it./ Think'st thou that I that saw the face of God/And tasted the eternal joys of heaven,/Am not tormented with ten thousand hells/In being deprived of everlasting bliss?' C. Marlowe, *Doctor Faustus*, Act I, scene (iii), Penguin Classics edition (1969), p. 275.

54   Genesis IV:12: 'When thou tillest the ground, it shall not henceforth yield unto thee her strength'.

55   E. Brontë, *Wuthering Heights* (1847), Penguin Classics edition (1995), p. 324.

Isabella, and she is an all-too-willing party to this act. It makes more sense, especially given the events of Lockwood's second dream, to equate the figure of Cain with that of Catherine Earnshaw.

In 1959, Edgar Shannon in his response to Adams' article pointed out first that Adams had mistaken the allusion, and second, that she had made the error of explicating the book in terms of the first nightmare alone; Shannon argues that 'the two dreams are inextricably linked'.[56] He considers that Genesis IV:24 has 'no relevance whatever to Branderham's pious discourse',[57] and suggests that the correct source of the allusion is Matthew XVIII:21-22:

> Then came Peter to him, and said, Lord, how oft shall my brother sin against me, and I forgive him? till seven times?
>
> Jesus said unto him, I say not unto thee, Until seven times: but, Until seventy times seven.

Shannon argues that this allusion is more likely to be the one Brontë had in mind for two reasons. Firstly, Branderham's sermon consists of four hundred and ninety parts, which is 'the product of seventy times seven'.[58] Secondly, Shannon notes that Lockwood specifically refers to 'the hypothetical brother of Peter's question':[59] 'it seemed necessary the brother should sin different sins on every occasion'.[60] I mentioned in chapter one Cathy's bemusement at being admonished for making herself comfortable when she hides in the dresser with Heathcliff. To name four hundred and ninety separate sins, one would have to see small sins everywhere, including the sin of making oneself comfortable on a Sunday. If, as I have suggested, Lockwood has changed places with Cathy during this first dream-sequence, then the reader sees that he, like Cathy, is bemused by both the number and nature of the sins, and, again like Cathy, he is finally punished for being bored by the 'good book'.

Shannon writes that the correct interpretation of the sermon 'advances the idea of an unpardonable sin beyond the ordinary scale of human wrongs'.[61] Cathy is the one who has apparently committed such an offence, and in Lockwood's second dream, the reader sees the consequences of her actions: Cathy is the Wandering Jew, the Cain-like figure, condemned to wander the

---

56   E. F. Shannon, 'Lockwood's Dreams and the Exegesis of "Wuthering Heights"' (1959), p. 95.

57   Ibid., p. 96.

58   Ibid.

59   Ibid.

60   E. Brontë, *Wuthering Heights* (1847), Penguin Classics edition (1995), p. 23.

61   E. F. Shannon, 'Lockwood's Dreams and the Exegesis of "Wuthering Heights"' (1959), p. 99.

earth for twenty years.[62] But what is the nature of her offence? Shannon suggests that the atmosphere of Gothic tradition in conjunction with a second biblical allusion in Lockwood's first dream identifies the crime as adultery. He writes that Branderham's words to Lockwood, '*Thou art the man!*', are 'the words of Nathan the prophet when he delivers God's rebuke to David for appropriating Bathsheba, the wife of Uriah the Hittite.'[63] If Lockwood has taken Cathy's place in this dream, then the charge of adultery is laid at Cathy's feet: she had been given Heathcliff but she took Edgar Linton instead. One may argue at this point that Heathcliff and Cathy do not actually commit adultery; but, says Shannon, Cathy's 'sin is marrying Edgar Linton, when she loves Heathcliff with a love that springs from a natural and elemental affinity between them'.[64]

To sum up: Lockwood's dreams contain two allusions that must be considered jointly if they are to be fully understood. The first allusion refers to a story in the New Testament in which the virtue of forgiveness for crimes committed is extolled and the second allusion identifies the crime as that of adultery. Cathy, having changed places with Lockwood in his dream, is charged with having committed adultery in abandoning the man she truly loved to marry another.

Lockwood's dreams are recounted at the beginning of the book but chronologically speaking the events related take place near the very end of Heathcliff's story. The key to understanding his story lies perhaps in the interpretation one places on the allusions in these dreams. It seems entirely possible that Shannon has correctly identified the two allusions. However, it is arguable that Adams' mistake is not entirely baseless: the fact that the wording *does* recall the Old Testament story of Cain may have some significance. In the text identified by Shannon, Jesus makes the point that forgiveness is better than vengeance and the reader is perhaps *intended* to recall the vengeance of Cain and his punishment for being unable to forgive his brother Abel. At the end of *Wuthering Heights*, it is Heathcliff who finally forgives Cathy, abandoning his plans of vengeance directed at her remaining family, and his reward is to join her in death. In this reading, both Heathcliff and Cathy are likened to the figure of Cain: both are excluded from the world or sphere they wish to inhabit until Heathcliff can learn forgiveness and abandon his plans for vengeance.

---

62   In Volume I, chapter 9, Cathy tells Nelly of her dream in which the angels, angry because Cathy is unhappy in heaven, fling her back to earth. It seems here that Cathy *chooses* to be an outcast, and in view of later events her dream can perhaps be read as a premonition: Cathy wishes to be back on earth because Heathcliff is there.

63   E. F. Shannon, 'Lockwood's Dreams and the Exegesis of "Wuthering Heights"' (1959), p. 100.

64   Ibid.

iii) Conclusions

In my brief overview of reader-response criticism it was noted that Fish places a great deal of emphasis on the role of the reader in his affective stylistics. Fish advocates the study of the reader's experience of reading rather than any attempt to extract meaning from the text, and he claims that it is imperative that one take into account the temporal left to right flow of the reading experience. Mailloux presents an argument that focuses on the reader less as an individual and more as a member of a reading community. He differs from Fish in his assertion that one cannot be a reader without also being a critic and that textual interpretation is the product of shared meaning-producing strategies.

It was seen that the displaced interaction between the encoder of the message, the author, and its decoder, the reader, is arguably one of the hallmarks of the literary text, as is the text's potential for supporting a plurality of interpretations. This potential is not limitless, however; the author takes pains to ensure that her message is decoded more or less as she intended, and to this end she acts as a guide for the reader. This argument is not incompatible with Iser's contention that the reader fills in textual gaps: this is indeed what happens, but the reader is not allowed to fill the gaps at random and is provided instead with hints and clues. Knapp and Michaels suggest that textual meaning and authorial meaning are one and the same and that it does not make sense to search for any additional meaning with reference to the author's biography or personal psychology: it suffices to believe that the author wrote what she meant. This argument can, I think, be cited in support of the claim that form and content are inseparable.

My investigation into the factors affecting reader response to individual word meaning also supports the claim that form = content in that it was demonstrated that words are not simply interchangeable. At first glance, it may appear that there is little difference between the words 'tourist' and 'traveller', but my small survey showed otherwise. Lexical choice is therefore as important in determining meaning as other textual factors such as syntactic arrangement and punctuation. A paraphrase of a literary work involves changes to these factors, resulting in an undesirable loss of the original meaning. Furthermore, I hope to have demonstrated that psycholinguistic study into the meaning of individual words can prove very useful to the student of literature. I discovered that the following factors have some bearing on word meaning: the reader's age, gender, nationality and attitudes; the time of year; current events; priming; the meaning of other, related words; the distance in time between the original encoding and the subsequent decoding – material for a diachronic study – and finally, the context in which the word appears.

The boundaries of what is understood by the 'content' of a literary text are stretched when it comes to a consideration of literary competence. It has been seen that specialised literary knowledge such as knowledge of literary schemata, genre, storylines, frames, and other texts is occasionally required to bridge the distance between the reader and the text. Linguistic research can help the student of literature in the study of the historical development of a language, which may sometimes be necessary to pinpoint the most likely meaning of a word or phrase at the time of writing, but leaving diachronic study aside, this is the area where the literary critic comes into her own. It must be concluded therefore, that the stylistic study of literary texts has to incorporate literary as well as linguistic analysis. For a full understanding of the text, linguistic analysis must be supported by specialised literary knowledge.

APPENDICES

Appendix A: Mervyn Peake's *Gormenghast* (1): Extract

Paragraphs are numbered for ease of reference.

(1) Titus is seven. His confines, Gormenghast. Suckled on shadows; weaned, as it were, on webs of ritual: for his ears, echoes, for his eyes, a labyrinth of stone: and yet within his body something other – other than this umbrageous legacy. For first and ever foremost he is *child*.

(2) A ritual, more compelling than ever man devised, is fighting anchored darkness. A ritual of the blood; of the jumping blood. These quicks of sentience owe nothing to his forbears, but to those feckless hosts, a trillion deep, of the globe's childhood.

(3) The gift of the bright blood. Of blood that laughs when the tenets mutter 'Weep'. Of blood that mourns when the sere laws croak 'Rejoice!' O little revolution in great shades!

(4) Titus the seventy-seventh. Heir to a crumbling summit: to a sea of nettles: to an empire of red rust: to rituals' footprints ankle-deep in stone.

(5) Gormenghast.

(6) Withdrawn and ruinous it broods in umbra: the immemorial masonry: the towers, the tracts. Is all corroding? No. Through an avenue of spires a zephyr floats; a bird whistles; a freshet bears away from a choked river. Deep in a fist of stone a doll's hand wriggles, warm rebellious on the frozen palm. A shadow shifts its length. A spider stirs...

(7) *And darkness winds between the characters.*

Appendix B: *Gormenghast* (2): Figure showing parallel constructions in extract (1)

Titus is seven.

His confines, Gormenghast.

Suckled	on shadows;
weaned, as it were,	on webs of ritual:
for his ears,	echoes,
for his eyes,	a labyrinth of stone:

and yet within his body something   other –

                  other than this umbrageous legacy.

For first and ever foremost

he is *child*.

A ritual, more compelling than ever man devised, is fighting anchored darkness.

| A ritual | of the blood; |
| | of the jumping blood. |

These quicks	of sentience owe nothing		to his forbears,
		but	to those feckless hosts, a trillion deep,
	of the globe's childhood.		

The gift	of the bright blood.				
Of blood	that laughs	when the tenets	mutter	'Weep'.
Of blood	that mourns	when the sere laws	croak	'Rejoice!'

O little revolution in great shades!

Titus the seventy-seventh.

Heir	to a crumbling summit:
	to a sea of nettles:
	to an empire of red rust:
	to rituals' footprints ankle-deep in stone.

Gormenghast.

Withdrawn and ruinous it broods in umbra:

>the immemorial masonry:

>the towers,

>the tracts.

Is all corroding?

No.

Through an avenue of spires   a zephyr floats;

>a bird whistles;

>a freshet bears away from a choked river.

Deep in a fist of stone   a doll's hand wriggles,

warm rebellious on the frozen palm.

>A shadow shifts its length.

>A spider stirs…

>*And darkness winds between the characters.*

Appendix C: *Gormenghast* (3): Paraphrase of extract (1)

Titus is seven years old. He lives in the castle of Gormenghast, which is both his territory and his prison. He has been reared within the castle, nourished and nurtured on its shadows and traditions. He hears echoes and he sees an endless maze of stone. But inside him there exists something alien, something else, something that is not the shadowy castle with its many rituals that he has inherited. Because the most important thing about Titus is that he is a child.

This 'something else' growing inside Titus is a ritual, but it is not like any of the rituals that are observed in Gormenghast; it has more appeal, more power than these man-made rituals. Within Titus there rages a battle between the rituals of Gormenghast and the more commonplace rituals of childhood. The rebellion is situated in Titus' blood, which pulses with life. These flashes of self-knowledge have not been inherited from his ancestors, but they have originated in the multitude of children all over the world.

The rebellion in Titus' blood is a gift from the world's children. This blood laughs when doctrine and tradition demand that it weep, and this blood mourns when the ancient laws command it to rejoice. A small show of defiance in the boundless shadow of Gormenghast's history and tradition!

Titus is the seventy-seventh Earl of Gormenghast. He will inherit a castle whose uppermost towers are gradually disintegrating: whose grounds are overgrown with weeds; he will inherit a domain of rusting metal: a domain in which the rituals must be observed. These rituals are imprinted upon the very stones of the castle.

Gormenghast.

The castle sits in shadow, decaying and isolated: the masonry ancient beyond memory or record, the towers, the vast regions within its boundaries. Is everything corroding? No. A breeze floats through the many spires of the castle; a bird whistles; a fresh-water stream flows away from a choked river. Inside the stones of the castle Titus' tiny hand wriggles; it is warm and rebellious against the cold stones of the castle. The day draws on and the shadows lengthen. A spider stirs…

And darkness winds between the inhabitants of the castle.

Appendix D: The Fictional Representation of Speech and Thought

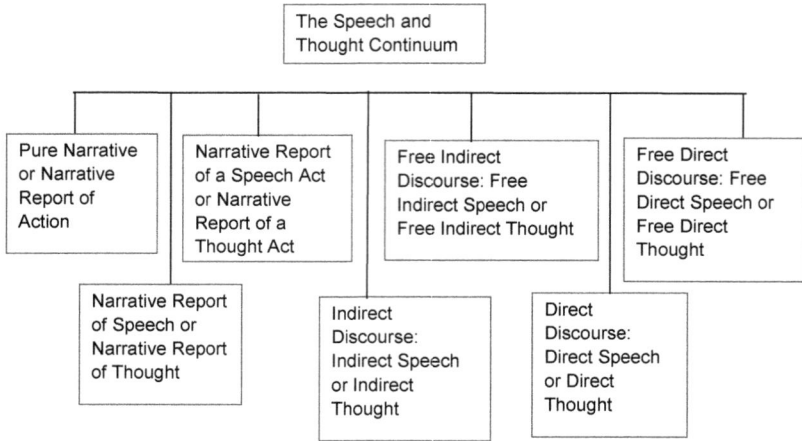

The Speech and Thought Continuum			
Pure Narrative or Narrative Report of Action	Narrative Report of a Speech Act or Narrative Report of a Thought Act	Free Indirect Discourse: Free Indirect Speech or Free Indirect Thought	Free Direct Discourse: Free Direct Speech or Free Direct Thought
	Narrative Report of Speech or Narrative Report of Thought	Indirect Discourse: Indirect Speech or Indirect Thought	Direct Discourse: Direct Speech or Direct Thought

Examples from Terry Pratchett's *Going Postal*:

PN: Vetinari looked down at the table again, and seemed to lose interest in Moist for a moment. (p. 27)

NRS: He nodded at Commander Vimes of the Watch, who whispered to another watchman, who pushed his way though [*sic*] the crowd and towards the door. (p. 335)

NRSA: In a silence punctuated by chuckles from the crowd, Pony tried to explain, in so far as he now had any grip of what was going on. (p. 320)

IS: Lord Vetinari told Mr. Pump to break one of Moist's fingers.*

FID: And what would you have done against a banshee? Moist had thought. You suspect Gilt. Well done. But people like Gilt don't bother with the law. They never break it, they just use people who do. And you'll never find anything written down, anywhere. (p. 244)

DS: 'Oh, dear.' The Patrician sighed. 'Mr. Pump, just break one of Mr. Lipwig's fingers, will you? Neatly, if you please.' (p. 27)

FDT: Welcome to *fear*, said Moist to himself. It's hope, turned inside out. You know it can't go wrong, you're sure it can't go wrong... But it might. *I've got you.* (p. 331)

*There are, to my knowledge, no examples of indirect speech in this novel. I have therefore rewritten the example of DS above as an utterance in IS.

Appendix E: Simpson's Transitivity Model

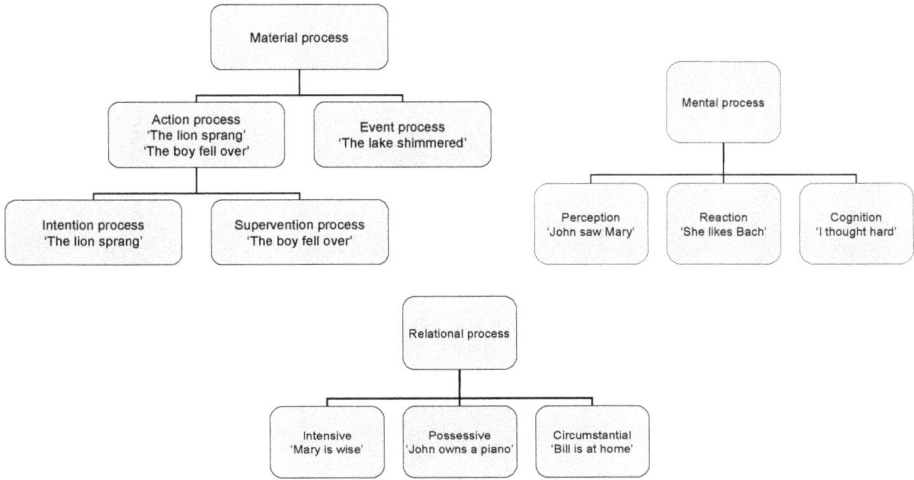

Process name	Process type	Participant role(s)		
			Obligatory	Optional
Material	'doing'	Actor	✓	
"	"	Goal		✓
Verbalisation	'saying'	Sayer	✓	
"	"	Target		✓
"	"	Verbiage		✓
Mental	'sensing'	Senser	✓	
"	"	Phenomenon		✓
Relational	'being'	Carrier	✓	
"	"	Attribute	✓	

Adapted from the categorisations outlined by Paul Simpson in chapter 4 of *Language, Ideology and Point of View* (1993), pp. 86-118.

Appendix F: Simpson's 'Relations Between Modal Categories'

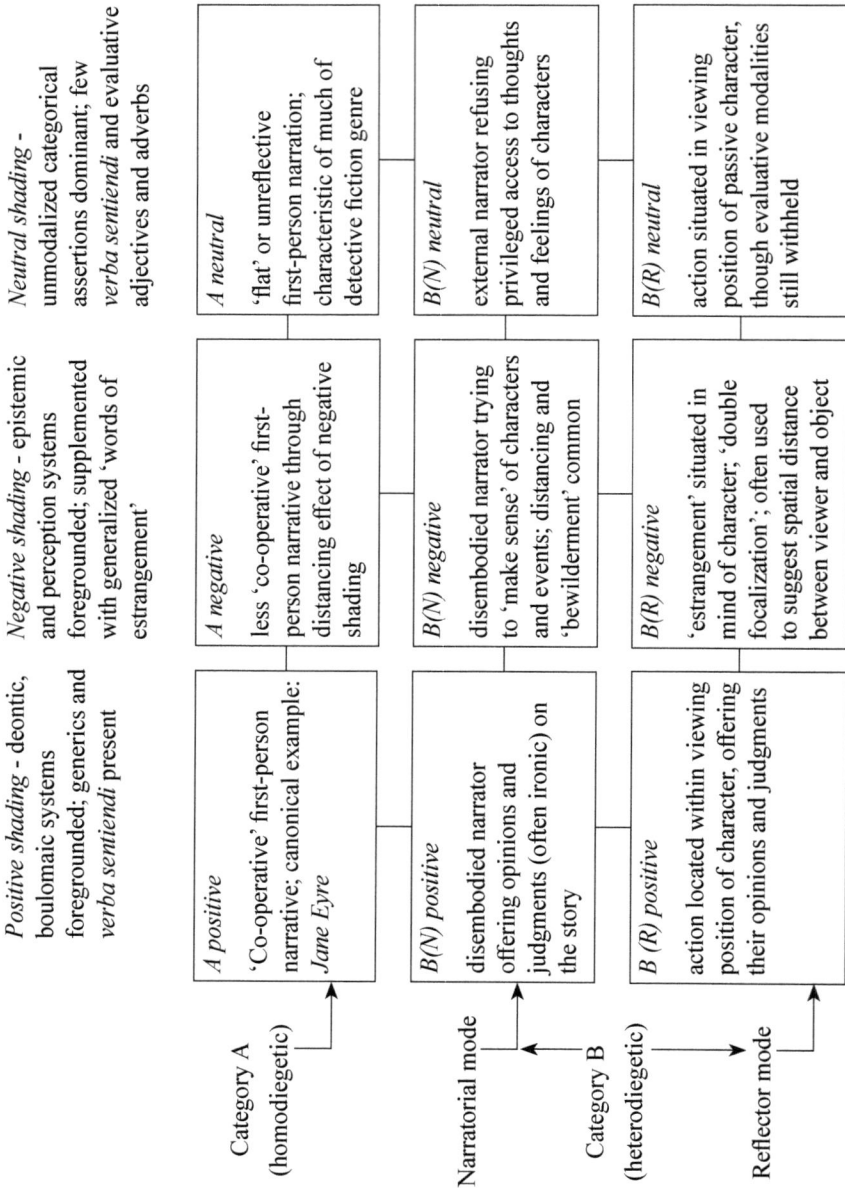

	Positive shading - deontic, boulomaic systems foregrounded; generics and *verba sentiendi* present	*Negative shading* - epistemic and perception systems foregrounded; supplemented with generalized 'words of estrangement'	*Neutral shading* - unmodalized categorical assertions dominant; few *verba sentiendi* and evaluative adjectives and adverbs
Category A (homodiegetic) / Narratorial mode	*A positive* — 'Co-operative' first-person narrative; canonical example: *Jane Eyre*	*A negative* — less 'co-operative' first-person narrative through distancing effect of negative shading	*A neutral* — 'flat' or unreflective first-person narration; characteristic of much of detective fiction genre
Category B (heterodiegetic) / Narratorial mode	*B(N) positive* — disembodied narrator offering opinions and judgments (often ironic) on the story	*B(N) negative* — disembodied narrator trying to 'make sense' of characters and events; distancing and 'bewilderment' common	*B(N) neutral* — external narrator refusing privileged access to thoughts and feelings of characters
Reflector mode	*B (R) positive* — action located within viewing position of character, offering their opinions and judgments	*B(R) negative* — 'estrangement' situated in mind of character; 'double focalization'; often used to suggest spatial distance between viewer and object	*B(R) neutral* — action situated in viewing position of passive character, though evaluative modalities still withheld

Adapted from the diagram appearing on page 75 of Paul Simpson's *Language, Ideology and Point of View* (1993).

List of references

Adams, Ruth M. 'Wuthering Heights: The Land East of Eden.' *Nineteenth-Century Fiction* 13.1 (1958): 58-62.

Aitchison, Jean. *Words in the Mind*. 3rd ed. Oxford: Blackwell Publishing Ltd., 2003.

Alexander, Gillian. 'Politics of the Pronoun in the Literature of the English Revolution.' *Language and Literature: An Introductory Reader in Stylistics*. Ed. Ronald Carter. London: George Allen & Unwin, 1982. 217-234.

Allott, Miriam, ed. *Emily Brontë 'Wuthering Heights' A Casebook*. Revised ed. London: Palgrave Macmillan, 1973.

Attridge, Derek. 'Closing Statement: Linguistics and Poetics in Retrospect.' *The Linguistics of Writing: Arguments between Language and Literature*. Eds. Nigel Fabb, et al. New York: Methuen, 1987. 15-32.

Austin, Frances. ' "Ing" Forms in "Four Quartets".' *English Studies* 63 (1982): 23-31.

---. 'Making Sense of Syntax: A Reply to Peter Barry.' *English Studies* 66 (1985): 167-168.

Austin, T. '(IN)Transitives: Some Thoughts on Ambiguity in Poetic Texts.' *Journal of Literary Semantics* 15 (1986): 23-38.

Bal, Mieke. 'Narrativity and Voice.' *Encyclopedia of Language & Linguistics*. Elsevier, 2006. 477-481.

---. *Narratology: Introduction to the Theory of Narrative*. 2nd ed. Toronto: University of Toronto Press, 1997.

Banfield, A. 'Narrative Style and the Grammar of Direct and Indirect Speech.' *Foundations of Language* 10 (1973): 1-39.

Barry, Peter. 'The Enactment Fallacy.' *Essays in Criticism* XXX.2 (1980): 95-104.

---. 'The Limitations of Stylistics.' *Essays in Criticism* XXXVIII.3 (1988): 175-189.

---. 'Making Sense of Syntax, Perhaps: A Reply Note to Frances Austin's ' "Ing" Forms in "Four Quartets" '.' *English Studies* 65.1 (1984): 36-38.

Basso, K. H. ' "To Give up on Words": Silence in Western Apache Culture.' *Language and Social Context: Selected Readings*. Ed. Pier Paolo Giglioli. London: Penguin, 1972. 67-86.

Bateson, F. W., and B. Shakevitch. 'Katherine Mansfield's "The Fly": A Critical Exercise.' *Essays in Criticism* 12 (1962): 39-53.

Berger, Carole. 'The Rake and the Reader in Jane Austen's Novels.' *Studies in English Literature, 1500-1900* 15.4 (1975): 531-544.

Binns, Ronald. 'Situating Gormenghast.' *Critical Quarterly* 21.1 (1979): 21-33.

Bolinger, Dwight. *Aspects of Language*. 2nd ed. New York: Harcourt Brace Jovanovich, Inc., 1975.

Bradbury, Malcolm. 'Towards a Poetics of Fiction: An Approach through Structure.' *Novel: A Forum on Fiction* 1.1 (1967): 45-52.

Brogan, Hugh. 'The Gutters of Gormenghast.' *The Cambridge Review* 95 (1973).

Brontë, Emily. *Wuthering Heights*. World's Classics. Oxford: Oxford University Press, 1976.

---. *Wuthering Heights*. Penguin Classics. London: Penguin, 1995.

Brooks, Cleanth. 'The Heresy of Paraphrase.' *The Well-Wrought Urn: Studies in the Structure of Poetry*. New York: Harcourt, Brace and Company, 1947. 192-214.

Brown, Keith, ed. *Encyclopedia of Language & Linguistics*. 2nd ed: Elsevier, 2006.

Brown, R., and A. Gilman. 'The Pronouns of Power and Solidarity.' *Language and Social Context: Selected Readings*. Ed. Pier Paolo Giglioli. London: Penguin, 1972. 252-282.

Burton, Ben, and Ronald Carter. 'Literature and the Language of Literature.' *Encyclopedia of Language & Linguistics*. Elsevier, 2006. 267-274.

Burton, Deirdre D. 'Through Glass Darkly: Through Dark Glasses.' *Language and Literature: An Introductory Reader in Stylistics*. Ed. Ronald Carter. London: George Allen & Unwin, 1982. 195-212.

Carter, Ronald, and Walter Nash. 'Language and Literariness.' *Prose Studies*. 6 (1983): 123-141.

Carter, Ronald, ed. *Language and Literature: An Introductory Reader in Stylistics*. London: George Allen & Unwin, 1982.

---. 'Style and Interpretation in Hemingway's "Cat in the Rain".' *Language and Literature: An Introductory Reader in Stylistics*. Ed. Ronald Carter. London: George Allen &Unwin, 1982. 65-77.

---. 'Responses to Language in Poetry.' *Literary Text and Language Study*. Eds. R. Carter and Deirdre Burton. Explorations in Language Study. London: Edward Arnold, 1982. 28-56.

Chalker, Sylvia. *A Student's English Grammar Workbook*. Essex: Longman, 1992.

Chapman, Raymond. *Linguistics and Literature: An Introduction to Literary Stylistics*. London: Edward Arnold, 1973.

Chatman, Seymour, ed. *Approaches to Poetics*. New York: Columbia University Press, 1973.

---, ed. *Literary Style: A Symposium*. London: Oxford University Press, 1971.

Cluysenaar, Anne. *Introduction to Literary Stylistics: A Discussion of Dominant Structures in Verse and Prose*. London: B. T. Batsford Ltd., 1976.

Collis, Louise. 'Memories of Mervyn Peake.' *Art and Artists* (1986).

Craig, G. Armour. 'On the Style of "Vanity Fair".' *Style in Prose Fiction*. Ed. Harold C. Martin. New York and London: Columbia University Press, 1958. 87-113.

Crowe Ransom, John. 'Criticism, Inc.' *20th Century Literary Criticism: A Reader*. Ed. David Lodge. London: Longman, 1972. 228-239.

Cruse, Alan. *Meaning in Language: An Introduction to Semantics and Pragmatics*. Oxford: Oxford University Press, 2000.

Culler, Jonathan. *Structuralist Poetics: Structuralism, Linguistics and the Study of Literature*. Routledge Classics. London: Routledge, 1975.

Dillon, George L. 'Whorfian Stylistics.' *Journal of Literary Semantics* 11.2 (1982): 73-77.

Dillon, George L., and Frederick Kirchhoff. 'On the Form and Function of Free Indirect Style.' *PTL* 1 (1976): 431-440.

Eagleton, Mary, ed. *Feminist Literary Theory: A Reader*. Oxford: Basil Blackwell, 1986.

Eagleton, Terry. *Literary Theory: An Introduction*. Oxford: Blackwell, 1983.

Eliot, George. *The Mill on the Floss*. Penguin Classics. London: Penguin, 1979.

Farr, Michael. *Tintin: The Complete Companion*. London: John Murray, 2001.

Fish, Stanley E. 'How Ordinary Is Ordinary Language?' *New Literary History* 5.1 (1973): 41-54.

---. *Is There a Text in This Class? The Authority of Interpretive Communities*. Cambridge, Massachusetts: Harvard University Press, 1980.

---. 'Literature in the Reader: Affective Stylistics.' *New Literary History* 2.1 (1970): 123-162.

---. 'What Is Stylistics and Why Are They Saying Such Terrible Things About It?' *Approaches to Poetics*. Ed. Seymour Chatman. New York: Columbia University Press, 1973. 109-152.

---. 'Why No One's Afraid of Wolfgang Iser.' *Diacritics* 11 (1981): 2-13.

Fowler, Roger, ed. *A Dictionary of Modern Critical Terms*. London: Routledge, 1987.

---. *The Languages of Literature: Some Linguistic Contributions to Criticism*. London: Routledge and Kegan Paul, 1971.

---. *Linguistic Criticism*. Opus. 2nd ed. Oxford: Oxford University Press, 1996.

---. *Linguistics and the Novel*. New Accents. Ed. Terence Hawkes. London: Methuen, 1977.

---. 'Linguistics, Stylistics; Criticism?' *Lingua* 16 (1966): 153-165.

---. *Literature as Social Discourse: The Practice of Linguistic Criticism*. London: Batsford Academic and Educational Ltd., 1981.

---. 'The New Stylistics.' *Style and Structure in Literature: Essays in the New Stylistics*. Ed. Roger Fowler. New York: Cornell University Press, 1975. 1-18.

---. 'A Note on Some Uses of the Term "Meaning" in Descriptive Linguistics.' *Word* xxi (1965): 411-420.

---, ed. *Style and Structure in Literature: Essays in the New Stylistics*. New York: Cornell University Press, 1975.

---. 'Style and the Concept of Deep Structure.' *Journal of Literary Semantics* 1 (1972): 5-24.

---. *Understanding Language: An Introduction to Linguistics*. London: Routledge & Kegan Paul, 1974.

Fowler, Roger, and F. W. Bateson. 'Argument II (Continued): Language and Literature.' *Essays in Criticism* XVIII (1968): 164-182.

---. 'Argument II. Literature and Linguistics.' *Essays in Criticism* XVII (1967): 322-347.

Freeman, Donald C., ed. *Linguistics and Literary Style*. New York: Holt, Rinehart and Winston, Inc., 1970.

Gilbert, S. M., and S. Gubar. *The Madwoman in the Attic: The Woman Writer and the Nineteenth-Century Literary Imagination*. New Haven and London: Yale University Press, 1984.

Golden, Catherine, ed. *The Captive Imagination: A Casebook on "The Yellow Wallpaper"*. New York: The Feminist Press, 1992.

Graddol, David, Jenny Cheshire, and Joan Swann. *Describing Language*. 2nd ed. Maidenhead & Philadelphia: Open University Press, 1994.

Green, Keith. 'Literary Theory and Stylistics.' *Encyclopedia of Language & Linguistics*. Elsevier, 2006. 261-267.

Greenbaum, Sidney, and Randolph Quirk. *A Student's Grammar of the English Language*. London: Longman, 1990.

Greenland, Colin. 'Mervyn Peake: Overview.' *St. James Guide to Science Fiction Writers*. Ed. Jay P. Pederson. 4th ed. St. James Press, 1996.

Gross, Maurice. 'On the Failure of Generative Grammar.' *Language* 55.4 (1979): 859-885.

Haddon, Mark. *The Curious Incident of the Dog in the Night-Time*. London: Vintage, 2004.

Hagan, John. 'Control of Sympathy in "Wuthering Heights".' *Nineteenth-Century Fiction* 21.4 (1967): 305-323.

Halliday, M. A. K. 'Descriptive Linguistics in Literary Studies.' *Linguistics and Literary Style*. Ed. Donald C. Freeman. New York: Holt, Rinehart and Winston, Inc., 1970. 57-72.

---. 'Linguistic Function and Literary Style: An Inquiry into the Language of William Golding's "The Inheritors".' *Literary Style: A Symposium*. Ed. Seymour Chatman. Oxford: Oxford University Press, 1971. 330-365.

Halliday, M. A. K. , and Ruqaiay Hasan. *Cohesion in English*. English Language Series. Ed. Randolph Quirk. London: Longman, 1976.

Hawkes, Terence. *Structuralism and Semiotics*. New Accents. Ed. Terence Hawkes. London: Routledge, 1977.

Hedges, Elaine R. 'Afterword to "The Yellow Wallpaper".' *The Captive Imagination: A Casebook on 'The Yellow Wallpaper'*. Ed. Catherine Golden. New York: The Feminist Press, 1973. 123-136.

Hewings, Martin. *Advanced Grammar in Use: A Self-Study Reference and Practice Book for Advanced Learners of English*. Cambridge: Cambridge University Press, 1999.

Hirsch, David H. 'Linguistic Structure and Literary Meaning.' *Journal of Literary Semantics* 1 (1972): 80-88.

Holquist, Michael. *Dialogism: Bakhtin and His World*. New Accents. Ed. Terence Hawkes. 2nd ed. London: Routledge, 2002.

Hunt, Bruce. ' "Gormenghast": Psychology of the Bildungsroman.' *The Mervyn Peake Review*. 6 (1978).

Irwin, Robert. 'Mervyn Peake: Overview.' *St. James Guide to Fantasy Writers*. Ed. David Pringle: St. James Press, 1996.

Iser, Wolfgang. *The Implied Reader: Patterns of Communication in Prose Fiction from Bunyan to Beckett*. Baltimore and London: The John Hopkins University Press, 1974.

---. 'Talk Like Whales: A Reply to Stanley Fish.' *Diacritics* 11.3 (1981): 82-87.

Jakobson, Roman. 'Closing Statement: Linguistics and Poetics.' *Style in Language*. Ed. Thomas A. Sebeok: M. I. T. Press, 1958. 350-377.

Jefferson, Ann, and David Robey, eds. *Modern Literary Theory: A Comparative Introduction*. London: B. T. Batsford Ltd., 1986.

Kafka, Franz. *The Trial*. Trans. Willa and Edwin Muir. London: Penguin, 1953.

Kennedy, Chris. 'Systemic Grammar and Its Use in Literary Analysis.' *Language and Literature: An Introductory Reader in Stylistics*. Ed. Ronald Carter. London: George Allen & Unwin, 1982. 83-96.

Keyes, Daniel. *Flowers for Algernon*. New York: Harcourt, Brace & World, 1966.

Knapp, Steven, and Walter Benn Michaels. 'Against Theory.' *Critical Inquiry* 8.4 (1982): 723-742.

Kress, Gunther. 'Ideological Structures in Discourse.' *Discourse Analysis in Society*. Ed. T. A. van Dijk. Vol. 4. Handbook of Discourse Analysis. London: Academic Press, 1985. 27-41.

Leavis, Q. D. 'A Fresh Approach to "Wuthering Heights".' *Collected Essays Volume I: The Englishness of the English Novel*. Ed. G. Singh. Vol. I. Cambridge: Cambridge University Press, 1983 (1969). 228-274.

Leech, Geoffrey N. *A Linguistic Guide to English Poetry*. English Language Series. Ed. Randolph Quirk: Longman, 1969.

---. ' "This Bread I Break" - Language and Interpretation.' *Linguistics and Literary Style*. Ed. Donald C. Freeman. New York: Holt, Rinehart and Winston, Inc., 1970. 119-128.

Leech, Geoffrey N., Margaret Deuchar, and Robert Hoogenraad. *English Grammar for Today: A New Introduction*. London: Macmillan, 1982.

Leech, Geoffrey N., and Michael H. Short. *Style in Fiction: A Linguistic Introduction to English Fictional Prose*. English Language Series. Ed. Randolph Quirk. London & New York: Longman, 1981.

Lemon, Lee T., and Marion J. Reis, eds. *Russian Formalist Criticism: Four Essays*. Lincoln: University of Nebraska Press, 1965.

Lodge, David, ed. *20th Century Literary Criticism: A Reader*. London and New York: Longman, 1972.

---. *Language of Fiction: Essays in Criticism and Verbal Analysis of the English Novel*. 2nd ed. London & New York: Routledge, 2002.

---. 'Towards a Poetics of Fiction: 2) An Approach through Language.' *Novel: A Forum on Fiction* 1.2 (1968): 158-169.

Lovell-Smith, Rose. 'Qu'a Donc Pu Lire Emily Brontë? Arrivals in the Waverley Novels and "Wuthering Heights".' *Brontë Society Transactions* 21.4 (1994): 79-87.

---. 'Walter Scott and Emily Brontë: The Rhetoric of Love.' *Brontë Society Transactions* 21.4 (1994): 117-124.

Lyons, John. *Introduction to Theoretical Linguistics*. Cambridge: Cambridge University Press, 1968.

MacPike, Loralee. 'Environment as Psychopathological Symbolism in "The Yellow Wallpaper".' *The Captive Imagination: A Casebook on 'The Yellow Wallpaper'*. Ed. Catherine Golden. New York: The Feminist Press, 1975. 137-140.

Mailloux, Steven. 'Learning to Read: Interpretation and Reader-Response Criticism.' *Studies in the Literary Imagination* 12.1 (1979): 93-108.

---. ' "The Red Badge of Courage" and Interpretive Conventions: Critical Response to a Maimed Text.' *Studies in the Novel* 10.1 (1978): 48-63.

Manlove, C. N. 'Mervyn Peake (1911-1968) - The "Titus" Trilogy.' *Modern Fantasy: Five Studies*. Cambridge: Cambridge University Press, 1975. 207-257.

Marlowe, Christopher. *The Complete Plays*. London: Penguin, 1969.

Martin, Harold C., ed. *Style in Prose Fiction*. New York and London: Columbia University Press, 1958.

Mason, Mary. 'Deixis: A Point of Entry to "Little Dorrit".' *Language and Literature: An Introductory Reader in Stylistics*. Ed. Ronald Carter. London: George Allen & Unwin, 1982. 29-37.

McGuinness, Mark. 'Gormenghast and Beyond: The Centre of Imaginative Gravity in Mervyn Peake's Titus Books.' *Peake Papers* (1994): 83-95.

McHale, Brian. 'Free Indirect Discourse: A Survey of Recent Accounts.' *Poetics and Theory of Literature* 3 (1978): 235-287.

---. 'Unspeakable Sentences, Unnatural Acts: Linguistics and Poetics Revisited.' *Poetics Today* 4.1 (1983): 17-45.

McIntosh, Angus. ' "As You Like It": A Grammatical Clue to Character.' *Review of English Literature* iv (1963): 68-81.

Mey, J. L. 'Literary Pragmatics.' *Encyclopedia of Language & Linguistics.* Elsevier, 2006. 255-261.

---. 'Pragmatics of Reading.' *Encyclopedia of Language & Linguistics.* Elsevier, 2006. 32-37.

Morris, Pam, ed. *The Bakhtin Reader: Selected Writings of Bakhtin, Medvedev, Voloshinov.* London: Edward Arnold, 1994.

Mukařovský, Jan. 'Standard Language and Poetic Language.' *Linguistics and Literary Style.* Ed. Donald C. Freeman. New York: Holt, Rinehart and Winston, Inc., 1970. 40-56.

Nash, Walter. 'On a Passage from Lawrence's "Odour of Chrysanthemums".' *Language and Literature: An Introductory Reader in Stylistics.* Ed. Ronald Carter. London: George Allen & Unwin, 1982. 101-114.

Nowottny, Winifred. *The Language Poets Use.* London: The Athlone Press, 1962.

Ohmann, Richard M. 'From Style to Meaning in "Araby": Reply.' *College English* 28.2 (1966): 171-173.

---. 'Generative Grammars and the Concept of Literary Style.' *Linguistics and Literary Style.* Ed. Donald C. Freeman. New York: Holt, Rinehart and Winston, Inc., 1970. 258-278.

---. 'Literature as Act.' *Approaches to Poetics.* Ed. Seymour Chatman. New York: Columbia University Press, 1973. 81-107.

---. 'Literature as Sentences.' *College English* 27.4 (1966): 261-267.

---. 'Prolegomena to the Analysis of Prose Style.' *Style in Prose Fiction.* Ed. Harold C. Martin. New York and London: Columbia University Press, 1958. 1-24.

Oliver-Morden, B. C. 'Mervyn Peake: Overview.' *Reference Guide to English Literature.* Ed. D. L. Kirkpatrick. 2nd ed. St. James Press, 1991.

Orwell, George. 'Politics and the English Language.' *The Penguin Essays of George Orwell.* Penguin Twentieth-Century Classics. London: Penguin, 1984. 354-366.

---. 'Politics Vs Literature: An Examination of "Gulliver's Travels".' *The Penguin Essays of George Orwell*. Penguin Twentieth-Century Classics. London: Penguin, 1984. 376-393.

Page, Norman. *Speech in the English Novel*. 2nd ed. Atlantic Highlands, NJ: Humanities Press International Inc., 1988.

Pateman, Trevor. 'Linguistics as a Branch of Critical Theory.' *UEA Papers in Linguistics* 14-15 (1981): 1-29.

Peake, Mervyn. *The Gormenghast Novels*. Woodstock: The Overlook Press, 1995.

Perkins Gilman, Charlotte. 'The Yellow Wall-Paper.' *The Yellow Wall-Paper and Other Stories*. Ed. R. Shulman. World's Classics. Oxford: Oxford University Press, 1995. 3-19.

Posner, Rebecca. 'The Use and Abuse of Stylistic Statistics.' *Archivum Linguisticum* xv (1963): 111-139.

Postal, Paul. 'Underlying and Superficial Linguistic Structure.' *Harvard Educational Review* 34 (1964): 246-266.

Pratchett, Terry. *Going Postal*. Discworld. London: Transworld, 2004.

---. *The Fifth Elephant*. Discworld. London: Transworld, 1999.

---. *Interesting Times*. Discworld. London: Transworld, 1994.

---. *Men at Arms*. Discworld. London: Transworld, 1993.

---. *Thud!* Discworld. London: Transworld, 2005.

---. *The Truth*. Discworld. London: Transworld, 2001.

Richards, Ivor Armstrong. *Practical Criticism*. London: Kegan, Paul & Co., 1929.

Richardson, Kay. 'Critical Linguistics and Textual Diagnosis.' *Text* 7.2 (1987): 145-163.

Riffaterre, Michael. 'Criteria for Style Analysis.' *Word* 15 (1959): 154-174.

---. 'Stylistic Context.' *Word* 16 (1960): 207-218.

Rimmon-Kenan, Shlomith. *Narrative Fiction: Contemporary Poetics*. New Accents. Ed. Terence Hawkes. London and New York: Methuen, 1983.

Rodger, A. ' "O Where Are You Going?": A Suggested Experiment in Classroom Stylistics.' *Language and Literature: An Introductory Reader in Stylistics*. Ed. Ronald Carter. London: George Allen & Unwin, 1982. 123-160.

Rolleston, James, ed. *Twentieth Century Interpretations of 'The Trial': A Collection of Critical Essays*. New Jersey: Prentice-Hall Inc., 1976.

Russell, John. 'From Style to Meaning in "Araby": Comment and Rebuttal.' *College English* 28.2 (1966): 170-171.

Rylance, Rick, ed. *Debating Texts: A Reader in 20th Century Literary Theory and Method*. Milton Keynes: Open University Press, 1987.

Searle, J. 'What Is a Speech Act?' *Language and Social Context: Selected Readings*. Ed. Pier Paolo Giglioli. London: Penguin, 1972. 136-154.

Sebeok, Thomas A. 'Style in Language.' Ed. Thomas A. Sebeok. Indiana University, Bloomington: M.I.T. Press and John Wiley & Sons, Inc., 1958.

Shakespeare, William. *Macbeth*. Arden Shakespeare. Ed. Kenneth Muir. 9th ed. London: Methuen, 1962.

Shannon, Edgar F. 'Lockwood's Dreams and the Exegesis of "Wuthering Heights".' *Nineteenth-Century Fiction* 14.2 (1959): 95-109.

Shen, Dan. 'Stylistics, Objectivity, and Convention.' *Poetics* 17 (1988): 221-238.

Short, Michael H. *Exploring the Language of Poems, Plays and Prose*. Learning About Language. Eds. Geoffrey N. Leech and Michael H. Short. London: Longman, 1996.

---. ' "Prelude I" to a Literary Linguistic Stylistics.' *Language and Literature: An Introductory Reader in Stylistics*. Ed. Ronald Carter. London: George Allen & Unwin, 1982. 55-61.

---. 'Stylistics and the Teaching of Literature: With an Example from James Joyce's "Portrait of the Artist as a Young Man".' *Language and Literature: An Introductory Reader in Stylistics*. Ed. Ronald Carter. London: George Allen & Unwin, 1982. 179-189.

Simpson, Paul. *Language, Ideology and Point of View*. The Interface Series. Ed. Ronald Carter. London: Routledge, 1993.

---. 'The Transitivity Model.' *Critical Studies in Mass Communication* 5.2 (1988): 166-172.

Sinclair, John. 'Lines About "Lines".' *Language and Literature: An Introductory Reader in Stylistics*. Ed. Ronald Carter. London: George Allen & Unwin, 1982. 163-175.

Smith, Stevie. *Novel on Yellow Paper or Work It out for Yourself.* Penguin Modern Classics. Harmondsworth: Penguin, 1972.

Spark, Muriel. *The Driver's Seat.* Penguin Modern Classics. London: Penguin, 1970.

Steinmann Jr., Martin , and Richard M. Ohmann. 'A Comment on Richard Ohmann's "Literature as Sentences" and Martin Steinmann's "Rhetorical Research": Replies.' *College English* 27.8 (1966): 635.

Strauss, Albrecht B. 'On Smollett's Language: A Paragraph in "Ferdinand Count Fathom".' *Style in Prose Fiction*. Ed. Harold C. Martin. New York and London: Columbia University Press, 1958. 25-54.

Sutherland, John. 'Is Heathcliff a Murderer?' *Is Heathcliff a Murderer?: Great Puzzles in Nineteenth-Century Literature*. Oxford: Oxford University Press, 1996. 53-58.

Swan, Michael, and Catherine Walter. *How English Works: A Grammar Practice Book.* Oxford: Oxford University Press, 1997.

Tanaka, Ronald. 'Action and Meaning in Literary Theory.' *Journal of Literary Semantics* 1 (1972): 41-56.

Taylor, Talbot J. 'Communication and Literary Style: The Principle of Inter-Subjectivity.' *Poetics Today* 3.4 (1982): 39-51.

Taylor, Talbot J., and Michael J. Toolan. 'Recent Trends in Stylistics.' *Journal of Literary Semantics* 13 (1984): 57-79.

Thomas, Jenny. 'Cross-Cultural Pragmatic Failure.' *Applied Linguistics* 4 (1983): 91-112.

Tibbetts, A. M. 'A Comment on Richard Ohmann's "Literature as Sentences" and Martin Steinmann's "Rhetorical Research".' *College English* 27.8 (1966): 634-635.

Todorov, Tzvetan. 'The Fantastic in Fiction.' *Twentieth Century Studies* 3 (1970): 76-92.

---. 'Structuralism and Literature.' *Approaches to Poetics*. Ed. Seymour Chatman. New York: Columbia University Press, 1973. 153-168.

Toolan, Michael J. *Narrative: A Critical Linguistic Introduction*. The Interface Series. Ed. Ronald Carter. 2nd ed. London and New York: Routledge, 2001.

---. *The Stylistics of Fiction: A Literary-Linguistic Approach*. London: Routledge, 1990.

Tube, Henry. 'His Nibs.' *The Spectator* 220.7283 (1968): 105-106.

Tytler, Graeme. 'Physiognomy in "Wuthering Heights".' *Brontë Society Transactions* 21.4 (1994): 137-148.

Ullmann, Stephen. 'Style and Personality.' *Review of English Literature* vi (1965): 21-31.

van Dijk, T. A., ed. *Discourse Analysis in Society*. Vol. 4. London: Academic Press, 1985.

van Ghent, Dorothy. 'On "Wuthering Heights".' *The English Novel: Form and Function*. New York: Harper & Brothers, 1953. 153-170.

---. 'The Window Figure and the Two-Children Figure in "Wuthering Heights".' *Nineteenth-Century Fiction* 7.3 (1952): 189-197.

Various. *Discworld Monthly*. Issue 109. May 2006.

Vendler, Helen Hennessy. 'Book Review: Essays on Style and Language: Linguistic and Critical Approaches to Literary Styles.' *Essays in Criticism* XVI (1966): 457-463.

Wales, Katie. 'Stylistics.' *Encyclopedia of Language & Linguistics*. Elsevier, 2006. 213-217.

Wall, Barbara. *The Narrator's Voice: The Dilemma of Children's Fiction*. London: Macmillan, 1991.

Watson, Melvin R. 'Tempest in the Soul: The Theme and Structure of "Wuthering Heights".' *Nineteenth-Century Fiction* 4.2 (1949): 87-100.

Watt, Ian. 'The First Paragraph of "The Ambassadors": An Explication.' *Essays in Criticism* 10 (1960): 250-274.

Wharton, Edith. *The Age of Innocence*. Penguin Twentieth-Century Classics. London: Penguin, 1996.

Widdowson, H. G. 'The Conditional Presence of Mr Bleaney.' *Language and Literature: An Introductory Reader in Stylistics*. Ed. Ronald Carter. London: George Allen & Unwin, 1982. 19-25.

---. 'Othello in Person.' *Language and Literature: An Introductory Reader in Stylistics*. Ed. Ronald Carter. London: George Allen & Unwin, 1982. 41-51.

Wimsatt, W. K., and Monroe C. Beardsley. *The Verbal Icon: Studies in the Meaning of Poetry*. Kentucky: University of Kentucky Press, 1954.

Yeoman, Ann. 'Playing Around with Shapes and Sounds: Reflections on Mervyn Peake and His Use of the Image in the Titus Books.' *Peake Papers* (1994): 61-81.

Muriel Spark: essays and blog posts

'Excluding the lumpen hoi polloi': The auto/biographies of Muriel Spark

The texts referred to below are Martin Stannard's 2009 biography, Muriel Spark's own autobiography *Curriculum Vitae*, which covers only the years before she really found fame, and Derek Stanford's volume of criticism and memoir. Spark instructed research students focusing on her work *not* to read the latter. Nevertheless, those students who disobey Spark's ruling will take Stanford's book with a pinch of salt once they have read *Curriculum Vitae*, because the ever-watchful Spark took steps to ensure that Stanford's memoir would not be taken seriously. She corrects more than a few of Stanford's mistakes: for example, Spark's grandmother did not have gypsy blood, and little Muriel was not breastfed for two years as Stanford claims; he also bungles the French of the title of Proust's major work (*Recherche dans le temps perdu*!).

In fact, Stanford was very fair to Spark in his 165-page memoir. Stanford himself emerges from contemporary accounts as a rather ridiculous figure, a dapper little bald fellow given to aping eighteenth-century speech mannerisms which never failed to irritate those with whom he conversed. Spark lampooned Stanford in *A Far Cry From Kensington* by casting him as the odious *pisseur de copie*, Hector Bartlett. After reading Spark's sharp, pared-to-the-bone prose and Stannard's lucid account of Spark's life, Stanford's written style reads as excessively elaborate and often contrived, but he attempts to do justice to his subject and is not insensitive as a critic: he gives a very plausible reading of Spark's poem, *The Rout* [Stanford, pp. 83-88]. However, his critical responses are more reliable when he is assessing Spark's poetry; when he moves on to her fictional prose, he flounders a little and it is clear that Stanford, steeped as he was in eighteenth- and nineteenth-century writing, didn't really have a critical grasp of the more modern forms of literature: some of his harsher judgements appear to stem from his own lack of comprehension. But Spark herself comes out well: Stanford depicts her as being delightful company, playful and humorous, yet determined to achieve her goals. In *Curriculum Vitae*, Spark, however, writes that she was concerned about Stanford's habit of inaccuracy: 'It was often small facts, dates and titles that Derek couldn't get right... In a literary collaborator, this carelessness puzzled me and worried me in those early fifties' [*CV*, pp. 189-190], so she was understandably concerned when she found out that Stanford was writing a biographical and critical study of her. Stanford caused more problems than simply getting a few minor dates wrong, however. After the Second World War, rationing continued in England until 1954, and Stanford cheerfully and regularly ate half of Spark's meagre rations, even though he was still living with his parents and she was evidently under-nourished. He cared for her when she suffered her breakdown and obtained on her behalf some money from Graham Greene to tide her over. However, when he let himself into her rooms in order to pack some belongings to take to Spark in her retreat, he helped himself to a couple of notebooks of juvenilia which he later sold for profit. He also betrayed Spark when he sold a large number of her letters, and the memoir too was an exercise in cashing in on the fame of a more successful writer to make money for himself.

Muriel Spark was intensely paranoid about, and fiercely protective of, her public image. She never doubted her own talent, that much is clear, but she did not trust other people to acknowledge it and was hypersensitive to any perceived criticism. Stannard's biography tells of a series of arguments and fallings-out that continued throughout Spark's lifetime, hence Ved Mehta's oft-quoted remark that Spark 'went through people like pieces of Kleenex' [Stannard, p. 322]. Spark resisted interviews following a first disastrous experience with Venetia Murray, but it was she who approached Stannard as a potential biographer after she had read and reviewed the second volume of Stannard's biography of Evelyn Waugh, a writer connected to Spark through both literary style and adopted religion. Spark instructed Stannard to treat her as if she were dead, but he tells us that she 'used up a great deal of her own time helping [him] to revise the first draft' [Stannard, p. xi]. A. S. Byatt reported, truthfully or not, that Spark went through the biography 'line by line' [O'Neill, p. 107]. James Campbell, reviewing Stannard's biography for the *TLS*, makes some acidic comments about this state of affairs in what is overall a rather harsh critique, and he also notes that Stannard's use of Spark's letters is limited to either very short quotations or paraphrase, although he has quoted liberally from letters written by others. Spark's personal correspondence would undoubtedly reveal more than she would wish the general populace to know. In reality, Stannard was probably not entirely at liberty to quote 'an unspecified amount from her unpublished writings, including the letters', as was the original arrangement with Spark [Stannard, p. xi].

In another review of the biography, Joseph O'Neill describes Stannard's unflinching defence of Spark as a means of 'awakening in the reader a prosecutorial instinct', and surmises that Spark 'foresaw her amiable assassination by Stannard and arranged for it'. This is an interesting conclusion, but O'Neill doesn't give us anything to go on: he doesn't really explain why he thinks Stannard's biography is so damning. He draws a clever likeness between Spark arranging her own biographical assassination, and the character of Lise, who arranges her own brutal murder in *The Driver's Seat*, Spark's most accomplished and most horrible novel. I like this line of reasoning very much, but I wish O'Neill had explored his conclusion in more depth. He was perhaps so enamoured of his clever comparison that he didn't dare examine it further in case his theory didn't hold water. On the whole, I think there is much that is good about O'Neill's review, but although he is quite right in asserting that 'postmodernism was around well before 1980', it took a little while for these new theories to take hold in the UK, so Stannard is justified in describing Spark as being ahead of her time. (She was. It's quite clear from reading contemporary reviews that a not inconsiderable number of critics just didn't know what to make of her.)

Alan Massie notes in his own book on Spark's oeuvre that a biography is 'something impertinent if done unsanctioned during its subject's lifetime, generally worthless if written with his [*sic*] co-operation' [Massie, p. 12]. So, by this reasoning, the Stanford book is impertinent and the Stannard worthless. As for Spark's autobiography, she 'determined to write nothing that cannot be supported by documentary evidence or by eyewitnesses' [*CV*, p. 11]. While this is an approach that has its merits, the end result is a book that is rather dry and humourless compared to her fiction; in fact, her barbed corrections of Stanford's errors make for some of the most entertaining passages – that, and her spat with Marie Stopes. Nevertheless, given Spark's concern for her public image, the volume of autobiography should be treated with caution. Jenny Turner hits home in her description of *Curriculum Vitae* as 'a debunking job...a pre-emptive attack' [online source]. Turner here anticipates O'Neill's conclusion that Spark, expecting the inevitable attacks to come, took care to arrange matters so that the presentation of biographical material was as much under her control as it was possible to be.

Muriel Spark did, in fact, lead a very interesting life. Born in 1918 and raised in Edinburgh, she left Scotland to marry Sydney Oswald Spark in Africa, where she gave birth to her son, Robin. Sydney Spark was a violent manic depressive: 'too mentally unstable to hold down a job, he also revealed himself as prone to gunplay and wife-beating' [O'Neill, p. 100], so Spark deserted her husband and obtained a divorce as soon as she could. The outbreak of the Second World War delayed Spark's return home, but she eventually managed to secure a passage back to England where she worked for the Foreign Office alongside Sefton Delmer, broadcasting falsified information intended to discourage the Germans. Once the war was over, Spark worked extremely hard to secure for herself a role in the world of literary London. She was offered the position of secretary for the clique-ridden Poetry Society, where she met the two men with whom she had the most intense love affairs, Howard Sergeant and Derek Stanford. She was eventually sacked from the Society, but she continued to write as often as she could while dealing with poverty, malnutrition and hallucinations brought on by her use of the slimming drug, Dexedrine. She converted to Roman Catholicism in 1954. When Macmillan commissioned a novel from her, she made use of her new-found Catholicism, and her hallucinatory experiences, in writing *The Comforters*, which was very well-received. From that point onwards, her star continued to rise until she finally achieved something like financial security with the success of *The Prime of Miss Jean Brodie*. She left England to take up residence first in New York, then Rome, and finally she settled in Tuscany with the painter Penelope Jardine, who was her companion for over thirty years until Spark's death in 2006 at the age of eighty-eight.

Stannard's biography cannot disguise the fact that Spark was driven by her sense of writerly vocation to the point of extreme selfishness: for example, her son Robin was brought up by his grandparents leaving Spark free to follow her literary career. She regularly sent money to her parents towards Robin's upkeep, but he was eventually cut out of Spark's will when he managed to offend her once too often. But, as O'Neill quite rightly points out, 'rarely is anyone much detained by the parental flaws of male writers' [O'Neill, p. 101], which will do quite nicely as the last word on the subject of Spark's parenting. Spark was a huge intellectual snob: the quotation in the title of this post comes from one of Spark's diary entries, and it more or less sums up her attitude to those who weren't her intellectual equivalent. For Spark, the world was full of dullards and timewasters. The reader is never encouraged to feel sympathy for any of Spark's slow-witted fictional victims. But there are worse crimes than snobbery and Spark saw such crimes during her years in Africa, the details of which she used in some of her short stories. Spark heard white colonials boasting about how a little black boy had been shot dead for peeping at a white woman breast-feeding, and she wrote about this killing in a story entitled *The Curtain Blown by the Breeze*. Another violent death provided the basis for yet another short story: by an enormous coincidence, Spark's old school acquaintance Nita, who bore more than a passing physical resemblance to Spark, had also relocated to Africa and Spark met up with her there, shortly before Nita was shot dead by her husband. In *Bang-Bang You're Dead*, Spark writes about two women, Desirée and Sybil, who look very much alike – so much so that Desirée is shot dead in place of Sybil, the intended victim.

Spark used autobiographical material in her writing, as do most authors: it makes sense, of course, to write about what you know. Stannard has conscientiously documented the points at which Spark's life meets Spark's fiction, and although the biography weighs in at 536 pages, it remains enjoyable throughout.

Adapted from an original version posted to www.auntymuriel.com on 19 August 2013.

List of references

Campbell, J., 2009. *Timorous Beasties*. [Online] Available at: http://www.the-tls.co.uk/tls/reviews/biography/article731655.ece [Accessed 11 September 2012].

Garland, N., 1988. *Muriel Spark*. London: The British Cartoon Archive.

Muriel Spark: Nicholas Garland in *The Observer*, 31 Jan 1988. The British Cartoon Archive, http://www.cartoons.ac.uk. Accessed 20 Jan 2013.

Kermode, F., 2009. *Mistress of Disappearances*. [Online] Available at: http://www.lrb.co.uk/v31/n17/frank-kermode/mistress-of-disappearances [Accessed 24 November 2012].

Massie, A., 1979. *Muriel Spark*. Edinburgh: Ramsay Head Press.

O'Neill, J., 2010. Killing Her Softly. *Atlantic Monthly,* September.pp. 99-107.

Spark, M., 1992. *Curriculum Vitae: Autobiography*. London: Constable.

Spark, M., 2002. *The Complete Short Stories*. London: Penguin.

Spark, M., 2007. *The Cahiers Series Number 2: Walking on Air*. Lewes: Center for Writers & Translators at the Arts Arena of The American University of Paris and Sylph Editions.

Stanford, D., 1963. *Muriel Spark: A Biographical and Critical Study*. London: Centaur Press.

Stannard, M., 2009. *Muriel Spark: The Biography*. London: Weidenfeld & Nicolson.

Turner, J., 1992. *She Who Can Do No Wrong*. [Online] Available at: http://www.lrb.co.uk/v14/n15/jenny-turner/she-who-can-do-no-wrong [Accessed 24 November 2012].

The Murder of Merle Coverdale

> He came towards her with the corkscrew and stabbed it into her long neck nine times, and killed her. Then he took his hat and went home to his wife.
>
> Muriel Spark, *The Ballad of Peckham Rye*, p. 36.

Many of Muriel Spark's readers have accused her of being cold in the treatment of her characters and in the case of Merle Coverdale in *The Ballad of Peckham Rye*, first published in 1960, Spark's position of callous indifference would appear to have been taken to an extreme: Merle is not only heartlessly disposed of, but the reader has arguably been induced to *not care* about it very much, through being constantly and relentlessly exposed to forewarnings of this event.

Merle is first presented to us as an absence: "'she works at Meadows Meade in poor Miss Coverdale's pool that was'" (12), and 'Miss Merle Coverdale, lately head of the typing pool, did not hear of it' (14). The reason Merle doesn't hear of Humphrey's return is because she is dead, murdered by her lover Mr Druce. This murder is heavily sign-posted from the very beginning of the novel and a great deal of repetition in the narrative centres around this event. The sign-posting, the repetition, and the flat delivery of the murder scene serve to deaden the reader's response to Merle's demise. We have looked for Merle's death for so long that when it happens we are largely unaffected by it, which is *not* the case with Dougal's imagined death scene, discussed below. But sympathy is always conspicuous by its absence in Spark's work.

It is not only in *Ballad* that Spark presents a character's end to us in so bald a fashion. Other examples of flatly-reported deaths in the Spark oeuvre include the casual and apparently motiveless murder of a woman in the final scenes of *The Girls of Slender Means*; the death by lightning of two bit-part characters in *Not to Disturb*; and the death of Needle (also heavily sign-posted) in the short story *The Portobello Road*: 'He looked as if he would murder me and he did' (412). Of the latter example, Stephen Schiff wrote in *The New Yorker*:

> It's a nasty piece of work, that sentence...for a moment the blow is difficult to absorb. The first clause is about a glance, the second about a catastrophe, yet both have the same nonchalant tone, and it is this evenness of tone that freezes the spine (1993: 36).

One might well wonder as to the nature of Spark's intention in disposing of her characters so coolly. A convincing explanation for Spark's chosen method lies in David Herman's suggestion that Spark has adopted for her own purposes techniques associated with Bertolt Brecht's *Verfremdungseffekt* (2008: 477), itself rooted in work done on 'defamiliarisation' by the Russian Formalists, Viktor Shlokovksy in particular, at the beginning of the twentieth century. The theory behind the *Verfremdungseffekt* is that the reader is 'alienated' from the characters and ceases to feel any regard for their fate, being encouraged instead to take a more conscious, objective view of proceedings. Any emotional involvement with the characters on the reader's part is stripped away by a laying-bare of the artificiality of the constructed text, and the reader is forced instead to make judgements on an entirely intellectual level. Alan Massie also suggests that Spark belongs amongst the rank of novelists

> who have attempted to understand the world by cultivating detachment; so that what they construct has a self-conscious artistry, which depends for its effect on the writer's oblique stance to his material. There is a clear preference for imposing form rather than interpreting what is immediately presented to the eye; it is the form which will give significance (1979: 94).

In practice, the attempt to create such an emotional distance is not always successful and the results can be unpredictable: notice, for example, Schiff's reaction to Needle's death above. What Schiff is responding to, however, is not the death of the character – we already know at this stage in the narrative that Needle is a ghost – but to the 'evenness of tone' the I-narrator adopts in relating her own murder. Schiff notes Spark's own comment on the sentence in question:

> 'There's something aggressive about it,' Spark admits. 'I've put a lot of tension into it, and I've left the emotion out. I don't really like very much writing about emotion. I like for it to be read between the lines.' (1993: 36)

As a self-proclaimed satirist, Spark may have found the technique of the *Verfremdungseffekt* intriguing. In addressing the American Academy and Institute of Arts and Letters in 1971, Spark gave a speech entitled 'The Desegregation of Art' (often quoted, and reproduced in Hynes, 1992: 33-37), in which she argues in favour of satire and ridicule in place of sentiment:

the power and influence of the creative arts is not to be belittled. I only say that the art and literature of sentiment and emotion, however beautiful in itself, however striking in its depiction of actuality, has to go. It cheats us into a sense of involvement with life and society, but in reality it is a segregated activity. In its place I advocate the arts of satire and of ridicule. (1992: 35)

Spark's argument runs along lines similar to those of Brecht: 'the liberation of our minds from the comfortable cells of lofty sentiment' will free us from 'the illusion that we are all essentially aspiring, affectionate, and loving creatures'. Ridicule, as opposed to sentiment, 'can penetrate to the marrow. It can leave a salutary scar. It is unnerving. It can paralyze its object' (1992: 36). So, in the case of Merle Coverdale's murder, Spark aims to underscore the horror of the act by deadening our emotional response to the victim. The latter is achieved by numerous forewarnings of the event to follow and by the deadpan way in which the murder itself is related, placed as it is in almost direct juxtaposition with the more sentimental imagined murder of Dougal Douglas.

From the very beginning of the novel, Merle Coverdale is a dead woman walking. Her untimely demise is marked out clearly for the reader in many ways. For example, Merle's death is sign-posted through the settings in which we see her: in chapter three, Dougal takes Merle for a walk through a cemetery, and on page 126, 'Miss Frierne [leaves] Miss Coverdale in that hall which was lined with wood like a coffin'. Secondly, Merle's epithet is an example of one of Spark's epithets that contain a hint of the plot. References to the attenuated length of Merle's neck appear every time she is mentioned. Dougal refers to Merle as an Okapi, a giraffe-like animal, and to Merle's neck itself as 'a maniac's delight' (101). Merle dies when she is stabbed in the neck nine times with a corkscrew. Thirdly, death in some shape or form is always mentioned, without fail, in close proximity to Merle's name: on page 34, '"That Miss Coverdale in the pool," said Mavis, 'is working Dixie to death..."'; on page 97, '"Killing herself," Merle said, "that's what she is, for money."'; on page 100, '"I've got a rotten life. Sometimes I think I'll swallow a bottle of aspirins."'; and lastly, on page 102, '"There's bodies of nuns down there, miss," the policeman said'. The cumulative effect of these repeated references to death is to point to Merle's own impending demise in an unequivocal fashion.

To sum up so far: we infer that Merle is marked for an untimely end through the references to death which surround her every appearance, and we have seen her placed in the settings of a cemetery and a coffin. We can guess at the manner of her death from the repeated references to her neck, which are so frequent as to constitute her epithet. The following examples demonstrate that we can also deduce early on who is responsible for Merle's death. In every scene featuring Merle and Druce, Druce looks at Merle with a sharp, pointed object in his hand, as follows:

p. 51: 'He turned, with the bottle-opener in his hand, and looked at her.'

p. 53: 'Mr Druce took a bread-knife from the drawer and looked at her.'

p. 82: 'Mr Druce lifted his paper-knife, toyed with it in his hand, pointed it at Merle, and put it down.'

p. 134: 'He turned to look at her with the corkscrew pointing from his fist.'

The four sentences above are constructed largely along the same lines, and it is interesting to note that the 'looking' of the first two examples turns into 'pointing' in the latter two – an indication that the threat posed by Druce is becoming increasingly serious. Druce touches, tickles or squeezes Merle's neck every time they are alone together: 'She put her hand up to her throat and moved it up her long neck. "Mr Druce squeezed it tight the other day," she said, "for fun, but I got a fright."' (100-101). We see, therefore, that long before the murder scene, the reader has been alerted through various kinds of narrative repetition that Druce will murder Merle by attacking her neck with a pointed object. By the time Druce looks at Merle 'with the corkscrew pointing from his fist', we know that *that corkscrew* will be the murder weapon.

Let us turn now to the murder scene itself, which is placed in juxtaposition with the scene of an *imaginary* murder. In chapter eight, both Merle and Elaine visit Dougal's room in scenes that open with an almost identical verbal exchange with Miss Frierne. Merle, Dougal's first visitor, is upset and tells Dougal '"God, if Mr Druce thought I was working in with you, he'd kill me."' (128). Elaine in her turn informs Dougal that there is a gang looking for him and Dougal imagines his murder at the hands of Trevor Lomas. This imagined murder is replaced in the following chapter with a real murder: Merle dies at Druce's hands, as she predicted.

The contrast between the two murder scenes, placed in such close proximity in the narrative, creates a bathos which contributes in no small measure to the overall alienation effect the reader experiences in relation to Merle's death. As one would expect from a character who spices up a dull autobiography with saucy tales, Dougal's description of his own imagined murder (130-131) is far more exciting than the deadpan narration of the killing of Merle. Dougal's own tale contains visually dramatic verbs (compare, for example, 'out jumps Trevor' with 'He came towards her'), sinister adjectives ('black concealing'), and melodramatic touches ('in the gutter'). Told in the present tense to give immediacy to the scene recounted, the reader is made aware of the position of each of the characters involved as an aid to visualisation, and is left to imagine the horror of the mutilated body. The policeman who finds Dougal 'pukes on the pavement' and his fingers are 'trembling' as he whistles for help. We see nothing like this in the murder of Merle Coverdale. Her death is indeed a gruesome one, but there are no sound effects ('rip rip rip'), or characters vomiting at the sight of the body: the final bathetic note sounds later in the narrative when Merle's corpse is discovered only because the neighbours are alerted when Druce's supper burns.

The actual murder scene is played out, but with a different ending, at an earlier stage in the narrative, when we see Druce and Merle meet for their usual Saturday night assignation in chapter four. It quickly becomes clear to the reader that there is no life left in this affair: the conversation is desultory and they watch a 'fragment' of a television play together, just as Mavis and Arthur do in a mirror-image dysfunctional relationship. Gerard Carruthers notes that:

> We see the pair sharing dull suppers together and Druce very neatly folding his trousers prior to their passionless lovemaking with the implication that they have lost not only a keen sense of goodness, but of badness too. (2008: 495)

The scene ends with a paragraph structured in parallel: 'She *went* into the scullery and *put on* the kettle while he *put on* his trousers and *went* home to his wife' (54, my emphasis). The parallelisms inject a blackly humorous note into the proceedings of this tawdry affair, but the reader will once again see Druce don an item of clothing and go 'home to his wife', this time leaving Merle's corpse behind him: 'He came towards her with the corkscrew and stabbed it into her long neck nine times, and killed her. Then *he took his hat and went home to his wife*' (136, my emphasis).

These parallel repetitions are part of a much wider structure of repetition at sentence-level here in these two scenes, and elsewhere in *Ballad*. A subject-verb-complement sentence structure constitutes the dominant feature of the opening chapter, as is the case in the assignation scene, and the murder scene. In the latter, there are at least 21 subject-verb-complement sentences connected with Druce, sometimes in rapid succession, as here:

He handed over her glass of wine. He looked at the label on the bottle. He sat down and took his shoes off. He put on his slippers. He looked at his watch. (135)

What is significant is that the sentence describing the murder itself is constructed in exactly the same way, with the addition of one final, horrible, clause: 'He came towards her with the corkscrew and stabbed it into her long neck nine times, and killed her' (136). The repetition of an identical sentence structure at this point places the murder on the same level as all the mundane actions described in the succession of subject-verb-complement sentences, and, even though the reader has been expecting Merle's death for a long time, it is still possible to be shocked at the casual way in which Merle is disposed of, much as the 'evenness of tone' used to tell us of Needle's death produces a chilling effect.

In conclusion, it is clear that there is an element of tension in operation between the narrator's delivery of the murder scene and the relative weight the murder is given in the text. After such a lengthy build-up, the flat delivery and anti-climax of the murder is startling and confusing, because it is not what the reader was expecting. Dougal's imagined murder fills that particular gap, and the reader is cheated of the high drama of the fantasised killing when finally called upon to witness Merle's long-awaited murder. An unresolved tension is generated also in the reader's response to the murder itself: as previously mentioned, the repetitive foreshadowing of Merle's death means that the reader is waiting for it and will not be surprised or affected by it when it comes. Humphrey and Dixie may well be the subject of the ballad that circulates in Peckham Rye, but the build-up to Merle's murder also fills its fair share of text-space. However, in spite of the reader being prepared for, and hardened to, the event to come, the calculated manner in which the murder is casually narrated, in an identical fashion to the description of Druce putting on his slippers, will cause the reader to suffer the same sort of 'blow' as that described by Schiff. In retrospect, the overly-dramatic, overly-literary nature of Dougal's imagined death is shown for what it is in comparison to the very pedestrian, but somehow much more *real* murder of Merle. We know how to respond to Dougal's 'murder', but our response to Merle's death is far more complicated, and the *Verfremdungseffekt* is thus brought into play.

Originally posted to www.auntymuriel.com on 6 April 2014.

List of references

CARRUTHERS, G. 2008. 'Fully to Savour Her Position': Muriel Spark and Scottish Identity. *Modern Fiction Studies,* 54, 487-504.

HERMAN, D. 2008. 'A Salutary Scar': Muriel Spark's Desegregated Art in the Twenty-First Century. *Modern Fiction Studies,* 54, 473-486.

HYNES, J. (ed.) 1992. *Critical Essays on Muriel Spark,* New York: Macmillan.

MASSIE, A. 1979. *Muriel Spark,* Edinburgh, Ramsay Head Press.

SCHIFF, Stephen. 1993. Cultural Pursuits, "Muriel Spark Between the Lines," *The New Yorker*, May 24, 36.

SPARK, M. 1999. *The Ballad of Peckham Rye,* London, Penguin.

Truth and the telling of stories: *The Twins*

An I-narrator recounts the events of a couple of visits to her friend Jennie's house, once when the twins are five and again when they are twelve. If we are to believe what the narrator tells us – and I'll explore this in more detail a little later on – the twins are born troublemakers whose angelic appearance belies their true nature. The story consists of six incidents in which it appears that a misunderstanding has occurred, but these 'misunderstandings' are in fact deliberately engineered to create disharmony amongst the characters. Eventually the narrator is moved to make an excuse to leave the house, without any intention of returning.

The six incidents are as follows: 1) the loan of a half-crown, in which little Marjie creates discord by not revealing all the necessary details; 2) the business with the tops, in which little Jeff lies outright; 3) Jennie reporting that Simon said the narrator looks ill and haggard, when the reader has overheard the conversation in question and knows he did nothing of the kind; 4) the biscuits and the mice – again, the reader knows that Jennie packed the biscuits and put them in the narrator's room; 5) the business with the petrol money; 6) the most serious incident of them all: Mollie and Simon's alleged misbehaviour in the kitchen.

The text world of *The Twins* is one in which everything can be questioned and even the most innocuous remark can cause great offence. This is a story about truth and about the telling of stories. And, what with it being a story, and being a story written by Muriel Spark, we mustn't forget that actually none of it is true anyway. The reader *believes* what she is told by the first-person narrator, because that is what readers are inclined to do, but there are instances when the narrator herself is less than honest, if her words are to be taken at face value. For example,

> When I returned, these good children were eating their supper standing up in the kitchen, and without a word of protest, cleared off to bed before the guests arrived [p. 323].

Knowing what we do about the twins at this stage, in what sense are they 'good' children? There are two possible answers here: 1) they *are* good children and we can't believe what the narrator has told us previously; 2) we are to understand that the word 'good' is heavily ironic in this sentence.

Another example of the narrator's possible duplicity occurs slightly previous to this episode on page 322:

> I munched [a biscuit] while I looked out of the window at the calm country sky, ruminating upon Jennie's perennial merits.

(Note the lovely inversion of the pathetic fallacy: the 'calm country sky' in no way reflects the tension running through the country home.) It is strange to find the narrator pondering Jennie's good points when she catches Jennie lying earlier that day:

> 'Thin and haggard indeed!' said Jennie as she poured out the tea, and the twins discreetly passed the sandwiches [p. 322].

Simon doesn't say 'thin and haggard' at all. What he says is: "'Why, you haven't changed a bit... A bit thinner maybe. Nice to see you so flourishing.'" [p. 322] But Simon's words are also part of what the narrator tells us, so whom can we believe?

For an explanation, we might look to the twins discreetly passing the sandwiches as the parent behaves in the way in which she has been taught to behave by her offspring, for this is a story in which the usual roles are topsy-turvy. "'You'll ruin those children,'" says Jennie to Simon, but in fact the reverse happens: the children ruin their parents in a startling role-reversal. The narrator tells us in the closing paragraphs that the twins gaze on their parents 'with wonder, pride and bewilderment', as they regard 'the work of [their] own hands' [p. 325]. But once again, this is what the narrator tells us, and the behaviour of all concerned is explained away in the narrator's tenuous comparison of an expression on the twins' faces with that of a portrait painter she once saw at the Royal Academy. But if these sentences were removed from the story, how could we explain the strange behaviour of Jennie and Simon? We rely on the narrator to tell us the truth, but there is no guarantee that what we are told is not a fabrication on the part of the narrator; the twins might well be the little angels everyone believes them to be and the narrator could be leading the reader by the nose just in order to have a good story to tell. Happy couples do not make narratives because there's no narrativity in contentment. So there are two ways in which we can read a sentence such as the following:

> In these surroundings she seemed to have endured no change; and she had made no change in her ways in the seven years since my last visit [p. 322].

We could take the sentence at face value: Jennie has made no change and all is as idyllic as before; or, the narrator is being disingenuous here and Jennie *has* changed – she has become the same kind of devious mischief-maker as her children. In the context of the rest of the story, the second option seems the most likely, but if we admit this, then we are admitting that the narrator has just lied to us. In addition, the tentative note of 'seemed' appears in the first clause, but not, as it should, in the second. If we admit then, that the narrator lies to us occasionally, how much more of this narrative is not quite true?

For the sake of moving the discussion on, let's assume that the narrator is indeed telling us the truth and that those moments of apparent disingenuousness are to be read and understood ironically. To be fair, the story is constructed so as to convince the reader of the narrator's veracity. The first incident which occurs to make us suspect the twins of not being quite so lovely is the episode in which Marjie asks for a half-crown. This coin is to provide Jennie with change for the baker's man, but Marjie does not reveal as much: she simply says that she wants it, which is not enough to induce the narrator to provide her with a coin, thus landing the narrator in some trouble with Jennie. Marjie is only five years old at the time, and we could believe that she has made a mess of this errand owing to youthful inarticulacy, had we not just been told how advanced the twins are for their years. (And in fact, Jennie herself says that she would never allow the children to ask for money when she has moments before instructed Marjie to do exactly that. No wonder the poor narrator is left floundering.)

Marjie's odd behaviour is still in the reader's mind when it comes to the fuss about the tops, which is why we accept the narrator's version of Jeff's behaviour so readily. The narrator provides us with two pieces of information which put together demonstrate that Jeff is telling an outright lie when he insists that he was playing with the blue top: Jennie points out that the top Simon has taken to pieces is the red one, and the red one belongs to Jeff; later, when the narrator goes outside, she sees 'the small boy spinning his bright-red top on the hard concrete of the garage floor' [p. 320]. From this, we can deduce that Simon *did* manage to piece together Jeff's top after he'd taken it apart, and that Jeff played with this top before taking it apart again in order to cause trouble between his parents. If it weren't for these two pieces of information, we could easily believe that Simon had broken Jeff's top and hadn't wanted to admit it.

Not that this incident does cause trouble between Jennie and Simon, of course – not on the surface, anyway. Everyone is too polite to make a fuss and this is precisely what allows the twins to get away with their little fibs and fabrications. Repeatedly we hear characters enjoin the narrator not to mention what has happened, or that words have been spoken, because Jennie doesn't want to upset Simon, and vice versa. When the narrator visits Jennie and Simon for the second time, it is no longer the twins causing trouble: it is Jennie and Simon, both of whom have adopted this behaviour from their creepy kids. And they are creepy: eerily beautiful, spookily well-behaved and exceptionally intelligent: we hear from Jennie when the twins have reached the age of twelve how both Marjie and Jeff have won scholarships. In a world where everything is suspect and every remark subject to scrutiny, Jennie's coments about Marjie's geography are potentially explosive: "'If it hadn't been for the geography she'd have been near the top. Her English teacher told me.'" In any other story world, this remark would be taken as ordinary parental boasting and perhaps also as a way to introduce the English teacher, Mollie Thomas, but in this world, the reader can easily imagine Jennie's comments becoming part of yet another fraught and private conversation in which one of the speakers uses the words 'Please don't say anything'. Each lie or half-truth opens up for the reader a little text world which may or may not exist: Simon and Mollie's alleged dalliance in the kitchen, for example – what happened here? The narrator says 'She's in the kitchen,' [p. 324] when Jennie asks where Mollie is, and before you know it, Simon is writing to the narrator berating her for insinuating that he and Mollie were 'behaving improperly' [p. 325]. The narrator by this time has quite sensibly cut her losses and left Jennie and Simon's troubled house, never to return.

Adapted from the original text posted to www.auntymuriel.com on 28 September 2013.

Spark, M., 2001. The Twins in *The Complete Short Stories*. London: Penguin.

Through a glass, darkly: Muriel Spark's *The Dark Glasses*

1 Corinthians 13:12

For now we see through a glass, darkly; but then face to face: now I know in part; but then shall I know even as also I am known.

The short story *The Dark Glasses* first appeared in 1961 in *Voices at Play,* a collection of Spark's stories and radio plays. The verse from the King James Bible quoted above is not directly referred to in the story, but it's always at the forefront of my mind when I read it, partly because the story was written at a time when Muriel Spark was still a recent convert to the Catholic faith, but mostly because the two characters in the story who wear coloured glasses - Joan with her dark glasses and Dorothy with her green - are the ones who really do 'see' (in the sense of 'understand') exactly what is going on. By comparison, Dr Gray, the psychologist who is insistent that Joan should remove her dark glasses, is adept at ignoring the evidence in front of her eyes because it suits her to do so: Joan remarks that '[t]hese fishers of the mind have no eye for outward things' [p. 379]. In fact, the implication is that Dr Gray has trained in psychology in order to enable her to reinterpret events in a manner of her own choosing.

(Incidentally, this is not the only dig at psychological practices to be found in Spark's writings: perhaps she felt that psychologists were attempting to encroach on an area - the human mind - that should be accessible only to God, or perhaps, as is suggested in this story, it was her view that psychologists state what is obvious and pass it off as science:

'"Didn't you know that when you married him? I should have thought it would have been obvious."

She looked at me again. "I had not studied psychology at that time," she said.

I thought, neither had I.' [*Complete Short Stories*, 2001, p. 379].)

Of course, the biblical verse doesn't quite fit with the story, but what *is* relevant is the idea of seeing and knowing. This is a story which explores the many different ways of seeing, and as I've already suggested, seeing is linked with understanding in the two characters who have problems with their sight: Joan, who needs reading glasses, and Dorothy, who goes blind in first one eye and then the other. The story begins when the I-narrator Joan recognises Dr Gray from the past and puts on her dark glasses to conceal the fact that she has identified the woman with whom she is taking a lunchtime stroll.

Joan is a familiar narrator in Spark: a confident, somewhat abrasive woman, easily bored and more than a little impatient with other people. She is thirteen when she goes to have her eyes tested and Basil Simmonds, the oculist, takes something of an unhealthy interest in her. Joan judges from his reaction when his sister Dorothy enters the dimly-lit examination room that his intentions were not honourable: 'Mr Simmonds removed his arm from my shoulder with such a jerk that I knew for certain he had not placed it there in innocence' [p. 368]. Dorothy later accuses Basil of attempting to blind her because 'she had seen something that he didn't want her to see, something disreputable' [p. 378]. By far the strongest implication in the narrative is that the 'something' mentioned here is Basil's attempted forgery of his mother's will, but it is undeniable that this 'something' could also be Basil's manhandling of Joan, an adolescent. And Joan's status as an adolescent at the early stages of the story is imbued with some importance later on in Dr Gray's lecture at the summer school on child-poltergeists: '"Adolescents in a state of sexual arousement," she said, "may become possessed of almost psychic insight."' [p. 377]. In spite of Spark's apparent debunking of psychologists in the story, there exists a narrative level at which the claim that adolescents have psychic powers is also true: Joan does, indeed, have a sense of what is really happening and she is able to visualise clearly not only the interior of the Simmonds' house, but also the enmity between brother and sister, worth quoting in full if only because it's one of my favourite passages in Spark:

> I invented for myself a recurrent scene in which brother and sister emerged from their mother's room and, on the narrow landing, allowed their gaze to meet in unspoken combat over their inheritance. Basil's flat-coloured eyes did not themselves hold any expression, but by the forward thrust of his red neck he indicated his meaning; Dorothy made herself plain by means of a corkscrew twist of the head - round and up - and the glitter of her one good eye through the green glasses [p. 370].

Of course, it would seem that it is Basil, rather than Joan, who is 'in a state of sexual arousement', but thirteen-year-old Joan is far from naive and she is seen to be going through a process of sorting 'right' behaviour from 'wrong' in her head. The narrative voice from Joan as a thirteen- and a fifteen-year-old is peppered with observations about whether or not the characters, including herself, are 'in the right', or 'in the wrong': 'Dr Gray swung her legs, she was in the wrong, sexy, like our morning help... Dr Gray swung her legs, and looked professional. She was in the right, she looked like our games mistress' [pp. 376-377]. It is Joan's growing *awareness* of sex and the sexual behaviour of other people rather than any possible attraction to Basil which marks her as sexually aroused.

However, rather more convincing than Dr Gray's theories about adolescent second-sight are the alternative explanations that Joan's insight is derived from her role as detective and her status as a narrator who is also a reader of books. Joan creates a story from what she knows of other stories.

James Naremore points out in his essay on Dashiell Hammett that 'in a general sense any fictional detective becomes the story's omniscient narrator and hence a type of God' [Benstock, 1983, p. 51]. Joan is not, of course, entirely omniscient, but in the general sense implied by Naremore, she certainly attains a degree of omniscience. Joan takes on the role of detective when she becomes intrigued by the brother-sister set-up in Leesden End, and she takes pains to find out as much as she can by encouraging other people to divulge what they know in the form of teatime gossip and, most importantly, in taking every opportunity to spy on the Simmonds' house. Like Dorothy, Joan sees what she shouldn't see, and we learn about the antipathy between brother and sister through Joan's snooping and Joan's imagined scenarios. The latter builds on the illusion of omniscience surrounding the figure of Joan because the impression created is that Joan can actually see into the minds of the other characters.

Joan also shares the omniscient narrator's ability to leap about in time. There are three distinct time periods to the story: Joan at thirteen, Joan at fifteen, and Joan as an adult recognising Dr Gray at the summer school. Spark's characteristic use of repetition as a time-marker guides the reader through Joan's narrative, but an additional effect is to create the impression of timelessness: events previously witnessed are seen again as if they hadn't happened.

The narrator is, of course, present-day Joan, but she takes on the voices of two other Joans who narrate different sections of the story: Joan at thirteen and Joan at fifteen, as previously stated. In the analeptic sections which make up the reminiscences of the two adolescent Joans, the present-day Joan breaks the usual illusion that the analeptic passages are taking place in the present by throwing in phrases which remind the reader that this section is a reminiscence:

'I can still smell the rain and hear it thundering about me' [p. 372]; 'I recall reading the letters... I recall Mr Simmonds squeezing my arm...' [p. 368].

On a narratorial level, then, Joan can see into the minds of others and she can jump about in time as she chooses. She is the omniscient detective who collects the facts and explains them to us. Of course, we are just getting Joan's view of things, and it is not inconceivable that a great deal of the story may be the product of Joan's imagination. She is clearly a reader of books with a flair for narrative: 'I knew he was going to select one sheet of paper from the sheaf, and that this one document would be the exciting, important one. It was like reading a familiar book: one knew what was coming, but couldn't bear to miss a word' [p. 372]. Basil does indeed select one sheet of paper and his subsequent actions may well be those of someone attempting to copy someone else's handwriting. And naturally, Dorothy catches him at it: 'I was not surprised, but I was thrilled, when the door behind him slowly opened. It was like seeing the film of the book' [p. 372]. The next day, something goes wrong with Dorothy's eye-drops and her one good eye is damaged almost beyond repair. Joan has her own ideas about what everyone else regards as an unfortunate mishap. She uses what she knows of stories to interpret the events she has witnessed:

'I said, "The bottle may have been tampered with, have you thought of that?"

"Joan's been reading books"' [p. 376].

We are not, on the whole, led to question Joan's reading of events, but it must be borne in mind that, as previously mentioned, one of the themes of the story is seeing and different ways of seeing. Seeing (or not-seeing) in this story is a memory, seeing in the mind's eye, a glance, watching, looking, testing one's sight, losing one's sight, ogling, spying, visualising, something camouflaged, a forgery, seeing as a child or through the eyes of an adult, interpreting, understanding, psychic insight, and of course, recognition - the story begins and ends with an act of recognition.

The story is also awash with doubles: Joan recognises Dr Gray from her reflection in the lake, and the two women stand there at the beginning of the story like two versions of themselves, past and present; Dr Gray's first husband was also Dr Gray; Joan's aunt and grandmother parrot each other and finish each other's sentences. Seeing can be deceptive: Basil turns his attempted caress of Joan into a movement more befitting an oculist; Basil attempts to forge his mother's handwriting in order to deceive the eye; Joan presses against the tree and wills herself 'to be the colour of the bark' [p. 372] as a form of camouflage in order to disguise her presence. Lastly, seeing does not always entail understanding, because it is necessary to be able to read and correctly interpret the signs. On a basic level, as an optician, Basil has pictures for illiterates who cannot read the letters. On a different level, Dorothy and Joan are both able to read the situation very quickly and interpret what they see accurately. But this is *their* truth, and everyone else in the story has a different truth. Dr Gray has usefully created two truths for herself - one as Basil's wife and one as a psychologist, the latter being more conducive to her peace of mind.

Given all this, it would seem that this is one more Spark narrative in which one of the major themes is the difficulty in getting at the real truth. Joan is not an unreliable narrator, but she is a storyteller nevertheless and the narrative calls attention to its own artfulness at several points and in various ways. By the end of the story, Joan is working as a historian, and the historian's job is very similar to that of the detective: the facts must be assembled and then interpreted. The resulting narrative is itself a creation and as such cannot be a *truthful* account of events.

Originally posted to www.auntymuriel.com on 31 March 2014.

List of references

Naremore, J., 1983. Dashiell Hammett and the Poetics of Hard-Boiled Detection. In: B. Benstock, ed. *Essays on Detective Fiction*. London: Macmillan.

Spark, M., 2001. *The Complete Short Stories*. London: Penguin.

Muriel Spark's ghost stories: *The Executor* and *The Portobello Road*

We meet a punitive ghost in Spark's *The Executor*, in the form of written messages from Susan's deceased uncle, a famous author. Susan is appointed as executor to her uncle's literary estate and following his death Susan sells almost his entire archive to 'the Foundation' – but she keeps back her uncle's final unfinished novel with the intention of completing and publishing it herself. Susan is punished for her greed when she finds messages addressed to her written in her dead uncle's handwriting, messages which clearly indicate that he knows exactly what she is doing and thinking at every moment. This persecution continues until the Foundation, having found evidence of the existence of this novel amongst the papers Susan sold to them, eventually contact her to enquire after the missing work. Susan hands it over, and her uncle leaves her a final message: '*Goodbye Susan. It's lovely being a speck in the distance.*' This message refers to a passage at the beginning of the story in which we are told that Susan's uncle once said to her that 'if you could imagine modern literature as a painting, perhaps by Brueghel the Elder, the people and the action were in the foreground...[but] in the distance...there he would be...a speck in the distance, which if you were to blow up the detail would simply be a vague figure, plodding on the other way.'

In Susan's uncle, we have an omniscient ghost: 'He even knew if I took a dose of salts and how long I had sat in the bathroom', but unlike *The Portobello Road*, this time we have a haunted I-narrator. Once again, though, it is the narrator who is the focal point of interest in the story, and what makes Susan so intriguing is the gap between her perception of herself and the way in which other characters perceive her, something that is made very clear to the reader. The different levels of awareness between reader and narrator generate humour and irony, and this is very much the case in another of Spark's tales, *You Should Have Seen the Mess*, in which the I-narrator Lorna cannot see beyond her upbringing and values only clean surfaces and good carpets. Susan is an older version of Lorna. They speak with the same voice. Both characters have limited, provincial minds: Lorna dates a wealthy painter, but ditches him when she realises that she just cannot cope with 'the paint oozing out of the tubes'; Susan appreciates letters written by 'Angus Wilson or Saul Bellow' only for their financial potential. As far as literature is concerned, she understands only that it can make money.

Susan's uncle, on the other hand, is well aware of the limitations of his niece. As the narrator of the story, Susan reports his barbed comments faithfully, without being conscious of their real meaning: 'I could see he was forced to admire my good sense. He said, "You remind me of my mother, who prepared her shroud all ready for her funeral."' The reader understands that when Susan's uncle refers to her as a 'Scottish puritan girl', he does not mean it as a compliment, but Susan remarks that 'at forty-one it was nice to be a girl and I wasn't against the Scottish puritanical attribution either since I am proud to be a Scot'. Irony is lost on Susan, but not on the reader, who joins the dead uncle in smirking at her.

The reader is prepared for the arrival of the ghostly messages in a narrative fashion that is very reminiscent of a conjuring trick: 'I looked through the rest of the notebook...all blank, I am sure of it.' So the audience has seen that the pages of the notebook are clean and empty, but when Susan next picks up the notebook, there is her uncle's handwriting, calling her a 'greedy little snoot'. Her reaction, oddly enough, is initially one of horror that her uncle seems to know about her affair with Jaimie, the hired help's son. It is only after this first shock has worn off that it occurs to Susan to wonder how the words came to be there at all.

As is the case with a great deal of Spark's fictional prose, we do not feel sympathy for the victim. Indeed, there is very little sympathy anywhere in Spark's work. We don't feel sorry for Needle, the ghostly narrator of *The Portobello Road*, because being murdered doesn't really seem to have affected her very much, and she is having such tremendous fun tormenting her murderer; we don't feel sorry for Lorna in *You Should Have Seen the Mess* because we are too busy laughing at her, and finally, we don't feel sorry for Susan, because frankly, she's mean-minded and greedy. Susan disapproves of her uncle's relationship with Elaine, because they are living together as man and wife without being married, yet she happily takes her clothes off for Jaimie because it is 'only Nature'. With a capital N. By the end of the story, the hired help has resigned after encouraging Susan to seek medical help, Jaimie is no longer welcome in the house, and Susan is drinking too much whisky to steady her shattered nerves. And after listening to Susan's poisonous little narrative, the reader can't help but think that it serves her right.

In *The Portobello Road* we have an I-narrator ghost, and in this story the murder victim haunts her murderer. This was one of Muriel Spark's favourite short stories, along with *The Executor*.

The Portobello Road tells the story of four friends: Kathleen, Skinny, George and Needle. In her youth, Needle found a needle in a haystack, which is why she came to be known as Needle. From that day forward, Needle is considered 'lucky' by the other characters, although in fact haystacks are associated with injury and death for her: the needle she chances upon in the story's first haystack drives deep into the cushion of her thumb creating a wound which bleeds copiously; Needle is suffocated with hay and her body buried in the second haystack. When her corpse is recovered, the headlines in the evening papers run '"Needle" is found: in haystack!'

Needle's haphazard, itinerant existence induces the other characters to remark that she is lucky. Needle makes her living by writing and in profiting from the occasional stroke of fortune, such as a fortuitous legacy, and the discovery of a diamond bracelet for which she is given a reward. Needle is a character we find often in Spark: an independent woman writer who is assured of her 'difference from the rest'. Spark is writing from her own experience, obviously, but she doesn't trouble to make this character likable. In fact, Needle treats George – her murderer – with malice and contempt, both before her death and after. But we are not led to have any sympathy for George, either. He is a ridiculous figure, marked from the outset as a threat by the narrator's repeated insistence on how large a man he is, and we are told often about George's full, sensuous red lips and white teeth. One can't help but think of vampires, and George does indeed drain Needle's life-force when he stuffs her mouth with hay and kills her. George's 'wide slit of red lips' reveals a sensuousness in his nature which marks him out as a man ruled by his passions. He takes up with Matilda and marries her because he 'needed the woman' and he murders Needle in a fit of anger when she refuses to keep quiet about George's projected bigamy. The murder itself is reported in the typically understated Sparkian fashion which is so devastatingly effective: 'He looked as if he would murder me and he did.'

So Needle exists as a ghost in order to haunt and punish George. She explains away the fact that she 'did not altogether depart this world' because there are 'odd things still to be done which one's executors can never do properly'. (This includes looking over papers which the executors have already torn up, so the papers are themselves ghostly.) Tormenting George is clearly one of the other 'odd things' to be accomplished, because Needle cannot be seen or heard by anyone other than George – she tells us that she 'wasn't in a position to speak to Kathleen', but that she 'had a sudden inspiration' to talk to George. We are given no more explanation than this. We do not know why

Needle can only address George, nor do we know who or what inspired her to do so. Needle does not speak very much to George beyond saying hello and telling him that he doesn't look very well, but her narratorial reporting of these encounters is gleefully disingenuous: 'I suppose from poor George's point of view it was like seeing a ghost when he saw me', and 'I suppose that was why he looked so unwell when I stood, nearly five years later, by the barrow in the Portobello Road'. But Needle knows exactly what she is doing, even if she chooses to give us a skewed version of events: 'The next Saturday I looked out for him, and at last there he was, without Kathleen, half-worried, half-hopeful. I dashed his hopes.'

The narratorial voice is a strange one, here as in almost everything else Muriel Spark wrote. What we have in this story is a first-person narrator who shares much of the knowledge of an omniscient third-person narrator, presumably because of Needle's status as a ghost. Needle reports the discovery of her own body and the results of the ensuing investigation, and she is also privy to the emotions and thoughts of other characters: Skinny feels sorry for the byre-hand who was one of the chief suspects; Kathleen doesn't like the snapshot George took of his friends on the day Needle discovered the needle; the police 'could tell from the way [George] was talking that there was something wrong with the man'. In the latter example, the narratorial voice slips easily into the perspective of the police following a straightforward description of action ('he went to the police and gave himself up'), which is the sort of thing you would expect from an omniscient third-person narrator, but not from an I-narrator. In fact, George is telling the police the truth at this point, but they don't believe him because he tells them that he has just escaped from a nursing home, and, as the narrator tells us, 'Dozens of poor mad fellows confess to every murder.' Needle's emotional detachment from even her own untimely demise is what gives the story its arch narratorial tone and its black humour. The malice which Needle directs at George, the most powerful emotion we sense from her, is engendered not as a result of his being her murderer, but is felt even when Needle was living, and throughout their friendship, because George so desperately needs the approval and company of others, whereas Needle considers herself 'set apart from the common run'.

Adapted from the original text posted to www.auntymuriel.com on 27 and 28 April 2013.

Spark, M., 2001. *The Complete Short Stories.* London: Penguin.

Repetition and narrative time in Muriel Spark's *The Bachelors*, *The Ballad of Peckham Rye* and *A Member of the Family*

Story time is not the same thing as narrative time. The Russian Formalists, active during the early years of the twentieth century, used the terms fabula and sjuzhet to refer respectively to the 'chronological sequence of events' and the 'order and manner in which [these events] are actually presented in the narrative' (Jefferson and Robey, 1986: 39). Scenes which occur once in story time, the fabula, can be repeated many times in the narrative, or the sjuzhet, and any such scene will be brought into prominence, or foregrounded, thereby inviting the reader to assign significance to it. Genette's work on frequency in the second half of the twentieth century is built on the foundations established by the Formalists. In his *Narrative Discourse*, first published in French as *Figures III* in 1972, Genette distinguishes three possible methods available to the writer for recounting events: the singulative, repetitive and iterative.

More recent work among narratologists has pinpointed the difficulties inherent in the fabula/sjuzhet distinction, briefly summarised as follows. The fabula is essentially a construct, put together by the reader at the time of reading and revised to create a final version once the text has been read. It has no external existence unless the fabula and sjuzhet can be seen to be absolutely identical. A 'primary' narrative must be identified to enable the construction of a fabula: this is not always straightforward, and disagreements cannot easily be resolved. In his 2012 article 'Experiencing meanings in Spark's *The Prime of Miss Jean Brodie*', Andrew Caink demonstrates how Teresa Bridgeman's analysis of the structure of this novel can be questioned, but there is no standard against which to measure the readings of either Caink or Bridgeman and no reason why one should be considered correct as opposed to the other. Mieke Bal suggests that the difficulties in extracting a primary narrative are not necessarily a huge obstacle to analysis because it suffices merely to be able 'to place the various time units in relation to each other' (1997: 88), but what does present a problem is when the 'anachronous are embedded in each other, intertwined to such an extent that it becomes just too difficult to analyse them'. Textual events themselves can also be difficult to categorise. Bal notes that false anachronies arise where the event has taken place in the consciousness of one of the characters (87), and similar anachronies can be found in direct discourse because the 'moment of speech is simply part of the (chronological) story'. In postmodern texts which lean towards the anti-narrative, it can often be impossible to judge whether an event took place at all. It should not be supposed that it is a simple matter to extract the fabula from the sjuzhet: some texts will lend themselves easily to this task, but others - particularly more modern texts - will prove far more resistant; for example, in Robbe-Grillet's postmodernist novel *Le Voyeur*, it is very difficult for the reader to work out what actually happened, or indeed, if any of the events depicted took place at all. Given that the title of Robbe-Grillet's novel refers to an essentially passive activity, it is possible that the 'events' of the novel all take place in Mathias' consciousness and have no place anywhere else.

Menakhem Perry notes that the attempt to separate fabula and sjuzhet necessarily involves the assumption that there is only one fabula. Perry argues that even the attempt to draw out a chronological depiction of events assumes there is only one 'story' to extract: '[t]his distinction assumes that a narrative text has one fabula only. But elements of the text may participate in several temporal frames at once' (1979: 39). A related problem is the value judgement this exercise inevitably entails in that the fabula, in being constructed from the sjuzhet, grows in stature accordingly and is assumed to be the superior of the two: 'the distinction between fabula and sjuzhet confers upon temporal order an exclusive role in the organization of narrative sequence' (1979: 39-40). Perry sounds a note of caution: it is not to be supposed that the fabula is superior to the sjuzhet, and that the latter has been constructed merely as some sort of code to be cracked in order to access the former.

Assuming that the story time can be extracted and arranged chronologically, it has to be constructed from a narrative time sequence which will in the majority of cases feature analepses, prolepses and instances of repetition, among other examples of the same kind of distortion of time, all of which Genette refers to as 'anachronies'. The fabula can only be realised once the sjuzhet has been activated in its entirety.

Any analysis based on the fabula/sjuzhet distinction must necessarily focus on an interpretation arrived at *after* the reading event, when the fabula is fully known, and current practitioners have chosen instead to highlight the activity of the reader in constructing meaning *during* the reading process (Bridgeman, Caink, Herman, Perry, Fludernik). Caink suggests that the interpretation of a text post-reading may well differ to an interpretation that prioritises the reading process. Perry describes the reader receiving the text as a process of 'concretization'. He argues that the linear character of language - the fact that the reader has to read one word after another - is not to be considered a drawback, but is a feature that writers can and do exploit as a means of guiding or misleading the reader. The reader can entertain several hypotheses about the text at once, some of which will be retained and some discarded as new information comes to light. The traces of the discarded hypotheses still remain, however, and Perry argues that these traces do not cease to colour the reader's impression of the text. Information is built up cumulatively:

> [l]iterary texts may effectively utilise the fact that their material is grasped successively; this is at times a central factor in determining their meanings. The ordering and distribution of the elements in a text may exercise considerable influence on the nature, not only of the reading process, but of the resultant whole as well: a rearrangement of the components may result in the activation of alternative potentialities in them and in the structuring of a recognisably different whole (1979: 35).

Perry sums up his position as follows: '[t]he effects of the entire reading process all contribute to the meaning of the work' and '[t]he reader of a text does not wait until the end before beginning to understand it, before embarking upon its semantic integration' (1979: 46). To put these arguments into the context of the concerns of this essay, repeated events will feature only once in the fabula, so the effect of their various appearances in the sjuzhet will not be taken into account in any reading that focuses primarily on the story as constructed post-reading.

Herman's notion of 'emplotment' is concerned with how the order in which events are related contributes to the meaning-making process. He asks '[w]hat is the relation between the temporal structure of events in the storyworld (insofar as that can be reconstructed) and the profile they assume in the process of narration?' He goes on to note that 'this question encompasses issues of emplotment, that is, the way events are, in being narrated, set out in a particular order that in turn implies a particular way of understanding causal-chronological relationships among them' (2012). The order of events in the text gives rise to meaning in that the reader interprets events in relation to what they have just seen, or seen before, or what they think they are going to see in future. Again, we can see that the causal-chronological links, established during the reading process, risk being overlooked if it is only the fabula under discussion.

Textual anachronies such as repeating prolepses can prove a useful and economical way of linking apparently unconnected narrative events, thus inviting the reader to draw a comparison and make interpretative inferences.

It is important, then, to acknowledge the limitations of the terms fabula and sjuzhet, but it must also be acknowledged that any discussion involving narrative time will inevitably have recourse to them. As Bridgeman points out in her article on prolepsis, this anachrony among others is a device necessarily bound up with the notion of fabula and sjuzhet because its 'essence…lies in the mismatch between the order of the narrative and a notional chronological story' (2005: 126).

Genette's analysis of frequency, based as it is on the fabula/sjuzhet distinction, 'investigates the relationship between the number of times events are inferred to have happened in the storyworld and the number of times that they are narrated' (*Routledge Encyclopaedia of Narrative*, 2005: 189). Events can be recounted singulatively (telling once what happened once), iteratively (telling once what happened many times) and repetitively (telling several times what happened once). Merle Coverdale's murder in *The Ballad of Peckham Rye* is an event recounted singulatively: despite the fact that this death is heavily signposted from the outset, the murder scene itself appears in the narrative only once. Bal notes that while the singulative frequency is the most recurrent, an entire narrative constructed like this would be very odd, hence a combination of frequencies is the normal practice (1997: 112). Michael Toolan explains that such combinations are possible because the reader can store and access many different timelines at once: 'we hold all the stories of all the characters in view; we recognise and overlook anachronies - the embedding of voice within voice' (2001).

Dixie and Humphrey's wedding is an example of the repetitive category: the wedding scene is actually narrated three times, and, as Toolan notes, 'an event or episode told with repetitive frequency will inevitably involve anachronies in terms of order' (2001). This will be discussed in more detail later on. An example of the second category, an iterative event, can be found in the first chapter of *The Bachelors*, in Ronald Bridge's deliberate act of memory.

Ronald believes he recognises Patrick when he sees him in the coffee bar but is at first unable to place him, and his concern for the functioning of his 'mental powers' (Spark, 1960: 10) brings to his mind the words of Dr Fleischer from fourteen years previously when Ronald discovers that his epilepsy is incurable. This episode of extradiegetic analeptic recall is something of a false anachrony (Bal, 1997: 87) because the event in question is a cognitive event, Ronald's act of remembering. It takes place in Ronald's consciousness, and is related to us by the same omniscient narrator who is able to reveal the exact state of mind of the specialist as he utters the words Ronald is to memorise and recall thenceforward:

> 'No,' the American specialist had said, irritable with the strain of putting a technical point into common speech, 'there is no reason why your intellect should be impaired except, of course, that you cannot exercise it to the full extent that would be possible were you able to follow and rise to the top of a normal career' (10).

Ronald's habit of calling to mind these words so important to him renders the event an iterative one in narrative time, clearly marked as such by the temporal adverbial phrase 'from time to time' in the following:

> Ronald had retained every one of these words importantly in his memory for the past fourteen years, aware that the specialist himself would possibly remember only the gist, and then only with the aid of his record cards. But Ronald held them tight, from time to time subjecting the words to every possible kind of interpretation (11).

The iterative nature of this event is further confirmed by the appearance in the same paragraph of a second temporal adverbial phrase ('at times throughout the years') and the modal 'would' of habitual activity (Toolan, 2001: 57): 'And anyhow, Ronald **would** think, I can manage' (11, my emphasis). Ronald's careful analysis of the specialist's words is enacted in summary for the reader, interspersed with remembered career advice from his friends. Ronald in this episode is one of Spark's many Job-like figures, surrounded by cheerless comforters who in effect do nothing but remind him of all the professions which are now closed to him because of his affliction.

In the fabula, or story time, Dr Fleischer's words will have been spoken only once, but, unusually for an iterative event, which 'envisag[es] in advance the whole series of occurrences that the first one inaugurates'(Genette, 1980: 72), Dr Fleischer's words are in fact encountered twice by the reader, once in the narrative present when Ronald brings them to mind after his failure to remember where he has seen Patrick before, and again in the narrative past, when the reader hears the specialist's words in a second analeptic sequence, this time instigated by the narrator. The first flashback, Ronald's act of remembering, is easily processed by the reader because the time-shift is '"naturalized" as the operation of memory' (Lodge, 1992). Narrative events can appear in the past and then again as a memory in the mind of a character without causing temporal confusion; Rimmon-Kenan notes that '[i]t is because of the present cognitive…act that such events retain, at least partly, their 'normal' place in the first narrative' (2002: 51), so there is a sense in which this kind of analeptic sequence is experienced by the reader as an event in the narrative present. In this instance, Ronald's act of remembering is actually witnessed before the event itself. The sequence of time-shifts beginning with the 'false' anachrony in Ronald's cognitive act paves the way for a second embedded analepsis in which the narrator turns to an account of Ronald's early twenties. The narrator takes the reader back to the time when Ronald's fits first began in another extradiegetic analepsis which extends further into the past - and further beyond the boundaries of the narrative - than the first, and provides us with more information about Ronald's personal history. Inevitably, we eventually reach the point in the fabula/story time at which Dr Fleischer speaks the words the reader has already encountered in Ronald's memory-event, and the repetition of these words not only underlines their importance for this particular character, but serves a practical function in that the reader is alerted to the fact that the time frames of the two analepses have now converged and the moment has been reached when Ronald hears the words he will recall for many years to come. It can be seen then, that Ronald's memory-event functions as both an iterative event and a repeating prolepsis: the words of the specialist are experienced proleptically out of chronological sequence and then once again in the rightful place.

In fact, Ronald's life consists of iterative events: the novel opens with a description of the London bachelors' routine and we first meet Ronald while he is doing his weekly shopping; Ronald's life is punctuated by epileptic fits; in the space of one chapter, he is twice seen to throw a shoe. Ronald holds the same conversations over and over: as a bachelor, he discusses food prices, dining arrangements, and whether or not one should marry; as a Catholic, he has compiled a repertoire of conversational sallies to counter attacks such as that which he is subjected to by Marlene; as a graphologist, he explains that someone's handwriting will not reveal their character or foretell their future, but the inking over the folds in the paper may well reveal a forgery. He has even been involved in the prosecution of Patrick Seton before the events of this novel: 'Ronald…managed to recall the last time he had heard Patrick speak. That had been at the Maidstone Assizes. Then, Patrick had mumbled' (199). Iterative presentation is the reverse of repetition, but here especially in the case of the words of the US specialist, the reader is presented with what is obviously an iterative event that is seen not once, but twice. In Bal's discussion of iterative anticipation, she notes that the event in question is presented in detail and the reader naturally understands that this is an example of something that will happen again and again in the future: the fuller the report, the less credible it becomes because recurring events cannot be exactly the same. However, the narrator is at pains in this novel to impress upon the reader that Ronald has remembered the words of the specialist exactly as they were spoken, and that this is how he experiences them each time he recalls the scene. The event being iterative renders it both analeptic and proleptic in nature: Ronald has recalled these words before and will do so again.

Far from there being any attempt to disguise the repetition by stylistic variation or perspective (Bal, 1997), the event itself - the specialist's diagnosis - is repeated verbatim. But here it is important to note that narratologists have long been aware that repetition is not really repetition. Genette writes that 'none of the occurrences is completely identical to the others, solely by virtue of their co-presence and their succession'. Even if all the words in the repeated account of the event are exactly the same and placed in exactly the same order, this cannot constitute a simple case of repetition, because the reader has seen the words before: the passage in question exists in another place in the same text and one rendition follows another. Bal paraphrases this as follows: 'The first event of a series differs from the one that follows it, if only because it is the first and the other is not'. Bridgeman describes the effect created by the reader's memory of the first encounter with the narrated event: 'repeating prolepsis will always carry within it an analeptic effect, for the eventual narration of an event in its appropriate place in the story always involves recall of the information already established by the *annonce*' (2005: 130). Rimmon-Kenan notes the inevitable change in meaning that will occur on the reader's second encounter with the event in question: 'Strictly speaking no event is repeatable in all respects, nor is a repeated segment of the text quite the same, since its new location puts it in a different context which necessarily changes its meaning' (2002: 57).

In the example under discussion here, the reader experiences the recollection of the specialist's words exactly as Ronald does, rendering the event iconic of memory in both temporal and experiential terms. Bridgeman notes that

> [a]ll reading is a combination of memory and anticipation. Our focus on whatever moment in the text we have reached will invariably be coloured by our memory of what has gone before and our anticipation of what is to come. The order in which events are presented in the text is therefore crucial to our temporal experience of narrative (2005: 57).

In this instance, exactly the same words are seen twice in the context of analeptic recall, and, as previously noted, the reader encounters Ronald's memory of the event before witnessing the event itself, so when the specialist's words are met for the second time, the reader already carries the memory of those words, and thus the experience of encountering them again mirrors Ronald's own experience.

It is crucial to an understanding of this novel that the reader recognises at the outset the centrality of the character of Ronald and his epilepsy. We are actively encouraged to do so in a variety of ways: the novel begin and ends with Ronald, and we are told more about his background than that of any other character. Bal notes that external retroversions, her term for analepses that extend beyond the timeframe of the narrative, can 'provide information about antecedents...which can be relevant for the interpretation of events' (1997). What we are given in the opening chapter of *The Bachelors* is a history of Ronald not only coming to terms with his epilepsy, but accepting that it is his vocation:

> Ronald does try to accept his epilepsy and incorporates its implications into his way of life. He decides not to marry a girl who attempts to shelter him from its consequences, and when Matthew asks him if he wants to marry, he says, 'No...I'm a confirmed bachelor'... The religious pun emphasises that Ronald begins to see the possibility of a vocation in his epilepsy and in his single state (Whittaker, 1982: 61).

The repetition of the specialist's words confirming Ronald's status as an incurable epileptic encourages the reader to assign significance to them, and following their second appearance, the narrator adds Ronald's rejoinder: '"Perhaps," Ronald said, "I'll be a first-rate epileptic and that will be my career"' (13). Ronald as vocational epileptic now takes centre stage, and Ronald's epileptic fits find their counterpart in the trances of the spiritualist medium, Patrick Seton. Indeed, Ronald's memory-event is an act instigated by this same antithesis and Ronald's initial failure to recognise him.

The discussion thus far has attempted to demonstrate how the repetition of a narrative event can be made to perform an interpretive and symbolic function within the wider context of the novel, and the second example to be considered from *The Bachelors* bears many similarities to the first. During the climactic trial scene which brings the events of the story to a close, Ronald suffers an epileptic fit and once again, this is an iterative event which also figures as a repeating prolepsis because the reader sees Ronald fall on pages 188-189 and once again on pages 197-198. As is the case with the specialist's speech, events are thrown out of chronological sequence and the reader witnesses Ronald's collapse proleptically *before* it takes place in the timeframe currently in operation, and the same fit is seen for a second time in its correct chronological position when the 'proper' time comes.

The 'range', or the length of time that elapses between the event witnessed first proleptically and then chronologically, is short in both examples, and in both instances, although more notably in the case of Ronald's collapse, the reader is able to judge the moment of the event's second appearance with a considerable degree of accuracy. Bridgeman notes that range relates for the most part to the timeframe of the story, that is, the probable amount of narrative time that must elapse before the event can be viewed in its correct place in the chronological sequence, but from the reader's perspective range also involves the physical space of the text, or how many pages must be turned, and the time of reading between the two occurrences measured in hours and minutes (2005: 134-135). Proleptic *annonces* with only a short range both create suspense and effectively sustain it: with only a few pages separating the *annonce* and the event itself, the reader's attention is bent on the forthcoming appearance of Ronald's anticipated fit in its rightful chronological place. Far from diminishing the effect of suspense, as has been claimed for proleptic episodes, the effect in this novel is to place the reader in the thematically-linked position of seer, or clairvoyant, and there is nothing for the reader to do but to watch anxiously as foretold events rapidly and inexorably unfold. We know that Ronald is 'the third witness for the Prosecution' (188), so it is simply a question of counting the number of witnesses until the moment when Ronald takes the stand and then waiting for him to fall. The narrator's omniscient and god-like manipulation of narrative time, to be discussed in more detail later on, is clearly demonstrated here: these events will happen, they have already happened, and nothing can stop them from happening.

Both examples under discussion feature short bursts of verbatim repetition, which in the first instance is iconic of the operation of memory, and in the second, as we shall see, the repetition plays out for the reader - again, in iconic fashion - Ronald's ever-repeating present, his life of endlessly repeated iterative moments.

Before Patrick's trial begins, the reader knows that the outcome means life or death for Alice and her unborn child. The question of whether Patrick did or did not defraud Freda Flower of her savings has become a matter of little importance. The reader has been induced from the very beginning to regard Freda Flower as a 'foolish' woman - the adjective is repeatedly attached to her - and Spark's narrators do not suffer fools gladly. Freda Flower is an object of ridicule from the outset. Even in a moment of acute psychological distress when she collapses at the end of a séance, the narrator makes Freda into a figure of fun: 'Freda then collapsed with a thud on the floor, where she continued her sobbing, her legs moving as in remorseful pain and revealing the curiously obscene sight of her demure knee-length drawers' (40). The reader is not invited to sympathise with Freda, but to laugh at her underwear. Freda's disastrously vague testimony, during the course of which she is persuaded to believe herself possessed of spiritualistic powers, heightens our contempt for this character and renders us indifferent to her eventual vindication. Alice's predicament is far more worthy of the reader's attention and she is kept constantly in the foreground as a reminder of what is at stake: Alice and Matthew's interspersed snippets of conversation perform a choric function throughout the trial and Patrick glances at Alice frequently as he imagines her demise at his hands. Nevertheless, the real focus of our attention is Ronald, whose epileptic fit at this important stage of the proceedings invites us to consider an alternative reading of the events taking place.

Ronald's role as witness for Patrick's prosecution 'is…mere setting for a match-up particularized throughout the novel' (Hynes, 1993: 39). The trial scene dramatises the action of the novel and the characters are placed under scrutiny in a secular counterpart to Ronald's mental courtroom of chapter eight. Ronald and Patrick are linked so effectively as to be each other's double, Ronald's fits and powers of observation while lucid mirroring Patrick's trances and prophetic utterances. Whittaker notes that

> The ancient beliefs in both the prophetic power and the demonic possession of epileptics are implied in the way Ronald functions in the novel. He is a graphologist, and as a detector of frauds he is placed in a clinal relationship with Patrick, a perpetrator of them. His powers of acute perception, analogous to those of a medium, are related to the illness from which he suffers (1982: 60).

Both Ronald and Patrick are gifted with powers of extraordinary perception and this link between the two men is consolidated when the judge asks 'Is this man a medium?' (198) as Ronald falls from the witness box in a fit. Patrick uses his powers to extort money from weak-minded people such as Freda Flower, whereas Ronald's gift is a cross he must bear: 'Ronald's disability, his wound, entails some compensatory penetration, has endowed him with more than ordinary perception: and…this gift can be uncomfortable, generating acrid states of mind' (Kemp, 1974: 65). Ronald sits in court 'with the demonic aftermath of his fit working within him' (121), and he silently accuses Martin Bowles of having swindled Isobel Billows out of twenty times the sum that Patrick has allegedly stolen from Freda Flower. Ronald's epilepsy marks him out as the novel's genuine truth-teller and in the final courtroom scene, it is Ronald's testimony as an epileptic, sitting in judgement on Martin Bowles among others, which is seen in the final analysis to hold far more significance than the evidence he gives as a graphologist.

The trial is an attempt to discover the truth, but as can be clearly seen, the characters all have their own version of the truth, none of which is entirely satisfactory. Detective-Inspector Fergusson's story is truthful only to a point at which it suits his own agenda, and his story is true only 'as far as the law is concerned' (187). Freda Flower's testimony becomes hopelessly confused as she is persuaded to alter her truth for one that suits Patrick's Defence Counsel. Patrick's truth is a version of events most likely to result in his acquittal and Father Socket's truth is an entire fabrication. The latter is countered by Elsie's truth, which is painted in the courtroom as a story motivated by malice. Even Ronald's testimony as an expert graphologist is cancelled out by that of Fairley, both accounts being equally plausible. As Hynes points out, the jury make the 'right' decision in that Patrick's conviction saves Alice's life, but it is not clear why a guilty verdict was returned: 'what [the jury] would seem to have relied upon as hard evidence came down to rival graphologists' readings necessarily unresolved' (40).

The trial provides a dramatisation of the search for truth, but we are simultaneously reminded of its essentially fictional nature:

> Patrick's trial has all the rituals and conventions of fiction, the opposing counsels each trying to persuade the jury that their version of the plot is the true one. And to achieve this the characters involved take on specific roles (counsel, judge, jury, prisoner) and even use the deceptions of dressing up in costumes and adopting temporary attitudes for their performance (Whittaker, 1982: 100-101).

Whittaker's perceptive observation can be pushed slightly further. The notion of play-acting is introduced early on in the trial scene with Alice and Matthew's comments on the perceptible change in Patrick's voice: '"I think he must be making a special effort," Alice whispered. "He feels a strong clear voice is called for".' (188). Ronald, Martin and Isobel are then placed in parallel with one another in the space of one paragraph, each shown to be wearing a costume of sorts. Ronald 'had put on his best dark suit for the occasion' (189) and Matthew's remark when he sees Ronald enter the courtroom is important: '"Here comes Ronald," said Matthew, "in his new dark chalk-stripe. He should have been a Civil Servant."' (196). The Civil Service is, of course, closed to Ronald as an epileptic, a fact of which we were informed much earlier in the narrative during one of Ronald's interior monologues: '"The Civil Service: closed to me"' (11). The chalk-stripe suit is significant, because Ronald's pills are in his other suit. If we put these two facts together, we see that Ronald takes the stand as an epileptic rather than a graphologist – and, after being seen in two parallel constructions to fumble first in his inner then his outer pockets for the pills which are elsewhere, Ronald duly suffers a fit.

Martin Bowles in his wig and gown is 'instantly wise, unimpeachable' (189), but we have already learnt from Alice that he has not made a success of the case for the Prosecution and Matthew refers to him as a 'clot' (193). Finally, Isobel Billows recites Portia's courtroom speech from Shakespeare's *The Merchant of Venice* when she tries on Martin's wig. So, Ronald dresses up as a graphologist, but underneath his suit he is an epileptic; Martin looks the part in his barrister's costume, but does not perform his role well; Isobel's actions with the wig and her recitation of a speech made by a character pretending to be a lawyer in another fiction featuring a courtroom finale reveals the purpose behind this juxtaposition of characters in costume: to emphasise that these are unreal people playing parts in a trial that is a fiction.

Correspondingly, the omniscience of the novel's narrator does much to undermine the illusion of realism and highlights instead the artificial nature of the fictional construct. Genette writes that prolepsis presents problems for 'the traditional fiction of a narrator who must appear more or less to discover the story at the same time that he tells it' (1980: 67), but Spark's narrator makes free and frequent use of temporal anachronies in what is often described as a 'god-like' fashion and as a result the reader is constantly adjusting and amending the constructed local and global situation models. In addition to the proleptic *annonce* revealing in advance the event of Ronald's fit, the narrator speaks directly to the reader in another *annonce*: 'Martin got up to re-examine her. "He'll make matters worse," Matthew said, **and he was right**' (196, my emphasis). The narrator also makes free use of the ellipsis within direct speech as a means of summary during the reading of the indictment and the opening of the case for the prosecution, a method used elsewhere in the novel. This has the effect of speeding up time, of course, but an additional effect in this instance is to give the impression of inattention on the character's part; we already know that Defence Counsel Hugh Farmer's mind is elsewhere, because the narrator has free access not only to an overview of the events of the story, but also to the consciousness of the characters. We are told that Hugh Farmer 'was thinking of his elder daughter, at the moment taking her most important examination in music' (189), and the narrator frequently reveals what is passing through Patrick's mind, speaking with his voice through free indirect discourse: '**the liberation of Alice's spirit** was so imminent, it was like a sunny radiance to distract his understanding from the proceedings of the court' (188, my emphasis).

The trial begins *in media res* with an iterative event belonging to Patrick, who visualises Alice's projected death on an Austrian mountainside at various moments throughout the chapter. Patrick's fantasies are prolepsis of a sort, a cognitive act such as Ronald's memory-event, but here we see a glimpse of what a character imagines or hopes the future to be (Toolan, 2001: 58), which is apt, of course, for a novel in which foretelling the future plays such an important role. The subject matter of *The Bachelors* means that this is a story in which many predictions concerning future events are made, so in a sense the default position is to see an idea repeated or worked over many times, and each prediction can be considered a moment of prolepsis. Predictions made during the course of the story invariably come true, but this is because these predictions frequently take the form of general, pat reassurances and remarks designed to flatter which serve to satisfy the vanity of clients and often become self-fulfilling. For example, Patrick tells Marlene while in a trance that, '"You were born to be a leader but you have not yet fulfilled yourself. Now is the time to start living your true life."' (29). Marlene subsequently assumes leadership of the Wider Infinity and purges it of 'cranks', all to Patrick's benefit. Alternatively, and more importantly, the predictions made form part of the story and are therefore narratorial in nature rather than clairvoyant. In effect, the characters are guessing at, and in some cases attempting to manipulate, the end of the story in which they feature, as Caroline Rose does in Spark's first novel, *The Comforters* (1957). Ronald anticipates Patrick's imprisonment and Matthew's subsequent marriage with Alice: '"I think you'll have a chance after Patrick Seton has served a few months of his prison sentence"' (83), and in chapter two, Mike accurately predicts Patrick's eventual conviction, the prophecy delivered in a quasi-Biblical register:

> But Mike, with his hands to his temples and head thrown back, began to intone. 'There will be weeping and gnashing of teeth. I see the prisoner

brought to judgement and cast into outer darkness. There will be a trial.
I see a young woman in distress and an older woman justified. I see – '
(39)

Whether or not we can believe that 'Mike's late overflowing of the soul
actually did evoke pronounced psychic talents' (150), the fact remains that what
we are given in each of these instances is one of those moments of prolepsis
so characteristic of Spark's work, the revelation of Lise's brutal death in *The
Driver's Seat* (1970) being the most well-known and notorious example.

The propensity of every character but Ronald to either fantasise about their
future or, in the case of Walter Prett, to rewrite their past, is in stark contrast
with Ronald's being fixed in an endlessly repeating present. It was noted above
that Ronald's life consists of a series of iterative events - his food shopping,
his graphological work, his conversations - and here at the climax of the story,
we witness the most important iterative event: Ronald's epileptic fit, repeated
for us here in a moment of repeating prolepsis in which the narrator employs
almost exactly the same words. The solipsism of the other characters is not,
as Massie claims (1979: 35), something to which Ronald is subject precisely
because he no longer expects his future to be any different from his past: his
only vocation is as an epileptic and he suffers the same fit repeatedly. The
narratorial repetition of Ronald's fit in the courtroom once again imbues the
text with an element of iconicity: Ronald's endlessly repeated fit is repeated in
full for the reader so that we too are forced to relive the moment.

Ronald's affliction places him firmly in the present and he does not try to
organise the world around his own wants and desires as the other characters
do. The glimpse given to us of Patrick's consciousness in chapter ten reveals
a man who has retained an adolescent's solipsism and who is 'emotionally
retarded', a man completely incapable of imagining the existence of the
minds of others. By way of contrast, during the episode of his mental trial
and judgement of his friends played out in chapter eight, Ronald is seen to put
himself in the shoes of others and to supply his friends' answers in their place,
in an effort to provide them with an opportunity to defend themselves. For this
reason, it seems curious to accuse Ronald of solipsism, a failing from which
many of Spark's characters suffer both in this novel and elsewhere. In rejecting
a solipsistic attitude and relinquishing the attempt to visualise or control his
future, Ronald accepts his role as a character in a pre-existing narrative. Indeed,
several readers have equated the figure of Ronald with that of the narrator
and author: Richmond likens the epileptic to the artist with 'a special vision

that brings moral responsibility' (1985: 85); Kemp compares Ronald with the novelist undergoing 'the vatic frenzies of the oracle or sybil' (1974: 64), or the satirist whose 'exhilaration at accomplished ridicule attractively antidotes any despondency at the nature of what is being ridiculed' (66); Cheyette argues that Ronald 'thinks like an author' and that Spark is 'exploring the extent to which the novelist's imagination and god-like pretensions are, in the end, depraved' (2000: 47). Ronald may certainly be acting as Spark's mouthpiece in his assumed role as implied author, but as a character, his epilepsy has wrested from him any vestige of control over events he may have had and his gradual acceptance of his vocation as epileptic is indicative of his recognition of this. He even rejects the controlling influence of Hildegarde so that he may pursue this vocation unimpeded. Hildegarde is herself tainted with that solipsism and tendency to worship false idols so prevalent in the other characters.

The examples of repetition in narrative time discussed so far take the form of iterative events presented as repeating prolepses. Bridgeman notes that the textual anachrony of an *annonce* means it is foregrounded, thereby inviting predictive inferences and carrying the implication that it is important to know whatever information is imparted now, at the present moment, rather than later (2005: 131). However, Spark would appear to be setting these temporal anachronies to a separate purpose. Prolepsis is used here to underline the significance of key moments in Ronald's life and to suggest a reading of the events of the novel in the light of Ronald's visionary role as vocational epileptic, emphasised for us through the repetition of the two moments discussed. The narrator's repetition of the exact wording of these proleptic scenes enables the temporal anachrony to function iconically: in the first instance as iconic of memory and in the second as iconic of an endlessly repeating iterative moment. It can be seen, then, that both blocks of time, Ronald's memory-event and his epileptic fit, are in fact curiously independent of time.

The first example to be discussed from the second novel under consideration in this essay - *The Ballad of Peckham Rye* (Spark, 1960) - is rather different in that it involves not verbatim repetition, but a second rendition of the same scene recounted from a different point of view. A character retelling a scene already witnessed fits Genette's framework as a repeated scene retold with a different 'focalizer'. In *The Ballad of Peckham Rye*, Joyce Willis' letter to Dougal recounts in more detail the encounter between Leslie and Richard Willis that Elaine has just described for Dougal's benefit: the letter informs Dougal of the substance of Leslie's conversation and Willis' response to the remarks made (131-132). The doubling and embellishing of this small narrative episode reinforces the larger, global theme of oral storytelling or ballad-making, and on a local level we are confronted with the many versions of Dougal - lover, duplicate employee, police informant - underlined by his response to Joyce's letter which is to improvise a variation on a remark he made much earlier to Merle Coverdale (29). Joyce's letter clearly serves a practical purpose in the narrative in that it fleshes out the bare bones of an incident previously related by an imperfect witness. The following example of a scene related more than once from a varying perspective differs in that it does not supply any new information as far as the plot is concerned: what it does do is to tell us more about the character of Mavis, to forge a link between Mavis and Trevor, and to re-enact for the reader the process of oral storytelling.

Mavis' opening conversation with Humphrey is repeated when Mavis tells the story of the encounter to Trevor Lomas later on (11). This scene is fresh in the reader's mind, having taken place only moments before in terms of reading time. Mavis' rendition of the encounter is a scene of analeptic recall: as is the case in the examples from *The Bachelors* previously discussed, we are given access to a character's memories, this time through the character's own direct speech. The repetition is partially disguised by Mavis' viewpoint, but it is obviously recognisable as the same scene and the differences between the two accounts are clearly foregrounded. Mavis freely embellishes her story. She is clearly anxious to give the impression that she faced down Humphrey rather more actively and conclusively than she actually did. Additional snippets of dialogue are introduced ('You just hop it, you' (11)) which the reader knows were not actually uttered at the time. Mavis recreates the encounter as she would have liked it to happen: she has included what she *would* have said to Humphrey had she thought of it at the time, or had she had the courage to do so. The way in which Mavis retells the story adds to the impression of her as a weak and ineffectual woman when her intention is to create quite the opposite effect. In fact, Mavis rapidly emerges as a relatively powerless character. Words describing Mavis' actions - 'slammed', 'burst out', 'arguing', 'quick little steps' (7-11) - have the cumulative effect of depicting a woman who exhibits uncontrolled, flamboyant, but essentially ineffectual behaviour. For all of Mavis' bluster, Dixie shows very little respect for her and Leslie is completely beyond either of his parents' control. In parallel with Mavis, Trevor also exaggerates his encounter with Humphrey, claiming to have 'knocked his head off' (11) when the reader has been told previously that the combatants 'suffered equal damage to different features of the face' before they were 'parted by onlookers' (9); Trevor and Humphrey are equally matched as potential suitors for Dixie, and this is further illustrated in Spark's use of tableaux. Both Trevor and Mavis choose to underplay Humphrey's performance and elaborate on their own, so we can attribute a level of bravado to each. More important than character-creation, however, is the element of storytelling in these episodes. What we see is an enactment of how people tell stories, and Spark's text demonstrates through these repetitions how oral narratives come into being. Here, Trevor and Mavis are actively creating the ballad of Peckham Rye.

Once again there is an element of textual iconicity in that the repetitions mirror the process of gossiping and rumour-mongering. The novel ends more or less where it begins, with the story of the jilted bride being repeated and passed from teller to teller, until the tale passes into local legend as the ballad of Peckham Rye. We are witness to the creative process as the story of Humphrey and Dixie passes from mouth to mouth and the tale gathers several different endings in the telling. We see how the story of Humphrey and Dixie is altered and amended as it moves from pub to pub in an echo of Humphrey's own movements. Eventually, the story takes on an existence in its own right and what really happened is no longer relevant. Ballads are narratives with an outcome, but Humphrey and Dixie's eventual marriage is not the outcome of this ballad, because the people of Peckham Rye do not agree on the ending of the story after Humphrey leaves Dixie at the altar:

> Some said Humphrey came back and married the girl in the end. Some said, no, he married another girl. Others said, it was like this, Dixie died of a broken heart and he never looked at another girl again. Some thought he had returned, and she had slammed the door in his face and called him a dirty swine, which he was. One or two recalled there had been a fight between Humphrey and Trevor Lomas. But at all events everyone remembered how a man had answered 'No' at his wedding (143).

The jilting scene itself is therefore the climax of the eponymous ballad to which the inhabitants of Peckham Rye supply their own individual resolutions. The dramatic resonance of this event and its status as the high point of the ballad merits its repetition. Spark's novel closely reflects the border ballads on which it is based:

> [t]hese poems are typically short to the point of being elliptical, show great narrative economy, make use of laconic dialogue and stylised description, and introduce scenes of death and often of violence and the supernatural. They are also transmitted by oral tradition and much

modified in the telling. All these qualities are to be found embodied or referred to in the novel, which affirms the connection between its story and the ballad or folktale tradition by drawing attention at the beginning and end to the way in which, even in a twentieth-century urban community, folklore and legend enjoy a vigorous life (Page, 1990: 28).

We see Humphrey's refusal to marry Dixie twice, three times if we include the episode in Dougal's room in which Dougal enacts the forthcoming wedding scene and supplies Humphrey with the words he is to speak when he jilts Dixie: 'Then he put the plate aside and knelt; he was a sinister goggling bridegroom. "No," he declared to the ceiling, "I won't, quite frankly."' (112). The extent of Dougal's influence over Humphrey is made clear, both here and in the response Humphrey gives to Arthur's enquiry after the jilting:

"She's blaming Dougal Douglas. Is he here with you?"

"Not so's you'd notice it," Humphrey said. (143).

In a sense Dougal *is* present at Dixie's wedding after all.

The opening chapter of *The Ballad of Peckham Rye* is enormously complicated in its organisation of narrative time and it is debatable whether this chapter should be taken as the main temporal frame or should be treated as an extended prolepsis. If taken as the main frame, then the events to follow are told in analepsis, right up until Dixie tells us that she has a cold, which is when the two temporal strands meet. Once Trevor and Humphrey have left the pub to fight in the car park, the jilting scene is seen for the first time in an analepsis which contains a brief prolepsis - Arthur Crewe's words on the wedding that didn't happen feature in the next day's newspapers (8) - and another analepsis within the framing analepsis, in which Dixie tells Humphrey about her cold. The latter serves the reader as another time marker much later in the novel, when, following the departure of Dougal, Dixie's complaint that she has a cold provides an indication that the wedding day is almost at hand. The reader is in this way made aware that narrative events have caught up with themselves. Changes in tense also guide the reader through the forest of analepses and prolepses: the switch to the simple past perfect - 'She had said' (8) - indicates that yet another time shift has occurred.

Repetition can be seen in this way to perform a practical function in aiding the reader to locate the end of a time shift, which will in turn contribute to the reader's construction of a global time frame. Repetition can also alert the reader that a temporal shift in the narrative has occurred. When Trevor and Humphrey start fighting, the barmaid is twice heard to order the two men outside (7,9). It is not to be supposed that the barmaid actually uttered her words twice; instead, the reader understands that the narrative has jumped forward in time from the jilting scene and Humphrey's subsequent departure to the moment when the analepsis begins, after Trevor and Humphrey have been ordered out of the Harbinger. What is notable here is that we are given two pieces of information when we only need one - it would have been enough merely to hear the barmaid say 'Outside', and yet we are shown the female bystander's comment twice as well: "'It wouldn't have happened if Dougal Douglas hadn't come here'" (7,9). In fact, the woman's comment is foregrounded in two ways: firstly, in that it is repeated, and secondly in that the speech adverbial 'remarked' breaks the pattern established prior to this moment. Until this point, every spoken comment is marked simply as 'said'. The change calls attention to the woman's remark, which is in fact an important one because it refers to Dougal Douglas for the first time. The responsibility for the events of the narrative to follow is placed squarely on Dougal's misshapen shoulders at this early stage. The 'remark' is also understood as an observation rather than a conversational turn. We do not know the identity of the woman's interlocutor, and she receives no reply. The narrative switches at this point to the aborted wedding scene, so the remark is left hanging in the air immediately before the reader sees the scene of the jilting for which Dougal is being blamed. The indefinite article – 'a woman' – spotlights the remark itself, not the speaker, as does the positioning of the remark in the sentence, which comes before we know who is speaking and to whom. The woman is not important. Her comment is, because it serves as the repeated refrain of a ballad, it introduces our hero as a troublemaker, and it sets up what is arguably the primary narrative.

We can see, therefore, that repetition in dialogue or direct speech can function as much more than a simple indication that a time-shift has occurred. The focus of Spark's short story *A Member of the Family* (2002) is a spoken invitation, which manifests itself throughout the text at various points and in several different forms: however, the invitation turns out to have an entirely unexpected outcome for the recipient. Trudy meets Richard Seeton, ostensibly by chance, while holidaying in Southern Austria with Gwen, and she embarks on a love affair with him. Trudy is very keen to meet Richard's mother, because for her, this will signify that Richard's intentions are serious. The invitation is not forthcoming, however, and Trudy becomes steadily more obsessed with the idea. It seems as if Richard is losing interest in the relationship, but finally,

Trudy is invited to meet Lucy Seeton. The meeting does not go as Trudy had envisaged: Richard doesn't stay, but leaves Trudy to dine with Lucy and Gwen. The following Sunday, Trudy has dinner with Lucy again, and this time there are two other women present as well as Gwen. The five of them spend the whole evening discussing Richard. Trudy finally realises that all these women – there are at least another three she has yet to meet – are Richard's ex-girlfriends, as, indeed, is she. Trudy, as one of Richard's exes who dines with his mother every Sunday, has become a 'member of the family'.

The opening scene of the story, including the all-important invitation, is reproduced below:

'You must,' said Richard, suddenly, one day in November, 'come and meet my mother.'

Trudy, who had been waiting for a long time for this invitation, after all was amazed.

'I should like you,' said Richard, 'to meet my mother. She's looking forward to it.'

'Oh, does she know about me?'

'Rather,' Richard said.

'Oh!'

'No need to be nervous,' Richard said. 'She's awfully sweet.'

'Oh, I'm sure she is. Yes, of course, I'd love – '

'Come to tea on Sunday,' he said. (2002)

The story opens at the defining moment when Richard invites Trudy to meet his mother – a moment which signals the end of the relationship, rather than its beginning, as Trudy is to discover later. This opening scene is repeated almost in its entirety about half-way through the story and when we see this scene for the second time, we already know that something is wrong. We have plenty of reason to suspect that Richard's commitment to the relationship is on the wane. The phrase 'a member of the family', which crops up on a regular basis, becomes more and more sinister as the story wears on and in fact, the story closes with these words, by which time both Trudy and the reader are aware of their true meaning. As noted in the introduction to this section, words and phrases are repeated in a sequence and the relative positions of successive repetitions within that sequence invite the reader to respond differently each time. Here, the repeated phrases quickly lose their innocence and their assumed meaning is gradually replaced by another.

In his biography of Spark, Stannard tells us that she stayed with Christine Brooke-Rose in the Austrian Alps, and when asked what she thought of the view, she replied 'It's just like Wales'. Stannard notes that everyone laughed, although 'privately [Brooke-Rose] thought it verged on bad manners in a guest' (2009: 214). Spark may or may not have picked up on Brooke-Rose's mild displeasure, but in any case this remark is given to Trudy, who tells Gwen that she thinks Southern Austria is 'all rather like Wales' (124). The reader already knows that Gwen and Richard talk about Trudy behind her back: 'as he told Gwen afterwards, this remarkable statement was almost an invitation to a love affair' (127). We can therefore infer that Gwen has also told Richard of Trudy's dull remark about Wales, because Richard himself makes this comparison while he and Trudy are out boating: '"It looks like Windermere today, doesn't it?... Sometimes this place,' he said, 'is very like Yorkshire, but only when the weather's bad. Or, over on the mountain side, Wales"' (128). It is obvious now to the reader that Richard is amusing himself at Trudy's expense because he elaborates and improvises on her original dull-witted observation: they are on a lake which looks like Windermere, another lake; the landscape of Southern Austria is similar to Wales because it has mountains, as does Wales; furthermore, the Austrian Alps look just like Yorkshire when it's raining because it rains in Yorkshire too. Trudy, of course, is completely unaware that she is being mocked.

In fact, Trudy is manipulated in a more calculated manner than this: Richard's appearance in Austria was most likely engineered, and the intention to recruit Trudy as a member of the family was there right from the start. Trudy was not ensnared purely by chance: she was deliberately targeted as the next victim. Even before Trudy meets Richard's mother, she is already cast as a member of the family in her relations with Gwen:

> Trudy wanted to move her lodgings in London but she was prevented from doing so by a desire to be near Gwen, who saw Richard daily at school, and who knew his mother so well. And therefore Gwen's experience of Richard filled in the gaps in his life which were unknown to Trudy and which intrigued her (129).

Already, Trudy spends much of her time discussing Richard in the company of another woman. So desperate is she for news of him that she suppresses her wish to change lodgings in order to have ready access to information about her lover from Gwen. Trudy is playing out by way of rehearsal what will be her role eternally once Richard has finished with her.

As previously noted, Richard's suggestion that Trudy come and meet his mother is very much the focus of the story and, for that reason, the invitation appears many times across the text, in one way or another. Trudy is made very anxious when the invitation is not forthcoming and the reader gradually comes to recognise the many repetitions of the invitation as iconic of Trudy's obsession with it.

Richard's invitation is heard twice in the opening scene, but the wording is slightly different each time: 'You must...come and meet my mother'/'I should like you...to meet my mother'. The difference between the two versions of the invitation is one of modality, and it is an important difference. In relating the conversation to Gwen, Trudy may prefer the second version to the first, for example, depending on how she wishes to depict her relationship with Richard. The first invitation – 'You must...come and meet my mother' – has a casual, throwaway air about it, whereas the second, 'I should like you...to meet my mother', is more formal and considered, and it expresses a direct wish on Richard's part, which the first invitation does not. The second of these two statements is expressive of a desire on the speaker's part to gain the addressee's approval. In fact, when Trudy does relate the conversation to Gwen, she opts for a modified version of her own: 'He said, "I want you to meet Mother. I've told her all about you', a version which places an even greater emphasis on Richard's imagined commitment to the relationship: 'should like' has become 'want' and 'I've told her all about you' is a more fanciful rendition of Richard's 'Rather,' in response to Trudy's question, 'Oh, does she know about me?' Trudy clearly wishes Gwen to believe – and is also perhaps trying to convince herself – that Richard has spent many hours regaling his mother with tales of Trudy and her delightful 'young way'.

In fact, we see at least three different versions of Richard's invitation. One is clearly Trudy's voice because it is rendered in direct speech and addressed to Gwen. That is Trudy's version of events. But we see two versions of the invitation in the opening scene, both in direct speech, and both uttered by Richard. It would be tempting to imagine that Richard simply repeated his invitation in the belief that Trudy had not heard or understood him the first time: one could argue that she is too 'amazed' to respond initially, but as we saw with the examples taken from *The Ballad of Peckham Rye*, it is not to be supposed that the character has actually made the utterance in question twice. It is a narratorial trick, altering the tale slightly in the telling. The character's words are heard by the reader again after a brief interlude in which the reader is supplied with a little more information, so that on hearing the words a second time, the reader's reaction to the utterance is modified in response to the narratorial intervention.

There is another alternative explanation: when telling stories, we don't necessarily remember verbatim what someone said, and will give instead a modified version of the original utterance which simply captures the gist. The narrator's trick here is to mimic that process, but in a written form – a form that usually purports to record events exactly as they occurred. The different versions of Richard's invitation seen here give a sense of the vague woolliness one would expect from a story told verbally. However, given that the narrator is supposed to know exactly what was said and to record it faithfully, one could argue that either Spark's narrator is not actually omniscient, or - and what is a more likely explanation given what else we know of Spark's concerns and preoccupations as a writer - the varying renditions of the invitation are there to remind the reader that this is fiction, and that the words were never actually spoken at all.

Conclusions

This essay has explored the ways in which Spark uses repetition in narrative time. A close examination of examples taken from the two novels published in 1960 and the short story *A Member of the Family* demonstrates that textual repetition in Spark's work functions on many different levels and is instrumental in the creation of meaning during the reading process. On a practical level, repetition marks time-shifts for the reader and can provide additional information about both plot and characters. Repeated sections of text were shown to be iconic of the function of memory and a continually recycled present in Spark's use of iterative events presented as repeating prolepses. Spark's particular use of prolepsis situates a flash-forward device in the past as memory, in the present as an iterative event, and in the future as a fantasy or a prediction. We also encountered the partial disguise of repetition through the reiteration of an event with a different focalizer. Repetitive structures in *The Ballad of Peckham Rye* were seen to reflect the structure of an external, informing text to which the text under consideration alludes. Repetition bestows significance and can serve as an aid to interpretation, which can in turn lead to accusations of didacticism: Cheyette describes *The Bachelors* as 'overly didactic and moralistic' (2000: 49) and Massie notes that 'the reader is more happily placed in his certainty of what is going on and how he is to judge it in *The Bachelors* than in any of…Spark's other novels' (1979: 43). Most importantly, repetition in Spark's writing works to highlight the artificiality of the fiction.

Originally posted to *www.auntymuriel.com* on 30 June 2015.

List of references

BAL, M. 1997. *Narratology: Introduction to the Theory of Narrative.* Toronto: University of Toronto Press.

BRIDGEMAN, T. 2005. Thinking Ahead: A Cognitive Approach to Prolepsis. *Narrative.* 13, 125-159.

CAINK, A. 2012. Experiencing meanings in Spark's The Prime of Miss Jean Brodie. *Journal of Literary Semantics.* 41, 121-138.

CHEYETTE, B. 2000. *Muriel Spark.* Tavistock: Northcote House.

FLUDERNIK, M. 2009. *An Introduction to Narratology.* London: Routledge.

GENETTE, G. 1980. *Narrative Discourse: An Essay in Method.* Ithaca: Cornell University Press.

HERMAN, D. 2012. *Narrative Theory: Core Concepts & Critical Debates.* Columbus, Ohio University Press.

HYNES, J. 1993. Muriel Spark and the Oxymoronic Vision. In: HOSMER, R. E. (ed.) *Contemporary British Women Writers: Narrative Strategies.* New York: St Martin's.

JEFFERSON, A. & ROBEY, D. 1986. *Modern Literary Theory: A Comparative Introduction.* London: Batsford.

KEMP, P. 1974. *Muriel Spark.* London: Paul Elek.

LODGE, D. 1992. Time-Shift. *The Art of Fiction.* Harmondsworth: Penguin.

MASSIE, A. 1979. *Muriel Spark.* Edinburgh: Ramsay Head Press.

PAGE, N. 1990. *Muriel Spark*. Basingstoke: Macmillan.

PERRY, M. 1979. Literary Dynamics: How the Order of a Text Creates Its Meanings [With an Analysis of Faulkner's 'A Rose for Emily']. *Poetics Today*. 1, 35-64 + 311-361.

RICHMOND, V. B. 1985. *Muriel Spark*. New York: Ungar.

RIMMON-KENAN, S. 2002. *Narrative Fiction: Contemporary Poetics*. London: Routledge.

ROBBE-GRILLET, A. 1958. *Le Voyeur*. New York: Grove Press.

SPARK, M. 1963 (1960). *The Bachelors*. London: Penguin.

SPARK, M. 1999 (1960). *The Ballad of Peckham Rye*. London: Penguin.

SPARK, M. 2002. *The Complete Short Stories*. London: Penguin.

SPARK, M. 2006 (1970). *The Driver's Seat*. London: Penguin.

SPARK, M. 2009 (1957). *The Comforters*. London: Virago.

STANNARD, M. 2009. *Muriel Spark: the Biography*. London: Weidenfeld & Nicolson.

TOOLAN, M. 2001. *Narrative: A Critical Linguistic Introduction*. London: Routledge.

WHITTAKER, R. 1982. *The Faith and Fiction of Muriel Spark*. London: Macmillan.

Literary Linguistics: collected essays

Schema theory, universal minds and the impossibility of the characterless character: a study of Katherine Mansfield's *The Man Without A Temperament*

Storyworlds are necessarily incomplete and work in recent years has investigated how the reader manages to plug the gaps. Schema theory (Culpeper, 2001; Schneider, 2001; Semino, 1997) and Palmer's twelve-point universal minds checklist (2007) complement one another in that both describe the reader's gap-filling activities in the creation of mental models which make up the fictional world of the text. Schemata are knowledge clusters formed from the reader's experience of the real world. They are activated by textual cues and trigger a set of default values, thereby enabling the reader to assume a great deal of information not explicitly stated. Once activated, schemata allow the reader to make inferences and predictions. Schemata are by no means static, however: they can be revised, expanded or rejected when new information is received. In a similar vein, Palmer's work focuses on how readers ascribe states of mind to characters in a story and he explores how readers use their experience of real people to create and maintain the fictional minds of characters across large stretches of text.

This essay uses these two theories to examine the presentation of the eponymous character of a short story by Katherine Mansfield. The circumstances of the story's production are briefly described before the discussion turns to a consideration of the main character's status as *actant* balanced against the view that emerges when Palmer's thought-action continuum is applied to a short scene. The investigation that follows explores how schemata are activated in relation to the characters and setting and how an ostensibly third-person narrative provides both aspectuality - the storyworld as experienced by a character - and access to a character's thought processes. The essay concludes with an examination of how metaphors associated with the characters operate within schema theory.

Mansfield suffered a pulmonary haemorrhage in February 1918 and in October of the following year she relocated to the Italian Riviera. Her husband, John Middleton Murry, remained behind (Mansfield, 1977: 138). For Mansfield, this was a desolate and lonely time and it was during this period that she wrote *The Man Without A Temperament* (165). This story of a man in exile abroad with his sick wife is told 'from the husband's perspective', and

Hanson and Gurr suggest that Mansfield's portrayal of Robert Salesby was an 'attempt at empathy' (Hanson and Gurr, 1981: 71) and a 'form of apology' (74) for her previous attack on Murry in a poem composed in December (Mansfield, 1977: 158). According to Hanson and Gurr, the story, originally entitled *The Exile*, was intended to counter-balance the poem's attack in that it represented an 'objective assessment' (1981: 74), Mansfield's 'generous… attempt at identifying what [Murry's] life in exile with her would be for him' (75). The final title reflects the story's focus on 'a man without a self…with no life and therefore no temperament of his own' (72). What follows is essentially an investigation into how this lifeless character has been created and if he is indeed the automaton suggested in Hanson and Gurr's description, or whether the reader is permitted to breathe some life into him.

In a 1972 article, Chatman explores the Formalist-Structuralist notion that characters are '*actants* or participants' and can be analysed purely in terms of what they *do* in place of any 'outside psychological measure' (1972: 57). Robert as character is subordinated to the actions he has to perform in caring for Jinnie, and this being the case he is potentially a prototypical example of the theory of character propounded by Formalist-Structuralist scholars such as Propp, Greimas and Todorov (Rimmon-Kenan, 2002: 34-36; Culpeper, 2001: 49-50). Such an extreme and reductive position can nevertheless be accommodated at the dehumanised end of the character scale (Culpeper, 2001: 11), but in practice, it remains the case that 'a genuinely pure behaviorist novel is very difficult to find', in part because 'apparently neutral descriptions of actions often contain references to the mental events behind the actions' (Palmer, 2007: 219-220). A significant number of verbs denoting Robert's movements or his manipulation of objects are indeed superordinate and 'apparently neutral' in tone: 'took his tea', 'sat down', 'turned away', 'carried it', and so on (Mansfield, 1981, all references which follow are to this edition). Very occasionally, a verb or verb phrase seems to contain its own adverb, for example, 'sauntered over' (134), but adverbs themselves are few and far between. Robert looks increasingly unfeeling and robotic against the background text-world of Mansfield's story, in which many inanimate objects are granted an unnatural animacy: the plant that is 'hungrily watching' the American Woman (129), the 'understanding biscuit', the 'unclaimed letters climbing the black lattice' (130). Nevertheless, behind many of Robert's actions the reader can infer his concern for Jinnie. In the scene where he goes to fetch her shawl (131), Robert's impatience and irritation is clearly marked in a passage of free indirect discourse ('Where the devil was the shawl!') and in the verb-choices, which in this particular instance are far from neutral: 'He *strode* across the room, *grabbed* the grey cobweb and went out, *banging* the door' (my emphasis). This verb-pattern is indicative of Robert's anxiety to keep Jinnie warm. However, there is more: using Palmer's notion of aspectuality, the reader can detect here the undercurrent of Robert's sense of humiliation that runs throughout. Palmer reasons that the storyworld 'is aspectual in the sense that its characters can only ever experience it from a particular perceptual and cognitive aspect at any one time' (2007: 216). The appearance of the room is described as Robert sees it, and once the reader is thus positioned inside Robert's version of the storyworld, it is natural to assume that the description of the servant girl's eyes comes also from Robert, not, as might otherwise be supposed, the narratorial voice: 'When she saw him her small, impudent eyes snapped'. It is Robert who supplies the adjectives here, Robert who interprets the girl's glance, and it is Robert who imagines that the room itself is staring at him: 'His eyes searched the *glaring* room' (my emphasis). The reader knows that the shutters have been put back to let the light in, but the use of 'glaring' as an adjective to modify 'room' in such close proximity to the hostile stare of the girl gives rise to the assumption that Robert feels himself to be scrutinised and ridiculed by his very surroundings. The verb in the reporting clause of the girl's speech - 'mocked' - indicates how Robert interprets her remark, and it is therefore he who imagines her boisterous singing following him as he leaves. From this brief exchange the reader can infer that Robert is aware of how he is judged by others in his present state of servitude and that he feels humiliated and isolated as an exile in this strange land. To return to the original discussion of the *actant*, Chatman concludes that the understanding of character depends on outside knowledge: 'The very inferences that are necessary to the recognition of character traits can only be formed by reference to the real world' (1972: 78). As seen in the example discussed here, the reader's knowledge of how real people behave can inform how fictional behaviours are to be interpreted.

The application of the reader's pre-existing knowledge structures to a text is referred to as top-down processing, in contrast with bottom-up processing which involves the reader using textual information to build up a mental model (Schneider, 2001: 611). The construction of these models is always the result of a combination of both processes in which the text and the reader's background knowledge interact: 'inferences result from the fact that particular elements in the text trigger the activation of certain schemata (bottom-up), and that activated schemata generate expectations that fill in what is not explicitly mentioned in the text (top-down)' (Semino, 1997: 125). Textual details encourage the reader to activate an OLD WOMAN schema for the Topknots, in spite of the fact that no age or gender is assigned to them: they act as one unit under the pronoun 'they'. Their moniker carries with it the image of a particular hairstyle formerly attached to a particular age-group, and the lexical items associated with the Topknots' 'decoction' transfer themselves to the characters: 'whitish', 'greyish', 'in glasses', 'little husks', 'speckled'. A faintly malevolent air is granted them through their 'two coils of knitting, like two snakes, slumber[ing] beside the tray' (129). This note of malignancy should not be dismissed because it provides a clue to the way in which the reader should understand the Topknots' comment: '*No* man is he, but an ox!' (135, emphasis in original). The way in which the characters regard each other is part of the process of characterisation and the discussion of this metaphor will be taken up again a little later.

The Topknots are singled out by their hairstyle and the American Woman by her nationality. She is a bundle of AMERICAN FEMALE stereotypes and the schema activated has more to do with evaluative beliefs than reality (Culpeper, 73). She is mocked according to her childish play-acting, her one-sided dialogue with the pet Klaymongso, her accent (both in English and French - 'knoo' (129) and 'voo' (135) respectively), her litigious nature and perceived privileged position as a US citizen. The attributes of her possessions - a 'torn antique brocade bag' and 'grubby handkerchief' (129) - bestow upon her a faded quality and indicate that she is past her best. (By way of an aside, Semino (1997) following Spiro (1980) notes that the activation of schemata and the ensuing application of default values can sometimes lead readers to 'confuse what was explicitly mentioned in the text with what they have inferred' (148). Hanson and Gurr confidently describe the American Woman as a 'widow' (1981: 74), but there is no mention of her marital status in Mansfield's text. This plausible error can in all likelihood be attributed to a schemata-based inference.)

To return to the discussion in hand, the Honeymoon Couple are a different matter entirely. Their function is twofold. First, their presence dispels any idea that the setting is a residential care home or sanatorium and the reader must revise their mental model of the setting in what has been termed a frame repair (Stockwell, 2002: 157) to make possible the presence of a honeymooning couple. A HOTEL schema is a likely candidate. Second, and more obviously, the Honeymoon Couple serve as a cruel reminder of how Robert and Jinnie used to be before Jinnie's illness. In fact, Jinnie herself is surely the subject of a frame repair when it is confirmed that she is, after all, Robert's wife, and not his mother or another elderly female relative. However, rejected hypotheses have nevertheless a part to play in the overall meaning of a text. Meaning creation is a dynamic process which begins as soon as the reader starts to read and Perry argues that 'rejected meanings continue to exist in the story even after their rejection, as a system of "hovering" meanings' (1979: 49). In this particular case, the idea that the Pension Villa Excelsior could have been a sanatorium or rest home and Jinnie Robert's mother will remain in the reader's consciousness and undoubtedly continue to colour their assessment of Robert as a character.

The schemata for the characters of the Topknots and the American Woman are activated through the objects with which they surround themselves, just as Jinnie's 'cobweb' shawl marks her fragility and transiency. Robert's key possession is - ironically - a signet ring. Such an object functions as a form of identity, but Robert has subsumed his own individual personality to devote himself to the care of his wife. The information one can collect on Robert is limited even under such broad headings as Culpeper's three social categories: personal (interests and preferences); social (role and function); and group membership (gender, race, age, and so on) (2001: 75-76). Robert is male, married to Jinnie, and doesn't like spinach (141). His profession is a mystery, but it is perhaps something literary (138). His only goal seems to be to keep Jinnie warm. Beyond this short list, very little can be confidently asserted except his ownership of the ring, an object to which the reader's attention is repeatedly directed. Robert's habit of turning the ring is foregrounded through repetition from the very first paragraph. The grammatically circular structure of this opening paragraph captures the shape of the ring and denotes the endless circle of entrapment in which Robert finds himself, which is also in evidence in some of the other fictional backdrops: the glassed-in veranda, the cage of the lift, the presence of mosquito nets in the final scene. The mental event behind Robert's ring-turning action is frustration and an ever-present awareness of his hopeless situation.

The final twist of the ring is delivered by Jinnie, and Hanson and Gurr read into this the 'denial of [Robert's] ego' (1981: 73). This reading is supported by the sudden shift into the present tense which occurs near the end of the story. The past tense is predominant before this shift into what Kokot refers to as the '*prasesens historicum*' (2011: 74); prior to this, the present tense features only in the three analeptic episodes as the text pushes and pops into and out of Robert's consciousness (Stockwell, 2002: 47). The rendering of Robert's memories in the present tense creates an impression that the past is far more real, far more *present* to him than his current reality, and thus the switch to the present tense in recounting the events of Robert's life with Jinnie in exile suggests his recognition, if not necessarily acceptance, of his new mode of existence.

To conclude, I turn to a discussion of the role of metaphor in schema theory and its relevance to the reader's mental model of Robert. Metaphor is the arena in which schemata interact and Semino argues that 'metaphors vary in their potential for schema refreshment, and...such variability can be captured in terms of a scale, from schema reinforcement at one end to schema refreshment at the other' (1997: 197). Mansfield's characters are metaphorically reimagined as various animals throughout the story: the Topknots are snakes, the American Woman a lapdog, the General a crow with his 'Caw! Caw! Caw!' (139), and other bird imagery flits between Jinnie, a small garden bird; the Honeymoon Couple, a larger, more robust seabird; and Robert, a 'broken bird' struggling to take flight (142). Even in the list of dilapidated bric-a-brac that lines the corridors of the *pension* does one find an animal metaphor in the umbrella stand shaped like a bear. This bear, given a shade of animacy in its 'clasp' of the walking-sticks, umbrellas and sunshades, is a metaphor for Robert: a powerful animal performing a servile function on behalf of those much weaker (130). The metaphors continue as the Topknots liken Robert to an ox (135), and in the final analeptic sequence, Jinnie, in begging Robert to accompany her, refers to him twice in quick succession as 'bread and wine' (143). The reader's real-world knowledge store will provide the information that both the ox and the reference to bread and wine are biblical in origin. The ox is a beast of burden, and in biblical terms, is the most valuable animal one could own. There is the sense of the ox bearing a yoke, of course, but the ox does so with enormous strength and inexhaustible stamina. Other schematic units are far less flattering: the ox is associated with a particular kind of brute stupidity and is castrated as a bullock. Given the malicious side to their personality evidenced by their metaphorical link with snakes, it is likely the Topknots mean to activate the less flattering units of the OX schema in their listeners. The reader's mental model will be subject to schematic refreshment upon encountering Jinnie's words. The OX schema will be recalled and reassessed in the light of this second metaphor, one which directly entails the schema of SACRIFICE. It is indeed possible, as Hanson and Gurr claim, that Mansfield wished to convey to Murry her acknowledgement of the sacrifice involved for him if he travelled to join her, but if this was her intention, the gesture backfired and Murry did not understand: in his next letter to Mansfield, he provided no comment on the story.

From this brief survey then, the following conclusions can be gleaned. A character cannot be just what they *do* because readers will ascribe mental events to the actions described no matter how neutral the description may appear to be. Although top-down processing is the preferred method of operating, if the reader cannot readily activate schemata then a mental model is constructed instead from what textual information is provided (bottom-up processing). It has been shown here how schemata can be activated from details such as a character's possessions and surroundings. Schemata can be revised and refreshed, but the original schema, although rejected, remains part of the text's overall meaning. Schemata can operate through metaphor and the text is thus enriched with a wealth of detail which is never explicitly stated, but which the reader supplies from a store of real-world knowledge - and of course, these knowledge-stores will differ from reader to reader, thus accounting in part for differing textual interpretations. A reader with a literary training will also be able to bring to the text schemata related to existing specialist knowledge (Schneider, 2001: 612). As far as Mansfield and Murry are concerned, however, one could surmise that Murry's misunderstanding originated somewhere in the activated SACRIFICE schema: Mansfield may have intended Murry to understand that she knew how much she was asking, but Murry could well have interpreted the story of the saintly Robert as a reproof.

List of references

Chatman, S. (1972) On the Formalist-Structuralist Theory of Character. *Journal of Literary Semantics* 1: 57–79.

Culpeper, J. (2001) *Language and Characterisation: People in Plays and Other Texts.* Harlow: Longman.

Hanson, C. & Gurr, A. (1981) *Katherine Mansfield.* London: Macmillan.

Kokot, J. (2011) The Elusiveness of Reality: The Limits of Cognition in Katherine Mansfield's Short Stories. In J. Wilson, G. Kimber, & S. Reid. (Eds.) *Katherine Mansfield and Literary Modernism.* London: Continuum, 67–77.

Mansfield, K. (1981) *The Collected Stories of Katherine Mansfield.* London: Penguin.

Mansfield, K. (1977) *The Letters and Journals of Katherine Mansfield: A Selection.* C. K. Stead. (Ed.) Harmondsworth: Penguin.

Palmer, A. (2007) Universal Minds. *Semiotica* 165: 205–225.

Perry, M. (1979) Literary Dynamics: How the Order of a Text Creates Its Meanings. *Poetics Today* 1(1-2): 35–64, 311–361.

Rimmon-Kenan, S. (2002) *Narrative Fiction* (2nd ed.) London: Routledge.

Schneider, R. (2001) Toward a cognitive theory of literary character: The dynamics of mental-model construction. *Style* 35(4): 607–640.

Semino, E. (1997) *Language and World Creation in Poems and Other Texts.* London: Routledge.

Spiro, R.J. (1980) Prior Knowledge and Story Processing: Integration, Selection, and Variation. *Poetics* 9: 313–327.

Stockwell, P. (2002) *Cognitive Poetics: An Introduction.* London: Routledge.

Focalization in verbo-visual texts:
Treat by Stephen Collins

The text under discussion here is a comic strip, a short 'verbo-visual' narrative (Saraceni, 2000) that can either take the form of a self-contained unit such as Collins' *Treat* or it can form part of a much larger narrative (Garry Trudeau's *Doonesbury*). These strips are published daily or weekly in newspapers and their purpose is to amuse, hence their former nickname, 'the funnies'. *Treat* is reproduced in full in Appendix A, and again in Appendix B with numbered panels for ease of reference, and a glossary of key terms.

In spite of the centrality of focalization as a concept in narrative theory, there is dissension amongst scholars as to the scope of this concept and whether or not it should include 'aspects of cognition' alongside more traditional considerations of purely visual perspective (Horstkotte and Pedri, 2011: 330). The argument presented here adopts Horstkotte and Pedri's conception of focalization as a 'cognitive operation related to aspectuality [Palmer, 2004: 194-200] that subsumes the narrower optical view' (2011: 332). In other words, focalization, or the filter through which the storyworld is presented, comprises processes of perception *and* cognition that are inseparable: an object or event is not merely placed before the reader as a fact, it is perceived in a way that is peculiar to the perceiving consciousness. The concerns expressed by Horstkotte and Pedri (2011) relating to the dominance of the visual facet of focalization at the expense of the cognitive are compounded when the text contains both visual and verbal elements, in which case the need is even greater for a more flexible approach. The perceptual facet of comics, or graphic narratives, obviously cannot be dismissed, but to restrict the analysis of focalization in these texts to a description of 'camera' angles alone is to do them an injustice. In this essay, I argue that focalization is realised in Collins' comic strip in three different ways. First, the vectors created by line of gaze describe a transitivity which places the boy wearing the devil-horns in subject position. This transitivity is also demonstrated through a variation of shot/reverse-shot editing, a filmic technique which aligns the object observed with the observer's visual perspective. Second, the reader is primed to accept the boy as focalizer by means of the reader's knowledge of the conventions of the fairy-tale genre which is established early on as a parallel secondary narrative. Finally, the boy is identified as focalizer in the second tier through repeated instances of a particular panel representing a narratively significant 'pregnant moment' (Kukkonen, 2013a: 48-50).

Focalization as a concept grew out of the need to differentiate between various competing narrative voices in purely linguistic texts (see Genette, 1980), and given the relative importance of focalization in narrative theory, there is justification for exploring how this concept might operate in graphic narratives. The relatively recent boost in academic interest in comics coincides with an accelerated proliferation of multimodal texts to the point where the co-existence of the verbal and the visual is arguably creating 'a new semiotic landscape' (Saraceni, 2000: 5; see also McCloud, 1993: 58-59; and Goodman, 2007: 113-146). Kukkonen claims that comics provide a useful test case for the new transmedial narratology, or 'the project of investigating how particular media constrain as well as enable storytelling practices' (2011: 34), and Ewert's sensitive analysis of the combined effect of the visual and the verbal in Art Spiegelman's *Maus* showcases the contributory potential of such work to narratological studies. Ewert's essay makes an eloquent case in favour of 'a poetics of the graphic narrative' (2004: 191), a framework which, though currently lacking, would greatly facilitate and enhance scholarly discussion. Practitioners such as McCloud and particularly Eisner laid solid foundations for future research in their own seminal publications, both of which, for example, discuss the different types of word/picture relationships occurring in graphic narratives (McCloud, 1993: 153-155; Eisner, 1985: 122-138). Saraceni adds 'semiotic blend' to this discussion, a word/picture combination in which verbal and pictorial elements acquire each other's characteristics (Saraceni, 2000:43), exemplified in *Treat* by the moon in panel 1 which doubles as a full stop. Other occasional instances of semiotic blend in this text occur against a background of 'mirroring, when the verbal and visual texts reinforce each other and can operate independently to tell the story' (Saraceni, 2000: 43). I shall return to this point later in the discussion of focalization and genre.

The first part of the analysis presented here focuses on the perceptual facet of focalization and how this can be realised in a verbo-visual text. Kress and van Leeuwen apply Halliday's work on ideational transitivity to the relation of objects in images (Halliday, 1994: 106-175), and they suggest that the interaction between objects can be 'visually realized by vectors' (Kress and van Leeuwen, 2006: 42). For example, the tail of a speech balloon in verbo-visual texts forms a vector between the character speaking and what was said, and the transitivity pattern in this case is that of the mental externalised process with a speaker and an utterance. In the second tier of *Treat*, a vector is formed by the boy's eyeline as he looks at the head: the boy's gaze and the direction of the vector travel left to right in accordance with the reading experience.

Although the stylised depiction of the boy renders his expression enigmatic, the direction of his gaze is not in doubt because the physical position of the dot which represents his eye changes as he looks up and down. When he looks up at the old woman, his eye-dot shifts up and to the right (compare panels 15 and 16). The transitivity pattern here is a mental internalised perception process (or 'reactional' in Kress and van Leeuwen's terms), with the boy as 'senser' (or 'reacter') and the head as 'phenomenon' (Kress and van Leeuwen, 2006: 67). The eyeline vectors establish the boy's act of looking as the *event* of silent panels 13, 15 and 20. If a vector is a visual realisation of an action verb (Kress and van Leeuwen, 2006: 46), then the boy is the subject of that verb, and because the verb denotes an act of perception, the boy can be identified as the perceptual focalizer at this stage of the narrative.

As previously stated, this transitivity of senser and phenomenon is also signalled by a shot/reverse-shot sequence played out over panels 13 to 21 as the 'camera' switches back and forth between focalizer in mid-shot and focalized in close-up. Kukkonen notes that in shot/reverse-shot editing 'readers can identify the middle image as being perceived from the perspective of the character' (2013a: 49; see also Saraceni, 2000: 200 and Mikkonen 2008: 312). A shot/reverse-shot sequence usually incorporates the focalizer's emotional reaction to the focalized and certainly the reader is invited to imagine the boy's response to the gift offered. I shall argue in the sections to follow that the boy's reaction is spread over a sequence of eight successive panels, thus requiring the reader to participate in this extended moment of indecision.

Before I discuss the playing-out of the boy's reaction, however, it is necessary to introduce some genre-related considerations, which have already been briefly touched on. Genre schemas can be evoked through textual clues (Kukkonen, 2013a: 69), and in this particular case, the fairy-tale genre is activated in the witch-like imagery (the pointed hat, an old woman giving sweets to children) and, most importantly, in the traditional structure-of-three. There are three trick-or-treaters, each of whom is offered a 'treat'. The first two are offered 'Nice' biscuits and the pattern is broken with the third child who is offered 'a lovely life-destroying cursed head in a jar'. The convention of the structure-of-three dictates that the reader will be expecting this change and will no doubt have already seen panel 12 before commencing a more detailed reading: after all, the whole strip is viewable at a glance (see Eisner, 1985: 40-41). Nevertheless, the positioning of the head at the end of the first tier creates a pause between the offering of the gift and the boy's reaction to it in panel 13 on the second tier, almost as if the tiers could be read like lines of poetry. The importance of the boy's reaction is therefore structurally marked both in this pause and in the anticipated break in the pattern as dictated by genre. Narrative progression can be partly guessed at once the fairy-tale genre is active, and this brings the argument back to the word/picture combination of 'mirroring' mentioned earlier. Both the visual and verbal components of *Treat* seem sufficient on their own to tell the story; however, one must ask what is lost if, for example, the words are removed from the pictures. Speech and thought representation is an important facet of focalization and the verbal component is vital 'in constructing the sense of a mind' (Mikkonen, 2008: 312). Here, the boy's voice works in postmodern contradiction to expectations aroused by genre. Kukkonen notes that '[p]ostmodern fairy tales [can]...subvert readers' expectations...by not following the narrative probabilities and modes of verisimilitude that genre decorum prescribes' (2013a: 80). The subversion of expectations in *Treat* is twofold: first, in the boy's obvious reluctance to accept the offered gift, and second, in his vocalisation of this reluctance. In traditional fairy tales, the narrator is usually the dominant narrative voice and fairy-tale characters are rarely allowed to speak for themselves. When they *do* speak, they express themselves only in bland or ritualised utterances and this convention no doubt stems from the oral origins of fairy tales which feature numerous formulaic and therefore memorable speeches. In *Treat*, the boy voices his disappointment that his gift is not also a biscuit both indirectly to the old woman and directly to his peers in the final panel. To summarise, the evocation of the fairy-tale genre primes the reader to anticipate that the third gift-offering will break the established pattern, and the third child will emerge as protagonist. The protagonist is not necessarily the focalizer, however: what singles the boy out as focalizer is his vocalised response to the 'treat' offered and the slow playing-out of his reaction in the panels of the second tier.

Both Eisner and McCloud devote entire chapters to the panel (Eisner, 1985: 38-99; McCloud, 1993: 94-117). The panel is 'a portion...of the narrative, where something actually takes place and time' (Saraceni, 2003: 7) and 'panel arrangements...are used to imply temporal sequence' (Kukkonen, 2011: 35). Each panel marks an indeterminate time-span which is dependent on variables both internal and external to that particular panel, including narrative context and reader input. For example, there is no dialogue to provide any indication of time-span in panels 13, 15 and 20, and the reader can determine for herself how much time passes. Panel shape and size adds another dimension to the illusion of narrative temporality and the removal of the panel's border altogether can create the impression of unlimited space or infinite time (McCloud, 1993:

102), as seen here in panel 12 with the introduction of the cursed head. Panel shapes in *Treat* are clearly divided into groups, and these groupings reflect semantically-linked narrative moments: for example, the proffering and acceptance of the biscuits is rendered in panels 6 to 11, comprising two groups of three duplicated frames. Panels 1 and 22 are the same shape and size, thus inviting comparison, and the content of these panels reflects the major narrative change, that is, the boy's acquisition of the head. In panel 1, the scene is an urban one, depicting human habitations picked out by street-lamps and lit from within. The street is lined with carefully-spaced trees and neatly-parked cars, and the trick-or-treaters stand on the doorstep, about to knock at the old woman's door. In the final panel, the houses and cars are nowhere to be seen, but the visually dominant trees tower over the silhouetted figures of the children in what has become a fairy-tale setting.

Equally important to the structure of graphic narratives is the space *between* the panels, known as the gutter, and it is always present even if the panels are adjacent (Saraceni, 2003: 9). If each panel is the grammatical equivalent of a sentence (Eisner, 1985: 28), then the gutter is the space between one sentence and the next, and it is a space in which the reader infers all that is missing from the narrative: 'just as you step across the gutter, your mind creates connections between the individual panels, by drawing inferences about how the action in the one can relate to the other' (Kukkonen, 2013b: 10). As is the case with purely linguistic texts, the reader infers that which the narrative does not tell. In fact, Collins' strip demonstrates unity of time in all but three places (between panels 1-2, 5-6 and 21-22), and it is here the reader uses real-world knowledge to fill the gaps. Nevertheless, the reader of *Treat* is required to perform only a minimal amount of inferencing to construct a coherent, meaningful narrative, for two reasons. First, the strip features a high level of visual repetition from one panel to the next, rendering it an enormously cohesive text: the repetition functions as an explicit marker of 'relatedness' (Saraceni, 2000: 101). Second, the movement between panels for much of the strip is what McCloud describes as a moment-to-moment transition, noticeably in the second tier when the boy's indecision is played out in detail (1993: 70).

It is at this stage that the function of panels 7 and 10 becomes clear. If they were to be removed from the strip, the moment-to-moment transition of panels 6 to 8 and 9 to 11 would become action-to-action transitions depicting the offering of the biscuit and its acceptance, and the loss of panels 7 and 10 would not occasion any confusion on the part of the reader. However, far from being redundant, the function of these two panels is to emphasise the moment between the proffering and acceptance of the old woman's gift, so that this moment can be extended over panels 13-20. The extension of this moment and the hesitation it depicts on the part of the boy clearly marks him as the text's internal focalizer. Mikkonen notes that in 'visual narratives we often *see* the mind in action from a focalized perspective' (2008: 316, emphasis in original) and that is precisely the case here. As previously stated, the boy's reluctance to accept the gift is played out over eight panels and this is a significant proportion in a text of only 22 panels: the moment between proffering and acceptance in this instance comprises just over a third of the whole strip (36%). This example of a 'sustained continuing-consciousness frame' (Mikkonen, 2008: 316) is a relatively straightforward feat for a short verbo-visual narrative such as the comic strip, but medium-specific constraints can curtail attempts to prolong internal focalization over longer stretches of text.

In this essay, I have claimed that the boy wearing the devil-horns can be identified as the internal focalizer of the events of the second tier of *Treat*, and that this identification is made possible through a combination of factors. The perceptual facet of focalization was explored in a discussion of the transitivity of the text created by eyeline-vectors, and a shot/reverse-shot sequence which coincides with the boy's viewpoint. Saraceni notes that the perspective through which the relationships between characters and objects are conveyed has an equivalent function to deixis (2000: 203), and deixis is defined by Simpson in relation to linguistic texts as 'features of language which function to locate utterances in relation to speakers' viewpoints' (1993: 13). The textual features discussed here locate the viewpoint as that of the boy. However, I argued earlier that the perceptual facet should be combined with the cognitive in order to fully encompass all that is implied by the concept of focalization. Saraceni makes a case for a merger of the perceptual with the psychological because access is needed to a character's mind in order to see what they see (2000: 172). The psychological facet is realised here in the playing-out of the boy's reluctance to accept the gift offered in a drawn-out moment of narrative significance. Finally, I have coupled the perceptual and psychological facets of focalization as evidenced in the text with the contribution brought to the narrative by the reader: that of the recognition of a secondary genre which informs the text and allows the reader to infer that the third child will receive a different gift. The reader can therefore anticipate in advance the boy's role as focalizer.

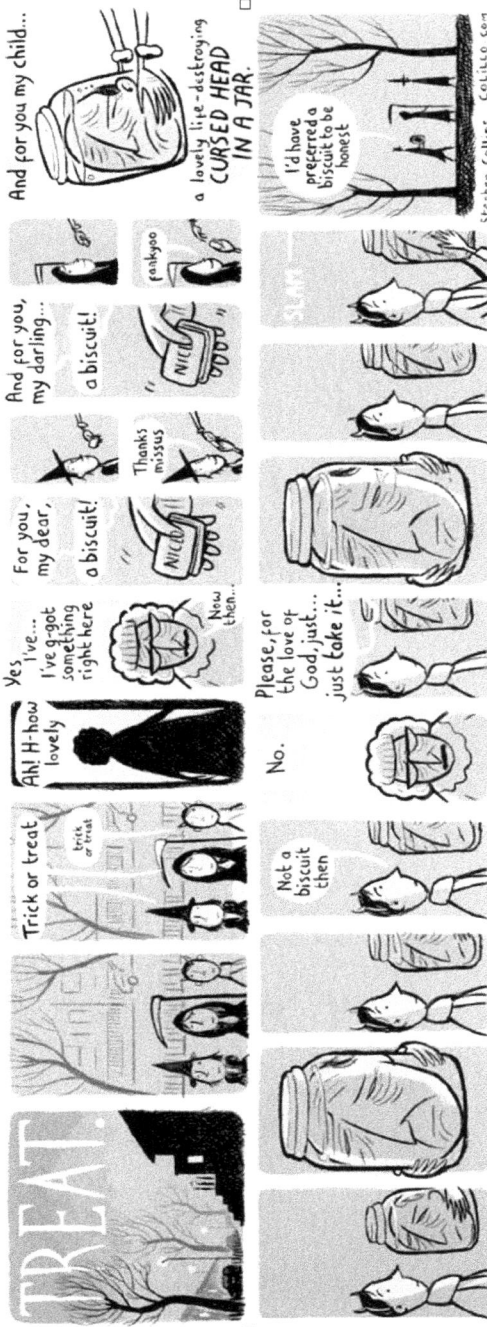

Appendix A
'Treat' by Stephen Collins
Available at colillo.com
Accessed on 18 February 2016 at 18:22

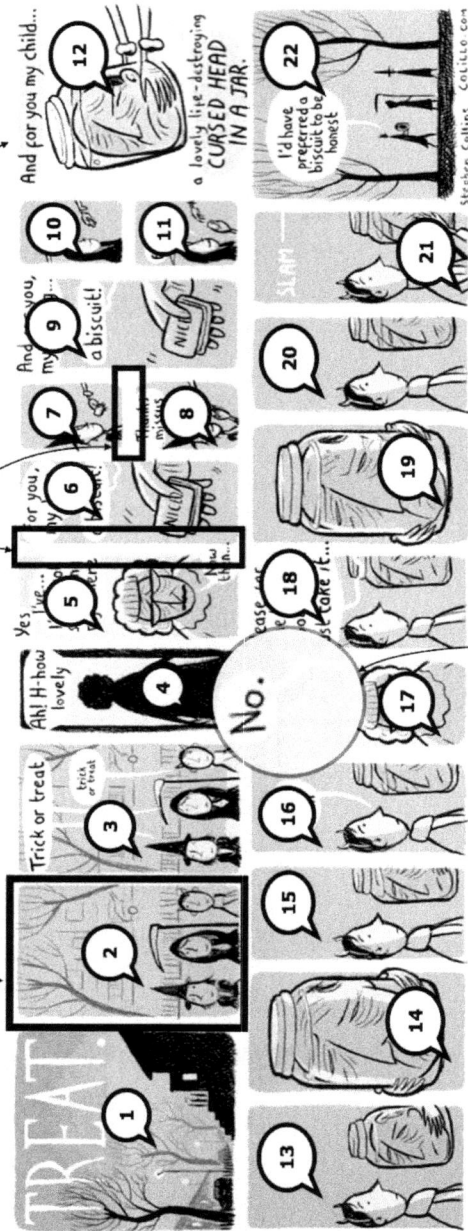

Appendix B
'Treat' annotated

PANEL or frame: a box which contains or displays a scene, moment or event. The BORDER is a line around the panel, but Collins marks out his panels here and elsewhere with blocks of colour.

GUTTER: the space between the panels. Note that gutters can, like the panels, be of any size and shape. Here the gutters are mostly vertical, but there are two horizontal gutters between panels 7 & 8, and 10 & 11.

Note that panel 12 does not have a border. Unconstrained as it is, the borderless panel can give the impression of infinite space and time.

BALLOON: a speech balloon contains the spoken dialogue of a character. Thought balloons (not shown here) contain the thoughts of a character, and are differentiated from speech balloons in that they take a different shape, usually clouds. The TAIL of the balloon indicates who is speaking or thinking. The rendition of balloons and tails can provide some indication of how an utterance is rendered; for example, here the wavering line of the old woman's balloon could portray her nervousness, or a quavering voice, or both.

TIER: a row of panels, travelling from left to right across the page for western readers. Here there are two tiers, consisting of panels 1-12 and 13-22.

List of references

Collins, S. *Treat*. Published in *The Guardian* on 26 October 2012. Available at http://www.theguardian.com/lifeandstyle/cartoon/2012/oct/26/2. Accessed 18 February 2016 at 18:22.

Eisner, W. (1985) *Comics and Sequential Art.* Paramus: Poorhouse Press.

Ewert, J. (2004) Art Spiegelman's 'Maus' and the Graphic Narrative. In *Narrative Across Media: The Languages of Storytelling.* Lincoln: University of Nebraska Press, 178–193.

Genette, G. (1980) *Narrative Discourse: An Essay in Method.* Ithaca: Cornell University Press.

Goodman, S. (2007) Visual English. In *Redesigning English.* Abingdon: Routledge, 113–159.

Halliday, M.A.K. (1994) *An Introduction to Functional Grammar.* (2nd ed.) London: Edward Arnold.

Horstkotte, S. & Pedri, N. (2011) Focalization in Graphic Narrative. *Narrative* 19(3): 330–357.

Kress, G. & van Leeuwen, T. (2006) *Reading Images: The Grammar of Visual Design. (*2nd ed.) London: Routledge.

Kukkonen, K. (2011) Comics as a Test Case for Transmedial Narratology. *SubStance* 40(1): 34–52.

——2013a. *Contemporary Comics Storytelling.* Lincoln: University of Nebraska Press.

——2013b. *Studying Comics and Graphic Novels.* Chichester: Wiley-Blackwell.

McCloud, S. (1993) *Understanding Comics: The Invisible Art.* New York: HarperCollins.

Mikkonen, K. (2008) Presenting Minds in Graphic Narratives. *Partial Answers: Journal of Literature and the History of Ideas* 6(2): 301–321.

Palmer, A. (2004) *Fictional Minds.* Lincoln: University of Nebraska Press.

Saraceni, M. (2000) *Language beyond language: Comics as verbo-visual texts.* PhD thesis. University of Nottingham.

—— (2003) *The Language of Comics.* London: Routledge.

Simpson, P. (1993) *Language, Ideology and Point of View.* London: Routledge.

The Battle of Maldon and Byrhtnoth's 'ofermod'

The historical battle of Maldon took place in 991 and was one of numerous viking attacks in England in the later decades of the tenth century. The policy of paying the sums of money demanded by the vikings in return for peace did nothing to deter further attacks and resulted only in yet more demands for steadily increasing amounts, from £10,000 in 991 to £72,000 paid in 1018 (Keynes, 1991: 100). *The Battle of Maldon* is not an accurate historical account, but a literary composition intended to inspire its contemporary audience and provide a behavioural model to emulate. I focus on the critical debate surrounding Byrhtnoth's *ofermod* and the necessity of assessing the meaning and implications of this word both in its context and according to the conventions of the heroic genre adopted by the poet. I discuss how alternative readings of *ofermod* can alter a perception of the poem's structure, its overall effect and its purpose. As part of this discussion, I describe the relationship between lord and retainer according to the heroic code, and the role played by the poem in immortalising the battle's participants. I suggest that the poem's major theme is loyalty, and I have argued for a positive reading of *ofermod* which pinpoints the crux of the poem as Byrhtnoth's death and Godric's disloyal flight for the safety of the woods. Following this climactic moment, the rest of the poem sets up the behavioural model Godric should have followed and the fragment ends with the loyal retainers engaged in their heroic final stand.

Years of relative peace and prosperity had made England an attractive prospect to would-be Scandinavian invaders (Keynes, 1991: 84), and the battle which took place at Maldon was among the first of a series of attacks which meant that 'the vikings maintained an almost constant presence in Æthelred's kingdom' (Keynes, 1991: 98). The invading forces demanded increasingly large sums of money or 'tribute' in return for peace, but the policy of paying tribute instead of mounting a military resistance was one which subjected the English people to 'an intolerable burden of taxation' and constituted an unsustainable drain on economic resources (Keynes, 1991: 99). Keynes suggests that *The Battle of Maldon* was composed 'against the background of such a debate' (1991: 91). The viking messenger in lines 29-41 sets out the argument for payment instead of bloodshed in battle, but Byrhtnoth's spirited response is to offer tribute in the form of 'gāras syllan / ǣttrynne ord and ealde swurd', or 'poison-tipped spear and seasoned sword' (Baker, 2012: 230, lines 46b-47, all subsequent quotations taken from the same edition). It is not to be supposed, after E. D. Laborde, that the words of the battle's participants have been accurately transcribed (Clark, 1968: 54); the *Maldon* poet has naturally invented the text of all the various monologues, which, as Pope notes, would be 'implausible' in a battle situation (2001: 76). Nevertheless, Byrhtnoth's reply is in essence historically accurate. Tribute was refused and the vikings' offer was met with resistance, and it is this heroic resistance which the *Maldon* poet sets out to celebrate.

The date of the composition of the poem is uncertain and opinion is divided as to whether the poem was written soon after the battle or some years later (Pope, 2001: 78). Scragg adopts a position of sensible compromise when he suggests that the poem should be considered a contemporary account of the battle 'until safe evidence of a later date is produced' (1991: 32). The contemporaneity of the text should not, however, encourage the reader to mistake *The Battle of Maldon* for reportage (Clark, 1968: 54). Indeed, in noting the textual lack of specific strategic information, Pope suggests that 'as a historical source the poem is a poor one' (2001:76). The poet's overall concern is not to provide the reader with an accurate military report of this crushing defeat for the English forces, but to depict events in a manner befitting a quite different agenda. *The Battle of Maldon* is a reimagining of the battle rendered according to the conventions of the heroic genre, and the poet's role is that of 'an omniscient narrator [who] judges the poem's actions from a vantage point appropriate to heroic legend' (Clark, 1968: 55). This nostalgic invocation of an ancient and more glorious past is made to serve a contemporary purpose: against the backdrop of an increasing number of similar viking attacks, the text provides a model of behaviour for the English armies to emulate. It is propaganda designed to inspire loyalty, to glorify those who fought to the end and to vilify those who fled.

Much of the debate surrounding the poem has centred on Byrhtnoth's problematic 'ofermōde' in line 89 (Cavill, 1995; Clark, 1968, 1979; Gneuss 1976). If *ofermod* is to be understood as something akin to 'excessive pride' (Baker, 2012: 348), it is difficult to reconcile the poet's portrayal of Byrhtnoth as an otherwise faultless hero with the image of a vainglorious man who makes a disastrous tactical blunder that costs him his life and the lives of those who fought beside him. Moreover, it has been suggested that in accusing Byrhtnoth of having committed the sin of pride, the poet leaves him 'in danger of damnation' (Clark, 1979: 265), but this clearly runs counter to the poet's objective of pitting the Christian Byrhtnoth, a man who prays for his soul at the point of death, against the pagan vikings, whose heathen status is spelled out as they cut Byrhtnoth down in line 181: 'Đā hine hēowon hǣðene scealcas' ('Then the heathen warriors cut him to pieces'). Byrhtnoth's *ofermod* must be set in context. Clark criticises what he terms 'the school of lexicographical criticism' (1979: 276) and argues that '[t]he meaning of a word in a work can only be ascertained in its context; other contexts of the same and closely related words can only suggest, not determine, the significance of *ofermode* in *Maldon*'. Clark concludes after an extended discussion that 'evidence for a "good sense" of *ofermod* exists, and in human languages speakers force new meanings on old words' (1979: 280). It is true, however, that Anglo-Saxon scholars are disadvantaged in that they are working with a limited corpus of written material and the scope for lexicographical error is therefore greater. Gneuss observes that scholars 'should patiently try to analyze the meaning of Old English words with the help of all available philological tools and all textual evidence, and…to avoid producing what Professor Robinson has very aptly called "a bit of literary criticism posing as lexicographical fact." ' (1976: 137). Nevertheless, the inherent and patently false assumption in this line of argument is that word-meaning is both fixed and constant according to its appearances in a concordance. Clark's observation that language users develop the meaning of existing words through usage is particularly true of those who write in a literary register and it makes for an attractive argument in this instance: there is, after all, no reason why a poet should not adopt an existing word for new purposes, nor why a critical insight should not shed new light on the way in which a particular word has been used. This line of reasoning renders it necessary to consider the use of *ofermod* in context, and to examine the motivation behind Byrhtnoth's decision in the light of the heroic genre adopted by the poet: '[t]he *ofermod* which impells [*sic*] Byrhtnoth to let the vikings cross the Pante is the same heroic spirit which drove him to choose battle instead of tribute; the second decision is implicit in the first' (Clark, 1979: 71). Having committed to the battle, it is unlikely that Byrhtnoth will refuse the vikings' request for safe passage, and simply wait for them to leave the scene only to launch an attack somewhere else. Whatever one may conclude about Byrhtnoth's *ofermod*, and even if it was the poet's intention to criticise his decision, the 'reverence and admiration' for the *eorl* is otherwise unequivocal (Pope, 2001: 78).

However, the tussle over the exact meaning of *ofermod* has greater ramifications than may at first appear. Critical opinion is divided over whether the poem - and the battle - turns on either the episode of Byrhtnoth's *ofermod* in lines 89-90, or Byrhtnoth's death and Godric's subsequent flight in lines 181-201 (Clark, 1979: 259). Those who incline to a negative view of *ofermod* favour an interpretation in which the moment when Byrhtnoth allows safe passage to the vikings is pivotal to the structure of the poem, but in countenancing a more positive interpretation, Clark necessarily takes the view that Godric's flight from the battlefield after Byrhtnoth's demise clearly marks a decisive turning point in the action. In support of his argument, Clark points to Offa's speech as confirmation that it is Godric's cowardice which decides the eventual outcome of the battle: 'Godric, the cowardly son of Odda, has deceived us all. Because he rode away on [Byrhtnoth's] splendid mare, many men believed he was our lord and for this the army has become divided in the field, and the shield-wall broken' (lines 237b-242a). Here the consequences of Godric's flight are spelled out in detail for the poem's audience, and Offa's words are followed by the speeches of those who, according to the codes of honour and loyalty, remain on the battlefield and fight to the end, revealing in their own behaviour what Godric's should have been. It is true that the English defeat is foreshadowed from the poem's outset in such formulaic phrases as 'þā hwīle þe hē mid handum healdan mihte / bord and brād swurd' ('for as long as he might wield his shield and broad sword in his hands', lines 14-15b) which naturally implies that the time will come when the warrior will no longer be able to hold his weapons, but Clark suggests that it is not until after Godric's flight that the *tone* of the poem changes to one of 'fighting without hope' (1968: 57). Furthermore, Clark is keen to emphasise that even though Byrhtnoth allowed the vikings 'landes tō fela' ('too much land') in line 90, the outcome of the battle is not a foregone conclusion at this point. Gneuss attempts to pin down the actual historical size of the invading force the English were facing, but the confusion which exists in primary sources makes this an impossible task (1976: 133). The traditional view is that the English army was vastly outnumbered, but there is little, if anything, in the text to support this claim. The poem is, of course, only a fragment of the original text, but even if the numbers involved had featured in the missing lines, this does not constitute historical fact and cannot be taken as such. It should not be taken for granted, then, that in allowing the vikings safe passage, Byrhtnoth was necessarily dooming his men to destruction.

The argument so far can be summarised as follows. The way in which Byrhtnoth's *ofermod* is understood is potentially crucial to a reading of the poem. If the pivotal moment of the poem is taken to be Byrhtnoth's poor decision as a result of his *ofermod*, then everything that follows is merely the inevitable outcome of that early decision and the poem feels unbalanced. In a negative-*ofermod* reading, the poem is structured as follows: two opposing armies line up and verbally challenge one another, one over-confident leader throws away a tactical advantage as early as line 90, and the remaining 235 lines list those who were slaughtered, including the brash leader. Godric's flight is rendered merely incidental. However, if a more positive, 'heroic' interpretation of *ofermod* is accepted, the poem's turning point is identified as Byrhtnoth's death and the emphasis switches to one of the poem's most important themes: the loyalty owed to the lord by his retainers. Godric's subsequent flight acquires both narrative and thematic weight as a result. The poem is now structured like this: a lord and his band of warriors (or 'comitatus', Scragg, 1991: 33) refuse to submit to the demands of an invading force and prefer battle to paying tribute. Finding themselves at a tactical disadvantage, the vikings parley their way across the causeway; Byrhtnoth cannot 'refuse the Viking request without failing in his duty' (Clark, 1979: 258). Byrhtnoth fights bravely, but is killed in the ensuing battle. Godric, who is cowardly and disloyal, flees the battlefield on Byrhtnoth's horse and many men follow him, believing Godric to be Byrhtnoth. The shield-wall is broken, the English army in disarray, and the action of the poem is henceforth concerned with extolling the virtues of those who choose to stay and die beside their fallen lord instead of running for the safety of the woods. This reading not only directly links structure to theme, but is more in keeping with the poem's rhetoric which strongly favours honourable death over dishonourable cowardice; furthermore, this more positive reading is more appropriate also to the *Maldon* poet's over-riding agenda: to inspire the beleaguered English to emulate an honourable tradition of heroism.

To fully understand the concept of loyalty as set forward by the *Maldon* poet, it is necessary to explore further the relationship between lord and retainer as understood in heroic literature. The *comitatus* system mentioned above was a ' "social contract" in which the lord bought the loyalty and the love of his followers with generous gifts, distributed at a feast when they vowed their allegiance publicly' (Scragg, 1991: 33). Such a feast is recalled by Ælfwine in lines 212-214 in words which are designed not only to inspire the men to honour their former vows, but to serve as a reminder of Byrhtnoth's hospitality and the debt of loyalty owed to their fallen lord. Noblemen in Byrhtnoth's position were expected to be generous with their gifts and are synonymously named in contemporary texts as 'bēahgifa' or 'ring-giver'. In return for his gifts and hospitality, the lord expected loyalty: '[i]n the transaction of the gift, the object given - ring, armour, horse or weapon - becomes the material reminder of the retainer's reciprocal obligation when war service or vengeance is required' (O'Keeffe, 1991: 108). Against this background of *comitatus*, the depth of Godric's dishonour is made manifest. His theft of Byrhtnoth's horse is made all the more despicable because Byrhtnoth had in the past given Godric horses as gifts: 'þone gōdan forlēt / þe him mænigne oft mearh gesealde' (he 'abandoned the good man who had given him many a horse', lines 187b-188). Byrhtnoth's generous gift of horses is repaid with theft of the same to compound Godric's cowardly act.

O'Keeffe locates the 'touchstone' of heroic life in 'the vital relationship between retainer and lord' (1991: 107). To be lordless ('hlāfordlēas', line 251), could mean isolation and dishonour, and the sorrow felt by one such lordless man is poignantly expressed in *The Wanderer*: 'I mourn the gleaming cup, the warrior in his corselet, / the glory of the prince. How that time has passed away, / darkened under the shadow of night as if it had never been' (Crossley-Holland, 1982: 52). When Byrhtnoth falls, variation across stressed alliterative lifts directs the listener's attention to the pathos of the moment. Byrhtnoth is described in terms of the roles he held, and the poet spells out what he represented to the various groups named and what they have now lost: 'Þā wearð āfeallan þæs folces ealdor, / Æþelrēdes eorl; ealle gesāwon / heorðgenēatas þæt hyra heorra læg' ('The army's leader had fallen, Æthelred's nobleman; everyone saw that the hearth-retainer, their lord was down' lines 202-204). Byrhtnoth was a military leader, a civic ruler, a loyal subject, a friend, patron and host, and for all this he expected the loyalty of his men in return. It can be seen, then, that the lord-retainer relationship was central to heroic convention, and to return to the discussion of *ofermod*, O'Keeffe adds her voice to those who claim that Byrhtnoth's *ofermod* is more likely to be viewed in a positive light if it is considered in its proper context: 'the note of complaint which the text seems to make in lines 89-90 arises out of the nature of the code which it ascribes to Byrhtnoth and his loyal retainers. The realm of the heroic lies apart from the mundane, and the poem locates the nobility of the English precisely in their excess' (1991: 123). Seen in this light, Byhrtnoth's 'excessive pride' is what one would naturally expect from a man in his position.

To conclude, it should be noted that *The Battle of Maldon* has its own part to play in cementing the reputations of the English fighters: on the English side, heroes and villains alike are named, regardless of rank. It should not be forgotten that although the poem itself is a literary creation, the events described have their basis in historical fact and some of the men named can be positively identified as real individuals (Locherbie-Cameron, 1991: 238-

249). In her discussion of heroic values, O'Keeffe notes that '[i]n the poetic articulation of the heroic ethos, a warrior's paramount goal is the achievement of a lasting reputation' (1991: 108). The *Maldon* poet bestows on the doomed men a succession of memorable monologues. Offa is permitted to denounce those who fled, thus ensuring their infamy, whilst Godric and his followers are denied a voice and the opportunity to explain their actions.

The ideals endorsed by the *Maldon* poet were not reflected in history. The attacks continued with ever-increasing ferocity and the scanty resistance put up by the English was plagued with treachery (Scragg, 1991: 93). The viking onslaught eventually forced Æthelred to make a treaty with the Danish Cnut, who became England's king after Æthelred's death.

List of references

The Old English font employed throughout for particular characters is Junius by Peter S. Baker. Downloaded on 14 September 2016 from fontspace. com.

All translations my own except for the quotation from *The Wanderer* translated by Kevin Crossley-Holland.

Baker, P.S. (2012) *Introduction to Old English.* (3rd ed.) Oxford: Blackwell.

Cavill, P. (1995) Interpretation of The Battle of Maldon, lines 84-90: a review and reassessment. *Studia Neophilologica* 67: 149–64.

Clark, G. (1979) The hero of Maldon: vir pius et strenuus. *Speculum* 54: 257–282.

Clark, G. (1968) The Battle of Maldon: a heroic poem. *Speculum* 43: 52–71.

Crossley-Holland, K. (Ed.) (1982) *The Anglo-Saxon World: An Anthology.* Oxford: Oxford University Press.

Gneuss, H. (1976) The Battle of Maldon 89: Byrhtnoð's *ofermod* Once Again. *Studies in Philology* 73(2): 117–137.

Keynes, S. (1991) The Historical Context of the Battle of Maldon. In D. Scragg. (Ed.) *The Battle of Maldon AD 991.* Oxford: Basil Blackwell, 81–113.

Locherbie-Cameron, M.A.L. (1991) The Men Named in the Poem. In D. Scragg. (Ed.) *The Battle of Maldon AD 991*. Oxford: Basil Blackwell, 238–249.

O'Keeffe, K.O. (1991) Heroic values and Christian ethics. In M. Godden & M. Lapidge. (Eds.) *The Cambridge Companion to Old English Literature*. Cambridge: Cambridge University Press, 107–125.

Pope, J.C. & Fulk, R.D. (Eds.) (2001) *Eight Old English Poems*. (3rd ed.) New York: W. W. Norton & Company.

Scragg, D. (1991) The nature of Old English verse. In M. Godden & M. Lapidge. (Eds.) *The Cambridge Companion to Old English Literature*. Cambridge: Cambridge University Press, 55–70.

Scragg, D. (Ed.) (1991) *The Battle of Maldon AD 991*. Oxford: Basil Blackwell.

Intertextuality and the poetry of John Heath-Stubbs

In this essay I explore the implications of T. S. Eliot's statement in 'Tradition and the Individual Talent' that '[n]o poet, no artist of any art, has his complete meaning alone'. Eliot imagines the entire collection of literary works as 'an ideal order' of 'existing monuments' (1920). Every new work is a product of that which has gone before, and, in circular fashion, the perception of existing works is affected by the arrival of the new. This essay is a study of that process and the discussion is informed by debates and issues concerning the concept of intertextuality, specifically what is understood by this term and what forms it can take. Selected poems by John Heath-Stubbs alongside his autobiography and literary essays provide the primary material, and all references are to Heath-Stubbs' *Collected Poems* (1988) unless otherwise indicated. The discussion focuses on Heath-Stubbs' use of intertextuality in the following particulars: the exploration and comparative study of the worlds of myth and natural history using the framework of ancient stories (*Polyphemus*); the appropriation of well-known literary characters (*Further Adventures of Doctor Faustus* and *Winter in Illyria*); and the adaption and expansion of a metaphor created by another writer (*Moving to Winter*). Implied in the discussion of the role of the author in this context is the question of where authorship begins and/or ends when the poet uses someone else's words or characters. I also consider the role of the reader, what kind of reader is implied in the poet's use of intertextuality and to what extent the reader/critic also takes on the mantle of authorship or creator.

The literary references of Eliot's *The Waste Land* (1940) operate a two-way effect in which the works alluded to infiltrate and resonate throughout the poem's lines, while simultaneously, Eliot's reformulation of literary fragments invites a re-evaluation of the original texts. This is entirely consistent with the logic of Eliot's argument in his 1920 essay 'Tradition and the Individual Talent', in that a new work of art stems from that which has gone before and, in being assimilated into the existing body of literature, affects how pre-existing works are perceived. The connection between Eliot's line of argument and intertextuality is encapsulated in Brée's description of Kristeva's version of intertextuality as 'the power of the written text to impose a reorganization of the corpus of texts that preceded its appearance, creating a modification in the manner in which they are read' (quoted in Orr, 2003: 10). In addition, Eliot's proposal that influence is bi- rather than mono-directional is reflected in Baxandall's suggestion that the newer text 'y' be redefined as 'agent', and that the original text 'x', which has been adapted to produce 'y', be considered therefore as 'contributory' (quoted in Orr, 2003: 84-85). As will be noted in the discussion of intertextuality to follow, this bidirectional flow of assimilation and re-evaluation entails a democratisation of texts with both x and y considered on the same footing. Before embarking on this discussion, however, I will consider briefly the life and work of the creator of the primary sources under consideration in this essay, and the poet's suitability as a subject for this topic.

John Heath-Stubbs (1918-2006) is a poet renowned for the extraordinary depth and range of his learning, in particular his remarkable knowledge of English literature. In an obituary written for *The Guardian*, one of Heath-Stubbs' university coevals Michael Meyer described him as 'unusually widely read and discerning' (2006) and, writing for the Royal Society of Literature, Sebastian Faulks noted that '[h]is encyclopaedic knowledge was legendary' (2006). Peter Avery, with whom Heath-Stubbs worked on translations of Hafiz and Omar Khayyám, wrote for a special edition of *Aquarius* dedicated to Heath-Stubbs that '[h]e has English literature at his finger-tips in a way I believe nobody else can equal'. In reference to the translations the two men produced, Avery notes that the 'apostolic approach' they adopted in regard to the original text raised difficulties which '[o]nly John's immense range of literary references…and his wide vocabulary [could] solve' (1978: 23). In spite of all evidence to the contrary, Heath-Stubbs insisted he was not 'erudite', but instead 'a magpie-like collector of interesting oddments' (Powell, 2006).

Heath-Stubbs struggled with poor eyesight from the age of three and was completely blind following the removal of his one remaining eye in 1978; nevertheless, he continued to publish poetry until the year before his death. Tape-recorders had their part to play in his compositional process, but more importantly, Heath-Stubbs was possessed of an exceptional memory. In an interview for *PN Review*, Clive Wilmer comments that '[i]nescapably, *memory* has played a major role in [Heath-Stubbs'] later development … the poems quite plainly draw on remembered knowledge' (1993:51). Heath-Stubbs has said of his use of literary references that '[w]hen I'm writing poetry…I almost make it a rule never to look things up, with the idea that the only real knowledge is what you can spontaneously remember' (Thompson, 1999). Even in the Google age where every reference is only a keyboard-search away, memory still has a central role to play in intertextuality; after all, the memories of authors and readers alike are repositories of previously-experienced texts and, to adopt Barthes' phrase, the 'already-read'.

Heath-Stubbs' poetry is rich in literary allusion. He notes in the preface to his *Collected Poems* that while studying at Oxford, he and his peers 'accepted that, amid the complexities of the twentieth-century, poetry, if it were to have any wide significance, should also be complex. It would be allusive and need not always be immediately accessible to rational analysis'. Heath-Stubbs also notes that he 'came to feel that since language is a convention which one shares with other speakers and writers, and not a separate mode of expression…the poem is in a certain sense carrying on a dialogue with other poems' (1988: 22). Heath-Stubbs is somewhat on the defensive in this preface. One senses the dissenting voice behind the text with which the poet is in dialogue, ostensibly with the aim of countering a charge of elitism. Heath-Stubbs cites Philip Larkin, his 'friend and contemporary at Oxford', who was puzzled as to the identity of Leporello in *The Don Juan Triptych*, and comments that 'I should have thought that it was not pedantry to suppose that at least some my readers might be acquainted with the operas of Mozart' (23). Heath-Stubbs gently makes clear his expectations of his readers: 'I can only ask my readers to be patient if they should come across in reading my poems references to matters which may be unfamiliar to them. I have already suggested that it might not be too difficult for them to find out, and that they might be gainers if they do, but if they are not so inclined, why not let it stand as a mystery or a riddle' (23-24). The tasks which fall to the reader to perform and questions of literary competence will be considered in due course, but the discussion turns now to an examination of what is meant by the term 'intertextuality' and what forms intertextuality can take.

Kristeva first coined the term by way of synthesising Saussure's structuralist work centring on the semiotics of *langue/parole* with Bakhtin's work on dialogism, and in practice it serves as a useful umbrella term for many 'forms of representation such as parody, pastiche, satire, caricature, travesty, that mimic by reversal but which are also distinguishable from plagiarism' (Orr, 2003: 99). The trilingual Kristeva was able to read the work of Bakhtin in its original form and her version of intertextuality is based on (but not identical to) Bakhtin's theories of 'heteroglossia' or the multi-voiced text (Vice, 1997). Barthes contributed to the debate, not least with his denial of the author (1977: 142-148), as did Riffaterre who wrote extensively about intertextuality and the reader. Another structuralist critic, Genette, responded to Kristeva's 'too overarching term' with his 'more nuanced taxonomies' (Orr, 2003: 6), namely the intertextual, metatextual, architextual, paratextual and hypertextual (Allen, 2000: 101-115), thereby reducing the scope of the term to 'issues of quotation, plagiarism and allusion' (Allen, 2000: 101). The post-structuralist position treats intertextuality as far more wide-ranging and all-encompassing. While structuralists laboured to demonstrate that intertextuality could stabilise textual significance by locating a text's sources, post-structuralists were concerned to show that intertextuality throws into confusion all 'notions of stable meaning' (Allen, 2000: 3-4). The post-structuralist position is in fact so inclusive as to render useless any attempt to locate the building blocks which have gone into a text's construction. In their overview of literary criticism and theory, Bennett and Royle write of intertextuality as a term which means 'that every word of every text refers to other texts and so on, limitlessly' (2009: 323); that texts are 'unfinished and unfinishable', and that 'texts are inevitably linked up with other texts and that there is no simple end (or beginning) to any text' (315). In spite of the divergence of opinion on the exact scope of the term, Orr notes that Kristeva's coinage was a success, and that this new term came as a challenge to 'pre-1968 ideologies', confronting amongst other things the notion of 'the pre-eminence of high-cultural expression' (2003: 1). This was possible because '[p]rior text materials lose special status by permutation with others in the intertextual exchange because all intertexts are of equal importance in the intertextual *process*' (28, emphasis in original). In support of this position, Allen notes that 'intertextuality reminds us that all texts are potentially plural, reversible, open to the reader's own presuppositions, lacking in clarity and defined boundaries, and always involved in the expression or repression of the dialogic "voices" which exist within society' (207).

The notion of heteroglossia or numerous voices present in any one text brings the discussion to Barthes' (in)famous essay on 'The Death of the Author' (1977: 142-148). Barthes draws on Kristeva's work on Bakhtin in arguing that the author's mind is full of language previously encountered and that this kind of knowledge, which includes a familiarity with literary conventions (Culler, 1975: 135), is unavoidable. As a result, the author simply 'arranges and compiles the always already written, spoken, and read' into a single textual space (Allen, 2000: 73). The resulting text is 'a tissue of quotations' (Barthes, 1977: 146). The restrictive extremism of such a position may be partially explained by an anxiety to discredit influence study on the part of those who have championed theories of intertextuality, dating from the work of the New Critics if not before. Orr points out that '[t]he term [intertextuality] reacted to most violently, and desired to replace and displace, was influence, with all its baggage of critical source-hunting and authorial intention' (2003: 15). The solution was to deny 'agents and intention altogether' (83). Almost sixty years before Barthes penned his essay, Eliot had acknowledged the debt poets owed to their forebears, but showed himself keen to retain the author figure through his metaphor of the poet's mind as a shred of platinum which acts as a catalyst in the presence of two gases to form 'sulphurous acid'. The poet's incorporation of already-written texts into the new provokes a readjustment in perception of the 'ideal order' of 'existing monuments' and Eliot's poet therefore shoulders 'great difficulties and responsibilities' (1920).

Eliot wants to make of the poet a literary torch-bearer, but Barthes' line of argument suggests that far from being a guardian who bequeaths received and acknowledged wisdom, the author is likely to be wholly unaware of her own specific sources of influence. In an interview for *PN Review*, Heath-Stubbs told Clive Wilmer that '[i]t's very difficult to know who has influenced you. I've sometimes had students who have been writing dissertations or theses on my work. They come to see me and the first question they ask is: "Who are your influences?" I say, "You're supposed to tell me!"' (1993: 52). The proponents of intertextuality promote the reader to a site of potential meaning; indeed, Barthes names the reader as the focal point of the existing multiplicity of writings (1997: 148), an 'I' that is 'already a plurality of other texts' (quoted in Culler, 1981: 113). For Barthes, authors and readers are one and the same: '[t]he intertextual nature of writing and of the text turns both terms of the traditional model, author and critic, into readers' (Allen, 2000: 75). Orr notes that accounting for the reader's prior knowledge presents researchers with a difficulty not easily resolved (2003: 39), and while it may indeed be impossible to accurately assess the literary competence of one particular individual, it is also true that readers are taught how to read literature as 'a second-order semiotic system which has language as its basis' (Culler, 1975: 132). As Culler points out in his chapter on literary competence, 'the notion of effect presupposes modes of reading which are not random or haphazard' (1975: 135). Knowledge of literary conventions enables the reader to 'identify various levels of coherence and set them in relation to one another'; the text then becomes subject to a 'different series of interpretive operations' compared with understanding an utterance outside the literary sphere (1975: 133). Jenny goes so far as to suggest that literature would be simply 'unintelligible' without intertextuality: '[u]nderstanding [the literary work] supposes competence in the decoding of the literary language, which can only be acquired by experience with a large number of texts' (1982: 34). This competence comprises knowledge of various conventions, which Culler identifies as those of metaphorical coherence, poetic tradition, thematic unity and the rule of significance (1975: 134). He adds that a poem should be 'thought of as an utterance that has meaning only with respect to a system of conventions which the reader has assimilated' (135). Similarly for Genette, literary works are not utterances that can stand alone, but 'particular articulations (selections and combinations) of an enclosed system' (Allen, 2000: 96), a system that is shared and understood and which to a certain extent even dictates reader-response. On reading as a social practice, Stockwell notes that '[i]ndividual sense experiences are partly shaped by our socialised sense of acceptable responses and appropriate articulations, from a very early point in processing' (2009: 78).

The notion of 'acceptable responses' is an important one for literary competence. As Culler points out, '[r]eaders do not have the freedom to read as they will. Poetic signs form patterns that cannot be ignored' (1981: 104). The reader is guided to complete the gaps in the text by means of 'secondary signals' which provide 'the thread leading to the solution' (65). Intertextual references, whether embedded or explicit, serve as such signals: '[i]ntertextuality is the recognition of a frame, a context that allows the reader to make sense out of what he or she might otherwise perceive as senseless' (Plottel and Charney quoted in Orr, 2003: 11). The text generates its own 'ideal reader', which is 'a theoretical construct, perhaps best thought of as a representation of the central notion of acceptability ... the possibility of critical argument depends on shared notions of the acceptable and the unacceptable, a common ground which is nothing other than the procedures of reading' (Culler, 1975: 144-145).

The ideal reader, then, should recognise a literary reference, or at least be able to spot that a frame of some kind is in use. Riffaterre refers to what he terms 'ungrammaticalities' in the text which enable a reader to do so. These 'ungrammaticalities' are markers which function as 'a nexus of significations' and they include the following:

> the remodelling of poetic paradigms, conventions of versification, stock images and epithets (conceits and blasons), or rhetorical overdeterminations such as paronomasia (the playing out of meanings of words that sound alike), catachresis (the improper use of terms in a given context), anaphora (repetition of certain words in subsequent clauses, extended metaphors), syllepses (words pertinent to two or more registers), hypograms proper (puns, anagrams, homophones, homonyms) and symbols (Orr, 2003: 38).

It should be noted, however, that the movement from identification to interpretation is not always straightforward. Riffaterre himself wrote an ingenious reading of a prose poem by André Breton, based on Riffaterre's knowledge of the conventions of the pastoral genre and his identification of intertextual references to the pastoral. The question to consider in such a case as this is whether Riffaterre's response constitutes an 'acceptable reading' of Breton's poem, or whether it is not, in fact, a response which is in itself an inventive and original piece of creative writing.

To return to Barthes, and his disregard for authorial authority of any kind, the Barthesian reader is a *reagent* of the text whose critical response is purely emotive (Orr, 2003: 35). It is not possible, however, to square this approach with the reality of readers' activities and their production of 'acceptable' readings, nor is it clear how Barthes would account for authorial use of quotation which is quite clearly intentional when the reference to another text functions as a 'shorthand cultural reference' (Orr, 2003: 88). Indeed, Genette argues for precisely the opposite approach in which the reader's function and priority is to follow the intertextual references, both embedded and explicit, to reassign the work its place in a closed literary system (Allen, 2000: 96). In the section to follow, I shall discuss examples from John Heath-Stubbs' poetry which make explicit intertextual references, thereby pointing the way very clearly for the reader to understand the poem in relation to the other texts on which it depends. I hope to demonstrate also that, in accordance with Eliot's claim, Heath-Stubbs' poetry draws on the works of the past to produce new works in the present and, in addition, encourages the reader to reflect on and perhaps reassess the literary sources adopted.

Literary archetypes such as myths and legends are texts which are 'constantly in flux, constantly metamorphosing in the process of adaptation and retelling ... Mythical literature depends upon, incites even, perpetual acts of reinterpretation in new contexts' (Sanders, 2016: 79-80). An artistic tendency to re-use and re-create ancient stories is well represented in Heath-Stubbs' work. In *Hindsights*, he notes that his exposure to *Hiawatha* and Kingsley's *The Heroes* 'opened up [his] mind to the possibilities of studying mythology and folklore in a comparative spirit' (1993: 34). In 'Polyphemus' (106), Heath-Stubbs explores the interface between the worlds of natural history and myth. Heath-Stubbs' Polyphemus is a lonely shepherd, loved by no one but his sheep. The poem leads the reader to several other sources - Homer, Lully, Handel, Ovid, Boccaccio - but the nature of Heath-Stubbs' eponymous character is distinct from Homer's man-eating monster who serves as an obstacle to Odysseus' journey. He is different again to the murderous spurned lover of Ovid, Lully and Handel who features in the stories of Galatea and her Acis.

The effect of painting a sympathetic portrait of Polyphemus is to encourage the reader to consider the well-known story from such an angle, and also to reassess the other characters in a corresponding light: Odysseus, known for his cunning and scheming in any case, is depicted here as needlessly violent and cruel, blinding Polyphemus for the sake of it rather than to save his own life and the lives of his men; 'brisk' Galatea is not Ovid's grieving nymph but a treacherous, wilful flirt who cruelly 'flaunts' Polyphemus. The last stanza turns the poem into a gentle lament for the loss of belief in these beings, now the subject of story and myth. Boccaccio's 'The bones of Polyphemus!' is dismissed in favour of the more practical explanation based in palaeontology which identifies Polyphemus' bones as those of an elephant. The irony is that the 'learned world' is mistaken according to the world of Heath-Stubbs' poem.

The switch required of the reader in the example above is to consider and compare different world-views and belief systems. Sanders notes that '[t]he transformation involved in seeing things from a different point of view is a driving force in many…appropriations of classic texts' (2016: 61). In 'Polyphemus', the reader is encouraged to sympathise with the cyclops in being reminded of his isolation and lonely death. Genette writes of this kind of creative move in *Palimpsests*: '[t]he revaluation of a character consists in investing him or her - by way of pragmatic or psychological transformation - with a more significant and/or more "attractive" role in the value system of the hypertext [the adaptive text or re-creation] than was the case in the hypotext [the source or original]' (quoted in Sanders, 2016: 62). In the examples to follow, Heath-Stubbs merges two characters into one, which has the effect of making both characters considerably *less* attractive.

In 'Further Adventures of Doctor Faustus', the character from Christopher Marlowe's play stages his own demise to escape his creditors, evading 'poor Mephistophilis' at the same time, to re-emerge as Prospero in Shakespeare's *The Tempest*. Both plays are referenced in Heath-Stubbs' text by proper nouns, plot references, direct quotation in italics and quotation marks, and quotation which is rather more indirect: 'nodding away / The butt end of his life, every third thought his grave' (103). Faustus and Prospero are both scholar-magicians and it is not inconceivable that they should be one and the same character, especially if one takes a rather dim view of Prospero's activities: 'being marooned, / Upon a desert island, he set it up / A mini-imperialist commonwealth, / Successfully enslaving and exploiting / The local aboriginals, of air and earth'. The 'local aboriginals' are, of course, Ariel and Caliban respectively. Both are set free at the end of Shakespeare's play, but prior to this event they are both bound to Prospero's will and any dissent is rapidly silenced by physical torture or accusations of ingratitude. In the final lines, Heath-Stubbs likens the magic in Faustus/Prospero's apparently still extant books to nuclear waste: a toxic residue that poisons the land and all who come into contact with it.

Heath-Stubbs performs a similar trick of merging literary characters in 'Winter in Illyria' (77). This short, bleak poem comprises six verses, each of two original lines followed by a third which, in each case a direct quotation from Shakespeare, has the function of a refrain. The first intertextual reference is of course in the name 'Illyria' itself. Illyria existed as an historical region, but it is more recognisably the setting for *Twelfth Night*. Each verse of this poem contains a visual and/or aural image, which structure arguably imitates 'the Persian manner of structuring a poem by means of a series of intuitive image-links, rather than logically and lineally' (Heath-Stubbs, 1998: 120), a literary tradition with which Heath-Stubbs, as co-translator of Hafiz and Omar Khayyám, would have been very familiar. The images are those of a drear desolation: a fountain choked with fallen leaves, the screech of a white peacock, and 'Remembered echoes' of 'lute-strings' and 'drunken singing'. The accompanying quotations to these images are drawn from Feste's songs, and in the fourth verse Fabian's line 'Carry his water to the wise woman!' follows the image of a 'tormented man' locked in a 'darkened room'. The man is of course Malvolio, and the tense shift in the fifth verse from present to past ('He left feckless Illyria') marks a movement from a remembering consciousness to an objective narratorial voice. The final quotation in the sixth verse is not from *Twelfth Night*, but *Othello*. Malvolio, with revenge in his heart, becomes Iago, that most inscrutable and ruthless of Shakespearean villains. Iago famously refuses to comment on the motivation behind his behaviour: 'Demand me nothing, what you know, you know, / From this time forth I never will speak a word' (Shakespeare, 1958 [?1604]: 194). In the poem-world imagined by Heath-Stubbs, that motivation becomes the need for revenge, irrespective of the identity of the victim. Babcock argues that Iago is a character who is peculiarly susceptible to social slights and that his behaviour is driven by a sense of inferiority (1965); the general premise of Babcock's argument is one that fits very well with Heath-Stubbs' experiment. Iago's motives have been the cause of much scholarly debate and Heath-Stubbs offers us a potential solution: Iago is the wronged Malvolio, bearing a grudge as a result of his former humiliation.

The final poem to be considered is one in which one poet's metaphor is adopted and expanded by another, and once again, it is a text which makes its intertextual reference explicit. There is no mistaking the source for *Moving to Winter*, given that Heath-Stubbs supplies both a name and the keywords necessary to locate the original poem: 'Edmund Waller's cottage of the soul' (36). The dereliction of the dwelling stands for the decrepitude of an elderly body, fulfilling the convention 'that one should attempt through semantic transformations to produce coherence on the levels of both tenor and vehicle' (Culler, 1975: 134). As mentioned above, this is one of the conventions with which readers comply when interpreting a text and it is an example of the type of learned, rather than innate, knowledge which forms part of a reader's literary competence. In comparing these two poems, the reader is required to engage with several metaphors on the theme of old age and the end of life. Waller's title asks the reader to imagine the life-span of an individual measured by the number of pages in a book (but it should be noted also that an EEBO search reveals this verse to have been printed at the very end of a book). The first line of Heath-Stubbs' poem comprises three different metaphors: life is represented as a journey in which the poet moves towards death; this is coupled with the conceit of one year representing a human life, where autumn is middle age and winter is old age; the third metaphor touches on Waller's soul-cottage in the phrase 'life-house'. In Old English, *feorhhūs* is 'life-house', or 'body', thus invoking a long tradition of verse and versifiers. As I hope to demonstrate, the figure of the poet is central to the hypertext.

Heath-Stubbs takes Waller's 'soul's dark cottage' metaphor as the theme of his poem, but there are some important differences. Heath-Stubbs drops the adjective 'dark' and substitutes 'eternity' for Waller's 'new light'. The binary opposition of dark and light in Waller is replaced in Heath-Stubbs with that of cold and warmth. The eternity which penetrates the holes of Heath-Stubbs' cottage is 'chill', compared with the still-burning fire representing warm life and a means of providing sustenance in the form of toasted cheese to feed poems, the crickets 'that chirp in the crannies'. Notable also is the shift from passive to active. Waller's soul-cottage passively receives ('Lets in') the 'new light', but Heath-Stubbs' eternity is an active agent which 'shines through' the chinks. Waller's passivity is in keeping with the tranquil tone of the poem as the speaker draws near his end with stoicism and calm acceptance, embodied in the second stanza's metaphor of quiet seas 'when the winds give o'er'. Waller's poem focuses on the wisdom gained in age and an imminent embrace of the 'eternal home', but there is nothing of this in *Moving to Winter*. Heath-Stubbs' cottage/body may be falling into disrepair, but it is still providing shelter and warmth. Waller, in the penultimate year of his life, is writing pietistic verse in seventeenth-century tradition, and his focus is on the imagined life to come. His cottage is empty of the angels, ghosts and folkloric spirits which make up the 'visitants' of Heath-Stubbs' cottage. Waller concerns himself for the most part with the passing of the 'batter'd and decay'd' body from one state to another, while Heath-Stubbs is focused on the life that remains to him.

Heath-Stubbs is not the only poet to have picked up on Waller's metaphor. As an admirer of the Augustan poets (Heath-Stubbs, 1993: 209), Heath-Stubbs will undoubtedly have known that Waller's lines were adapted by Alexander Pope in Book IV of *The Dunciad*. Pope imagines the body of the poet to be maimed and perforated by critics: 'And you, my Critics! in the chequer'd shade, / Admire new light through holes yourselves have made' (Pope, 1743). Pope's poets put their critics in the shade, but the critics' destructive activities create chinks through which they can themselves enjoy some of the sunshine. What both Pope and Heath-Stubbs have done is to identify the speaker specifically as a poet, and the light as a source of threat or attack. The poet-speakers do not welcome death, because their passing will deprive the world of their poetry.

This essay has explored Eliot's 1920 description of bi-directional literary influence through discussion of the concept of intertextuality with reference to the poetry of John Heath-Stubbs. Intertextuality is a term whose scope ranges from Genette's narrow distinctions (quotation, plagiarism, allusion) through to a poststructuralist plurality which encompasses every word of every text. Barthes' author/reader was pitted against Eliot's literary torch-bearer in an examination of the author's role, after which the discussion turned to the notion of the 'ideal reader' who produces an 'acceptable response'. The final section of the essay comprised an examination of several poems which make explicit their intertextual references, and readings were produced by way of demonstrating the response required from the reader to such references. I conclude by turning once again to Eliot's claim that just as new works respond to and draw on the old, the perception of existing literature is affected by the arrival of the new. In the poems examined, the reader is encouraged to view the cyclops as a persecuted solitary being instead of a man-eating monster; Faustus and Prospero are merged into one, as are Malvolio and Iago, thus potentially eliciting a reappraisal of all four characters; and finally, Waller's metaphor is adopted and expanded to incorporate the voice of a poet under attack.

List of references

Allen, G. (2000) *Intertextuality*, London: Routledge.

Avery, P. (ed.) (1978) In Honour of John Heath-Stubbs. *Aquarius*, 10.

Babcock, W. (1965) 'Iago - An Extraordinary Honest Man'. *Shakespeare Quarterly*. 16(4): 297–301.

Barthes, R. (1977) 'The Death of the Author' in *Image Music Text*. London: Fontana Press: 142-148.

Bennett, A. & Royle, N. (2009) *An Introduction to Literature, Criticism and Theory*. 4th ed. Harlow: Pearson.

Culler, J. (1981) *The Pursuit of Signs*. London: Routledge.

Culler, J. (1975) *Structuralist Poetics*. London: Routledge.

Eliot, T.S. (1920) 'Tradition and the Individual Talent'. *The Sacred Wood: Essays on poetry and criticism* [online]. Available at: https://archive.org/details/sacredwoodessays00eliorich (Accessed 2 January 2017).

Eliot, T.S. (1940) *The Waste Land and other poems*. London: Faber and Faber.

Faulks, S. (2006) 'John-Heath Stubbs Remembered'. *The Royal Society of Literature* [online]. Available at: http://rsliterature.org/fellow/john-heath-stubbs-obe/ (Accessed 26 February 2017).

Heath-Stubbs, J. (1998) *The Literary Essays of John Heath-Stubbs*. T. Tolley (ed.) Manchester: Carcanet.

Heath-Stubbs, J. (1993) *Hindsights: An Autobiography*. London: Hodder & Stoughton.

Heath-Stubbs, J. (1988) *Collected Poems 1943-1987*. Manchester: Carcanet.

Jenny, L. (1982) 'The strategy of form'. In T. Todorov (ed.) *French Literary Theory Today*. Cambridge: Cambridge University Press: 34–63.

Meyer, M. (2006) 'John Heath-Stubbs'. *The Guardian*. 29 December [online]. Available at: https://www.theguardian.com/news/2006/dec/29/guardianobituaries.booksobituaries?CMP=share_btn_link (Accessed: 26 February 2017).

Orr, M. (2003) *Intertextuality: Debates and Contexts*. Cambridge: Polity Press.

Pope, A. (1743) 'The Dunciad' [online]. *Google Books*. Available at: https://books.google.co.uk/books?id= a2JXAAAAcAAJ&pg=PA244&lpg=PA244&dq=you+critics+chequered+shade+pope&source=bl&ots=LEg6OGZPFO&sig=QaTGijsQiv5qb9fDJsAmOf1eWp0&hl=en&sa=X&ved=0ahUKEwibycnUhfzSAhWHCcAKHdMaDFwQ6AEIMzAE#v=onepage&q=you%20critics%20chequered%20sha&f=false (Accessed 29 March 2017).

Powell, N. (2006) 'John Heath-Stubbs'. *The Independent*. 27 December [online]. Available at: http://www.independent.co.uk/news/obituaries/john-heath-stubbs-429904.html (Accessed 26 February 2017).

Riffaterre, M. (1990) 'Compulsory reader response: the intertextual drive'. In *Intertextuality: theories and practices*. Worton & Still (eds.) Manchester: Manchester University Press, 56-78.

Sanders, J. (2016) *Adaptation and Appropriation*. 2nd ed. London: Routledge.

Shakespeare, W. (1958 [?1604]) *Othello*. M. Ridley (ed.) London: Routledge.

Stockwell, P. (2009) *Texture: A Cognitive Aesthetics of Reading*. Edinburgh: Edinburgh University Press.

Thompson, R.H. (1999) 'Interview with John Heath-Stubbs'. *The Camelot Project* [online]. Available at: http://d.lib.rochester.edu/camelot/text/interview-with-john-heath-stubbs (Accessed 21 February 2017).

Vice, S. (1997) *Introducing Bakhtin*. Manchester: Manchester University Press.

Waller, E. (2017 [1686]) 'Of the Last Verses in the Book'. *Poetry Foundation* [online]. Available at: https://www.poetryfoundation.org/poems-and-poets/poems/detail/45439 (Accessed 22 February, 2017).

Wilmer, C. (1993) 'Clive Wilmer in conversation with John Heath-Stubbs'. *PN Review*, July/August: 51–54.

Worton, M. & Still, J. (eds.) (1990) *Intertextuality: theories and practices*. Manchester: Manchester University Press.

Contextual frame theory and Shirley Jackson's *A Visit*

Contextual frame theory explains 'how readers track reference to characters and events through the process of reading' (Stockwell, 2002: 155). To summarise the essence of this approach, the reader constructs mental images, or 'contextual frames', containing characters and objects which are said to be 'bound' to that frame. The binding process enables the reader to monitor who and what appears in a particular textual location. Characters and objects become 'primed', however, when they form the focus of the reader's attention (Emmott, 1997: 123), and 'textually overt' when mentioned. As new information is received, the reader must perform various revisions such as adding to or amending entity representations for characters and locations. Frame modifications are necessary when characters enter or leave the frame; frame repairs occur when the reader learns that she has made an incorrect assumption, such as, for example, the gender of the protagonist; frame replacements (Stockwell, 2002: 158) are an extreme version of the latter in which an entire frame must be revised or scrapped altogether. In this essay I use contextual frame theory to explore one of Shirley Jackson's most Gothic stories. I begin by examining the Gothic trope of the splintered self in the context of entity representations. I show how the orientational information necessary to contextual frame theory is repurposed to bewilder the reader and I examine how contextual frame theory can explain the calculated deception practised on the reader. I contend that contextual frame theory runs into difficulties when presented with an unreliable narrator, but the necessary repair-work is nevertheless integral to the experience of reading and forms part of the story's meaning.

'A Visit' (1950) appears in a collection of Jackson's work entitled *Come Along With Me* and was also anthologised as 'The Lovely House' in *American Gothic Tales,* edited by Joyce Carol Oates, herself a writer in the same tradition.[1] Jackson achieved fame as a writer working within the Gothic genre, and given both the identity of the writer and the context of publication, it is crucial that the Gothic genre is taken into account in any discussion of this story. Gothic genre conventions dictate reader expectations: there is, after all, some truth in Kosofsky Sedgwick's playful comment that '[o]nce you know that a novel is of the Gothic kind…you can predict its contents with an

---

1   Carla's family name appears as 'Rhodes' in the version published in the 2013 Penguin edition, and 'Montague' in the Oates anthology. I have used the name 'Rhodes' throughout.

unnerving certainty' (1986: 9). Many readers of the Gothic, and the Female Gothic in particular (Fleenor, 1983; Wallace and Smith, 2009; Wallace, 2013) will be familiar with the themes and tropes of Jackson's story, including an imprisoned female protagonist, a splintered or fractured self, live burial and a labyrinthine dwelling, but few perhaps will foresee the twist in Jackson's tale, and most readers will have to perform frame repairs and replacements. A first reading of the story will therefore be an entirely different experience to every subsequent reading. Readings other than the first will draw on repaired and modified frames in the light of acquired knowledge.

The story is narrated in the third person, but there are no scenes in which Margaret is not present and the reader follows Margaret's subjectivity throughout. The reader has access to Margaret's thoughts, but the minds of the other characters are kept closed except for what the reader can infer from their reactions and behaviour. The story begins when school-friends Margaret and Carla arrive at Carla's home, where Margaret is to spend the summer months, and together Margaret and Carla explore the seemingly endless rooms. Carla speaks of the time when her brother will visit and when Paul and the captain arrive, the reader is led to believe that *Paul* is Carla's brother. However, when the time comes for the men to depart, the reader discovers that it is *the captain* who is Carla's brother. Neither Paul nor great-aunt Margaret in the tower have ever been present, and the very nature of their existence is brought into question.

Plausible readings of the story within the context of the Gothic genre include the possibility that the main female character is the subject of a split personality, and that the house and its occupants represent different facets of just one fractured mentality. For example, Bowman's 'structuralist inquiry' into the work of Victoria Holt asserts that the characters surrounding the Gothic heroine represent 'projections of her inner ambivalences' (Bowman, 1983: 69), and similarly, Punter and Byron suggest that the architecture in Gothic fiction embodies an externalisation of a character's emotions (2004: 179). If the house and its characters represent aspects of Margaret's unconscious self, it should be noted in addition that there exist at least five versions of the character 'Margaret', all of whom may or may not be the same person. Hattenhauer does not doubt that the great-aunt is an older version of Margaret, and suggests that '[w]hen the madwoman in the attic appears as Margaret's double, the theme of Margaret trapped in the history of her disunity as a subject emerges' (2003: 56). The various Margarets can be identified as follows. The first is Carla's school-friend, the Margaret who has a mother and sisters, who is embroidering a pair of slippers for a friend and who has a home to send to for more clothes. This Margaret is referred to, but never seen in the narrative. The second is the Margaret who visits Carla at her home during the school summer holidays. The third is the Margaret whose face is depicted on the floor of the tile room, the Margaret who died for love. The fourth is the great-aunt, the Margaret in the tower, and the fifth is the image of Margaret that Mrs Rhodes is preparing to weave into her tapestry at the end of the story. The shared name should not be overlooked: Punter and Byron suggest that 'repetitions of names… produces a doubling that repeatedly works against any sense of narrative division' (2004: 213)[2]. According to contextual frame theory, the reader uses details provided in the text to construct a character, or an 'entity representation' (Emmott, 1997). The doubling provoked by the naming of the tiled image and the great-aunt prompts the reader to conflate the various Margarets into one entity representation. As Margaret's growing fondness for Paul becomes evident, it becomes more likely that she will indeed turn out to be the Margaret who died for love, and whose tiled image now resides permanently in a tiled image of the tower. This conflation of the entity representation with a mosaic image rendered from chips of the very materials from which the house has been constructed provides a valuable clue as to the true nature of the house and its occupants, to which I shall return in due course.

In her full-length study of contextual monitoring, Emmott notes that the reader retrieves 'orientational information' from the text, including details such as where and when the action is located (1997: 103). However, both the temporal and spatial locations of 'A Visit' are difficult to identify with any certainty. There are very few clues available, for example, to enable the reader to place the events of the story within a historical timeframe. Margaret arrives with Carla at the house, but no indication is provided of the girls' means of travel, whether by rail, car, or horse and carriage; the reader is merely told that Margaret 'alighted with Carla' (Jackson, 2013 [1950]: 101)[3]. Paul appears in uniform, and the presence of the 'captain' leads the reader to infer that the uniform is a military one and the two men are soldiers; beyond this, however, no further assumptions can be conclusively drawn. As the story progresses, the reader's sense of temporal disorientation is compounded by elements of narrative repetition, particularly in the dialogue. When Margaret grasps the

---

2   This comment appears in a discussion of Emily Brontë's *Wuthering Heights*, a novel that, along with Charlotte's *Jane Eyre*, operates as a Gothic ur-text which has inspired many imitations (Stoneman, 1996). Cf. Hattenhauer's reference to the great-aunt in the tower as 'the madwoman in the attic' (2003: 56).

3   All subsequent references are to this edition.

hands of her namesake in the tower, she hears the words that will be spoken and heard again on Paul's departure. Carla speaks often of what they will do when her brother arrives, and she begins this refrain again almost as soon as he has departed. The pattern of arrival and departure established in relation to the two men means that by the end of the narrative, it is unclear whether the title of the story refers to Margaret's visit, the captain's, or Paul's.

The confusion caused by the narrative's circular temporality is compounded by the maze-like spatial location within which the action takes place. The house, with its many rooms and corridors, is an unimaginable space. It is not a *home* but an anthropomorphised construction with its 'long-boned structure' (101); it is also an endlessly repeated exhibit of itself. In a fairy-tale like episode, Carla shows Margaret two identical rooms, one in gold and one in silver, and when Margaret enquires who uses the rooms, Carla replies 'No one' (103). (One expects the third room in this sequence to be of bronze, but instead it is the room of mirrors.) In sum, both the spatial and temporal details provided can be described, with some justification, as *deliberately* unhelpful.

In the section which follows, I refer to contextual frame theory to demonstrate how it is that the reader of Jackson's story is so comprehensively hoodwinked into believing that Paul exists and that he is Carla's brother. Emmott's work with contextual frames shows how readers use the information stored in these frames to correctly identify the referent of pronouns (1997). Margaret is the focalizer of the story, but the depth to which the ostensibly third-person narrative is immersed in Margaret's consciousness is not immediately evident to the reader. Only at the end of the story is the reader made aware that Paul and the great-aunt exist only for Margaret, prompting many frame repairs; in addition, the reader realises that the scene in the tower could not have taken place when the tower is described (for the first and only time) as 'ruined' (124). The reader must then perform a frame replacement and substitute instead a scene in which Margaret *tries* the door of the tower but is unable to gain entry. From the moment Paul arrives, the reader is led to believe that he is Carla's brother:

> …and Carla said, "Brother, here is Margaret." *He* was tall and haughty in uniform… Next to him stood his friend, a captain (108, my emphasis).

The 'He' which follows on immediately from Carla's introduction refers to a man who is not the captain. Moreover, the captain is never referred to by name, which allows the reader to assume that Carla means Paul whenever she refers to her brother. In the scenes which follow Paul's arrival before

Margaret's visit to the tower, a pattern is established in which the characters are scrupulously bound into every frame in careful descriptions such as the following: 'They went for a picnic, Carla and the captain and Paul and Margaret, and Mrs. Rhodes waved to them from the doorway as they left, and Mr. Rhodes came to his study window and lifted his hand to them' (111). In this sentence, all the characters mentioned by name are primed, bound and textually overt. Mr and Mrs Rhodes, however, will not be present for the picnic and are bound out of the frame from this point onwards. Paul, however, remains bound, and is textually overt in his conversations with Margaret. In the reader's mind, Paul exists as much as Margaret, Carla and the captain. On subsequent readings, the reader must perform frame repairs in striking each of Paul's utterances and considering how each scene plays out without him. Textual clues previously unnoticed become evident: for example, Carla refers to Margaret as 'odd' and looks at her 'strangely', and the reason for this is that she does not hear Paul's remarks, such as his offer to show Margaret the rose garden. Carla, in her refusal to respond to Margaret's curiosity regarding the tower, is established as someone with a habit of ignoring the utterances of others when it does not suit her to reply; as such, her lack of response to Paul's conversational turns is not sufficient on a first reading to alert the reader to any possible anomaly. There are other clues in sentences such as the following: 'After dinner they played charades, and even Mrs. Rhodes did Achilles with Mr. Rhodes, holding his heel and both of them laughing and glancing at Carla and Margaret and the captain' (109). The reader assumes 'they' to refer to Paul as well as the named characters in this sentence, so even though he is not textually overt as the others are, he is still bound and primed into the frame, and in fact becomes textually overt in the sentence which follows when he speaks to Margaret. There is another example of the same tactic here: 'And they played word games in the evening, and Margaret and Paul won, and everyone said Margaret was so clever' (109). The 'everyone' in this sentence is assumed to include Paul, so he remains bound and primed to the frame, even though his own cleverness has apparently been ignored by those assembled. The most blatant clue, however, is provided in the scene in which Margaret is watching Mrs Rhodes sew while 'Carla and the captain bent over a book together'. Paul is not bound into this frame and is therefore assumed *not* to be present. Carla gently rebukes Margaret with the words 'Margaret, do come and look, here. Mother is always at her work, but my brother is rarely home' (110). If the reader weren't convinced by this stage that Paul is Carla's brother, this is a clear indication that Carla is referring to the captain. On first reading, the reader might perhaps believe that Carla's intention is to criticise Margaret's inattention to the other guests in the house and thus Paul and the captain are included together in her reference to 'my brother'. When the narrative reaches its conclusion and the captain is positively identified as Carla's brother, the resulting confusion renders indecipherable the pronouns used by Paul in his closing remarks before departure. He claims to 'care for [the house] constantly, even when *they* forget', and states that nothing in the house can be replaced: 'All *we* can do is add to it' (123, emphases in original). It would seem that Paul is referring to himself and the Rhodes family, but in touching Mrs Rhodes' embroidery frame as he speaks, he appears to imply that Mrs Rhodes adds to the house as she embroiders its image. If Paul is including the Rhodes family in his 'we', then Carla and the others presumably share the same status as Paul, who claims that without the house he 'could not exist' (123). Epistemological uncertainty reaches such a peak at this point that contextual frame theory cannot help the reader sort through the increasingly tangled jumble of what is to be believed and what can be discredited.

There is textual evidence to support the reading that the house and its occupants, including Margaret, are nothing but figures woven into a tapestry, just as words are woven into a story. Margaret witnesses the creation of 'doors and windows, carvings and cornices' under Mrs Rhodes' hands, and indeed, Margaret's own entrapment: '[t]he small thread of days and sunlight…that bound Margaret to the house, was woven here as she watched' (110). The grounds of the house are included: the 'proper forest' with its 'neat trees' and too-green moss is also part of a tapestry on display in the breakfast room (111). Margaret is afraid of the room of mirrors because 'it was so difficult for her to tell what was in it and what was not' (104). The objects in this room such as the table and the wooden bowl which are bound, primed and textually overt may not have any tangible presence at all, and, of course, as elements in a fictional text, the table and bowl exist only as signifiers to evoke an image of the signified in the mind of the reader. Margaret partially guesses the truth when she uses a metaphor of the house as a story: 'perhaps, she thought, from halfway up the stairway this great hall, and perhaps the whole house, is visible, as a complete body of story together, all joined and in sequence' (102). Coupled with this metaphor are numerous references to patterns and images that are too large to be seen except from far away, just as one must read the whole story to understand its import. In another scene, an anthropomorphism connected with Margaret's world-view hints at the possibility of conscious life in inanimate images: 'Margaret felt surely that she could stay happily and watch the small painted people playing' (107). The same device is used in the scene depicting the morning after the ball:

> the gay confusion of helping one another dress…seemed all to have happened longer ago than memory, to be perhaps a dream that might never have happened at all, as perhaps the figures in the tapestries on the walls in the dining room might remember, secretly, an imagined process of dressing themselves and coming with laughter and light voices to sit on the lawn where they were woven (121).

In the final scene, both Carla and Margaret are still wearing their ball gowns, and Carla - laughing - invites Margaret to sit beside her on the lawn as models for Mrs Rhodes' tapestry.

The discussion in this essay has made use of contextual frame theory to account for the numerous adjustments the reader is required to make on reading 'A Visit', and has suggested a possible reading in which the house and its occupants are no more than figures in a tapestry. It has been noted how contextual frame theory falters when confronted with unreliable narration and the resulting epistemological uncertainty. However, it should be noted that frame repairs and replacements do not efface original impressions and the reader is left with the idea of a living consciousness trapped within a woven image. To place the story in its Gothic context once more, the conventions of this genre are employed here to express the living death experienced by women expected to immerse themselves in the home and devote their lives to it. Wallace writes of the civil death which was the legal status of married women in 1765 (2013: 2) and Jackson herself struggled with the domesticity expected of women in post-war America (Smith, 2009: 152-161). Margaret's 'death', therefore, can be read figuratively not as a physical death from a broken heart, but as the death of what Margaret's life *might* have been had she not been bound to the house.

List of references

Bowman, B. (1983) Victoria Holt's Gothic Romances: A Structuralist Inquiry. In J. E. Fleenor (ed). *The Female Gothic*. Montréal: Eden Press, 69–81.

Emmott, C. (1997) *Narrative Comprehension: A Discourse Perspective*. Oxford: Oxford University Press.

Fleenor, J.E. (ed). (1983) *The Female Gothic*. Montréal: Eden Press.

Hattenhauer, D. (2003) *Shirley Jackson's American Gothic*. Albany: State University of New York Press.

Jackson, S. (1996 [1950]) The Lovely House. In J. C. Oates (ed). *American Gothic Tales*. New York: Plume, 204–225.

Jackson, S. (2013 [1950]) A Visit. In S. E. Hyman (ed). *Come Along With Me: Classic Short Stories and an Unfinished Novel*. New York: Penguin, 101–125.

Kosofsky Sedgwick, E. (1986) *The Coherence of Gothic Conventions*. New York: Methuen.

Punter, D. & Byron, G. (2004) *The Gothic*. Oxford: Blackwell.

Smith, A. (2009) Children of the Night: Shirley Jackson's Domestic Female Gothic. In *The Female Gothic: New Directions*. London: Palgrave, 152–165.

Stockwell, P. (2002) *Cognitive Poetics: An Introduction*. London: Routledge.

Stoneman, P. (1996) *Brontë Transformations: The Cultural Dissemination of 'Jane Eyre' and 'Wuthering Heights'*. London: Prentice Hall.

Wallace, D. (2013) *Female Gothic Histories: Gender, History and the Gothic*. Cardiff: Cardiff University Press.

Wallace, D. & Smith, A. (eds). (2009) *The Female Gothic: New Directions*. London: Palgrave.

Fictional consciousness in comics: Ascribing a mind to Iris Pink-Percy in Rachael Ball's *The Inflatable Woman*

1. Introduction

The expansion of Anglo-American comics scholarship in recent years derives in part from a long-overdue recognition that comics deserve study as a medium in their own right. A more enlightened generation of comics scholars have voiced protests against the conflation of comics with literature because such comparisons are misguided, unhelpful, and ultimately stem from an unnecessary anxiety about the status of comics as a fitting subject for study at higher educational levels. Comics are often subject to the criticism that their medium-specific immediacy renders them ill-suited for the kind of intellectual and critical analysis to which purely verbal texts lend themselves. Instead of treating comics as an inferior subset of literature as it is represented by prose narratives, a more productive line of enquiry involves a rejection of the assumption that narrative is independent of the medium in which it appears and to develop analytical approaches and frameworks which enable the scholar to focus on storytelling as dictated by the constraints and possibilities of the medium in which the story is told. The study of narrative across media is today led by such luminaries as Marie-Laure Ryan and David Herman, and it opens up opportunities for interdisciplinary exploration and academic collaboration with scholars from other fields of enquiry such as film, art, psychology, and the cognitive sciences.

This study takes for its focus the creation of fictional consciousness in comics and explores aspects of visual storytelling in order to account for how a comics reader ascribes a mind to a visually-rendered character. Focalization is central to the study of fictional consciousness and comics scholarship brings a fresh perspective to this concept, one which has occasioned much debate in the study of prose narratives. The application of previous focalization research to a different medium expands the scope of the discussion and entails the possibility of fresh insights. I begin by placing the primary text under discussion in its context as a member of the canon of publications in the genre of graphic medicine, and its status as an autobiographical text. I discuss how genre and public discussions surrounding cancer discourse might affect or even dictate reader expectations, and to complement this discussion I examine the book's critical reception and real reader responses to the character of Iris. There follows a very brief discussion of current debates in comics scholarship and a cautionary note regarding the omission of any discussion of page layout in this study; discussion of the same features heavily in most comics scholarships, but is not pursued here. I then turn to a more detailed exploration of three areas which contribute to character construction in comics: the depiction of face and body, speech and thought representation, and pictorial metaphor. The final section investigates the concept of focalization in relation to the construction of a fictional mind and endorses the suggestion from film theory that images can simultaneously display several levels of narration.

The primary text for this study is Rachael Ball's *The Inflatable Woman* (hereafter *TIW*) published by Bloomsbury in 2015. Where illustrations are featured to support the argument, all page references are to this edition. The author of this study is a reader in the Western tradition, hence comments relating to reader response to images and reading paths should be understood within the conventions of this tradition. There are numerous terms used for the kind of narrative under discussion here, many of which are tainted by the value judgements of those who coined them; for example, 'graphic novel' has become popular with publishers who wish to capitalise on adult enthusiasm for such narratives, but who do not wish to use the descriptor 'comics' for fear that this term is associated with publications aimed for consumption by children and superheroes enthusiasts. I have no problem with the word 'comics' and I use it wherever possible throughout, as a catch-all term which encompasses every kind of graphic storytelling, including the text under discussion.

Summary of the story

Zookeeper Iris discovers two lumps in her right breast and is diagnosed with cancer. While Iris is undergoing a mastectomy and receiving treatment, she enters into an online correspondence with 'sailorbuoy-39', or Henry, who describes himself as a lighthouse keeper. Iris, or 'balletgirl42', tells him that she is a prima ballerina. Iris and Henry meet for a date, following which Iris buys a wedding veil. Iris' friend Maud urges her to tell Henry how she feels, but when Iris writes to Henry that she loves him, Henry responds with the news that he has been posted to a lighthouse in the North Pole with no internet or telephone reception and he must say farewell forever. Iris breaks down during her next hospital appointment.

Maud and Granma Suggs drive Iris to The Helping Hand, an alternative clinic for cancer sufferers. Iris finds it impossible to communicate with the other women present, inspiring those running the clinic to take drastic action:

Plan X, or The Early Death Experience. The women dig a huge hole in the garden, and Iris is tricked into spending the night there. Polly, one of the other patients, arrives with wine and talks to Iris about the purpose of the exercise. Iris is visited in the night by all the nightmarish visions which have haunted her throughout her illness, but emerges from the hole the next day to cheers and congratulations. Iris leaves the clinic and takes the train back to the zoo. The journey is peaceful until Iris spots Henry standing at a station. He calls and waves to her, and she waves back as the train pulls out, but she knows the dream has gone: as the reader is already aware, Henry is not a lighthouse keeper after all.

The story closes a year later, when crowds fill the zoo for a sold-out World Tour: Maud plays the violin while the penguins perform acrobatics, and Iris, dressed in a tutu, leaps onto the stage to tumultuous applause.

2. Context

This section explores the contextual background of *TIW* and will consider the following topics in turn: the genres of graphic medicine and autobiography; public discourses surrounding cancer and other comics which deal with the same subject; and finally, the book's critical reception and real reader responses to the character of Iris.

The contextual background of *TIW* is relevant to the purposes of this study in that the character whose fictional consciousness is under discussion is an avatar of an author writing through the comics medium about her experience of cancer. *TIW* therefore belongs to two genres: its subject matter places it within the genre of graphic medicine, and its basis in lived experience means the book cannot help but be considered autobiographical. Iris as character stands in not just for the author, however, but for all those who are living with cancer; as a cancer patient, Iris signifies on a level beyond the personal. Naturally, the reader's experience with public discourse surrounding cancer will encourage a certain amount of projection onto the character, and the nature of this projection is arguably pre-determined by narratives which are sanctioned through repetition to the exclusion of other narratives which do not fit the pattern. Any negative reader-response to Iris could well be the result of the pre-conditioning occasioned by the prevalence of entrenched and regulated cancer narratives. Reviews from critics and real readers are included in this section to gauge the kind of reaction and response to the character of Iris on the publication of *TIW*, but, by way of a tangential observation, it should be noted that the critical response highlights the inadequacy of language used about comics: professional reviewers were struggling even to follow the plot in some cases, and comments proffered as insightful reveal only a lack of engagement with the medium. Real reader responses to the character oscillated between whole-hearted acceptance and disappointment.

Stories of trauma, loss or illness expressed through the medium of comics has become such a popular and rapidly growing trend that 'graphic medicine' is now fully recognised as a separate genre. Baetens and Frey offer the observation that 'the graphic novel seems to have an elective affinity with stories of the self, the self in crisis because of history or trauma, maybe because…the self is harder to remove when a work is drawn as well as narrated' (2015: 177). Personal experiences dealt with to date in this medium have included epilepsy (David B's *Epileptic*), obsessive compulsive disorder (Ian Williams' *The Bad Doctor*), grief (Nicola Streeten's *Billy, Me & You*), eating disorders and sexual abuse (Katie Green's *Lighter Than My Shadow*), rape (Ravi Thornton and Andy Hixon's *The Tale of Brin and Bent and Minno Marylebone*), depression (John Stuart Clark's *Depresso*), and cancer (Miriam Engelberg's *Cancer Made Me A Shallower Person* and Marisa Acocella Marchetto's *Cancer Vixen*). Rachael Ball's novel is positively identified as a contribution to this genre in Andy Oliver's review for the online blog *Broken Frontier*, in which he describes the novel as 'a visionary entry in the graphic medicine canon' (2017).

Many publications categorised as 'graphic medicine', including those listed above, are autobiographical accounts, and Ball's novel is no exception. *TIW* recounts Ball's own experience of breast cancer, mastectomy, and the process of reconstruction which is referred to in the book's title. Rocío Davis notes that 'the subjects of the autobiographical comics are, most often, graphic artists themselves. The reader is privileged to participate in the performance of both memory and art, and the complex interaction between them' (2005: 269), and Martha Kuhlman, who provides an overview of some important contributions to the genre in her 2017 essay, writes that '[l]ines drawn by hand register the state of mind of the cartoonist, and thus represent the subjective nature of one's changing sense of self in the grip of illness' (119). This observation has relevance for any discussion of artistic style as a carrier of meaning, and it underlines the very personal nature of the experience of producing this book, because Iris, Ball's stand-in, has to be continually re-drawn.

In his 2007 book *This Book Contains Graphic Language*, Rocco Versaci devotes a chapter to the 'special reality' created by comics memoirists, the phrase itself taken from Will Eisner's autobiographical work *To the Heart of the Storm*: 'fact and fiction became blended with selective recall and result in a special reality. I came to rely on the truthfulness of visceral memory' (Eisner, 1991: xi). Versaci pursues Eisner's comments in his discussion of the relationship between memoir and the representation of the truth. He references the work of Hayden White, who has famously claimed that history is fiction in his *Tropics of Discourse,* and notes that Paul Eakin makes similar arguments with respect to the practice of autobiography in *How Our Lives Become Stories* (Versaci, 2007: 57). Expressions of the past are not unfiltered and narratives retold in the present become coloured by the operations of perspective and re-creation. Versaci summarises this very succinctly: 'the "facts" of a life are altered by their translation into some representational medium [and] "telling the truth" in memoir is not always a straightforward process' (57).

Versaci notes that a variety of first-person perspectives are available to memoirists, and that comics memoirs 'have additional ways to express and layer the first-person perspective' (48), including an additional signifier, namely the artistic style of images. He claims that 'the visual component… allows…memoirists to represent the complicated and shifting nature of the self' (49). This shifting self can include a split self, a self as defined by others, or a self as constructed by a culture and social community.

In her work on split selves in fiction, Catherine Emmott comments that this split 'commonly occurs at times of personal crisis' (2002: 153), and she examines research on metaphor analysis in the portrayal of a split self. For example, Emmott mentions Lakoff's container metaphors (156) and there is an example of exactly this sort of metaphor in *TIW* (see figures 1a and 1b below). When Iris has been brought to her lowest point, she no longer recognises herself and describes herself as 'a hollow thing', similar to an empty container.

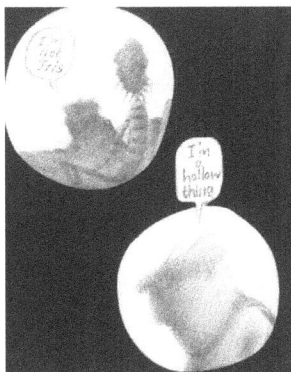

Figure 1a, p. 436

251

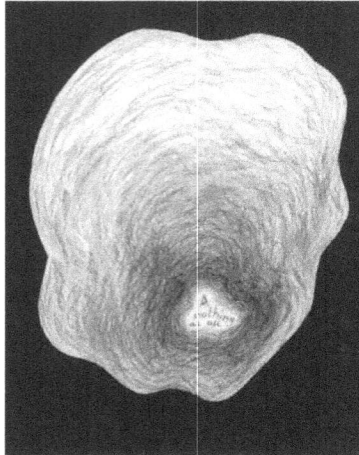

Figure 1b, p. 437

In section 4.4 below, I examine pictorial metaphor as a way of expressing one's own truth. The visual depiction of a metaphor or an analogy to express emotion is widely used in comics and it presents no problem to habitual readers of such texts: Versaci perceptively notes that 'readers already view comic books as "unreal," so any further distortion of reality becomes a mere extension of the form' (2007: 76). Leigh Gilmore explores the limitations of language in the expression of trauma and asserts that trauma survivors, in repeatedly testifying verbally to their emotional experience, create 'a conscious language that can be repeated in structured settings' (2001: 7), but which is inimical to the unconscious lived experience of trauma. This telling of pre-determined stories in a sanctioned setting is reflected in Judy Segal's research on the public discourse surrounding cancer narratives.

In the context of an article on the subject of Marjane Satrapi's *Persepolis*, an autobiographical account of Satrapi's own experience of the Iran-Iraq war (2008), Rocío Davis writes that 'autobiographical comics cannot...be read solely as a personal account, the cultural connotations of the stories and the narrative choices signifying on the level of national drama and attesting to the complex interweaving of the strategies of meaning' (2005: 270). Similarly, cancer narratives contribute to an existing public discourse on illness. In studies published in 2007 and 2012, Segal investigates the more sinister side of cancer narratives. She concludes that personal narratives often take on standard plots and features of existing cancer stories which have already been rehearsed many times, such as an opening scene in which a lump is discovered (this is indeed true of *TIW*). These stories focus on the cure rather than the cause, and the cancer sufferer is often described metaphorically as a warrior in battle against an implacable enemy. The problems inherent in these stories are manifold, not least of which is the entailment that the cancer patient who does not recover is in some way to blame for simply not fighting hard enough. Segal focuses on the regulatory function of these stories, and how one of their most insidious effects is the sidelining of other narratives which do not follow the prescribed pattern. The accepted stories provide information for sufferers, but they also evaluate and govern. Naturally, the generic and conventionalised ways in which illness is discussed generates reader expectations with regard to such narratives and reader response can be dictated by the extent to which the story matches these expectations.

Other cancer narratives in comics format include Miriam Engelberg's *Cancer Made Me A Shallower Person* (2006) and Marisa Acocella Marchetto's *Cancer Vixen* (2006), both of which have gained some critical attention (Segal, 2007, 2012; Stoddard Holmes, 2014; Tensuan, 2011). Ball's novel is very different from these two publications in many respects, the most obvious departure being that the protagonist, Iris Pink-Percy, is an avatar for the author, whereas Engelberg and Marchetto draw representations of their physical selves. Iris' diagnosis, treatment and recovery are expressed through metaphor, caricature and grotesque mockery, which is indicative of mental activity either on Iris' part or on the part of her creator. As such, the purpose of the book feels different to that of the other two titles mentioned: Marchetto's book is genuinely informative about the disease, as is Engelberg's to a lesser extent. Ball's novel is less a self-help guide than a genuine attempt to capture the experience of illness and to express it in a unique way. The comics medium both permits and invites the exploitation of the interplay of verbal and visual layers as a way of evoking experience. Martha Stoddard Holmes notes that a minimalist representation of characters allows for the depiction of an unstable self (2014: 148), and Andy Oliver notes in his very perceptive review that Ball's 'forceful visual symbolism…uses an ever shifting sense of warped perspective to underline those moments when Iris feels dehumanised or overawed by the realities of her situation'. Oliver writes that 'as readers we become fully invested in Iris…as she adapts to the challenges ahead' (2017).

Amongst the many reviews of *TIW*, Oliver's is by far the most perceptive. Many reviewers produced overly-simplistic assessments or a selection of catch-all statements which will hardly satisfy a competent comics reader. Sarah Gilmartin writing for the *Irish Times* produced the observation that '[p]encil drawings against a black background highlight Iris's predicament as the world turns bleak around her' while blithely ignoring the fact that the only colour sequence in the book is Iris' terrifying vision of the paper dolls coming to attack her, all of whom are bleeding red from the breast. Michelle Martinez (*The New York Journal of Books*) recognises that the book is unlike other comics on the same theme; however, this particular reviewer's response is interesting because her confusion around Henry's online catfishing reveals that she has not understood the scene in which Henry rows his boat towards shore after his date with Iris and drives away in a car, which tells the reader that Henry is not the lighthouse keeper he pretends to be. As a consequence, perhaps, of her lack of experience in reading comics, Martinez does not consider Iris to be a fully-rounded character. She comments, '[f]urther attention to building Iris as a character would have created stronger engagement in this fast-paced story'.

Reviews written by the book's audience rather than its critics appear on the Goodreads site (https://www.goodreads.com). Most of these reviews are very positive, with many readers extolling the artwork. One reader comments on the use of pictorial metaphor (see section 4.3 below) as follows: 'Powerful symbolism is incorporated, such as illustration of train = giving up while emergency stop pull = will to live' (see figures 2a and 2b below). Another reader writes about their response to the character of Iris: 'Iris, the protagonist, is someone you connect with instantly, even if she may not be relatable'; however, a third reader found their expectations disappointed: 'a technically decent book, I was hard pressed to find its heart'.

Figure 2a, p. 76

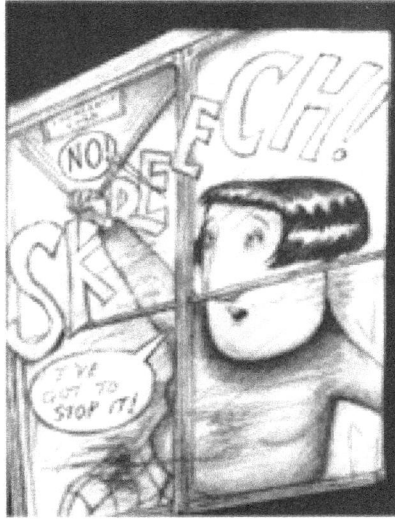

Figure 2b, p. 80

3. Current Debates

Owing to spatial constraints, the scope of this section is limited to only three areas of comics scholarship which are the focus of current debate: word/image parity, status anxiety, and sequentiality versus network, or 'braiding'. Finally, I have explained why page layout is not considered in this study.

One of the most hotly contested issues in comics scholarship is undoubtedly the relationship between word and image. Most comics theorists will have some kind of take on this issue, but psychologist Neil Cohn is one of the most vocal and vociferous supporters of word/image parity and the establishment of a 'visual language' of comics (2013). Compelling though his arguments might be, his theories of a visual language system are perhaps better suited to Japanese manga comics which feature a highly codified set of images. Cohn's choice of examples are often created by himself for the purposes of his argument; examples taken from real texts are limited in scope and not applicable to any graphic narrative which does not make use of the symbols discussed. Hannah Miodrag praises Cohn's linguistic awareness over that of other critics (Miodrag, 2013: 109), but she is very clear on her position that words and images belong to two different systems, one arbitrary and the other motivated.

Miodrag's book is a refreshing addition to comics scholarship in that she boldly debunks some dubious but widely-accepted claims. She holds that the all-too frequent comparisons between literature and comics have come about as a result of needless status anxiety, and notes that this approach takes no account of the specificities of comics as a medium. Along with word/image parity, Miodrag rejects the emphasis on sequentiality so beloved of Scott McCloud and his followers, and privileges instead the web or jigsaw approach over linear progression; this position is much more in keeping with Thierry Groensteen's influential work on braiding (Groensteen, 2007, 2013).

The fragmentary nature of comics and the format of page and panels is another area which attracts a great deal of critical comment. McCloud's notion of closure relating to the gutters has generated some lively discussion on the subject of narrative time in comics, much of it in rebuttal of McCloud's rather limited theories. While the subject of page and panel layout is a fascinating one, I do not intend to pursue it here for the following reason. Rachael Ball posted a single panel from *TIW* online, on a daily basis, as part of her search for a publisher, and the book's final appearance - over 70% of its pages feature only one panel - is a result of this activity. When more than one panel appears on a page in *TIW*, this is the result of an editorial decision. While I do not wish to argue that it is therefore impossible to comment on the aesthetic effect of layout given the circumstances of production, it would be disingenuous to claim that these effects were the result of authorial intention, and given the spatial constraints of this essay, I will turn instead to a discussion of other medium-specific considerations which in the case of this particular text more closely reflect the outcome of an artistic process.

4. Introduction: Three Medium-Specific Characteristics of Comics

The following section focuses on three medium-specific characteristics of the formal properties of comics: the portrayal of the character's face and body, speech and thought presentation through speech balloons and other devices, and pictorial metaphor. Each aspect will be explored in relation to the text under discussion following a brief outline of that aspect as it is represented in comics scholarship.

It is important to note from the outset that comics is a medium, not a genre (Wolk, 2007: 11; Baetens and Frey, 2015: 7). Comics resists the attempt at explication in terms of literature, film, or art, and remains a separate storytelling medium with its own inherent complexities. Nevertheless, as Baetens and Frey point out, 'many aspects of narratology apply to the graphic novel, and it would be absurd not to benefit from the existing narratological research on storytelling' (2015: 163). Relevant scholarship from related disciplines can provide a helpful springboard, certainly, but comics research makes it clear that narrative cannot be studied independently of the form it takes; for example, concepts such as world-making, space and characterisation throw up new issues when applied to graphic narratives (164). Miodrag makes a similar point on the application of other analytical paradigms to the study of comics; she writes that 'we cannot simply build comics theory from pieces of existing theory without attuning these to the art form's particularities' (2013: 60), and she goes on to add that 'comics weave a connective tissue that enmeshes a multitude of textual fragments that can never be summarized by a single (or even taxonomic set of) "core" feature(s) that will comprehensively account for how we read them' (67). I have chosen the three aspects under scrutiny in this section because each has something pertinent to offer to the discussion of fictional consciousness and the creation of the character of Iris Pink-Percy.

4.1 Face and Body

Readers ascribe mental activity to characters in comics in watching their actions and in reading their facial expressions as a gauge of the character's emotional response to events. This section begins with reference to the work of Harry Morgan, who maintains that character acts as a cohesive force in this medium, binding the narrative together with the repetition of the character's image in each panel and across the pages; equally, Jan Baetens and Hugo Frey also note that the character is constantly before the reader's eyes. Alan Palmer argues in his influential monograph on fictional minds that every action performed by a character has mental activity behind it, and it is therefore possible to assess fictional consciousness without necessarily being given access to a character's life by a narrative intermediary. Paul Ekman claims that six basic human emotions are easily identifiable by the facial expressions which accompany these emotions, and Ed Tan suggests that more complex comics avoid any schema of recognisable emotions. Moreover, empirical research carried out by Charles Forceville and his colleagues reveals difficulties with the interpretation of facial expression not anticipated by Scott McCloud's proposed taxonomy. This leads the discussion to a consideration of representational versus caricatural depiction, and the representation of emotion through visualisation of conceptual metaphor.

In a 2009 article, Harry Morgan, author of *Principes des littératures dessinées* and one of the leading theoreticians of graphic storytelling, argues that character is the only real constant in such narratives: '[i]t is the character that gives the image sequence its semantic cohesion and it is around the character that the storytelling is organised' (35). Morgan writes that character provides the reference point for a reading of frame and sequence, allowing the reader to understand temporal and spatial sequential logic. In other words, the character is the first thing the reader looks for, and the reader follows the character frame by frame: where they are, what they do and when they do it. Baetens and Frey support this claim in their assertion that '[e]ven if graphic novels do tell stories, their first concern is not infrequently the portrait of the characters and the multiperspectival representation of their bodies' (2015: 176). They refer to the structuralism of the 1960s which reduced characters to agents or actors 'in abstract structural diagrams' (174); as such, a character's appearance or psychological profile would be of little importance. A character in comics, however, is constantly present before the reader's eyes in a series of portraits. Baetens and Frey understand this as a characteristic of comics which marks them out as a very specific form of storytelling with an important contribution to make to contemporary thought and the 'rediscovery of the body in cultural theory' (177), and they refer to the rising popularity of the 'actionless' or 'abstract' comics (180) to support this argument; however, their claim that what the reader is confronted with is the character's *body* and *face* and not the character's *thinking* (174) is perhaps more contentious. For example, this separation of mind from body is not easy to square with Alan Palmer's work on fictional minds, and his claim that '[u]ltimately, it is impossible to separate physical actions from the mental life that lies behind them' (Palmer, 2007: 214). Palmer's concept of 'situated identity' maintains that 'we are not so much what we say we are, but what we do. Action is public and so is a fairly reliable, though not infallible, basis on which other individuals can judge the workings of our minds' (Palmer, 2004: 168-169). In prose narratives '[an] action will be described in a certain way for a particular purpose, and different descriptions of the same action can obviously vary greatly in the ways in which they ascribe agency, responsibility, praise, criticism, blame, and so on' (Palmer, 2007: 215). It is surely the case that the same holds true for comics if the way in which an action is depicted within a panel or sequence of panels is equivalent or comparable to a prose description.

What follows is an examination of the possible ways in which a reader could construe a character's inner life from the depiction of a physical form. I consider Ekman's work on basic emotions and Tan's article in response to this research on the 'recognition of emotional expression in characters'; this is followed by a discussion of Forceville's empirical consideration of McCloud's theory of facial expression which leads in turn to considerations of caricature, and the visual rendering of conceptual metaphors to depict emotion.

In 1992, emotion psychologist Paul Ekman put forward an argument for six basic emotions which are in turn identified by each having nine characteristics, all of which must be present. Ekman claims that these six emotions are anger, fear, sadness, enjoyment, disgust, and surprise, although he acknowledges that there is some dissent over this number on the part of other scholars (170). Ekman argues convincingly that emotions are the product of evolution: 'the primary function of emotion is to mobilise the organism to deal quickly with important interpersonal encounters, prepared to do so in part, at least, by what types of activity have been adaptive in the past' (171). Emotions provide information about 'antecedent events, concomitant responses, and probable next behaviour', and are 'crucial to the development and regulation of interpersonal relationships' (177). Ekman also groups emotions into families. He has identified more than sixty 'anger' expressions (172). The more contracted the facial muscles, the more intense the emotion experienced (173). Ekman claims that there 'is robust, consistent evidence of a distinctive, universal facial expression for anger, fear, enjoyment, sadness and disgust' (175), but the 'evidence for a unique facial expression for surprise and contempt is not as firm' (176).

Ed Tan is interested in the application of Ekman's theories to comics (2001), and he focuses on the recognition of emotional expression in characters. He concludes that it may well be the case that comics he describes as 'popular' employ a schema of 'facial cues' that supply recognisable emotions, but, more interestingly, he also suggests that '[t]he more complex graphic novel may renounce from using the schema altogether, either because it is too explicit, or because the emotions that characters have are too complex to be 'told' through the face' (45).

Forceville, Stamenković and Tasić put these theories to the test in 2018, and conducted an experiment to test Scott McCloud's claim in *Making Comics* (2006: 80-101) that the six basic emotions identified by Ekman can be drawn by competent artists, and that readers can recognise both these emotions and the degree of the emotion's intensity. McCloud contends also that artists can draw combinations of the basic emotions to produce depictions of many more complex emotions; Forceville, Stamenković and Tasić note that McCloud is suggesting that the potential combinations should yield '2300 different drawn faces' (2018: 6). The data obtained from the experiment, however, demonstrates that McCloud's claim cannot be wholly substantiated in practice. While McCloud's competence as an artist is not in doubt, respondents did not recognise emotional expressions in line with McCloud's claims. The identification of the basic emotion expressions demonstrated reasonably consistent results, but more complex expressions proved far more controversial, to the extent that 'participants sometimes saw other components not intended to be there - in certain cases, these elements even overruled the effects of the intended primaries' (16). The result was 'a considerable degree of unpredictability' (19). Of course, facial expression is not the only criteria by which people assess other people's mental state, and, as acknowledged by Forceville, Stamenković and Tasić, a participant in an experiment viewing a decontextualised face is presented with an artificial situation that never arises in real life (or in comics). Facial expression is interpreted in conjunction with a host of other clues such as utterance, posture, background story, and so on. Forceville, Stamenković and Tasić also note that 'we should not underestimate the degree to which, both in real life and in comics, we *anticipate* fellow humans' or comic characters' emotions' (21)

What has not been touched upon as yet is the actual rendering of faces in comics, which more often than not leans toward caricature instead of faithful representation. To return to Harry Morgan's article entitled *Graphic Shorthand*, he notes that 'characters can be reduced to a few fixed traits, so as to be identifiable at first sight', and in fact, 'complexity comes at the expense of clear characterisation' (2009: 24). Stuart Medley contends that 'in experiments intended to determine what kinds of images allow for easy identification of objects, the most realistic image has been persistently demonstrated *not* to be the most communicative' (2010: 55, emphasis in original). Medley points to the 'sense among some comics critics, and many creators, that…realism is not the pictorial ideal' (67) and he seems to be implying that comics are inherently caricatural in nature: '[t]he degree of distillation or abstraction, the removal of realistic detail that all comics artists must address, is important to the way comics are perceived' (68).

Emotions can be represented metaphorically in visual images. In a 2005 article, Forceville asserts that comics have the ability to 'privilege aspects of ICMs [Idealized Cognitive Models] that are less dominant, or even absent, in its linguistic manifestations' (69). The example he chooses to explore is that of anger as depicted in the Astérix album *La Zizanie* (*Asterix and the Roman Agent* in its English translation). Forceville refers to the work of Zoltán Kövecses, who, like Ekman, suggests that 'conceptualizations of emotions are to a considerable extent universally shared' (Forceville, 2005: 71). Forceville lists the visual, non-linguistic features representative of anger in this album and demonstrates how these features exemplify the conceptual metaphors associated with anger, such as ANGER IS THE HEAT OF A FLUID IN A CONTAINER (for example, a character goes red and begins to emit steam as if physically boiling). He notes, however, that it 'is important to emphasize that no pictorial sign single-handedly cues anger: signs combine to suggest anger and the more signs are used, the more clear-cut and/or the more intense the anger is' (84). Equally, it is not the case that a particular sign always denotes anger. In another context, the same sign could convey a different emotion altogether.

I have provided below three images from *TIW* to exemplify the points discussed here. Iris' features, with the exception of her eyes, are caricatured rather than representational. The first example (see figure 3 below) presents the reader with a relatively easy passage to decipher. Iris sends a message, and waits for a reply. Her expression in its basic outlines is legible as 'anxious' in conjunction with the position of the hand at the mouth, and in context with the preceding panel. Similarly, Iris' relief and joy when the new message arrives is easy to read. As she smiles and clicks on the icon to display the message, a small love heart (a symbolic sign in Peirce's framework, outlined in section 4.3 below) flutters to the right of the panel. This love heart will be the last thing the reader reads on this two-page spread and is therefore in a position of maximum weight and significance.

Figure 3, p. 128-129

Susan Osborne, writing for *A Life in Books* (2015), noted that 'the skinny spectres of death pop up frequently', and the second example (see figure 4 below) shows the two grotesque figures who follow Iris from the point of diagnosis until she purges them during her Early Death Experience at The Helping Hand. Iris' expression in this image shows the defining features of fear identified by McCloud: her brows are lifted over wide eyes, and her lips are 'tightly stretched apart and opened' (McCloud 2006: 93). One might ask, however, whether this expression would be recognisable as fear when removed from its context. What makes the emotion legible in this case is arguably dependent on other factors such as the presence of the two *memento mori* figures with skull-like features. Iris stands in a spotlight with a strong shadow cast behind her, rendered speechless by the utterance of the smaller death figure, and she is trapped by patterns of stripes, bars and checks. (In fact, this latter detail is in evidence throughout many of the book's images.)

Figure 4, p. 78-79

Iris' emotional state is interpreted through both visual and verbal tracks in this section's final example (see figure 5 below). She is very small, and situated in a room that is sparsely furnished with only an uncomfortable-looking chair and a mirror, and she is seen as if at a distance or from a great height. In conjunction with the recitation of a poem from a narratorial voice-over whose speaker is a child addressing its mother, the visual imagery highlights Iris' fragility and vulnerability at this point. The visual and verbal tracks work together in this example to show the reader Iris' mental activity: she feels alone, she has no visible comforts, she is afraid, she feels vulnerable, and she exhibits a sense of guilt that is related to a child's fear that they are being punished for an unknown misdemeanour.

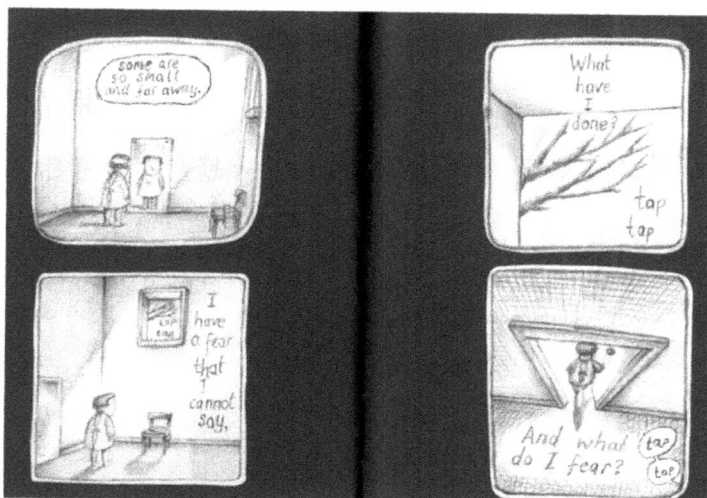

Figure 5, p. 42-43

Just as readers ascribe mental activity to a character by watching that character's actions and facial expressions, readers also make assessments based on a character's utterances both in the form of speech and thought.

4.2 Speech and Thought Representation

In their immensely popular and seminal work *Style in Fiction* ([1981] 2007), Geoffrey Leech and Mick Short set out a taxonomy of the ways in which speech and thought can be represented in prose fiction. While not all of their categories can be accommodated by the comics medium, it is worthwhile to investigate the points of cross-over and divergence. The speech categories are as follows (Leech and Short, 2007: 268):

NRSA	IS	FIS	DS	FDS
Narrative Report of a Speech Act	Indirect Speech	Free Indirect Speech	Direct Speech (norm)	Free Direct Speech

If Direct Speech (DS) represents the words of the character, then any move to the left on this continuum indicates an increased narratorial presence in the utterance, and movements to the right of DS demonstrate a stripping-away of the narrator; utterances in Free Direct Speech (FDS) therefore, are in prose fiction devoid of any narratorial markings such as quotation marks, and the utterance is presented as if produced entirely of the character's own volition. It is arguable that Indirect Speech (IS) can only occur in graphic narratives when one character is recounting the words of another. Both IS and FIS (Free Indirect Speech) require the presence of a narrator, and this is a highly contentious area in comics studies.

I have provided examples below from *TIW* to exemplify two of Leech and Short's categories of speech representation. The first, and most obvious, is the use of the speech balloon to represent DS. In figure 6 below, Iris is in conversation with Granma Suggs. The reading path in the Western tradition travels across the image from left to right and top to bottom, and the conversation between Suggs and Iris follows this path. Suggs makes five utterances and Iris two in this single image, but the direction of the tails of the speech balloons and the spatial layout makes it clear who says what when. Of note here is Ball's idiosyncratic use of speech balloons to encapsulate sound effects ('knock knock'), although in this instance it is entirely possible that Dr Magic does actually utter these words.

Figure 6, p. 160

The example in figure 7 below shows how NRSA (Narrative Report of a Speech Act) can be employed in this medium. The utterances of those wearing the 'I kicked the ass of cancer' T-shirts cannot be heard by Iris, a fact which is reinforced by the verbal track (her question 'What?'). The speech balloons do not contain recognisable lexical items, but indecipherable symbols. This device, used several times and in various circumstances throughout *TIW*, constitutes an NRSA because while the reader is aware of the utterance and the context in which it has been made, the actual words used remain a mystery. In this particular example, it is clear that Iris cannot hear the words spoken because she is distanced from those speaking; however, when those on the platform issue a collective 'Bye!', as indicated by the speech balloon with more than one tail, Iris can just about hear this word, demonstrated by the fractured appearance of the lettering.

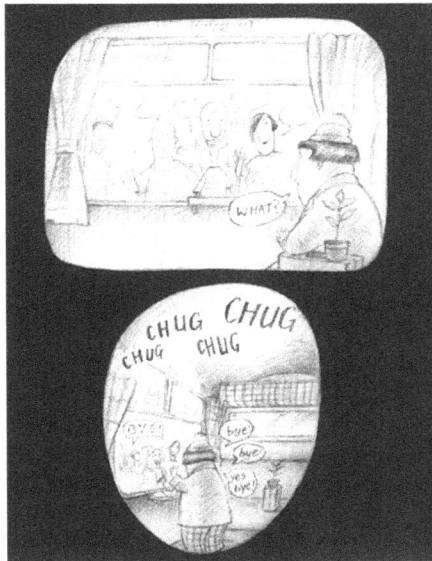

Figure 7, p. 502

The image in figure 8 provides an interesting example of an utterance that is a mixture of DS and NRSA: Iris' stricken explanation is offered in between sobs, inside a segmented speech balloon. It is possible that the words written here present Iris' utterance in its entirety, but it is equally possible that her conversation is truncated into a series of subject headings to convey to the reader the substance of a far longer utterance as Iris tells Maud of her diagnosis and her fears. Iris' words are represented as NRSA but with elements of DS: the reader knows an utterance was made and is also cognisant of some of

265

the words used, from which the substance of a much lengthier speech can be guessed at.

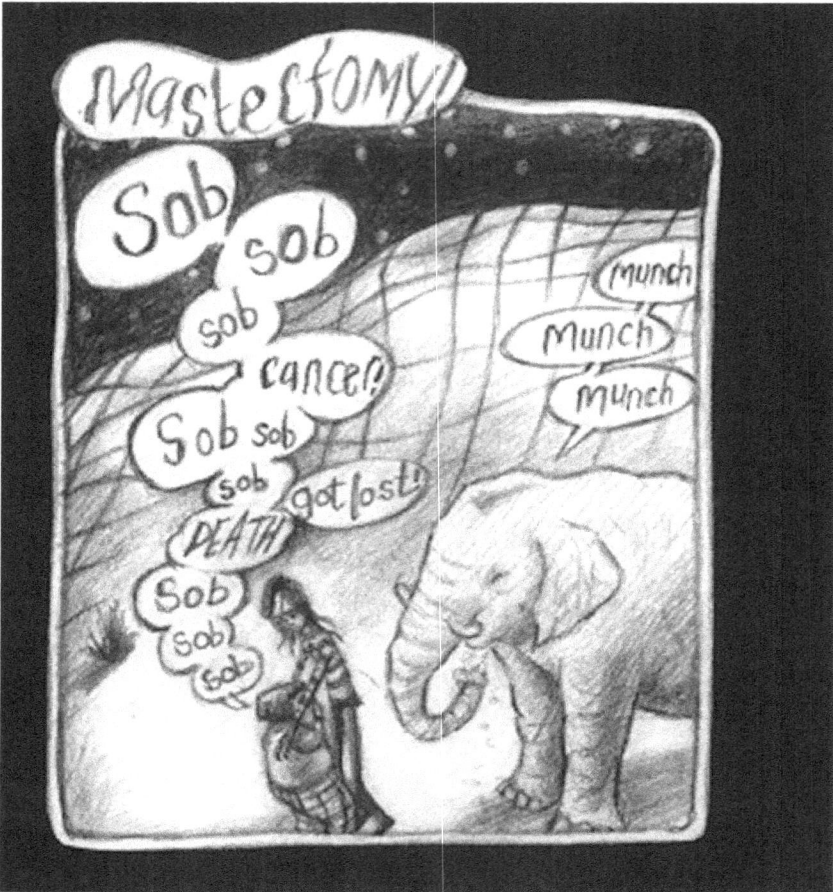

Figure 8, p. 86

The comics medium in general offers only limited space for verbal utterances and Ball has found an economical solution here. Lengthy utterances encroach on the image inside the frame and risk tipping the balance too far in favour of the verbal track. This latter consideration explains in part the relative scarcity of thought balloons in comparison with utterances in DS; this observation refers to *TIW* and other comics in general, although exceptions can, of course, always be found. For example, Guy DeLisle tells a fictionalised account of the story of Christophe André's kidnap and escape in *Hostage*, in which utterances in captions represent the thoughts of a man who cannot communicate with others because he is a prisoner and because he cannot speak either Chechen or Russian. The eponymous hostage is left alone for long stretches of the narrative. He talks out loud to himself on occasion, but by far the majority of his utterances are rendered in a form of Direct Thought (DT): words that appear in a caption that is a coloured differently from the rest of the text. This form of caption-box in comics is conventionally reserved for the narrator's voice, but in this particular story, the captions communicate both narrative information and the protagonist's thoughts. The reader is thus informed of narrative developments, and in the same manner is apprised of the hostage's anxiety through his mental cogitations. Without the latter, DeLisle's text would lack both tension and narrativity.

Having touched on the mechanisms for representing thought, I return briefly to Leech and Short in order to reproduce their categorisations of thought presentation as shown below (2007: 276).

NRTA	IT	FIT	DT	FDT
Narrative Report of a Thought Act	Indirect Thought (norm)	Free Indirect Thought	Direct Thought	Free Direct Thought

Leech and Short point out that in prose fiction, Indirect Thought (IT) is the norm for thought presentation, as opposed to DT being the norm for speech presentation. The reason is simple: the rendering of a character's thoughts verbatim is perceived as highly artificial in prose fiction (277), and it is more usual for a character's thoughts to be filtered in some way through the narrator. Many comics arguably lack a narrator entirely, and the option of IT in comics is therefore problematic, to say the least. Writers and artists do, however, make use of DT, but its use is necessarily localised. If used too often, DT very quickly appears contrived, and, as is the case with lengthy spoken utterances, risks overloading the verbal track at the expense of the visual. If the verbal track is allowed to significantly outweigh the visual, there comes a point where the identity of the text as a comic comes into question and the visual track is reduced to mere illustrations of the verbal. Even here, however, exceptions can be found: Posy Simmonds makes free and abundant use of passages of prose text in conjunction with stretches of narrative that is more recognisable as comics in format. (Simmonds, 2001, 2009, 2018). The panel in figure 9 below shows an example of DT in *TIW*, one of only a handful of similar examples in the book.

Figure 9, p. 17

Other thought balloons do appear from time to time, often containing nothing more than a question mark to indicate confusion on the part of a character. What has not yet been touched upon is the use of silence in comics. Baetens and Frey note that 'the number of graphic novels including large wordless sections and sequences is steadily increasing' (2015: 152). Some texts, such as Shaun Tan's enduringly popular *The Arrival*, are entirely wordless (Tan, 2006), and this silence 'invite[s] the reader to gain understanding through observation and deduction, and to decode the narrator's (or the protagonist's) intentions, to let symbols and icons "talk", [and] to deliver information on the implicit level' (Adler, 2011: 2278). Indeed, in *TIW*, approximately 40% of over 700 panels have no dialogue (although a percentage of this figure includes panels which feature a sound effect). This figure represents a high proportion of panels which exclude the verbal track, forcing the reader to engage with the visual, and to follow Iris' story through what can be deduced from her facial expressions, postures, gestures and actions. As Adler points out, '[s]ilence functions…not only as a simple absence of speech…but also as a vehicle of a large variety of emotions and mental states connected to the protagonists'

(2011: 2278). Figure 10 shows Iris, exhibiting hair loss from chemotherapy, in the hole at The Helping Hand. Polly, a resident at the clinic, visits Iris and advises her to 'think about all that sadness and tomorrow, leave it down here' (*TIW*, 481). The three wordless images in figure 10 are powerfully eloquent of Iris' silent despair.

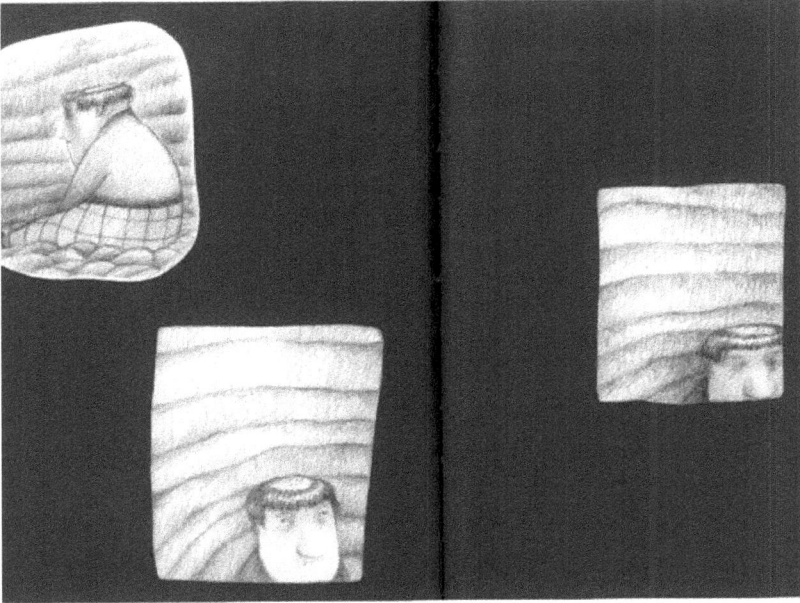

Figure 10, p. 482-483

Speech and thought balloons are capable of rendering far more than just the lexical items of a verbal utterance: the visual track can be deployed to communicate tone, volume, and other extra-linguistic information besides. Baetens and Frey mention 'grammatextuality', a concept coined by French theoretician Jean-Gérard Lapacherie, which refers to the visual form of the words in comics (2015: 153). The concept includes 'the form of the lettering, the configuration of the words in the speech balloons and the insertions of these balloons in the panels, the presence of letters and other written symbols within the fictional world, [and] the presence of...onomatopoeias' (154). An example from *TIW* is shown in figure 11 below. Iris has been told that her right breast is to be removed following the discovery of two cancerous tumours. The appearance of the hand-lettered word 'mastectomy' which hangs over Iris' head communicates to the reader Iris' misgivings about the operation. This is emphasised in the visual track by Iris' wide-eyed expression and the absence of the lower half of her face as a visual pre-echo of the removal of her breast.

269

Figure 11, p. 64

In another example from the same moment in the narrative, Iris' understanding of her situation is rendered as shown in figure 12. Iris is asked if she understands the information she has just been given. This panel gives us the response 'yes' and 'I've got breast cancer'. The word 'yes' appears to come from the tree which features as part of the text's many pictorial metaphors, but the words 'I've got breast cancer' form the tree's roots, thus rendering visually Iris' understanding that the cancer is rooted within her and is growing inside her breast; the breast itself is represented as the hill upon which the tree (the nipple) is standing.

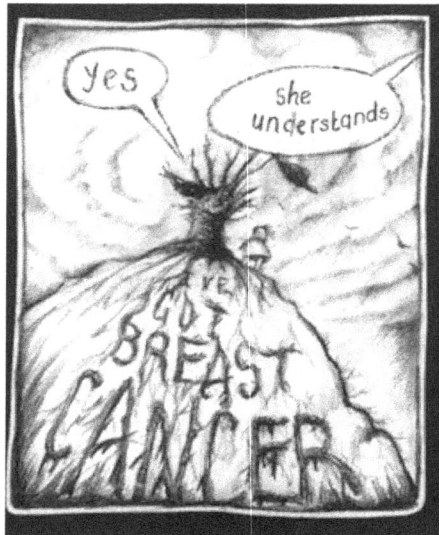

Figure 12, p. 60

Miodrag notes that 'bold format, underlining, capitals, and shifts in text size visualize the modulations of tone that are natural to speech' (2013: 71). The convention of using capital letters for the equivalent of shouting has passed into more modern forms of communication such as email and text messages: the larger the font and the heavier the type, the louder the volume. Miodrag is careful to note however that '[s]pacing and typography…are vital elements in comics' visual arsenal, but do not operate as signs standing in for an identifiable signified' (78). Her main concern, as we have seen, is to dismiss arguments that insist on the parity of word and image, but she concedes that 'the speech balloon remains a convincing proponent of comics-as-language (or, at any rate, as symbol system) insofar as it reads as a conventionalized sign, recognized as a visual signifier of sound whose border and script affect how we interpret particular instances of its use' (101). Miodrag notes that the speech balloon is exclusive to comics and that readers recognise 'by learned convention their relationship to the diegesis: not visible in the world-of-the-work as they are to the reader, these forms represent diegetic material nonetheless, visualizing for the reader what is audible for characters' (100-101). Achim Hescher also mentions this quality of speech balloons: '[b]alloon speech is verbal (as speech or writing) *and* pictorial (in its outline or shape), and diegetic *as speech*; the balloons, in contrast, are non-diegetic (for the characters see no speech balloons floating around them)' (2016: 149).

4.3 Pictorial Metaphor

This section is concerned with 'the literal depiction of textual metaphors' (Miodrag, 2013: 92) and how this can contribute to the construction of a fictional consciousness in the visual portrayal of an emotion or a state of mind. Versaci writes that 'we see comics as a metaphoric interpretation of reality and are therefore accepting - whether we are aware of it or not - of the subjective nature of "truth" in comics' (2007: 74). We saw an example in section 2 of a real reader interpreting a visual metaphor in an episode from *TIW*, in which the image was held to be directly representative of the character's mental activity. The use of pictorial metaphor is a very particular and medium-specific method of revealing fictional consciousness, and the deployment of visual metaphor can show emotional response in an immediate and visceral fashion.

Many critical studies of comics refer to the work of American philosopher, semiotician and scientist Charles Peirce (1839-1914), who differentiated three categories of sign: iconic, indexical and symbolic. Iconic signs are motivated and resemble that which they signify. Peirce's indexical sign is, as Miodrag notes, 'causal, based on real connection' (2013: 173), and Forceville describes indexical signs as having 'a metonymic relation' with their referents: he gives the example of footprints in the sand, which 'indexically signify the person who left them' (2005: 73). Symbolic signs, however, are entirely arbitrary and purely conventional. Any one sign may feature qualities of all three classifications listed above and may not fit comfortably into a single category. Peirce's work is naturally interesting to comics scholars because comics exhibit all three of these signs in many and various ways.

In her 2009 article on the interpretation of political cartoons, Elisabeth El Rafaie testifies to the 'prevalence of symbols and metaphors' (181) in such texts and examines the necessary competences to understand these cartoons. She concludes that 'interpretation is a matter of drawing on many different types of literacy, ranging from a familiarity with cartoon conventions and a broad knowledge of current events to the ability to draw analogies' (182). When presented with three political cartoons, the responses of participants in El Rafaie's experiment differed according to their final interpretation of the cartoon and 'what they actually *saw*' (182, emphasis in original). To explain these results, El Rafaie raises the question of abstraction. Cartooning always features a degree of abstraction, which 'involves reducing resemblance in order to amplify meaning', and the 'greater the degree of iconic abstraction, the more interpretative work and knowledge of cultural conventions are required on the part of the viewer' (183). Reader competency, therefore, involves not only the ability to interpret iconic abstraction, but a level of familiarity with conventions of the medium, one of which is a set of commonly-used signs which Forceville labels 'pictorial runes' (2011).

According to Peircean descriptors, the status of pictorial runes occupies a curious middle ground between the arbitrary 'through endless reuse', and the motivated in the original reasons behind their appearance (Forceville, 2011: 887). Forceville defines runes as 'non-mimetic graphic elements that contribute narratively salient information' (2011: 875). They are a limited set of elements and they can work in combination. Runes therefore share some characteristics with linguistic systems in that they are a relatively closed set of fixed forms which display a rudimentary syntax (876). Runes are the 'pictorial equivalents of what in language would be labeled metaphors, metonymies, or other tropes' and take the form of 'abstract-looking flourishes' (876) which seldom communicate meaning on their own. Forceville lists runes as speed lines, movement lines, runic droplets, spikes, spirals and twirls. Speed lines show the trajectory and velocity of an object or a character, whereas movement lines show trajectory in connection with a body part or object. Runic droplets appear around a character's head and represent water, sweat, tears or spit. Spikes are similar to droplets, and indeed, these two runes are often seen together; the primary function of spikes, however, is to indicate the production of sound. Spirals show negative emotions such as anger, disgust, or frustration, and twirls, which are more 'loopy' than spirals, can indicate movement, or dizziness and confusion if appearing above a character's head.

Nevertheless, the use of runes is not unambiguous. Different artists can use runes in different ways, and usage can differ even across and within the work of the same artist. The positive identification of runes is also not entirely unproblematic, as can be seen in the example from *TIW* below (figure 13). On the morning of her mastectomy, Iris dreams that she rows out to sea, past the lighthouse where she was hoping to find Henry, and reaches instead an island where a strange monkey-like figure asks her to mend a small doll by sewing its leg together. Iris does so, only to witness the monkey-man tear the doll's torso so 'the soul can get in…and out' (*TIW* 194-195).

Figure 13, p. 192-193

The same spiked lines accompany the monkey-man's action and Iris' reaction, evoking a different emotion in each case: the ripping of the doll is an horrific, shocking act and the spikes highlight the aggression with which this action is carried out. On a verbal level, the 'RIP' sound effect in this context could also be read as the abbreviation of 'Rest In Peace', given that what the reader is witnessing here is clearly an anxiety dream about Iris' forthcoming surgical procedure. Iris' horror is clear from her expression: eyes and mouth open, hands raised to her face, and the spikes emphasise her shocked response. In both panels, the spikes also serve to direct the reader's eye in framing the central image. Three spikes emanate from the tear in the doll's side, but it should be clear by now that none of the spikes discussed in this example are the runic spikes which indicate the production of sound. The purpose of these spikes is solely one of emphasis and directing the reader's eye. To conclude this section, the following examples provide a selection of the pictorial metaphors used in *TIW*, all of which contribute to the construction of Iris' consciousness. We have already seen in section 4.1 above that Iris is pursued throughout by two grotesque figures which represent Death, and reference was made in section 4.2 to the proliferation of breast-like images in the novel. One of the novel's more insightful reviewers, Sheila Pham, notes that '[t]he breast is a recurring image, analogous to different objects, such as a mound with a tree growing on top where the nipple would be' (2015, and see figure 12 above). As Iris rows away from the island under lowering skies in the nightmare sequence discussed above, she accidentally decapitates the 'baby' with her paddle. The doll-baby's head with its halo of blood has the appearance of an excised breast, the two small dots for eyes representative of Iris' two tumours (figure 14).

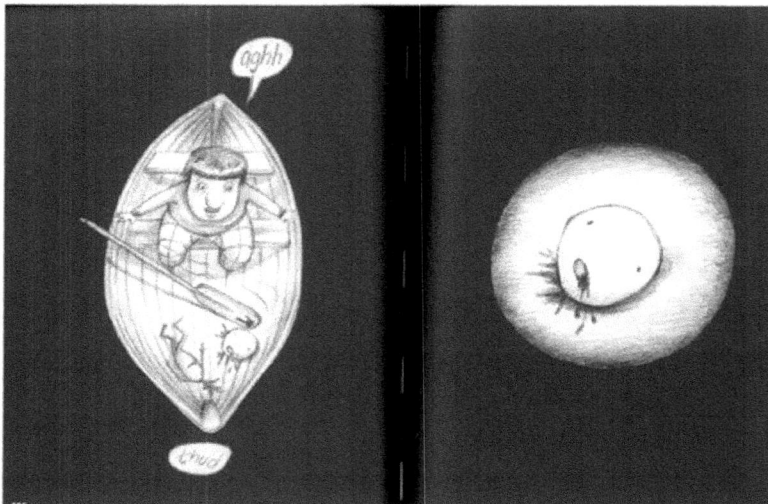

Figure 14, p. 200-201

When Iris is told she will have to undergo a mastectomy, two round breast-like panels show the doctor's mouth where the nipple should be (figure 15). Iris' metaphorical transformation into a moth at this moment is indicative of her feelings of physical fragility and temporal intransigence. The Iris-moth flutters towards the light of hope which is 'reconstruction' only to burn when Nurse

Bobby cruelly points out that the surgeons are 'not rocket scientists' (*TIW* p. 68 and see figure 16). Bird imagery pervades the novel, with Iris herself often represented by a motherless baby bird to convey both her vulnerability and her sense of fragility and isolation. As for Henry, his appearances are often filtered by Iris' consciousness, and this point is pursued further in the section on focalization below.

Figure 15, p. 62-63

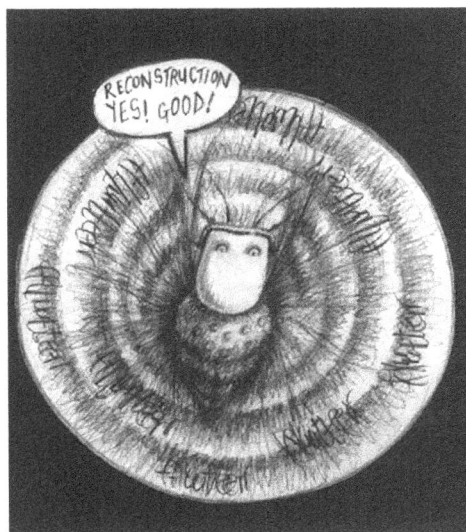

Figure 16, p. 67

5. Focalization

The concept of focalization is central to discussions of fictional consciousness in prose narrative, but as we shall see, its application to the same in comics is problematic without some medium-specific adjustment. In the section to follow, I outline Genette's theory of focalization and discuss conceptual modifications imported from film scholarship to address the difficulties created by the constantly shifting focalization in visual narrative. Included in the discussion is Branigan's assertion that several different narrations can run simultaneously in images, and Borkent's exploration of the concept of embodiment from cognitive linguistics demonstrates how visual modality allows the reader to construct composite viewpoints.

In a 2008 article which takes for its subject the presentation of minds, Mikkonen concludes that frameworks for the exploration of mind construction current in literary scholarship require some reassessment if they are to be usefully and productively applied to comics. The concept of focalization as it exists in research devoted to prose narratives is one such concept which requires a medium-specific reevaluation if it is to be a helpful tool in the study of fictional consciousness in texts which comprise a visual as well as a verbal track. Gérard Genette's theory of focalization continues to provide the basis for investigation of fictional consciousness in spite of the many subsequent revisions it has undergone since the publication of *Narrative Discourses* in 1972 (1980 in English translation), and Ann Miller devotes a chapter of her 2007 book *Reading Bande Dessinée* to the application of Genette's theory to French-language comic strips, with some modifications adopted from film scholarship.

Miller begins by restating that focalization falls under Genette's 'mood', a category which reflects the linguistic concept of modality in that it 'enables information to be affirmed with greater or lesser degrees of certitude or subjective investment' (Miller, 2007: 105). Focalization, according to Genette's model, is displayed in the processes of selection and restriction by which narrative information is conveyed. Genette separates the focalizer (who sees?) from the narrator (who speaks?), and he divides focalization into three types depending on the level of restriction to information, where zero focalization is an entirely unrestricted omniscient point of view, internal focalization presents the view of a particular character, and external focalization is limited to strictly behaviourist accounts with no access to mental processes.

In zero focalization, the narrator has knowledge of the character's thoughts. As we have seen, in the comics medium thoughts can be rendered by way of various devices such as thought balloons, dreams, visions and fantasy sequences. In figure 17 below, Iris is seen contemplating her forthcoming mastectomy and how it will affect her fantasy persona; in figure 18, Iris' dream features a metaphorical pre-echo of her imminent cancer diagnosis in the form of a huge boulder which is heading her way.

Figure 17, p. 215

Figure 18, p. 11

In the case of internal focalization, the information rendered is dependent on and coloured by the orientation and perspective of one of the characters. What is narrated is likely incomplete and possibly unreliable, but in representing that particular character's experience of being in the story world, the narration is endowed with its own epistemological veracity. In terms of purely physical viewpoint, internal focalization can take the form of the restricted field of vision of a particular character; in comics, this means that the panel shows the reader only that which the character can see at that moment. An example from *TIW* (see figure 19 below) shows Iris in hospital following her mastectomy. The image shows her hands and the rest of her body under the bedcovers, and the reader is positioned in a way which makes it clear that the image represents Iris' field of vision. Mikkonen notes how it is possible to reveal this subjective viewpoint by the inclusion of body parts which belong to the character doing the seeing at the edges of the image (2017: 161).

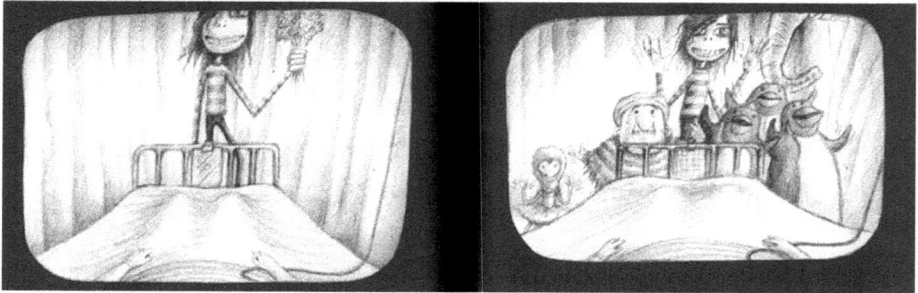

Figure 19, p. 262-263

Conversely, characters are only seen from the outside in cases of external focalization. This category is exemplified in behaviourist fiction, in which no access is granted to the inner life of the character apart from that which the reader can glean through observing the character's actions and speech. Figure 20 below shows Iris after having made an appointment with the doctor. Iris herself says nothing, but the reader can deduct from the worried expression created by her frown and lowered brows that Iris is anxious about the outcome of the examination. The constant tapping of Iris' pencil demonstrates her mental distraction, and the sequence of the panel triad will lead the reader to assume that Iris has been tapping her pencil continuously for an hour; the clock in the first panel reveals the time to be 3pm and Iris' appointment is at 4pm. Pictorial runes exaggerate the effect of the tapping pencil: the pencil's movement is shown through repeated versions of its form alongside motion lines, and the volume of the tapping sound is increased by the echoes which shadow the sound effect.

Figure 20, p. 30

Genette discusses five categories in all: order, duration, frequency, mood and voice. The first three categories are largely concerned with narrative time; as we have seen, the mood category deals with narrative perspective, and the final category of voice 'addresses the question of who tells the story, and what traces of the narrator's presence may be discerned in the text' (Miller, 2007: 105). Heterodiegetic narrators are external to the storyworld and can utilise all three types of focalization; by contrast, homodiegetic narrators exist within the storyworld and cannot logically use zero focalization (with, as always, the exception of experimental texts).

Although Genette's work remains a popular starting-point for further enquiry, it has been subject to numerous revisions and refinements by narratologists and interested parties from other disciplines. Genette himself reformulated 'who sees?' as 'who perceives?' in his 1988 revision of *Narrative Discourse*; Mikkonen notes that this was an attempt to capture not only what is seen, but to represent the 'affective, perceptive, and conceptual centre orienting the narrative' (Mikkonen, 2017: 151). In other words, this was a revision which represents a movement away from the purely visual aspect of focalization implied by earlier formulations. Mieke Bal, one of Genette's earliest revisionists, preferred to jettison external focalization altogether, and redefined this category in terms of the relation between the seer and the seen. Bal's modifications to Genette's framework have been well-documented, and others have debated what should be understood and encompassed by the term focalization: Shlomith Rimmon-Kenan (2002) argues in favour of the inclusion of mental processes and ideological orientation alongside the purely perceptual facet of focalization, a position that is opposed by first-generation narratologist Seymour Chatman (1978). Achim Hescher (2016) would discard focalization entirely in the case of comics, but this position is certainly opposed by Mikkonen (2017) and Baetens and Frey (2015), who argue that while existing narratological theories are obviously unsuited in their present form for wholesale transferral to the study of comics, they contain much that is useful nevertheless, provided medium-specific adjustments and additions are implemented.

By way of adapting Genette's work to render it more suitable for application to comics, Miller supplements Genette's framework with the work André Gaudreault and Francis Jost, who argue that Genette's three categories of focalization refer to knowledge, whereas 'ocularisation' represents the visual perspective of a character, thus separating what a character knows from what they see. Furthermore, Gaudreault and Jost identify a subcategory of ocularised shots which 'bear traces of the subjectivity of a character through deformation' (Miller, 2007: 106), as can be seen in figure 21 below. As Iris succumbs to the anaesthetic, the sides of the frame gradually encroach across the panel until an entirely black panel indicates that Iris is now unconscious. The numbers of the surgeon's countdown also become increasingly wobbly and malformed as the surgeon's voice become fainter and more indistinguishable for Iris.

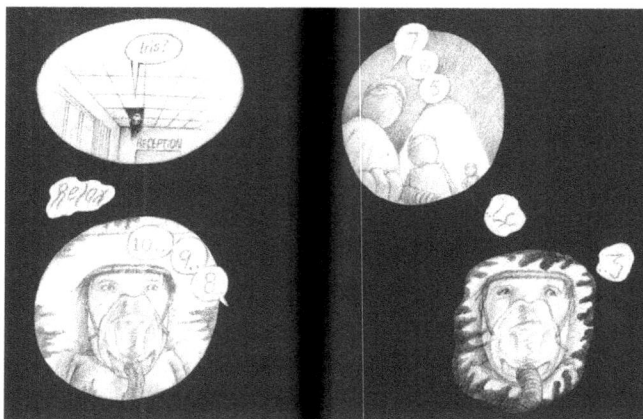

Figure 21, p. 242-243

Subjective traces 'may be further extended through images which represent purely mental processes such as dreams' (Miller, 2007: 106). Gaudreault and Jost argue that the status of these images is made clear by modalisation operators such as a foregrounded change in the panel's shape to indicate a dream sequence, but if these operators are not present, the reader has to distinguish between what is real in the storyworld and what is real to the character: internal focalization presents character perception as fact. Iris' second dream in chapter 8 features a deliberately misleading opening sequence which shows Iris waking on the morning of her scheduled mastectomy. The dream-status of the following episode is uncertain for perhaps twenty panels. Iris' encounter with the paper dolls in chapter 5 is even more puzzling: Iris is intoxicated, of course, and this sequence could be written off as a drunken nightmare if it were not for the continued presence of the paper doll bearing the personal ad which leads Iris into communication with Henry. The doll can be seen pinned to the wall above Iris' computer from this point onwards, and it is Iris' action of discarding and burying the doll in chapter 16 which marks the end of her fantasy-romance. The doll's sudden appearance in an unfamiliar location at this crucial juncture in the narrative imbues it with metonymic significance: the doll is a stand-in for Henry and the fantasy world Iris formerly cherished. Nevertheless, the question of the doll's physical existence in the storyworld remains unclear.

It would be useful at this point to summarise that which has been discussed so far. Graphic storytelling allows for zero, internal and external focalization in heterodiegetic narration. Panels that are externally focalized naturally do not include subjective imagery or a point-of-view shot which would suggest the filtering consciousness of a character. Characters are depicted from an external viewpoint and thought balloons do not feature in externally focalized images because this device allows access to a character's mental activity. At the other extreme, zero focalization implies omniscience and access is given to the characters' inner life, although it is rare that all characters are treated equally in this regard (Miller, 2007: 110). It is more common that one or two characters will be selected for such privileged access. In *TIW* the reader has access to Iris' thoughts and feelings, and very occasionally those of Maud, although in the case of the latter access is usually restricted to a thought balloon containing a question mark to indicate Maud's confusion or her frustrated attempts to understand Iris' behaviour.

Internal focalization provides access to one particular character's mind. However, 'it is rare that images are restricted to the ocular viewpoint of that character' (Miller, 2007: 109), although examples can be found. In figure 22 below, the reader sees Maud from Iris' perspective, indicated by Maud's gaze and her placement in the frame, and the tails of Iris' speech balloons which point to the speaker at a position somewhere outside of the panel's frame. Film theorist Edward Branigan, whose work I shall turn to shortly, contends that the point-of-view shot is composed of two shots (Branigan, 1984: 103). Following Branigan's analysis, Iris' presence at the window is established as a point in space in the panel on page 296. In the next panel, her glance is directed towards an 'off-camera' object, in this case, Maud. The 'camera' is located from Iris' position in the panels on pages 298 and 299 and focuses on Maud-as-object. Maud's thought balloon on page 299 indicates her puzzlement that Iris could have forgotten her hospital appointment. (In fact, the presence of this thought balloon in an ocularised image means that the reader is presented with two inner lives simultaneously: Iris' field of vision and Maud's mental confusion.)

Figure 22, p. 298-299

Ocularised views such as the example discussed above are possible in localised instances, but while it is a relatively simple matter to sustain one particular fictional consciousness in prose texts, it is impractical, difficult, and arguably undesirable to do so in comics (Mikkonen, 2008: 316). Focalization in comics is constantly shifting and as a result of this perpetual movement, Miller states that graphic storytelling 'tends to exhibit a certain permeability between inner and outer worlds' (2007: 119). Film scholars have noted a similar phenomenon with respect to their own medium, and Branigan cites the example of Robert Montgomery's 1946 film *Lady in the Lake*, which sustains the point of view of the investigating detective, Philip Marlowe, throughout its duration (Branigan, 1992: 142-160). Montgomery as Marlowe is visible onscreen only in reflections or when his hands come into the frame, and the camera renders as accurately as possible this character's ocularised view. However, cinema audiences quickly wearied of the experiment and found the viewing experience to be frustrating. A far more successful experiment with first-person consciousness can be found in Channel 4's sitcom *Peep Show*, which features ocularised shots simultaneously with voice-overs, so the viewer sees what the character can see and hears what the character is thinking. This inner access is restricted entirely to the two main characters, Jeremy and Mark, played by Robert Webb and David Mitchell respectively. The popularity of this show attests to its success, unlike the now infamous failure of Montgomery's film. *Peep Show*'s appeal rests on the fact that internal focalization is often deployed to set the visual and verbal tracks against each other for comic effect, and the shifting viewpoint between the two leads allows the audience to witness Jeremy and Mark from external as well as internal positions.

The work of film scholar Edward Branigan has already been briefly touched upon, but I wish to consider in more detail now his argument that several different narrations can operate simultaneously. Branigan defines the character as an agent who provides information by simply living in their world and talking to other characters who inhabit the same world, and focalization depends upon that character *experiencing* something. Branigan draws a distinction between looking/listening, which is intersubjective and can be reported by a narrator, and seeing/hearing, which is a personal experience and can only be recounted through means of internal or external focalization.

Character experiences can be rendered internally through point of view shots and dream sequences, or externally through close-ups and eyeline matches. As well as seeing and hearing, Branigan notes that focalization extends to 'thinking, remembering, interpreting, wondering, fearing, believing, desiring, understanding, feeling guilt' (Branigan, 1992: 101).

On the question of different narrations running concurrently, Branigan quotes fellow film scholar Stephen Heath, who argues that there is no real dichotomy between a subjective point of view shot and an objective non-point of view shot. The latter can be the basis over which the former runs, and an external shot can be overlaid with consciousness. This line of reasoning has enormous consequences for the interpretation of visual narrative in that it removes the onus to positively identify a single focalizing source for each panel, and it becomes possible to describe an image in terms of numerous levels of focalization. As previously stated, visual narratives feature numerous transitions from panel to panel and cannot sustain the depiction of a single consciousness without contrivance. Heath's argument suggests there is ground for claiming that fictional consciousness in visual narrative could be sustained over extended passages if it is transposed over a basis of externally rendered images.

To exemplify this point, figure 23 from *TIW* presents an apparently objective narratorial third-person perspective because Iris is not present and there is nothing to suggest that this is an ocularised image based on her field of vision. Nevertheless, traces of Iris' subjectivity are present and her mental preoccupations are clearly reflected in the symmetry of the image which is neatly divided into two. Her computer takes centre-stage, with Henry's kiss forming the focal point of the entire panel. The paper doll seen to the left of the computer represents the fantasy world of Iris' online romance, but the letter from the hospital which is pinned above the computer on the right-hand side provides a stark reminder of the reality of Iris' cancer and her imminent mastectomy. The panel following (figure 24) shows continuity of spatial arrangement in that the computer screen is still visible, thus indicating to the reader that the location is identical to the previous panel but the 'camera' has moved closer to the letter so that its text is fully legible. This refocusing of the reader's attention on Iris' real situation is a narratorial move to underline the escapist nature of her fantasy.

Figure 23, p. 140

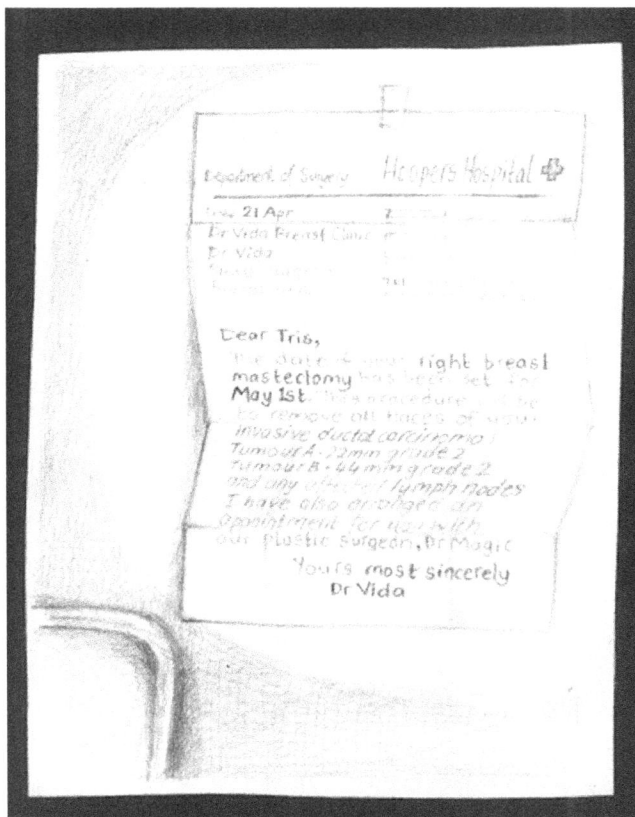

Figure 24, p. 141

To demonstrate composite viewpoints over a more extended sequence, I refer below to pages 131-139 in *TIW*, which depicts a messaging conversation between Iris (balletgirl42) and Henry (sailorbuoy-39). The reader is aware that Iris has misrepresented herself to Henry, and she is writing as balletgirl42, a persona she has invented as a distraction from her diagnosis. What is unapparent to the reader on a first reading, however, is that Henry's persona, sailorbuoy-39, is also a fiction: he too, is not what he claims to be. The voices of the two characters - or at least, their personae - appear onscreen in the form of messages, and the messages are depicted as panels within the wider surrounding panel. As such, the frame of each message operates in the same way as a speech balloon. The frame of the panel on page 132 (figure 25) takes the form of the computer screen and water drips from the bottom, leaking out of the frame's dimensions. The frame's contents have also switched, and now include an image of the lighthouse Henry is describing.

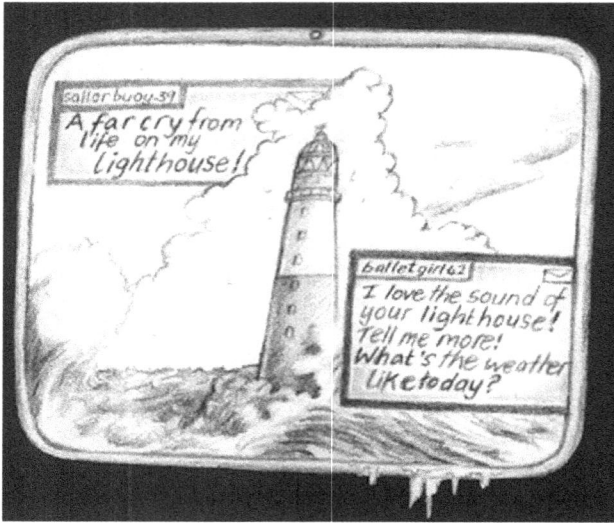

Figure 25, p. 132

Horstkotte and Pedri would likely label this a shift in visual vocabulary (2011), and this shift marks the movement into Iris' consciousness and her fantasy of Henry. (Of course, it is also true that these images represent Henry's own fantasy version of himself.) The reader reads Henry's words and witnesses Iris' fantasy simultaneously (figures 26a and 26b). On another narrative level, the reader knows that Iris has been diagnosed with cancer and is shortly to undergo a mastectomy; this narrative level is still present throughout Iris and Henry's conversation, and resurfaces in the image of the letter from the hospital.

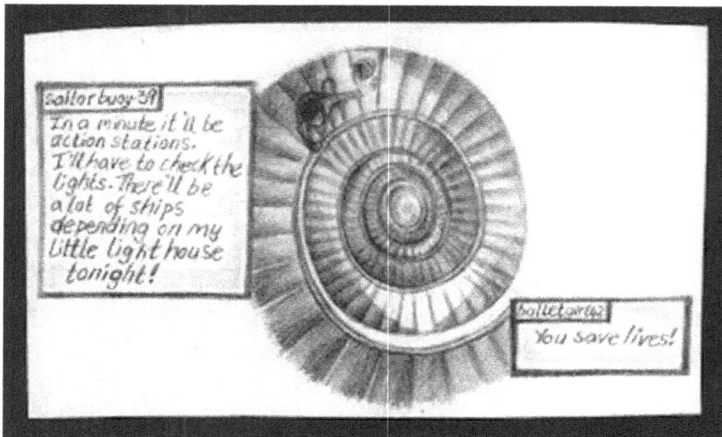

Figure 26a, p. 135

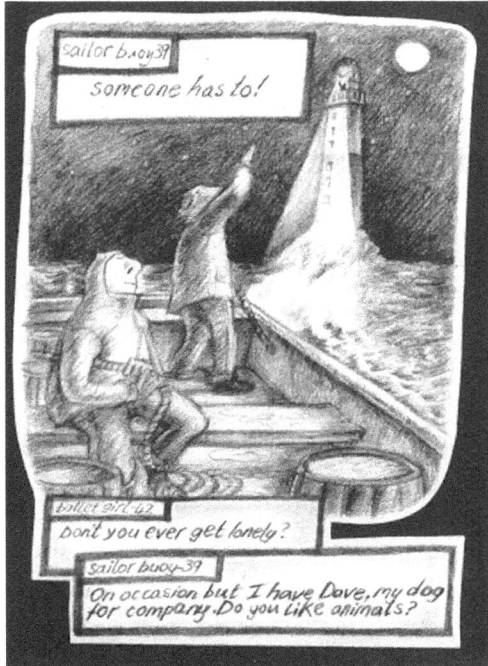

Figure 26b, p. 136

In a 2017 article published in the journal *Cognitive Linguistics*, Mike Borkent considers how viewpoints are constructed from 'multiple modalities' (2017: 539) and he brings more recent cognitive theories to the study of focalization. He argues that theories of 'embodiment, domains, mental simulation, and mental space blending' (2017: 539) can provide a framework for the analysis of multimodal viewpoint construction in comics. Borkent considers carefully the communicative and expressive possibilities of the comics medium and notes that the range of signs through which comics relay their narratives (referred to previously in the discussion of Peirce's classifications) have their own 'viewpoint prompting features and conventions' (2017: 541). Images communicate through iconicity and on the surface seem to do little more than point to the storyworld existence of an object through the depiction of something resembling that object, but even in this case, Borkent maintains that the 'variable formal features' of such images 'can significantly reconstrue content' (2017: 540). Iconic signs in comics interact with other signs in turn to construct viewpoints that are multimodal and multilayered.

Borkent uses the cognitive linguistic concept of embodiment to explain how comics readers 'activate lived experiences - from basic sensorimotor schemas up to cultural knowledge - to flesh out and interpret limited communicative cues' (2017: 542). This is to say that readers' gap-filling activities extend far beyond mentally completing the spaces, or gutters, between panels. Real-world knowledge is drawn upon to complete the information given in the panel. Borkent notes that the panel itself 'acts as a window of attention' (544; cf. Cohn 2013, Bridgeman, 2005, and Jahn, 1996) presenting a view into the storyworld that is not unfiltered: the composition of the panel and its style of presentation can be mobilised to influence the reader's inference processes. Such processes might include completing a half-shown image, filling in a blank background, and importing 'cues from prior panels to contextualise the action' (Borkent, 2017: 544), all of which is reminiscent of Catherine Emmott's work on contextual frame theory which focuses on how readers build mental frames of reference in relation to characters, settings, and so on, to create, maintain and update a storyworld (1997). An artist does not have to produce endless replications of one panel because the reader will assume that information not shown is still present; furthermore, this kind of ellipsis enables the foregrounding of communicative signs which contain salient narrative information. In addition, readers interpret signs with the aid of domain networks. The concept of 'domains' originates from research in semantics, and refers to pockets of stored information which people activate whenever that particular domain is encountered. In the example from *TIW* discussed in this section, the domain is 'online dating', activated by the images of the personal ad on pages 125 and 126 (see figures 27a and 27b below). The reader is able to make inferences connected with this domain, concerning roles, values, interactions and ideology. Given that Iris and Henry are both less than honest about their true identities, the sub-domain of catfishing is also activated for those readers who are aware of such things.

Figure 27a, p. 125

Figure 27b, p. 126

6. Conclusions

This study has investigated the construction of fictional consciousness in texts comprised of a visual as well as a verbal track through consideration of the following. The existing discourses relevant to the work's genre and subject matter should be considered when taking account of a reader's activity in constructing a fictional mind, particularly when sanctioned pre-existing narratives are likely to interfere with this process. The novel under discussion was placed in its wider context in section 2 to explore possible external influences on the reader and to provide examples of real-life responses in the form of critical reviews and comments posted online. Section 3 provided a brief overview of some of the issues which comprise current debates in comics scholarship by way of showing how this particular field of enquiry differs from research devoted purely to prose narratives. Having highlighted some of the issues raised in comics research, three of those issues were explored in more detail in section 4.

The visual rendering of a character's face and body was discussed in section 4.1. It was suggested that readers construct a fictional consciousness in part from watching the character's actions. However, it was shown that the reading of facial expression in comics is not as simple as has previously been supposed. Facial expression in comics tends towards the caricatural and is interpreted in the immediate and wider context, and in the presence of other visual and verbal clues. Furthermore, the medium allows for other devices to assist the reader in interpreting characters' feelings, such as the visual depiction of conceptual metaphors of emotion. Readers assess fictional consciousness in watching what characters do and listening to what they say, and the representation of speech and thought in comics was explored in section 4.2. The work of Geoffrey Leech and Mick Short provided the basis for the discussion, the focus of which was the speech/thought balloon and the opportunities this device affords for the comics writer. Of particular note was the option to depict the tone and attitude of the speaker through typographical variants of the balloon and its contents. Pictorial metaphor provided the focus for section 4.3, with reference to Peirce's work on signs which he categorised as iconic, indexical, or symbolic. El Rafaie's study of the reading of political cartoons provided some insight into the kind of reader competencies necessary for the interpretation of signs, and Forceville's taxonomy of pictorial runes exemplified the kind of medium-specific conventions with which comics readers should be familiar. Examples of pictorial metaphor in *TIW* were provided to show how Iris' fictional consciousness and her emotional response to her illness can be represented through the visual track.

The final section took the concept of focalization for its subject, a concept that is central to the study of fictional consciousness in prose narratives. It was suggested that this concept as it exists in research devoted to literature, specifically in Genette's theory, requires some adjustment before it can be usefully applied to narratives in other media, and the work of film scholars was brought in to expand the concept to include visual images. Film researchers have claimed that an image or a sequence can be constructed of composite viewpoints with more than one narrative level running concurrently. This removes the onus to identify a single focalizer for an image and conveniently accommodates the continuous shifts and transitions in viewpoint inherent in comics. In addition, the problem of not being able to sustain a single consciousness over an extended sequence in comics can be countered if an external point of view can be the basis over which a subjective viewpoint runs. There is justification for arguing that a single consciousness is conceivably ever-present on one or more of the narrative levels. Furthermore, all potentially troublesome claims to an entirely objective viewpoint or an aspect-neutral background can be disregarded if every image is regarded instead as a composite viewpoint. Focalization has to take into account what the reader brings to the image and Borkent adds the concepts of embodiment and domains to represent how the reader fills out a two-dimensional image into something that approximates a real-world event occurring in space and time. This study thus begins and ends with the reader in terms of the existing knowledge that is brought to the text.

The field of narratology, although focused primarily on prose narratives, contains much that is useful for the study of comics and narratives in other media, providing medium-specific adjustments are made. Directions for further research should include a more positive and thorough engagement with European comics scholarship, which has a much longer history than its Anglo-American counterpart and has reached greater levels of sophistication; this could help in shaking the influence of Scott McCloud, who is still widely referenced without question. McCloud remains a pioneer of comics studies and deserves recognition as such, but his theories do not always stand up to greater scrutiny. His prioritisation of sequentiality is particularly troublesome because it denies comics one of their defining aspects. A key feature of comics is the non-linear nature of the reader's path through the text. Miodrag notes that by contrast 'Groensteen's notion of arthrology describes the relationships, both linear and translinear, between panels' (2013: 109) and she goes on to suggest that 'it is these non-linear relations that truly distinguish comics from other forms of narrative sequence' (112). Future research should also include studies of fictional consciousness in a far wider range of texts, including those which lean towards the abstract rather than the representational.

List of references

Primary sources

B., David. (2005) *Epileptic*. London: Jonathan Cape.

Ball, R. (2015) *The Inflatable Woman*. London: Bloomsbury.

Clark, J.S. (2010) *Depresso*. London: Knockabout.

Delisle, G. (2017) *Hostage*. London: Jonathan Cape.

Eisner, W. (1991) *To the Heart of the Storm*. New York: W. W. Norton & Company.

Engelberg, M. (2006) *Cancer Made Me A Shallower Person: A Memoir in Comics*. New York: Harper.

Goscinny, R. & Uderzo, A. (1970) *Asterix and the Roman Agent*. London: Hodder & Stoughton.

Goscinny, R. & Uderzo, A. (1970) *La Zizanie*. Paris: Dargaud Editeur.

Green, K. (2013) *Lighter Than My Shadow*. London: Jonathan Cape.

Marchetto, M.A. (2006) *Cancer Vixen: A True Story*. New York: Pantheon Books.

Peep Show. Channel 4. 19 September 2003- 16 December 2015.

Satrapi, M. (2008) *Persepolis: The story of a childhood and the story of a return*. London: Vintage.

Simmonds, P. (2001) *Gemma Bovery*. London: Jonathan Cape.

Simmonds, P. (2009) *Tamara Drewe*. London: Jonathan Cape.

Simmonds, P. (2018) *Cassandra Drake*. London: Jonathan Cape.

Streeten, N. (2011) *Billy, Me & You: A Memoir of Grief and Recovery*. Brighton: Myriad Editions.

Tan, S. (2006) *The Arrival*. London: Hodder & Stoughton.

Thornton, R. & Hixon, A. (2012) *The Tale of Brin and Bent and Minno Marylebone*. London: Jonathan Cape.

Williams, I. (2014) *The Bad Doctor*. Brighton: Myriad Editions.

Secondary sources

Adler, S. (2011) Silence in the graphic novel. *Journal of Pragmatics* 43: 2278–2285.

Baetens, J. & Frey, H. (2015) *The Graphic Novel: An Introduction*. New York: Cambridge University Press.

Bal, M. (2017) *Narratology: Introduction to the Theory of Narrative*. 4th ed. Toronto: University of Toronto Press.

Borkent, M. (2017) Mediated characters: Multimodal viewpoint construction in comics. *Cognitive Linguistics* 28(3): 539–563.

Branigan, E. (1984) *Point of View in the Cinema*. Berlin: Mouton.

Branigan, E. (1992) *Narrative Comprehension and Film*. London: Routledge.

Bridgeman, T. (2005) Figuration and configuration: mapping imaginary worlds in BD. In C. Forsdick, L. Grove, & L. McQuillan. (Eds.) *Francophone Bande Dessinée*. Amsterdam: Edition Rodopi, 115–136.

Chatman, S. (1978) *Story and Discourse: Narrative Structure in Fiction and Film*. Ithaca: Cornell University Press.

Cohn, N. (2013) *The Visual Language of Comics: Introduction to the Structure and Cognition of Sequential Images*. London: Bloomsbury.

Davis, R.G. (2005) A Graphic Self: Comics as autobiography in Marjane Satrapi's 'Persepolis'. *Prose Studies* 27(3): 264–279.

Eakin, P.J. (1999) *How Our Lives Become Stories: Making Selves*. Ithaca: Cornell University Press.

Ekman, P. (1992) An Argument for Basic Emotions. *Cognition and Emotion* 6: 169–200.

El Rafaie, E. (2009) Multiliteracies: how readers interpret political cartoons. *Visual Communication* 8(2): 181–205.

Emmott, C. (1997) *Narrative Comprehension: A Discourse Perspective*. Oxford: Oxford University Press.

Emmott, C. (2002) 'Split selves' in fiction and in medical 'life stories': Cognitive linguistic theory and narrative practice. In E. Semino & J. D. Culpeper. (Eds.) *Cognitive Stylistics*. Philadelphia: John Benjamins, 153–181.

Forceville, C. (2005) Visual representations of the idealized cognitive model of 'anger' in the Asterix album 'La Zizanie'. *Journal of Pragmatics* 37: 69–88.

Forceville, C. (2011) Pictorial Runes in 'Tintin and the Picaros'. *Journal of Pragmatics* 43: 875–890.

Forceville, C., Stamenković, D. & Tasić, M. (2018) Facial expressions in comics: an empirical consideration of McCloud's proposal. *Visual Communication* 0(0): 1–26.

Genette, G. (1980) *Narrative Discourse: An Essay in Method*. Ithaca: Cornell University Press.

Genette, G. (1988) *Narrative Discourse Revisited*. Ithaca: Cornell University Press.

Gilmartin, S. (2015) Book Review: The Inflatable Woman, by Rachael Ball. *Irish Times*. [Accessed October 27, 2017].

Gilmore, L. (2001) *The Limits of Autobiography: Trauma and Testimony*. Ithaca: Cornell University Press.

Groensteen, T. (2007) *The System of Comics*. Jackson: University Press of Mississippi.

Groensteen, T. (2013) *Comics and Narration*. Jackson: University Press of Mississippi.

Hescher, A. (2016) *Reading Graphic Novels: Genre and Narration*. Berlin: De Gruyter.

Horstkotte, S. & Pedri, N. (2011) Focalization in Graphic Narrative. *Narrative* 19(3): 330–357.

Jahn, M. (1996) Windows of Focalization: Deconstructing and Reconstructing a Narratological Concept. *Style* 30(2): 241–267.

Kuhlman, M. (2017) The Autobiographical and Biographical Graphic Novel. In S. E. Tabachnick. (Ed.) *The Cambridge Companion to the Graphic Novel*. Cambridge: Cambridge University Press, 113–129.

Leech, G. & Short, M. (2007) *Style in Fiction: A Linguistic Introduction to English Fictional Prose*. 2nd ed. Harlow: Pearson.

Martinez, M. The Inflatable Woman. *New York Journal of Books*. Available at: https://www.nyjournalofbooks.com/book-review/inflatable. [Accessed October 27, 2017].

McCloud, S. (1993) *Understanding Comics: The Invisible Art*. New York: HarperCollins.

McCloud, S. (2006) *Making Comics: Storytelling Secrets of Comics, Manga and Graphic Novels*. New York: Harper.

Medley, S. (2010) Discerning pictures: how we look at and understand images in comics. *Studies in Comics* 1(1): 53–70.

Mikkonen, K. (2008) Presenting Minds in Graphic Narratives. *Partial Answers: Journal of Literature and the History of Ideas* 6(2): 301–321.

Mikkonen, K. (2017) *The Narratology of Comic Art*. Abingdon: Routledge.

Miller, A. (2007) *Reading Bande Dessinée: Critical Approaches to French-language Comic Strip*. Bristol: Intellect Books.

Miodrag, H. (2013) *Comics and Language: Reimagining Critical Discourse on the Form*. Jackson: University Press of Mississippi.

Morgan, H. (2009) Graphic Shorthand: From Caricature to Narratology in Twentieth-Century Bande Dessinée and Comics. *European Comic Art* 2(1): 21–39.

Oliver, A. (2017) The Inflatable Woman - Rachael Ball's Debut Graphic Novel is a Visionary Entry in the Graphic Medicine Canon. *Broken Frontier*. Available at: http://www.brokenfrontier.com/the-inflatable-woman-rachael-ball-bloomsbury/. [Accessed October 27, 2017].

Osborne, S. (2015) The Inflatable Woman: Ways without words. *A life in books*. Available at: https://alifeinbooks.co.uk/2015/10/the-inflatable-woman-ways-without-words/. [Accessed October 27, 2017].

Palmer, A. (2004) *Fictional Minds*. Lincoln: University of Nebraska Press.

Palmer, A. (2007) Universal Minds. *Semiotica* 165: 205–225.

Pham, S. (2015) The Inflatable Woman. *Graphic Medicine*. Available at: http://www.graphicmedicine.org/comic-reviews/the-inflatable-woman/. [Accessed October 27, 2017].

Rimmon-Kenan, S. (2002) *Narrative Fiction*. 2nd ed. London: Routledge.

Segal, J.Z. (2007) Breast cancer narratives as public rhetoric: genre itself and the maintenance of ignorance. *Linguistics and the Human Sciences* 3(1): 3–24.

Segal, J.Z. (2012) Cancer Experience and its Narration: An Accidental Study. *Literature and Medicine* 30(2): 292–318.

Stoddard Holmes, M. (2014) Cancer Comics: Narrating Cancer through Sequential Art. *Tulsa Studies in Women's Literature* 33(1): 147–162.

Tan, E.S. (2001) The Telling Face in Comic Strip and Graphic Novel. In J. Baetens. (Ed.) *The Graphic Novel*. Louvain: Leuven University Press, 31–46.

Tensuan, T. (2011) Up from Surgery: The Politics of Self-Representation in Women's Graphic Memoirs of Illness. In M. A. Chaney. (Ed.) *Graphic Subjects: Critical Essays on Autobiography and Graphic Novels*. Madison: University of Wisconsin Press, 180–193.

Versaci, R. (2007) *This Book Contains Graphic Language: Comics as Literature*. London: Continuum.

Wolk, D. (2007) *Reading Comics: How Graphic Novels Work And What They Mean*. Philadelphia: Da Capo Press.

Shorter writings and blog posts, 2012-2018

"It's SOMEONE'S fucking fault": social responsibility in J K Rowling's *The Casual Vacancy*

The Casual Vacancy (hereafter *TCV*) was Rowling's first novel for the adult market, but on reading it I couldn't help feeling that she hadn't quite shaken off the mantle of 'children's author'. First, it is undoubtedly a heavily moralistic book. A great deal of children's literature is moralistic or didactic in tone because it's supposed to be edifying and educational. Second, a non-adult narrative viewpoint is an important feature of YA fiction/children's literature and *TCV* features a number of teenage characters with whom we spend a great deal of time. The liberal use of free indirect discourse (FID) gives the reader access to the thought processes of most of the characters, adults and children alike. Third, the novel dishes up for a younger audience the sort of stuff that those readers like best, namely, a bunch of kids teaching stupid adults the error of their ways. Three of the novel's teenage characters enter into open battle with the adults, posing online as the Ghost of Barry Fairbrother to admonish their parents: first Andrew, then Sukhvinder, then Fats. So far, so Harry Potter.

However, the novel's Wikipedia page suggests that Rowling would respond unfavourably to the idea of *TCV* being a YA novel in disguise, noting that at the time of publication, '[c]ritics questioned whether younger *Harry Potter* fans might be drawn into wanting to read the book…Rowling responded saying, "There is no part of me that feels that I represented myself as your children's babysitter or their teacher. I was always, I think, completely honest. I'm a writer, and I will write what I want to write".' So let us take Rowling at her word and assume that at least as far as authorial intention is concerned, the moral lesson of the book is aimed at adult readers. (Incidentally, you know you're in the hands of a moralist when one of the characters is called 'Fairbrother'. George Eliot did the same in *Middlemarch* with Camden Farebrother.)

Rowling has in fact made no secret of the fact that this is a book intended to remind its readership of the responsibilities that come with living in a community made up of other people. In an interview for *The New Yorker* she comments, '[t]his is a book about responsibility. In the minor sense— how responsible we are for our own personal happiness, and where we find ourselves in life—but in the macro sense also, of course: how responsible we are for the poor, the disadvantaged, other people's misery'. So how does the moral message of the book manifest itself? I've mentioned a couple of things already: the novel's avenging 'ghost' and the use of FID which allows us to see into the minds of the characters. And as well as being able to read their minds, the reader can see into the characters' histories: the narrator provides the kind of background knowledge that promotes an understanding of why the character behaves the way s/he does. Terri Weedon (played by Keeley Forsyth in the BBC mini-series) is the one that springs to mind. Terri, a drug addict and neglectful parent, inspires little but revulsion until you learn the details of her past, the most shocking part of her backstory being how as a little girl she was happy to be in hospital being treated for the burns inflicted by the man who was supposed to be caring for her, because at least she wasn't being raped and beaten at home. No wonder she turned to heroin for comfort.

The television audience was spared these details as it was also spared the ending of the novel, the original being considered 'too grim' for a Sunday night audience. Adaptations of novels for film and television tend to suffer problems of compression when the screenplay tries to cover everything and obviously a great deal of the novel had to be cut in order to squeeze it all into three hours' worth of telly, *but* I do think it rather prissy of Auntie Beeb to skirt around the real tragedy of the book: the death of the innocent, Robbie Weedon, already unadoptable at the age of four. In the TV adaptation, Robbie is spotted by Vikram Jawanda while out on his morning run, this routine of his established early on in the series so as to render Robbie's rescue credible. In the book, Robbie drowns in the river - and the real tragedy is that there are *three* people who saw him, and who could have saved him, but who did nothing.

One of these three is Shirley Mollison, wife of Parish Councillor Howard Mollison and mother of Miles, contender for Barry's seat on the council (the eponymous casual vacancy), played with a beautifully pitched line in hard icy cruelty by Julia McKenzie for the mini-series. Shirley is spiteful and small-minded, desperate to cultivate an air of gentility because her mother had a reputation for promiscuous behaviour and the young Shirley was bullied because of this. In spite of this mitigating factor, we do not like Shirley: she bullies her daughter-in-law, sucks up to the appalling local gentry, scores points off her friends wherever possible and alienates her gay daughter. Shirley learns nothing from the events that play themselves out, and her part in them. The following exchange is very revealing:

> '[T]he boy was right by the river when I saw him. A couple of steps and he'd have been in.'

Something in Maureen's expression stung her.

'I was hurrying,' said Shirley with asperity, 'because Howard had said he was feeling poorly and I was worried sick. I didn't want to go out at all…I was absolutely distracted, and all I could think was, I must get back to Howard…'

These excuses will not bring Robbie back from the grave, and Shirley is not telling the truth in any case: in actual fact, the reason she was so distracted at that point was her discovery of Howard and Maureen's affair. She had intended to murder Howard – but she lies to herself about this, as well. Shirley is punished with public shame and the certain knowledge of her husband's infidelity.

Gavin Hughes also sees Robbie wandering alone by the river. Gavin is the boyfriend of social worker Kay, although his character does not appear in the mini-series. In the novel, he is the reason for Kay's relocation to Pagford (much to the chagrin of Kay's daughter Gaia), but he doesn't love Kay and treats her with a disdain that stems from his essential cravenness. He pursues Mary Fairbrother instead, the widow of his best friend Barry. Gavin's self-absorption is so complete that he cannot even remember seeing Robbie. He is punished with solitude: his best friend is dead, and he is rejected by Mary and eventually Kay.

Samantha Mollison is the third character who sees Robbie that day, and she is the only one to internally acknowledge the part she played in Robbie's death. She is shaken out of her selfish frustration at the loss of her youth and expresses a wish to take part in local politics alongside her husband. Her renewed interest in her previously failing marriage is her reward. (In the mini-series, Samantha is sympathetically portrayed by Keeley Hawes – an actor always worth watching.)

So, to return to the discussion around the novel's moral content, we can see here a clear pattern of reward and punishment. This extends beyond the three characters discussed above, with perhaps the worst fate meted out to Fats Wall. Objectionable enough in the mini-series, this character is far worse in the novel: he bullies Sukhvinder so viciously that she is induced to self-harm; he treats his adopted father with heartless disdain; he feeds his nut-allergic best friend a disguised peanut just to see what will happen; he snogs the girl he knows his best friend fancies and he uses Krystal Weedon for sex. Fats is punished severely for his burgeoning career as a sociopath which is embodied in his pursuit for 'authenticity'. Fats is humbled and forced to realise that you simply cannot bludgeon your way through life pretending that other people don't exist, and he is brought to terms with this in the hardest way imaginable: he is indirectly responsible for the death of Robbie, and also that of Krystal, who commits suicide soon after her brother's body is dragged from the river.

There is no justice, no reward, no possibility of escape for Krystal – not without Barry Fairbrother. She, perhaps, could have dragged herself out of the mire in which she was forced to live, and to have subsequently made a new start for herself with Robbie, but events conspire against her: she is raped by her mother's drug dealer, the repulsive Obbo (thank goodness the BBC spared us that scene), and she is terrified a similar fate will befall Robbie. The death of her Nana Cath leaves her nowhere to turn and she concocts a plan that will lead inexorably to the final tragic events. Krystal is not spared in the mini-series either: fearlessly depicted by Abigail Lawrie, she drowns after jumping in the river, believing that Robbie has fallen in. Her legs become entangled in the cables of a stolen television, dumped in the river by Andrew's brutal, violent father.

I want to finish with reference to what is, for me, the most resonant line of the mini-series, and it belongs to Sukhvinder. Sukhvinder's role is very much reduced in the adaptation for television. In effect, she is become a Chorus figure: hers is the voice of the narrator, a heterodiegetic voice-over. Its function is not only to remind the viewer of what has happened previously, but to comment on the action, just as is the case with the Chorus figure from Greek tragedy. It is another Harry Potter touch that an adolescent character was chosen for this role, but it works really well. Sukhvinder herself is almost entirely silent throughout the series (something of a mercy, given the garbled quality of the voice-over) and she is apparently completely isolated from the action: she wears headphones all the time, so she is kept separate and apart, but at the end, you realise that she has been observing closely in spite of her detached air. She has only one homodiegetic line – that is, only one line that is spoken within the narrative itself – and this comes after Krystal's body has been retrieved from the river and Vikram Jawanda, Sukhvinder's father, has rescued Robbie. The little boy has been taken into care as a result and Sukhvinder overhears her mother telling Vikram 'It's not your fault... anyone would have done the same.' 'Whose fault is it then?' asks Sukhvinder. 'Because it's someone's fucking fault.'

And this is the point. Things don't just happen. There is no such thing as fate, or destiny, or any such tripe. It is always SOMEONE'S FUCKING FAULT. You can call it karma if you wish because what goes around certainly comes around. What happens to Krystal and Robbie in the novel is not only the fault of the characters such as Krystal's rapist, their drug-dependent mother, the three people who saw Robbie and did nothing – no, it is also the fault of those people who routinely put their own concerns first, who think that caring for and about others is someone else's responsibility, who put their heads in the sand and pretend that other people's misery doesn't exist.

Adapted from the original text posted to www.auntymuriel.com on 10 May 2015.

Masculinity and Metaphor in *Teen Wolf*

I revisited *Teen Wolf* very recently and, perhaps the first time, I understood what a multi-faceted narrative it actually is. It's a *Bildungsroman*, of course, a coming-of-age story, and the film is positively dripping with symbolism at every corner; each symbol in itself is worked over and over so that it becomes maximally meaningful. What follows is a discussion of the film's metaphors, how these metaphors are presented, and how repetition and parallelism guide the viewer towards a particular understanding of these metaphors and, by extension, of the narrative as a whole.

The story is a simple one. High school student Scott Howard (Michael J. Fox) notices that he is undergoing some physical changes - not the *usual* ones - and one night, when there is a full moon, he changes into a werewolf. His father, also a werewolf, tells Scott that the Wolf is a part of himself that he must accept and learn to deal with. Scott changes into the Wolf unintentionally during a basketball game and goes on to achieve the kind of popularity he had never enjoyed as plain Scott Howard. But being the Wolf comes with its own set of difficulties and Scott eventually rejects what the Wolf can offer him when he decides to play the basketball championship as himself. The game is won and Scott's transition to manhood is complete. (I've capitalised 'Wolf' throughout because there is a very real sense in which the Wolf is a separate character: he is Scott's *alter ego*, Hyde to his Jekyll, Batman to his Bruce Wayne, and he deserves a capital letter.)

It should be fairly obvious even from the simple synopsis above that Scott's transformation into the Wolf, and his subsequent absorption of the Wolf which allows him to become Scott again, is a metaphor for his transition from puberty through adolescence and into maturity. This is a male *Bildungsroman*, as I said before, and *Teen Wolf* has a great deal of 'maleness' about it, involving scene after scene of some kind of confrontation. The film opens and closes with young men engaged in competitive sport, and throughout the film a great deal of combat takes place on the basketball court in both a literal and a metaphorical sense. Scott's team makes the transition from losing to winning team, by way of indicating that Scott has fought his demons and emerged victorious. When Scott chooses to play the final game as himself instead of the Wolf, the viewer is presented with an exact replica of the opening scene: Scott, in slow-motion, bouncing the ball in preparation for a vital penalty shot. This is a neat and economical way of heightening the tension because when we first see this scene, Scott loses. The Wolf would win it - we know that - but can *Scott* do it? We've seen him lose before, and this time we know that much, much more is at stake - this is not just about the championship, this is Scott's moment to prove himself. This is his initiation ceremony. This is the point when he asserts his right *not* to be the Wolf.

On a more literal, surface level, the most obvious confrontation - and the most physical - is that with Mick, the 'Neanderthal' twenty-year-old who is still at school because he has 'done time', and the boyfriend of Pamela, the object of Scott's young male desire. That said, Scott runs up against almost all the other characters at one point or another - his father, Vice Principal Rusty Thorne, girlfriend-in-waiting Boof, the man from the liquor store, the whole basketball team - but the central confrontation is of course that between Scott and the Wolf, the hitherto unknown side of himself. Scott has to learn to control the Wolf, not to let it control him - and this is true of all of us during our formative teenage years. We all have to confront our own wolves at this stage in our lives and we all have to decide who we want to be. And of course, when you're sixteen or seventeen, you just don't know who you want to be. Moreover, you don't know who *other people* want you to be, and a battle rages between the need to conform and to be part of a community, the desire to please others, and the absolute necessity of finding your own voice. 'Everybody likes the Wolf,' says Scott, but this is not entirely true, nor in the end is it entirely relevant. The point is whether or not *Scott* likes the Wolf.

In one reading of the film, Scott's exploration of his burgeoning sexuality includes the possibility of his being homosexual, with this latent tendency being represented by the Wolf. This is rather an outlandish reading, but there is textual support for it in the script and also by way of precedent in numerous other texts. Many of the most popular teenage fictions feature vampires and/ or werewolves, and their presence is almost always metaphorically sexual. For example, it has been noted elsewhere (*Reading the Vampire Slayer,* ed. Roz Kaveney) that the scene in which Buffy reveals to her mother Joyce that she is a vampire slayer is intentionally scripted to read like a daughter-to-mother coming-out scene: all you have to do is replace 'slayer' with 'gay' and there you have it. And Joyce's response comes straight out of the same script: 'Have you tried *not* being a slayer?' This scene has its less subtle counterpart in *Teen Wolf* when Stiles' response to Scott's request for a listening ear is to assume that Scott is going to tell him that he's gay:

STILES: Wait a minute, are you going to tell me you're a fag?

SCOTT: No, I'm not a fag...I'm a werewolf.

It's nowhere near as clever as the *Buffy* script, but it deals with the same idea: the presence of the Other (slayer or werewolf) which is mistaken for homosexuality. The night Scott transforms into the Wolf for the first time is the same night Stiles asks him 'What's it like coming out of the closet?' after Scott has been shut away in a cloakroom with Boof as part of a party game. Scott returns home in some physical distress, and, locked in the bathroom, he 'comes out of the closet' when he transforms into the Wolf. The next morning, Mr Howard attempts to comfort his son by telling him that 'Werewolves are people too'. Again, the dialogue in this scene could easily be read with 'the werewolf' acting as a metaphor for homosexuality. And the Wolf polarises opinion in a way that could be translated into a first experience of homophobia directed at someone who has recently come out. The Wolf is almost universally popular, but there are those who reject Scott's new persona: Rusty Thorne, Lewis, Boof, and especially Mick, who tells Scott 'Stick with your own kind, freak!'

It is tempting to accept this reading, but to do so one would have to interpret the film's ending as a rejection of homosexuality in favour of a return to a more 'acceptable' way of life and an insipid relationship with the girl-next-door. While this is not entirely out of the question, I don't think there's enough textual evidence to support such a reading beyond making a tentative foray into the possibility of the Wolf's being representative of a homosexual Other, as I have done here. On the whole, it is far more likely that the Wolf symbolises the increase in a young man of both sexual hunger and prowess; the eventual suppression of the Wolf becomes possible once Scott has completed his rite-of-passage in (presumably) losing his virginity to Pamela.

Let's take a closer look now at *Teen Wolf*'s women. There isn't really any room in this film for women. Pamela and Boof are both cyphers, non-characters, there simply to be symbols for the choices open to Scott and what he chooses to reject in himself - although, to be fair, this is also largely true of the male characters. Apart from Pamela and Boof, the only other female character is Scott's mother, who is conspicuous by her absence. Her appearance in the narrative can be categorised in five different ways, as follows: firstly, of course, she is the woman who is no longer there. Scott is apparently being raised by his father alone. There is no woman in the home to act as a counterfoil to all this *maleness*. Scott's mother is the woman who accepted, and became accustomed to, having a werewolf for a mate; she is also the woman who was fought over and won, thereby providing a parallel narrative for Scott's own courting years in Mr Howard's confrontation with Rusty Thorne. In *Mick's* narrative, she is a woman who had her head blown off for stealing chickens; this latter is a 'your mother' type of taunt with which Mick goads Scott at the dance. Finally, Scott's mother leaves a gap for Boof to fill. Scott's parents were also childhood sweethearts, as Boof and Scott finally prove to be, and Boof is the successor to Scott's mum as the werewolf's mate. She begins to take on this role in her relationship with Mr Howard: Scott comes home one afternoon to find Boof 'shooting hoops' with his father. This is an obvious attempt on Boof's part to ingratiate herself with Scott, but the whole set-up has a distasteful smell of Oedipus about it.

Or, I don't know, perhaps it's just a scene that doesn't work. Boof's pursuit of Scott is so *naked*, and here she is saying 'I'm a much better match for you than Pamela, because look how well I get on with your father!' As if that mattered. I'm not sure whether it's just me, but I think a big problem with this film is that we *don't like Boof*. I'm not sure whether this is a question of the actor's performance or the script with which she had to work, but to be honest - well, she's a pain in the backside. She's a nag. She's humourless. She stomps off in a strop at least three times. She's everything Scott is trying to escape at the beginning of the film: she's average, she doesn't mind him being average, she thinks his father is 'a great guy', she likes the town in which they live. Boof is also *basketball* - emphasised for us in the 'shooting hoops' scene just mentioned - whereas Pamela is the school play. We see Scott approach the basketball team coach in an early scene to talk to him about quitting the team. Scott doesn't want to be on a losing team: he wants to be something special, something different, and all these connections are made in his conversation with Boof immediately following his chat with the coach. Scott's frustration at the poor performance of his team quickly turns to a discussion of his perceived 'averageness' and the fact that Pamela won't talk to him. Boof's responses (before she flounces away in a huff) forge links which will remain in the minds of the viewer throughout: Boof at this stage *is* everything Scott would like to get away from.

So, in wishing to dump the basketball team in favour of the school play, Scott is expressing a preference for Pamela over Boof. Scott can only appear in the school play as the Wolf, whereas he plays basketball in both his personae. When he appears onstage as himself following the showdown with Mick at the dance, he explains to the bemused drama teacher that he wishes to play the role as himself, but this request is refused because 'that wouldn't be theatre'. No

Wolf, no part. Scott walks offstage, rejecting both the play and, by implication, Pamela. The drama teacher's association of the Wolf with theatre encourages the viewer to categorise the Wolf with that which is not real: Pamela, the Wolf, the play - it's all show and no substance. Scott abandons the play to return to basketball, and by implication, Boof.

Pamela is Boof's physical antithesis - she is blonde to Boof's brunette - and she is cruel and selfish. She shamelessly plays Scott and Mick off against each other and her relationship with the drama teacher has its sexual undertones. I can't trace which play it is that Pamela's acting in, but there's an awful lot of talk about 'ravishing'. Pamela is Scott's initiation into the adult world of sex and their dressing-room liaison ends with Scott/Wolf howling with pleasure. (This howl is heard - of course - by Rusty Thorne, the man thwarted in love by Scott's father.) By contrast, there are two scenes in which Scott kisses Boof when they are alone together and in both instances, Scott is physically chastised afterwards. When they are locked in the cloakroom during the party, Scott's growing sexual excitement causes a partial transformation and Boof slaps his face when Scott claws her back with his Wolf fingernails. Boof and Scott kiss briefly at the dance and Mick punches Scott when the two reappear. In the context of the film's narrative, Scott's final rejection of Pamela for Boof would appear to be on some level a rejection of sex altogether, because in choosing Boof, he is choosing to be punished, rather than rewarded, for any sexual acts he may instigate.

Scott's rejection of Pamela is in some respects a frustrated narrative: the boy gets the girl, but in the end he doesn't want her. And Scott's relationship with his coach is arguably another frustrated narrative. This is no *Karate Kid* scenario. The coach is one of many potential male role models with which Scott is presented, and on two occasions the coach is seen to give Scott advice, but this advice is either confused or irrelevant and when Scott refuses to play as the Wolf at the end, this is an acknowledgement on Scott's part that his coach *doesn't* know best and that he must trust to his own instincts. It has to be said though, that the scenes in which the coach doles out his useless advice are really very funny.

'It doesn't matter how you play the game, it's whether you win or lose. And even that doesn't make all that much difference'

'Let me give you a little advice. There's three rules that I live by. Never get less than twelve hours' sleep, never play cards with a guy who's got the same first name as a city, and never go near a lady who's got a tattoo of a dagger on her body. Now you stick with that, everything else is cream cheese.'

Other potential role models include Stiles, of course, and Scott briefly tries out 'being' Stiles when he 'surfs' as the Wolf on top of Stiles' van (or 'Wolfmobile'). Mick represents the aggression which would dominate Scott if he chose to remain as the Wolf, but after the fight at the dance, this is not an option for Scott any longer. The Wolf's rage has frightened him as it once did Mr Howard many years ago in his confrontation with Rusty Thorne, and it is inevitable from this point that the role model Scott will adopt is his own father. Scott rejects the Wolf, and in doing so, repeats his father's history. And just in case we are left in any doubt as to how Scott will cope without the Wolf, we are shown a scene in which Mr Howard demonstrates that he himself no longer needs to transform. When Scott's father confronts Thorne for a second time at the dance in order to protect Scott, he does so as himself - not the Wolf - and yet the end result of this second interview is the same. All Mr Howard has to do is let out a low growl and Thorne wets himself in terror.

The film's ending is in many ways problematic. Scott's decision is touted as 'the right thing', but he is rejecting everything he craved at the film's opening and settling for an ordinary life instead of an extraordinary one. Yes, everything within the context of the metaphor works out just fine, but there remains a sense that the viewer is being force-fed an ideology in which the individual's capacity for difference and his or her potential for greatness must be suppressed in order to meet the needs and requirements of the community in which s/he lives. Scott's a team player. The Wolf is not. But I suppose the counterweight to this argument lies in the fact that the Wolf's achievements are empty: the theatre is only make-believe, Pamela is cold-hearted and vain, and his basketball victories are Pyrrhic in that they lose him the friendship of his team-mates.

Adapted from the original text posted to www.auntymuriel.com on 27 September 2014.

King Gary and his court: repetition and prolepsis in *The World's End*

The World's End is the final film in Simon Pegg and Edgar Wright's Three Flavours Cornetto Trilogy and what binds the films together, apart from the Cornetto references, is that all three are about attempted takeovers in which human beings are assimilated and homogenised. In *Shaun of the Dead*, those affected by a zombie plague turn other people into zombies; in *Hot Fuzz*, the attempt to build a utopian village means that those who don't fit in are murdered; in *The World's End*, the utopian theme is present again when an alien force known as 'The Network' (voiced by Bill Nighy) turns people into robot versions of themselves when they refuse to comply. As the character of Basil says,

> It's not an invasion, it's a merger. They don't want to get rid of us, not if they can help it. They just want to make us more like them. Change the way we think. Bring us into line with all the others. Become another link in their chain. Which is fine - unless you say no.

Given the underlying theme of the trilogy - that of assimilation - visual and verbal repetition naturally features strongly in all three films and it takes both spatial and temporal forms in *The World's End*. Spatially, repetition is seen in the 'Starbucking' of Newton Haven: chains such as Starbucks have taken over and the pubs are identically furnished, right down to the same fake chalk handwritten signage. Basil refers to The Network's wish to incorporate humanity as another link in the 'chain', and this wish is metaphorically embodied in the homogenisation of the spaces in the film. In the final scene, Gary and Andy confront The Network with its 'Starbucking' of human beings: each identical pub has a robot landlord who, in an identical movement to all his robot counterparts, slaps a bar-towel over his shoulder.

Temporally speaking, Gary (Simon Pegg) is an ideal hero, because he is hopelessly stuck in the past: he wears the same clothes, drives the same car, listens to the same music (on the same cassette tape!) and still possesses the same map as that which was consulted when the five friends didn't quite finish the Golden Mile over twenty years ago. Gary persuades his friends to join him in the ill-fated recreation of 22nd June 1990 and the short vignette into the past which accompanies Gary's voiceover at the beginning of the film more or less provides the reader with the entire storyline (minus the robots). This vignette is a kind of proleptic *annonce,* as described by structuralist and narratologist

Gérard Genette: it's a narrative flashforward, containing information about the characters' future. As the film progresses, the viewer watches the characters re-enact the events of that night, and although the presence of the robots means that everything is essentially different while only appearing to be the same, the narrative structure of the vignette is broadly identical to the larger storyline of the film. And beyond the confines of the film's story, there is even more repetition on a grand historical scale: The Network tells Gary and Andy that mankind endlessly repeats the same cycles of self-destruction.

You are children and you require guidance. There is no room for imperfection.

Here's Gary's opening monologue in full, courtesy of IMDB:

http://www.imdb.com/title/tt1213663/quotes

[opening monologue] Ever have one of those nights that starts out like any other but ends up being the best night of your life? It was June the 22nd, 1990. Our final day of school. There was Oliver Chamberlain, Peter Page, Steven Prince, Andy Knightley, and me. They called me "The King". Because that's my name - Gary King. Ollie fancied himself as a bit of a player but really he was old man. We called him "O Man" because he had a birth mark on his face that was shaped like a six. He loved it. Pete was the baby of the group. He wasn't the kind of kid we would usually hang out with, but he was good for a laugh. And he was absolutely minted. Steve was a pretty cool guy, we jammed together. Chased the girls. I think he saw us as rivals. Sweet really. And Andy. Andy was my wingman. The one guy I could rely on to back me up. He loved me, and I'm not being funny, but I loved him too. There was nothing we were going to miss about school. Maybe Mr. Shepherd, he was one of the good guys. He used to ask me what I wanted to do with my life. I told him I just wanted to have a good time. He thought that was funny. It wasn't meant to be, not that night. Newton Haven was our home town, our playground. Our universe. And that night was the site of a heroic quest. Our aim? To conquer the Golden Mile - 12 pubs along the legendary path of alcoholic indulgence. There was the First Post, the Old Familiar, the Famous Cock, the Cross Hands, the Good Companions, the Trusty Servant, the Two Headed Dog, the Mermaid, the Beehive, the King's Head, the Hole In The Wall, all before reaching our destiny - The World's End. We took my car into town that night. We called her "The Beast" because she was pretty hairy. And so our journey into manhood began. We were off. We didn't waste any time, we hit pub

one and we hit it hard. There was drinking, there were laughs, there was controversy, there were ladies, there were shots, there was drama, and of course there was drinking. By pub 5 we were feeling invincible, and decide to purchase some herbal refreshment from a man we called "The Reverend Green". Pint 6 put O Man out of commission, so we carried on without him. Good thing, I bumped into his sister at the next pub and we went into the disableds, and then I bumped into her again. Sam tagged along for a while, but then I had to let her go, I had another date that night. And her name was Amber. Nine pints in and it was us against the world. Things got mental in the Beehive so we tailed it to the Bowls Club, or as we called it "The Smoke House", which is where it all went fuck up. Everyone got paranoid and Pete chucked a whitey so we had to bench him. In the end we blew off the last three pubs and headed for the hills. As I sat up there, blood on my knuckles, beer down my shirt, sick on my shoes, knowing in my heart life would never feel this good again.

[*shows Gary in a group therapy setting*]

And you know what? It never did.

Here we are introduced to the friends as they existed in the past, and during the opening credits, we see them as their adult selves more than twenty years after the events of that night.

Gary is a king with his court. In conversation with Peter, he makes reference to *The Once and Future King*, who, of course, is King Arthur in T. H. White's novel of the same name. Gary's attempt to conquer the Golden Mile is elevated to the level of a quest and many of Gary's speeches have an epic tinge to them:

> Tonight, we will be partaking of a liquid repast as we wind our way up the Golden Mile. Commencing with an inaugural tankard in The First Post, then on to The Old Familiar, The Famous Cock, The Cross Hands, The Good Companions, The Trusty Servant, The Two-Headed Dog, The Mermaid, The Beehive, The King's Head, and The Hole in the Wall for a measure of the same, all before the last bittersweet pint in that most fateful terminus, The World's End. Leave a light on good lady, for though we may return with a twinkle in our eyes, we will be in truth be blind - drunk!

In the final confrontation, The Network refers to Gary as King of the Humans, and as previously suggested, Gary is the perfect leader and hero of this tale because he hasn't grown up or moved on, and he doesn't want things to have changed since 1990. He embraces the biggest change when it comes because it takes him backwards in time, not forwards, and he ends by recreating his court with the robot versions of his friends when they were young.

King Gary's Court

A *page* is a young male servant, an apprentice to a knight, and Peter Page (played by Eddie Marsan) is the baby of the group. His death is foretold in the opening vignette: everyone gets paranoid in The Smoke House as before, but on this occasion it's because they can't be sure that everyone present is still human. Peter gets benched at this stage of the Golden Mile as he did twenty years ago when he is entrapped by his childhood bully in robot form and distracted for long enough to enable the robots to close in. His friends can only look on in horror. Earlier in the film, Pete predicts his own demise in a proleptic announcement: "We could end up dead in a field. I hate fields." But it's not quite all bad: the adult Peter is seen in the opening credits looking very uncomfortable in the company of his offspring and hiding behind a newspaper to avoid his parenting responsibilities, but the robot Peter is seen having fun entertaining these children with his detachable hand at the end.

A *chamberlain* is an officer in charge of managing the household of a sovereign, and the adult Oliver Chamberlain (Martin Freeman) has become an estate agent and works, therefore, with property. His trademark mobile phone is first a brick-like device and then an in-ear piece. Oliver's death is also signposted for the attentive viewer: it was the sixth pint which put young Oliver out of action, and, twenty years later, after pint six in The Trusty Servant, it isn't Oliver who returns from the toilet. Robot Oliver is seen showing a couple around a property at the end of the film, and in fact this is the same young couple who couldn't afford the house priced at £1.2 million during one of the film's opening sequences.

A *knight* is a vassal who serves as a fighter for a lord, and Andrew Knightley (Nick Frost) is the most ferocious brawler of the five friends. Andy fights bravely in the toilet when five robots line up western-style facing the five humans; things get 'mental' in The Beehive as they did before, and it is Andy who begins the fight. He and his wife 'go organic' at the end, a reference to an earlier conversation, and this is what allows the fleeting Cornetto reference when a discarded wrapper of the same sweeps past Andy's nose. Gary narrates the story for us at the opening, but it is Andy who is our closing narrator.

The *prince* is one who will eventually take over from the king, as Steven Prince (Paddy Considine) does when he wins the heart of Samantha in an echo of the Lancelot and Guinevere narrative. Both the young and adult Gary repeatedly shove Steve out of the way to get to Sam, but Steve wins in the end. Steve is shown with his 26-year-old fitness instructor in the opening credits and in his shack with Sam at the close.

Repetition and prolepsis

Everything in the film is a repetition of something that has gone before, even down to its framing Arthurian narrative: we already know this story. The pub names are repeated in sequence over and over again, like a verbal map of the quest as recited during an oral narrative. The five friends have their spoken catchphrases and almost every conversation is a repetition of something previously said: Steve repeatedly mentions his 26-year-old fitness instructor; Oliver has his WTF?; Andy with his references to selective memory and his rebuff, 'It's pointless arguing with you'; Gary keeps telling Steve to write down potential band names. Numerous visual images are repetitions of something that has gone before: the landlords with their bar-towels have already been mentioned; Gary ringing the doorbell and running away; Gary jumping over objects and obstacles (not always successfully, and in fact, this is a running gag throughout the trilogy); the 'Starbucked' pubs, the view of Newton Haven from the road…and in fact, it is a repeated visual image that tells you something is very wrong. The sequence of pedestrians who walk past the five friends is identical in two separate instances: it's not just that the woman with the pram is still out walking her baby after dark that gives the viewer the shivers, it is the fact that she is seen in the same position in the sequence of passers-by. This is not normal. This is Uncanny Valley. Something is Going On.

There are other proleptic *annonces* signposting the deaths of Oliver and Peter outside of the opening vignette. The Beast herself, Gary's car from the 1990s, is a metaphorical *annonce*: more or less everything on this car has been replaced, so although it looks like the same car, it isn't. The car, therefore, is a metaphor for the robots: they look the same as the human they replaced, but the likeness is only superficial. The Oliver and Peter we see after they have been replaced look more or less the same as they always did, but they are nothing more than mechanical facsimiles of their human selves.

In addition, the two deaths are foretold in the many and various references to *The Three Musketeers* which are voiced throughout the film:

Gary King: And here we go! Just like the Five Musketeers!

Steven Prince: Three musketeers, wasn't it?

Peter Page: Four, if you count d'Artagnan.

Gary King: Well, nobody knows how many there were, really, do they?

Oliver Chamberlain: You do know that *The Three Musketeers* was a fiction, right? Written by Alexandre Dumas?

Gary King: A lot of people are saying that about the Bible these days.

Steven Prince: What, that it was written by Alexandre Dumas?

Gary King: Don't be daft, Steve! It was written by Jesus!

Gary then goes on to say that five musketeers would have been preferable to three because 'Two could've died and they'd still have three left', and, of course, this is exactly what happens. The film ends with the most famous quotation from Dumas's novel when Gary, surrounded by his new court of the robot versions of his friends, insists that the landlord in The Rising Sun serve all five of them with pints of water because it's 'All for one and one for all'.

The last point I'd like to make is just about a nice little bit of scriptwriting. The friends drunkenly discuss pronouns in one of the pubs - I forget which - and later on, one pronoun becomes very important.

Steven Prince: We need to be able to differentiate between them, them and us.

Peter Page: Yeah, I think the pronouns are really confusing.

Gary King: I don't even know what a pronoun is.

Oliver Chamberlain: Well, it's a word that can function by itself as a noun which refers to something else in the discourse.

Gary King: I don't get it.

Andrew Knightley: You just used one.

Gary King: Did I?

Andrew Knightley: "It" is a pronoun.

Gary King: What is?

Andrew Knightley: It!

Gary King: Is it?

Andrew Knightley: Christ!

A *change* in pronoun features in a later conversation and provides a clue as to the events to follow. In The Mermaid, the robots have been able to access the DNA of Gary, Peter and Andy. All the pub names in *The World's End* carry some significance, and here the mermaids are of course the two blondes and the redhead which make up the Marmalade Sandwich, but their role is really that of the Sirens: the robots knew that these three would not be able to resist a school uniform. (Mermaids and Sirens are not the same thing, but they have long been conflated in the collective consciousness. Sirens are in fact bird-like creatures and not mermaids at all.) When the friends exit The Mermaid, Gary challenges Oliver with not having lasted this long on the previous pub crawl. Oliver is of course Robot Oliver by now, and Gary has hit on the truth without realising it - he has given the viewer the clue that he can't quite work out for himself. In fact, Oliver is just about to be outed as a robot version so this is an *annonce* of a sort: if the viewer hasn't already spotted the switch, it will become obvious during this exchange. Outside the next pub, Oliver says to Andy 'It can't start without you,' which he changes to '*We* can't start without you,' when Andy asks him to repeat his remark. The change in the pronoun is significant - the friends are about to be directly 'invited' to join the robot community by a robot version of Mr Shepherd - and Andy knows what a pronoun is, even if Gary doesn't. 'It' is more likely to refer to something *outside* of the group of friends, in this case, the issuing of the invitation, whereas 'we' conceivably refers to the five friends partaking of their next round. Andy has all the clues he needs now to put two and two together: Steve's information from Basil about how the robots collect human DNA in order to create robotic clones, Gary's challenge to Oliver and Oliver's curious response, then Oliver's slip over that pronoun. That's why it's Andy who spots that Oliver's birthmark has returned. Then he knocks Oliver's robot head off.

Adapted from the original text posted to www.auntymuriel.com on 27 September 2014.

A potential development for cognitive poetics: text world theory and verbo-visual narratives

Multi-modal texts are increasingly prevalent in today's media-rich society and this in itself provides the justification for further research into how readers make sense of such texts. Kress and van Leeuwen (2001, 2006) explore the modality of images, and Peeters (1991) investigates the representation of emotions and thoughts, which can be depicted either iconically or linguistically, or through a combination of words and images. Analysts of verbo-visual narratives (comic books, graphic novels, etc.) such as Neil Cohn (2013), Scott McCloud (1993), Thierry Groensteen (2007, 2013), Benoît Peeters (1991), Mario Saraceni (2000, 2003) and others, have researched and constructed frameworks designed to facilitate discussion of texts composed of words and images. Teresa Bridgeman (2005) draws on the work of Catherine Emmott (1997) and Paul Werth (1999) in suggesting ways in which frame theory and text world theory can also inform the reading of such texts. What follows is an overview of Bridgeman's work with additional examples and ideas from my own reading.

I. The role of the reader of verbo-visual texts

Bridgeman opens her argument with a comment on the perceived inferior status of verbo-visual texts in comparison with texts composed entirely of words, because, like film, the verbo-visual text has an immediacy that limits the extent of interpretative work required by the reader. In some senses this is true, but it is not the case that the reader of graphic novels is merely a passive recipient. For example, the linearity of the reading process does not necessarily apply to verbo-visual texts. The reader can see much more of the story at a glance and the eye can be drawn to many points on the page before a conventional left-to-right and top-to-bottom reading is undertaken. (Cohn in particular has undertaken research using eye-tracking to investigate this aspect of verbo-visual texts more closely.) Bridgeman contends that the 'panoramic view' available to the reader means that textual elements can be processed 'first as potentially accessible details in a whole, and then as individual centres of experience'. Both readings are generated by the same 'word-image combination', and therefore 'the work of construction of meaningful relationships between world elements must be the reader's' (2005: 126).

There is other work for the reader to do besides. Bridgeman notes that there exists a relationship between 'fictional "fact"' and 'modalised subjective experience'. The reader tracks which character is experiencing what and assigns epistemological and/or ontological status to textual elements, differentiating between what is known and what is understood or believed (2005: 115). In dealing with the numerous text worlds present in one verbo-visual text, the reader allocates textual elements and sequences to various worlds and constructs relationships between them.

In addition, the reader constructs an imagined world *outside* the frame. Scott McCloud's famous example of the interpretative activity which is undertaken by the reader in the space between two frames, or the 'gutter', is that of the reader who swings the axe. Similarly, Kessler points out how the reader completes the stages of an action in *Astérix Légionnaire*, where Uderzo has drawn only the opening and closing stages of the action in question. Obelix kicks the tree and the frame which follows shows the tree lying on the ground, but it is the reader who imagines the tree in the act of falling.

Bridgeman refers to Emmott's work on priming in her explanation of the need to take into account sequence and ongoing processing (Bridgeman, 2005: 120; Emmott, 1997). The notion of priming must be modified somewhat when discussing verbo-visual texts because much of the information required is visually available to the reader – the characters are visually present in the frame – but, as Bridgeman points out, the reader must be able to recognise that character as the *same* character. In a scene from *Harrow County*, the Skinless Boy has penetrated the house where Emmy is being held captive. He is recognisable in the frame only by his yellow eyes, with which the reader is already familiar. The Skinless Boy is also present in the frame following, but only as a shadow above Emmy's head. Nevertheless, the reader will connect this shadow with the appearance of the Skinless Boy in the previous frame and will know in advance that rescue is at hand for Emmy.

The discussion will now take a closer look at the different types of text worlds as described initially by Werth and adapted by Bridgeman (see Appendix A), how movement is effected between text worlds and how different text worlds can be processed simultaneously.

II. Different types of text world

Bridgeman notes that Werth uses a Chinese box model of worlds and Marie-Laure Ryan a model with a world and satellites 'with degrees of remoteness from the centre' (2005: 118-119). Both models can be represented in verbo-visual texts. In default mode, the dominant frame represents the textual-actual-world with embedded subworlds of the thought and speech of characters, following the Chinese box pattern (119). In other words, the different text worlds are physically represented on the page by means of the frames around each image and each speech and/or thought bubble. A two-page spread from *Fables* has been discussed at some length by Karin Kukkonen in her exploration of comics and the discourse of postmodernism (2013: 48-50). The reader is given access to the fictional mind of the Frog Prince via an attitudinal subworld. The focus closes in on the Frog Prince's eye as his thoughts are revealed. The subjective experience of the character creates a subworld within the larger textual-actual-world (see Appendix A). A change in colour scheme indicates that the events witnessed are taking place only in the Frog Prince's 'mind's eye' as he considers a possible and imagined future; the subworld is closed when the colour scheme returns to normal. As Bridgeman notes, 'the world continues to be that set up at the entry point, unless evidence to the contrary is provided' (2005: 122), in this case, the switch in colour scheme.

a) The Narrative World: *Spirits of the Dead*

Spirits of the Dead is a collection of Edgar Allan Poe's tales adapted and retold in verbo-visual form. The narrator figure is present throughout the volume, but s/he occupies an unusual position which is sometimes internal and sometimes external to the narrative. In this particular adaptation of Poe's *The Masque of the Red Death*, the androgynous narrator – a type of Tiresias figure – is internal to the story. S/he is a storyteller seeking a story when s/he finds a hooded figure wandering through the misty ruins. This shadowy figure tells his story while the reader listens in. The reader is therefore twice displaced as narratee, listening to someone telling someone else a story. On the story's final page, the man telling the story is revealed as King Prospero, meaning that he is a character in the story's text world.

Prospero does not step out of his textual-actual-world (see Appendix A). His telling of the story is part of his own world, as is his death at the end. For the Tiresias figure, his/her conversation with Prospero is the discourse world, and the story is the text world. For the reader, the discourse world is the book containing all the adaptations of Poe, and the text world includes the Tiresias figure's narrative world (which is collapsed into the story's text world because this traveller/listener is a character) and Prospero's textual-actual-world.

By way of contrast, in an adaptation of another of Poe's tales, the Tiresias figure is *external* to the story. Although s/he is present in the frame and is apparently watching events happen, s/he does not communicate directly with any of the characters and comments only on the action of the story, winding up events for the reader. The paratextual addition of the words 'The End' in a demarcated box occur a level up from the narrative world to take place in the discourse world. The author(s) inform the reader that this particular tale has reached its end.

b) The Narrative World: *Lighter Than My Shadow*

Lighter Than My Shadow is an autobiographical memoir in which writer and artist Katie Green explores her battle with anorexia. At the opening of the narrative, the reader sees a present-day enactor of the author-figure sitting at her desk in the act of creating the book the reader is reading. The images of the naked figures in foetal position represent an earlier author-enactor figure, dating from the time when Katie Green was struggling with anorexia. The next page in the book shows the black squiggle behind the naked figures being drawn down into the author-enactor's pen, and the final image in the sequence shows the black squiggle, now an ink-substitute, emerging from the pen onto the paper. This black squiggle is a feature of the entire book: it grows over Katie's head and remains with her throughout until she learns how to defeat it. This sequence informs the reader that the author is writing about this period from her life in an effort to purge herself of the memories which haunt her, and that the experience of producing this book is, for Katie Green, one of catharsis.

The text world thereby incorporates aspects of the discourse world. The reader is reading an autobiographical memoir in which the author has demonstrated here in a sequence of images the very personal reasons behind the production of this book, and the reader sees on the page the author in the process of writing. The text world itself is Katie's story, beginning when she was a small girl and bringing her story up to the present day.

c) Narrative World: *Dotter of Her Father's Eyes*

The levels of narration in this text are rather complicated. The writer Mary Talbot is an academic married to Bryan Talbot, author and illustrator of many successful graphic novels. At the beginning of the story, the fictional counterpart of the real-life Mary is seen reading the biography of Lucia Joyce by Carol Loeb Shloss. These details are part of the text's discourse world: Mary and Bryan Talbot are real, Mary's father was real and the book by Shloss is real. The Talbots' book tells of two dysfunctional father-daughter relationships. The story of Mary and her 'cold mad feary father', an eminent

Joycean scholar, is told alongside that of Lucia Joyce, daughter of the famous James, whose promising career as a dancer is cut tragically short with her parents being in no small way to blame. The reader must therefore follow three separate text worlds: the story of Lucia Joyce, the story of Mary's childhood, and the present-day world of Bryan and Mary. These three worlds are represented by three different colour schemes. Lucia Joyce's story is told in black and white; Mary's childhood is rendered in sepia with occasional splashes of red; and Bryan and Mary's present-day is in full colour. Considered chronologically, the colour scheme moves through black and white into sepia and finally into full colour, as if the reader were looking at a century's worth of old photographs. Splashes of colour dribble into the sepia colour-scheme, and these splashes become increasingly dominant as Mary and Bryan's history begins to catch up with the present time.

III. Signalling a shift between worlds

Devices to signal a shift between worlds include the following: modification of the frame pattern, such as using a semi-permeable dotted line or wavy shapes to indicate that the character is dreaming; inclusion of place and date in the space demarcated for narratorial comment; use of different colour schemes as seen above in *Dotter of Her Father's Eyes* and *Lighter Than My Shadow*; voice-over narration and contrasting contents as exemplified in a sequence from *Harrow County*. This sequence appears close to the end of the first volume, when protagonist Emmy has discovered her real identity as a second incarnation of the witch Hester Beck, who was murdered eighteen years ago in retribution for her activities by the inhabitants of Harrow County. Emmy has inherited Hester's healing powers and a couple shown have overcome their suspicion of Emmy and are seeking her help with a sick child. The couple follow Emmy into the house, but the main focus of this image is the calf which is captured in the action of running from right to left across the frame, counter to the left-right reading path. The calf's face points towards the blue box to the top left of the frame which contains Emmy's spoken words to the couple as they move towards the house at the back of the frame and away from the reader.

The reader assumes this calf to be the very same animal healed by Emmy at the story's opening, and its appearance in this section of the narrative serves as a reminder of Emmy's power to do good. Emmy's voice continues as they move inside the house and is 'heard' over this frame: 'She's gonna be just fine'. The dialogue has moved into the space usually reserved for the narratorial 'peripheral world' described by Bridgeman (2005: 119). Emmy's 'voice-over' continues into the next frame with the words 'There's nothing to worry about', and, as in the previous frame, this dialogue occupies the same peripheral space and is demarcated by a blue box. In addition, the quotation marks placed around both remarks help the reader to understand that the words represent Emmy's utterances to the worried parents. But there is a difference between the two remarks. The words 'She's gonna be just fine' are *supported* by the accompanying image: Emmy's remark refers to the sick child who at present is feverish, but also to the calf, who has recovered completely and is shown happily cantering across the foreground. The implication, of course, is that the child will make a full recovery just as the calf did. In the next frame, however, Emmy's words are 'heard' over an image of a very different text world. Harrow County has been replaced with a city scene where it is pouring with rain and the streetlights are illuminated to pierce the gloom. Emmy's claim that 'There's nothing to worry about' is true in relation to the child and her parents, but untrue in relation to the image it accompanies: in the second volume of *Harrow County*, Kammi, an inhabitant of this city world, provides Emmy with plenty to worry about. Emmy's words in the latter frame are undermined by the image. She is talking about the child, of course, but the reader's attention is grabbed by the sudden intrusion of a visual image of a completely different text world, and it is natural for the reader to consider in what way Emmy's words might relate to this new world, and to draw the conclusion that this new world does indeed contain something to worry about.

The shift between text worlds itself is effected over the two frames, with Emmy's 'voiceover' linking the two. Emmy's voice works in tandem with the drawing-back of the 'camera' to pull the reader out of the text world of Harrow County, but the continuation of this voice in the new text world of the rainy city links the two worlds as the transition is made from one to the other. We cannot be said to be wholly in the rainy-city text world until the frame following the one shown, where Emmy's voice can no longer be heard.

IV. Simultaneous sequences in more than one world

Bridgeman notes that '[t]he graphic layout of BD not only allows more than one world to be present in a single frame, it also allows sequences in more than one world to be presented as simultaneous' (2005: 123). In the example explored below, this use of simultaneous sequences occurs at the climax of the narrative and reveals an important truth about the nature of some of the characters.

Livestock is Hannah Berry's third graphic novel, and it tracks the career of Clementine Darling, singer and political spokesperson. Berry's political dystopia explores how public opinion is both created and controlled by the media through adored celebrities such as Darling, who are used time and time again to distract public attention from the political issues of the day. Berry's celebrities are in fact directly affiliated with political parties and are manipulated into endorsing whatever policy is currently making the headlines. The policy which forms the subject of Berry's tale is that of cloning. Politicians and scientists have secretly endorsed the cloning of human beings, and, as a character who is an opponent of cloning points out, 'sentient clones created by these companies wouldn't be recognised as free citizens - technically these people would be classed as "livestock"'. Berry's tale takes its title from this observation.

Towards the end of the story, the narration presents two simultaneous sequences, first in parallel frames. The central frame depicting the moon in the night sky which overlaps the two frames below is an indication that the events depicted are taking place at the same time on the same evening. On the left, the frame shows the crowds gathering for a protest at which singer Nina Malick is going to speak. On the right, the crowds assemble for an awards ceremony called the Tammies and various celebrities are depicted on the red carpet.

As the two events progress, gradually the text worlds merge and both worlds can be accessed in each single frame. The speech bubble at the top *without* the tail represents Nina Malick's words delivered during the protest. The speech bubbles *with* tails represent the utterances of the celebrities shown receiving their Tammies. Malick's eloquent speech is about the creation of an unthinking public controlled by the press via a constant stream of vacuous irrelevances concerning the celebrities they worship. She names in the bubbles here some of the ways in which the public have been hoodwinked and manipulated by the 'partisan media', which itself holds sway over the politicians. If the reader has not worked out before this point that the celebrities who act as political spokespeople are themselves clones, this is made obvious by the juxtaposition here of Malick's speech with images of those celebrities receiving their awards and spouting platitudes to a placid audience. In the closing pages of the narrative, Clementine is sacrificed to distract the public from Malick's campaign, and her body is discarded in a skip marked 'clinical waste'.

In this essay, I have provided an overview of the work of Teresa Bridgeman on text world theory and its application to verbo-visual texts. I have considered the interpretative work required of the reader to make sense of these texts and I have explored examples of different types of text world, with a focus on the narrator-world level. Finally, I have examined how shifts are effected between text worlds and also how text worlds can operate simultaneously.

Appendix A: Bridgeman's breakdown of the different types of text world

'DISCOURSE WORLD: the context for the "communication event" of the text, constituted by "participants" (here being author(s) and readers), and those parts of their environment which are relevant to the act of communication.

TEXT WORLD: the world constructed from the text itself, including the narrative world (if there is one), the textual-actual-world, and various subworlds. The text world may also include aspects of the discourse world, through reference to them.

NARRATIVE WORLD: Werth calls this the narrative envelope, suppressing its importance in fiction as a potentially discrete area of common ground between narrator and narratee (although he does distinguish between character-accessible subworlds, and participant-accessible subworlds). As all who are familiar with Genette (1972) are aware, the narrative world may be presented as either external or internal to the textual-actual-world, and this has significant implications for the way in which the reader builds it into his/her world model.

TEXTUAL-ACTUAL-WORLD: this is the world the characters inhabit and which they consider to be the discourse world.

SUBWORLDS: Werth describes three kinds of subworld: deictic, attitudinal and epistemic. The first group are "departures from the basic deictic "signature" of the conceptual world, e.g. "flashbacks", direct speech, "windows" on to other scenes". The second comprise "notions entertained by the protagonists, as opposed to actions undertaken by the protagonists in the discourse". Epistemic subworlds are produced by "modalised propositions expressed either by participants or characters" (Werth 1999: 216).'

Transcribed from Bridgeman 2005: 117-118.

List of references

My Top Five Favourite Comic Books, an Outsider: 'Dotter of Her Father's Eyes' by Mary and Bryan Talbot. (17 February 2014). [Blog] auntymuriel. com. Available at: https://auntymuriel.com/2014/02/17/my-top-five-favourite-comic-books-an-outsider-dotter-of-her-fathers-eyes-by-mary-and-bryan-talbot/ [Accessed 5 Jul. 2017].

Berry, H. (2017) *Livestock*. London: Penguin.

Bridgeman, T. (2005) Figuration and configuration: mapping imaginary worlds in BD. In C. Forsdick, L. Grove, & L. McQuillan (eds.) *Francophone Bande Dessinée*. Amsterdam: Edition Rodopi, 115–136.

Bunn, C. & Crook, T. (2015) *Harrow County Volume 1: Countless Haints*. Milwaukie: Dark Horse Books.

Cohn, N. (2013) *The Visual Language of Comics: Introduction to the Structure and Cognition of Sequential Images*. London: Bloomsbury.

Corben, R. (2014) *Edgar Allan Poe's Spirits of the Dead*. Milwaukie: Dark Horse Books.

Emmott, C. (1997) *Narrative Comprehension: A Discourse Perspective*. Oxford: Oxford University Press.

Goscinny, R. & Uderzo, A. (1967) *Astérix Légionnaire*. Paris: Dargaud Éditeur.

Green, K. (2013) *Lighter Than My Shadow*. London: Jonathan Cape.

Groensteen, T. (2007) *The System of Comics*. Jackson: University Press of Mississippi.

Groensteen, T. (2013) *Comics and Narration*. Jackson: University Press of Mississippi.

Kessler, P. (1995) *The Complete Guide to Asterix*. London: Hodder Headline.

Kress, G. & van Leeuwen, T. (2001) *Multimodal Discourse: The modes and media of contemporary communication*. London: Hodder Education.

Kress, G. & van Leeuwen, T. (2006) *Reading Images: The Grammar of Visual Design*. 2nd ed. London: Routledge.

Kukkonen, K. (2013) *Contemporary Comics Storytelling*. Lincoln: University of Nebraska Press.

McCloud, S. (1993) Understanding Comics: The Invisible Art. New York: HarperCollins.

Saraceni, M. (2000) Language beyond language: Comics as verbo-visual texts. PhD thesis. University of Nottingham.

— (2003) The Language of Comics. London: Routledge.

Talbot, M.M. & Talbot, B. (2012) *Dotter of Her Father's Eyes.* London: Jonathan Cape.

Werth, P. (1999) *Text Worlds: Representing Conceptual Space in Discourse*. London: Longman.

Willingham, B. (2008) *Fables Volume 10: The Good Prince.* New York: DC Comics.

Elizabeth reads Darcy's letter

The account of his [Wickham's] connection with the Pemberley family, was exactly what he had related himself; and the kindness of the late Mr. Darcy, though she had not before known its extent, agreed equally well with his own words. So far each recital confirmed the other: but when she came to the will, the difference was great. What Wickham had said of the living was fresh in her memory, and as she recalled his very words, it was impossible not to feel that there was gross duplicity on one side or the other; and, for a few moments, she flattered herself that her wishes did not err. But when she read, and re-read with the closest attention, the particulars immediately following of Wickham's resigning all pretensions to the living, of his receiving in lieu, so considerable a sum as three thousand pounds, again was she forced to hesitate. She put down the letter, weighed every circumstance with what she meant to be impartiality - deliberated on the probability of each statement - but with little success. On both sides it was only assertion. Again she read on. But every line proved more clearly that the affair, which she had believed it impossible that any contrivance could so represent, as to render Mr. Darcy's conduct in it less than infamous, was capable of a turn which must make him entirely blameless throughout the whole.

Jane Austen *Pride and Prejudice*
Oxford World's Classics edition (1990) p. 182

This passage represents a turning point in the narrative: first Darcy and then Elizabeth are forced to reassess their own embedded narratives (Palmer, 2004) in order to incorporate that of the other. Darcy has spent much of the night writing an explanatory letter to Elizabeth after she has given her reasons for refusing his proposal of marriage, and the excerpt under discussion shows Elizabeth's reaction on reading this letter and learning a different sort of truth to the one she has previously upheld. The world-view of each character alters dramatically, and this change is reflected also in the situation of the reader, who is forced to revisit and reassess the novel's events up to this point at the same time Elizabeth does so, and is therefore subject to the same reading experience as Elizabeth. Many of Elizabeth's memories will tally with the reader's recollection of events, and the reader, alongside Elizabeth, will revise formerly-created contextual frames (Emmott, 1997). It is now that the reader will realise that many of these memories were not, in fact, impartially formed, but were coloured by Elizabeth's perception of events. She is the novel's

327

focalizer, and at this point she is also the *focalized* while she examines her recollections and even her conscience: this passage occurs shortly before Elizabeth famously cries out: 'Till this moment, I never knew myself' (185). It is at this moment in the novel that the difference between the narrator and focalizer is apparent, and once this difference is recognised, the reader is also cognisant of the extent to which the two were previously confused. The narrator has encouraged the deception of the reader through discreet use of the focalizer-character's world-view to distort the creation of memory as the novel's events occurred, thus enabling the narrator to administer a salutary corrective to both Elizabeth *and* the reader when Darcy's letter is read and the ugly truth about Wickham's character known.

The narrator states that Elizabeth has to collect herself before re-reading the letter, an activity described as a 'mortifying perusal of all that related to Wickham' (182). Although Darcy is not yet exonerated for his part in Bingley's rejection of Jane, the narrator indicates here that he is in no way to be held accountable for Wickham's misfortunes, and that Elizabeth knows this to be the case even before she embarks upon reading the letter for a second time. In writing the letter, Darcy has provided his own defence against Wickham's aspersions, and Elizabeth is to judge between the two narratives. The passage under consideration shows Elizabeth weighing the evidence before passing judgement. Sections of Darcy's letter reappear in paraphrase: for example, 'Wickham's resigning all pretensions to the living, of his receiving in lieu, so considerable a sum as three thousand pounds'; thus the reader receives the same information twice in quick succession having read Darcy's letter in the chapter preceding, and these reiterations now serve as a makeshift summing-up. In addition, these paraphrases are iconic of Elizabeth's own experience of re-reading Darcy's words, as she also repeatedly encounters the same information in her several attempts to digest the contents of the letter.

The written form of the chosen passage also mirrors the meaning in a more immediate sense. Vocabulary choices reflect both language of a legal character, and the act of comparing two differing accounts of the same events and weighing or measuring one account against the other: *exactly, equally, confirmed, difference, on one side or the other, read and re-read, put down, weighed, deliberated, probability, each statement, both, assertion, every line proved, impossible, represent, entirely, the whole*. On a syntactical level, Elizabeth's mental gymnastics are encapsulated in the way in which her initial thoughts are each time balanced against another statement introduced with the co-ordinating conjunction 'but', which appears four times in this short excerpt.

The 'written' nature of the passage reveals to the reader the presence of a narrator beyond Elizabeth's consciousness, and if this were not enough, the narrator's voice actively intrudes three times to make it clear to the reader that Elizabeth is mentally fighting against the information newly-received, and in the process is doing her best to retain her former mind-set: 'for a few moments, she flattered herself that her wishes did not err'; 'weighed every circumstance with what she meant to be impartiality'; and thirdly, the twisty final line of the passage contains a subordinate clause which comprises 23 words - exactly the same number as the main clause. Darcy is found to be 'blameless' in the more important main clause, but the lengthy subordinate clause represents the depth and rigidity of the opinion Elizabeth had willingly formed beforehand. She finds her previous opinion difficult to relinquish, as demonstrated here in the syntax of subordinate clause (former beliefs) versus main clause (new beliefs). While Elizabeth struggles hard to exonerate Wickham, in the end she cannot do so, and is therefore confronted not only with the downfall and disgrace of her former favourite, but also the humiliating knowledge that she herself has judged wrongly and has allowed her prejudice to blind her to the reality of the situation: 'Pleased with the preference of one, and offended by the neglect of the other, on the very beginning of our acquaintance, I have courted prepossession and ignorance, and driven reason away, where either were concerned' (185). Elizabeth now joins the narrator in balancing her words: *pleased/offended; preference/neglect; ignorance/reason.*

Until this moment, the narrator has colluded with the focalizer-character to mislead the reader, and now the narrator takes a step back to uncover the deception. Elizabeth's desire for Wickham to be innocent is clearly acknowledged by the narrator, tied as this circumstance is to Elizabeth's self-respect, and her partiality is revealed. In staying close to Elizabeth, the narrator has before this moment presented her views as if they were the objective truth, but in retrospect, both the reader and Elizabeth can see that her emotional response at the time of previous meetings with the two men was instrumental in the formation of her memory of each event (Wiltshire, 2014). Darcy's revelations force Elizabeth to confront the folly of her behaviour and she says in conversation with Jane: '"the misfortune of speaking with bitterness, is a most natural consequence of the prejudices I had been encouraging"' (200). In accepting without question Elizabeth's view of Darcy and Wickham before Darcy writes his letter, the reader has also been hoodwinked and is complicit in Elizabeth's shame. Austen's narrator is one who deceives in order to instruct, a point to which I shall return later.

In terms of the story, this is a moment when nothing is happening. Elizabeth is merely reading and re-reading Darcy's letter while remembering and reassessing former events. Genette would refer to this as a *pause* in the story (1980), but this is not to say that the same is true of the *narrative*: in actual fact, there is an enormous amount of *mental* activity happening at this point which will determine how future events play themselves out. It is, as previously stated, a pivotal moment in the narrative. Elizabeth is made aware of her error and from this point onwards she begins to fall in love with Darcy. In Proppian terms, this is the moment when the hero is recognised and the false hero or villain exposed (Toolan, 2001: 19-20).

It is notable also that Elizabeth's mental activity at this crucial juncture is linked to one of the much wider themes of the novel. Wiltshire argues that *Pride and Prejudice* is a novel about memory and how memories are created (2014: 51-71), and the whole of chapter thirteen of Austen's novel, from which this extract is taken, is given over to Elizabeth's musings on reading the letter. Elizabeth examines her memory of events and makes several corrections in the light of what she now knows. The reader is not strictly witnessing flashbacks, but the narrator actively points the reader to previous episodes where Elizabeth interprets events according to the background context entertained at the time, which leads to the creation of a memory coloured by an emotional response: the relevant parts of the text are 'was exactly what he had related himself'; and 'agreed equally well with his own words'; but then the vital difference emerges in relation to Darcy's father's will and 'What Wickham had said of the living'.

As mentioned above, Austen is a narrator who deceives in order to instruct, which is a very different approach to the didactic satirical method adopted by Swift in *Gulliver's Travels*. Austen chooses to *involve* the reader instead of actively preaching and the linear character of the reading experience is very much taken into account by Austen's wily narrator. Austen is well-known as an accomplished exponent of free indirect discourse, and it is through liberal use of such that voices of narrator, focalizer and character become intermingled and indistinguishable; thus when the rebuke comes for Elizabeth Bennet and Emma Woodhouse, the reader feels it just as keenly. Re-reading Austen is a very different experience to an initial reading of her novels. The pleasure in re-reading is in retracing exactly how the deception was carried out.

List of references:

Austen, J. (1990 [1813]) *Pride and Prejudice*. Oxford: Oxford University Press.

Emmott, C. (1997) *Narrative Comprehension: A Discourse Perspective.* Oxford: Clarendon Press.

Genette, G. (1980) *Narrative Discourse: An Essay in Method.* Ithaca: Cornell University Press.

Palmer, A. (2004) *Fictional Minds.* Lincoln: University of Nebraska Press.

Swift, J. (1967 [1726]) *Gulliver's Travels.* J. Chalker & P. Dixon. Eds. London: Penguin.

Toolan, M. (2001) *Narrative: A Critical Linguistic Introduction.* 2nd ed. London: Routledge.

Wiltshire, J. (2014) *The Hidden Jane Austen.* Cambridge: Cambridge University Press.

Focalization in Chaucer and Swift

The passages explored in this essay are reproduced in full on pages 337-338.

Chaucer's portrait of the lawyer is traditionally viewed as satirical. The editor of *The Riverside Chaucer* notes one or two exceptions to this trend (Benson, 1988: 811), but my personal inclination is towards the less favourable picture of this particular pilgrim.

On first reading this passage, I divided up the description into four sections as follows: 1) the lawyer's wisdom and professional reputation; 2) his activities as a buyer of land; 3) how his learning enables and facilitates his land-buying activities; 4) his relatively humble attire. I considered also the placing of the lawyer in between the Clerk (or university student) and the Franklin. The Clerk has devoted his life to study and possesses very little; the Franklin is a landowner and an Epicurean. The lawyer shares traits with both these characters: he is learned, like the Clerk, but he uses his learning to facilitate the purchase of land thereby consolidating his wealth and position. The lawyer is a landowner like the Franklin, but while the Franklin enjoys a reputation as a *bon viveur*, the lawyer appears avaricious and miserly in his 'medlee cote'. The lawyer's reputation is that of a 'greet...purchasour' (land-buyer), contrasted with the Franklin who is known as a 'worthy vavasour' (feudal landholder).

Lawyers had equal status to knights in Chaucer's time (Benson, 1988: 811) and the Sergeant of the Law's position is entrenched by his knowledge of existing legislation and precedence dating back to the days of King William, approximately 350 years before *The Canterbury Tales* appeared. The lawyer represents a societal stratum which reinforces and perpetuates the *status quo* out of self-interest, and he acquires land apparently without restraint: 'Al was fee symple to hym in effect'. His belt with its stripes ('barres') serves as a metaphor for the system the lawyer serves, a system that is impregnable, unimpeachable, which both debars those not learned from entry and protects those it encompasses.

In considering the presence of irony in this passage, I came to the following conclusions. It seems unlikely that the lawyer would have presented his land-buying activities in this way and it is not clear how the narrator has gained this knowledge, unless it be by former acquaintance with the lawyer and his reputation ('So greet a purchasour was nowher noon'). A conversation between the narrator and the lawyer could be imagined, but the reporting of the lawyer's character and the conclusions drawn would seem to belong entirely to the narrator. There is a throwaway observation in 'And yet he semed bisier than he was' which undermines and corrodes the portrait painted so far, as does the reference to the lawyer's 'purchasyng' which interrupts the description of his work as a 'Justice'. The statements made in relation to the lawyer's land-buying activities are unproven and could be based purely on hypothetical imaginings on the narrator's part, but the reader takes it on trust that these statements are true. A pilgrimage is evidently a democratic activity, but the lawyer does not represent a democratic order and the ironic tone of the narrator perhaps highlights this. The lawyer's words are reported as 'wise', but the reader is not allowed to hear the lawyer speak in the passage under consideration. His story, when he tells it, is one of justice being meted out by the gods and, given the evidence in the narrator's portrait, the reader may be inclined to wonder whether this is how the lawyer imagines his own position in society. The use of irony or satire means taking a stance in relation to the character and it does seem that the narrator is acting as a moral judge. The pilgrims of *The Canterbury Tales* represent sections of Chaucer's society and they all come under the scrutiny of a narrator who is a long way from being impartial.

There is a conflict between the narrator's position as pilgrim and the extent of knowledge possessed about the other travellers, as is clearly demonstrated in the passage describing the lawyer. I understood the focalizer to be the voice of Chaucer's pilgrim, and the narrator to be the voice who presents all the information not available to the focalizer. This is one and the same voice, however: what is presented here is an internal focalizer with the attributes of an external focalizer who can penetrate the consciousness of the focalized. The pilgrim is one of the characters and therefore should be limited to external observations and restricted knowledge of the other characters, but this is not the case. The *focalized* is both internal and external which means that Chaucer's pilgrim can provide the reader with the same kind of information that would be available to an omniscient narrator. Rimmon-Kenan notes that focalization and narration are separate in first-person *retrospective* narratives (2002: 74), which could account for the stance presented here if the time of narration could be confidently asserted, but *The Canterbury Tales* remains unfinished and without an ending, the reader cannot know whether or not the relation of this pilgrimage is synchronous with events as they unfold.

In the pilgrim's description of the lawyer it is possible that what is presented is two separate views of the lawyer's reputation, because there certainly seems to be the expression of a collective voice in line 318: 'So greet a purchasour was nowher noon'. Lines 309-317 show the lawyer as a professional man and a wise judge, whereas lines 318-327 paint a different picture - the lawyer as land-grabbing opportunist who makes use of his legal knowledge to ensure that no protest against his large-scale purchase of land is possible. If this view were accepted, it may be possible to argue for two different focalizers: an internal focalizer for lines 309-317 and an external focalizer for lines 318-327. The portrait ends with an external focalizer who describes the details of the lawyer's dress in lines 328-330, but this placing of such a description is calculated. It does not come at the beginning of the portrait as one might have expected, but appears after the reader has learned of the lawyer's acquisition of land through his legal know-how, and in the light of this knowledge, the reader may feel inclined to consider this modest dress as a disguise or a mask rather than a mark of humility on the lawyer's part; as previously stated, the lawyer's silk belt decorated with stripes functions symbolically as the bars which exclude others not of the same status from an impenetrable 'club'. It is strange that the narrating pilgrim should so decidedly clam up over the lawyer's appearance ('Of his array telle I no lenger tale') when some very pointed insinuations have already been made about his methods of buying land. It is notable also that the lawyer does not wear his purse on his belt as many of the other pilgrims do; his wealth does not lie in coinage, but in the knowledge of legal cases and judicial decisions that allows him to manipulate the law for his own purposes.

The voice of the focalizer intrudes into this short portrait at three points: in lines 313, 322 and 330. The use of 'semed' in lines 313 and 322 suggests that the inner state of the focalized is implicit by external behaviour (Rimmon-Kenan, 2002: 82), and the modality of these two lines casts doubt on the portrait painted: the lawyer only *seems* to be wise and his apparent busyness is flatly contradicted. In sum, there is a very clear ideological stance from which the lawyer is assessed. The modality of the pilgrim's interjections suggests that there is reason to doubt the lawyer's integrity, and the structure of the portrait places the lawyer's professional work in direct juxtaposition with his activities as a 'purchasour'; these activities fall no doubt within the law, but it is clearly intimated in the assertion that no one would stand a chance of questioning these land-purchases that there is something distasteful or perhaps immoral about the way in which the transactions are performed. The spatiotemporal orientation is fairly easy to pinpoint - that of Chaucer's pilgrim - but the source of the psychological and ideological orientation is much more complicated. In recognising this, however, the reader becomes more attuned to the satire of *The Canterbury Tales* and is far less likely to take the text at face value without question.

Gulliver's Travels is another satirical work, but by way of contrast, the narrator-focalizer is very much internal. In fact, this text is perhaps one of those for which 'it is debatable whether we need to posit a focalizer *position* distinct from the narratorial one' (Toolan, 2001: 63). Gulliver's point of view is represented throughout, and the satirical intent of the work is therefore displaced up a level - the satirist is Swift, the author, not Gulliver, the narrator-focalizer. The focalizer is internal, and the *focalized* external. Everything is rendered from Gulliver's viewpoint as and when he encounters each new event, and as such, he is the spatiotemporal 'zero point'. In terms of Rimmon-Kennan's analysis, the perceptual facets of space and time are both internal (limited and synchronous); the cognitive element of the psychological facet is internal (restricted); and the emotive element of the psychological facet is also internal (subjective and involved). The ideological facet is more complicated: the text functions as a satire on another text (Defoe's *Robinson Crusoe*) and as a blistering attack on humankind in general. *Gulliver's Travels* is not to be read in the same way as *Robinson Crusoe*, because the story related could not possibly be true. Defoe's novel stretches credibility, but it is not the fantasy that Swift's work represents. For Swift, Gulliver's voyages are a way of exploring the true subject: the shortcomings of human beings and human society.

In analysing this short passage from Swift's novel, I found Emmott's contextual frame theory to be rather more fruitful than the analysis based on focalization and point of view, and Emmott's theory threw up a very intriguing question in relation to a proleptic statement which I shall discuss shortly.

As is the case in *Robinson Crusoe*, the distance travelled by the hero and the time taken to do so are carefully documented, thereby suggesting a kind of map and a hint that the reader may be able to mimic the journey undertaken if inclined to do so. When Gulliver awakes after the shipwreck, he is quite literally bound into the frame. He can only see the sky, but the reader can see him and the 'Ligatures' that bind him to the ground. (Gulliver's hair is also tied down, and according to Emmott's framework, the statement that Gulliver's hair is long and thick is the only piece of non-episodic information throughout the passage; the remainder is specific to the frame in question and is therefore episodic in nature.) At this point, and consistent with the internal narrator-focalizer, the contents of the frame are limited entirely to what Gulliver himself can see, feel and hear. The Lilliputian who first climbs onto Gulliver's left leg is bound into the frame when Gulliver becomes aware of him, but because Gulliver cannot see the Lilliputian, the reader's first assumption may well be that the small man is some kind of insect. When the other Lilliputians follow, the reader accepts Gulliver's conjecture that these beings are more of the same and binds them into the frame accordingly. Gulliver does the only thing he can do and shouts aloud, which startles the Lilliputians and causes them to jump off. This leads to a proleptic moment in the text: 'and some of them, *as I was afterwards told*, were hurt with the Falls they got by leaping from my Sides upon the Ground' (my emphasis). In the context of Emmott's framework, this prolepsis is extremely interesting. The reader will create a frame, but personal expectations will dictate what frame is created. Clearly Gulliver survives the current episode, but what does the reader imagine will happen next? If Gulliver is being reprimanded for hurting the Lilliputians who fell, is he still in danger? Is he still in shackles? The 'telling' of 'as I was afterwards told' is reported in the passive voice, so the reader does not know who is doing the telling and in what context. This allows for many imaginative possibilities. Any frame that the reader forms of Gulliver's future at this point must be integral to that particular reader's narrative expectations and perhaps also their hopes concerning the character of Lemuel Gulliver.

List of references

Chaucer, G. (1988) The Riverside Chaucer. L. Benson. Ed. Oxford: Oxford University Press.

Emmott, C. (1997) Narrative Comprehension: A Discourse Perspective. Oxford: Oxford University Press.

Rimmon-Kenan, S. (2002) Narrative Fiction. 2nd ed. London: Routledge.

Swift, J. (1967, 1726) Gulliver's Travels. J. Chalker & P. Dixon. Eds. London: Penguin.

Toolan, M. (2001) Narrative: A Critical Linguistic Introduction. 2nd ed. London: Routledge.

Passages in full

Geoffrey Chaucer *The Canterbury Tales*

General Prologue lines 309-330: The Sergeant of the Law

309 A Sergeant of the Lawe, war and wys,

310 That often hadde been at the Parvys,

311 Ther was also, ful riche of excellence.

312 Discreet he was and of greet reverence -

313 He semed swich, his wordes were so wise.

314 Justice he was ful often in assise,

315 By patente and by pleyn commissioun.

316 For his science and for his heigh renoun,

317 Of fees and robes hadde he many oon.

318 So greet a purchasour was nowher noon:

319 Al was fee symple to hym in effect;

320 His purchasyng myghte nat been infect.

321 Nowher so bisy a man as he ther nas,

322 And yet he semed bisier than he was.

323 In termes hadde he caas and doomes alle

324 That from the tyme of kyng William were falle.

325 Therto he koude endite and make a thyng,

326 Ther koude no wight pynche at his writyng;

327 And every statut koude he pleyn by rote.

328 He rood but hoomly in a medlee cote,

329 Girt with a ceint of silk, with barres smale;

330 Of his array telle I no lenger tale.

Jonathan Swift *Gulliver's Travels*

I lay down on the Grass, which was very short and soft, where I slept sounder than ever I remember to have done in my Life, and as I reckoned, above nine Hours; for when I awaked, it was just Day-light. I attempted to rise, but was not able to stir: For as I happen'd to lye on my Back, I found my Arms and Legs were strongly fastened on each side to the Ground; and my Hair, which was long and thick, tied down in the same manner. I likewise felt several slender Ligatures across my Body, from my Armpits to my Thighs. I could only look upwards, the Sun began to grow hot, and the Light offended mine Eyes. I heard a confused Noise about me, but in the Posture I lay, could see nothing except the Sky. In a little Time I felt something alive moving on my left Leg, which advancing gently forward over my Breast, came almost up to my Chin; when bending mine Eyes downwards as much as I could, I perceived it to be a human Creature not six Inches high, with a Bow and Arrow in his Hands, and a Quiver at his Back. In the mean time, I felt at least forty more of the same kind (as I conjectured) following the first. I was in the utmost Astonishment, and roared so loud, that they all ran back in a Fright; and some of them, as I was afterwards told, were hurt with the Falls they got by leaping from my Sides upon the Ground.

Ghost Stories

1: The structure of ghost stories - the punchline

The Scooby Doo stories are an excellent example of how a ghost story can be structured. The stories always follow the same basic pattern with the four narrative phases shown on the graph below. The vertical axis shows the reader/viewer's level of excitement, which you could think of perhaps in terms of your heart rate; thus, your heart rate is highest at the climactic moment of the story. The horizontal axis shows narrative time. (Story time and narrative time are not the same thing, but in the Scooby Doo stories time is mostly linear and we move from the beginning to the end with very little deviation.)

The Scooby Doo Graph

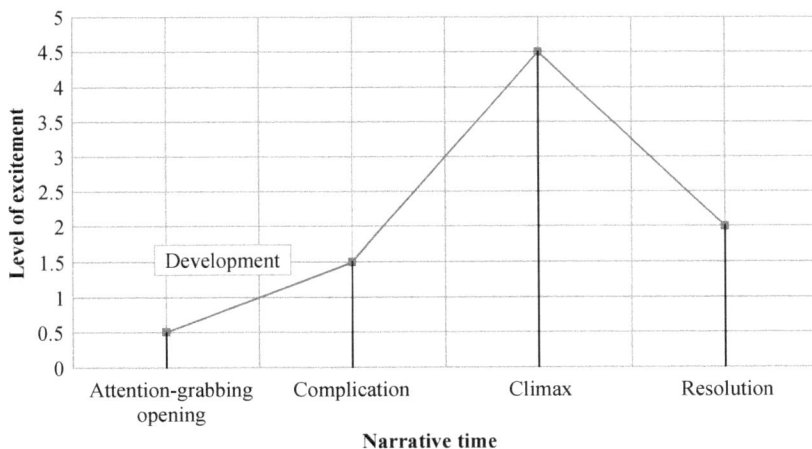

This is how the four narrative phases manifest themselves in a Scooby Doo mystery...

- **The attention-grabbing opening.** We are thrown right into the heart of things with little or no explanation. We see the ghost/monster/vampire etc. in action and lots of terrified people.

- **Following a period of development there comes a complication.** The Scooby Gang arrive in the Mystery Machine and are filled in on what's been going on. They split up and there's a lot of running around before Thelma finds a clue. This is the complication, because it suggests there is an alternative explanation and that the monster may not be what it seems.

- **The climax.** Following a lot more running around and an elaborate plan which goes a bit wrong, the character we saw very briefly at the beginning of the story – usually the janitor/caretaker – is unmasked and revealed as the villain.

- **The resolution.** This is where we get the details, all the Why and the How. Very often we'll see a clip of an earlier event (a flashback within an otherwise linear timeframe), but this time we witness events from a different perspective, which enables us to see what really happened. And then the janitor/caretaker says, 'I would have got away with it if it hadn't been for you meddling kids.' The End.

Not all ghost stories follow this pattern, of course. Many stories containing an element of horror or the supernatural finish at the climax, the high point of the story, and when the reader's level of excitement is at its peak. The stories of Edgar Allan Poe, for example, rarely have a resolution, and end just when the horror is at its most intense. When a short story is structured in this way, the climax is similar to the punchline of a joke: the punchline is delivered at the end of a narrative and the reader is left to fill in the rest of the details in order to arrive at a full understanding of the text. By way of illustration, the following story was presented to me as a joke, but it's really a horror story in miniature:

A man was dragging a small boy through the dark wood in a bitter storm. 'I'm frightened!' wailed the boy. '*You're* frightened?' said the man, 'I've got to come back on my own!'

Once the reader has realised the full implication of the man's words, the response can only be one of horror.

I'll finish with a quick look at how one of Muriel Spark's stories follows the punchline structure. The story is, of course, *The Girl I Left Behind Me*. The story opens with the I-narrator leaving the office with the tune her boss has been whistling still going round in her head. She catches the bus, all the while feeling invisible amongst the crowd of other tired people returning home for the evening and experiencing a nagging sensation that she has left something behind at the office. When she gets back to her digs, she realises that she cannot bear the thought of the unsavoury repast awaiting her, and the nagging sensation has become so strong now – this is the complication – that she feels she must go back to the office and find out what it is she has left there. She travels on another bus and when she arrives, she finds her own strangled body. The story ends at the climax, with the narrator embracing her body 'like a lover'. At this point, the reader re-evaluates the narrative in what those who study cognitive poetics term a 'frame refresh': now that we know the I-narrator has been a ghost right from the very beginning, we understand how she travelled twice on a bus without paying a fare, why the man whose foot she stood on didn't react, and why she felt invisible in the presence of other people. We can see that the odd behaviour and dream-like state of Mr Letter, her boss, was in fact symptomatic of his murderous instinct rising, and that he was so fascinated by his tie because it is the murder weapon: the narrator last sees Mr Letter 'swinging his tie in his hand, beside [her] desk'. The tune she can hear in her head – the tune her boss was singing – is the last thing she hears before she is murdered. The tunes featured in the story have sinister titles themselves: *Softly, Softly, Turn the Key*, which is what the narrator does first when she enters her digs and again as she re-enters her office, and, of course, *The Girl I Left Behind Me*, which we now understand in its double sense. Outside the story this is probably the title of a romantic ditty, but as part of the text, Mr Letter has left a murdered girl behind him, and the narrator has left a girl behind her in the form of her murdered body.

In conclusion, then, the way in which a ghost story is structured can add to its inherent 'scariness'. The lack of resolution can leave the reader at the most intense part of the narrative. The structure can mimic that of a joke and guide the reader towards a punchline which comes as a chilly shock and necessitates a re-working in the reader's mind of earlier events: Oh! – she was dead all along! (As a final note, Spark re-works this idea on a larger scale in her 1973 novel *The Hothouse by the East River*, in which it is revealed towards the end of the story that *all* the characters are dead, having been killed by a V2 bomb in WWII.)

2: The reader's imagination – filling in the gaps, or Don't Show The Monster

A story or a film is far more frightening if the nasty bits are left to the reader/viewer's imagination. It's far *less* scary if we actually *see* the monster. This is the essential difference between horror and splatterfest: horror is scary, splatterfest is just yuck, featuring gore for gore's sake. So the lesson is, don't *show* us the monster, let us *imagine* it – and I'm going to use three ghost stories to illustrate the effect of letting the reader's imagination do the work.

My starting point is H G Wells' *The Red Room*. In Wells' story, a foolhardy protagonist of the kind you always get in ghost stories has volunteered to spend the night in the Red Room, which is rumoured to be haunted. We meet him *in media res*, in conversation with the three old retainers who wind him up good and proper with their portentous pronouncements of 'It's your own choosing' and 'This night of all nights!' Our hero makes his way to the Red Room along a thoroughly spooky corridor and is duly shut in for the night. Left alone, he conducts the obligatory 'systematic examination of the place', and lights as many candles as he can. He is by now 'in a state of considerable nervous tension' and, just after midnight, the candles begin to go out. The light diminishes as each little flame disappears, and our hero dashes around the room desperately trying to relight the candles. Eventually, every single candle has gone out and the only light in the room comes from the fire in the grate, but as the man moves towards it, the flames dwindle and vanish, leaving our hero in darkness. Terrified, he makes a rush for the door, but he misjudges its location and knocks himself out cold when he bashes into 'some other bulky furniture'. The three retainers find him at dawn and bandage him up. They ask him what he saw in the room and he tells them there is nothing in there, except the Fear (with a capital letter) that he took in there with him: 'Fear that will not have light nor sound, that will not bear with reason, that deafens and darkens and overwhelms. It followed me through the corridor, it fought against me in the room –' One of the retainers, whose words provide the story with its close, insists on believing that the 'Fear' is due to a curse placed upon the 'poor young countess', but my general feeling about this story is that we are being pointed in another direction: we are being shown how powerful the human imagination can be when it is sufficiently worked upon.

In spite of the stories that surround the room concerning a 'timid wife and the tragic end that came to her husband's jest of frightening her', I still believe we should take the young man at his word when he says there is nothing in the room. Remember, he is badly frightened before he has even reached the Red Room. First, he is spooked by the retainers, whose 'very existence was spectral; the cut of their clothing, fashions born in dead brains'. He is further frightened on his journey to the Red Room, startled by the shadow of a 'bronze group', and 'a porcelain Chinaman on a buhl table, whose head rocked silently'. And this is where I come back to the candles: yes, it seems odd that the candles all go out, but we need to bear in mind here that candles will, of course, go out at some stage. They don't last forever. The fact that they apparently go out *simultaneously* is potentially a mark of supernatural intervention, but this too can be explained by the state the young man is in. He is a first-person narrator and our instinct is to trust that which first-person narrators tell us, but it is arguable that by this stage in the story he has become an *unreliable* narrator: because he is so frightened, he is no longer an impartial judge of events. The candles may perhaps be going out simply because they have burned down naturally, and there is no question of their being deliberately extinguished by 'an invisible hand' as the narrator imagines.

What I'd like to do now is to take a look at two more stories, one of which is more successful than the other. Not surprisingly, both stories involve empty houses. Let's begin with the not-so-successful story, *The Empty House* by Algernon Blackwood. The premise is very simple: a chap called Shorthouse agrees to spend the night in a haunted house with his Aunt Julia, who is extremely curious about the house, but too afraid to spend the night there alone: 'Three tenants have come and gone in the last few months, and the house is said to be empty for good now.' Of course, the house was previously the scene of a horrible murder: 'a jealous stableman...had some affair with a servant in the house. One night he managed to secrete himself in the cellar, and when everyone was asleep, he crept upstairs to the servants' quarters, chased the girl down to the next landing, and before anyone could come to the rescue threw her bodily over the banisters into the hall below.' The stableman, we are told, was caught and hanged. Shorthouse and Aunt Julia make their way to the house and, once inside they decide to search the place. At this point, the story is still genuinely scary, and there is one terrifying moment when, having opened some folding doors, Shorthouse and Aunt Julia are making their way upstairs: 'From the room they had left hardly ten seconds before came the sound of doors quietly closing.' This sentence made my blood run cold. Not only is there definitely something in the house with them, but also, whatever it is resents their intrusion. And another thing...it is tangible enough to be able to close a pair of heavy folding doors. This threat is very real.

Unfortunately, the story goes downhill from here. It becomes clear that what Shorthouse and Aunt Julia are going to see is a re-enactment of the murder scene. They have already heard a man cough, and seen a spectral woman, and now they hear 'a sound of rushing feet' before their candle is extinguished – but not before Shorthouse has seen 'a face working with passion; a man's face, dark, with thick features, and angry, savage eyes'. But...well, a man's face isn't scary, is it? And it doesn't really matter how evil-looking the narrator tells me this man's face is, I still think the doors closing on their own is scarier. Shorthouse and Aunt Julia stay in the house long enough to witness the ghostly protagonists act out the murder before rushing back out into the street in terror, but my heart rate had long since returned to normal before this point. I just knew too much to be frightened any longer. Right, so the ghosts of the hanged man and the murder victim act out the murder every night. Ho hum. Got that.

But if you know who the ghosts are – or were – and you know what they're going to do, where's the suspense? It's far more frightening if you have lots and lots of questions and absolutely no answers. That's why W. F. Harvey's *The Clock* is more successful.

The I-narrator of this story is genderless, but for the sake of convenience, I'm going to assume that she's female. So, the narrator is staying with her aunt, and has planned a trip to Lewes. Her aunt has another house-guest, a Mrs Caleb, 'recuperating after a series of domestic upheavals, which had culminated in her two servants leaving her at an hour's notice, without any reason'. The narrator takes a dislike to Mrs Caleb, but agrees to carry out a small errand for her in Lewes: to fetch from Mrs Caleb's house a travelling clock inadvertently overlooked and left behind. Once the narrator has gained access to Mrs Caleb's house, she takes a dislike to that too: it is stuffy and oppressive from having been shut up for twelve days and a monkey puzzle tree obscures a great deal of light, making the rooms gloomier than they might otherwise have been. The clock is eventually located in an older part of the house, 'ticking away merrily'. And this is where it starts to go wrong. Why is the clock still ticking? Why hasn't it wound down? The house has been unoccupied since Mrs Caleb left. The narrator speculates that perhaps it's a fourteen-day clock, but when she tries the winder, she 'had scarcely turned the winding-screw twice when it stopped...the hands had been set in motion probably only an hour or two before'. The narrator is badly frightened – she knows the house to be empty, and yet the clock has undoubtedly been recently wound – and she is just wondering what to do next when she hears a noise. 'It was very faint at first, and seemed to be coming from the stairs. It was a curious noise – not the noise of anyone climbing up the stairs, but...of something hopping up the stairs, like a very big bird would hop.' It gets worse. The noise stops once it reaches the landing, then 'there was a curious scratching noise against one of the bedroom doors, the sort of noise you can make with the nail of your little finger scratching polished wood. Whatever it was, was coming slowly down the corridor, scratching at the doors as it went.'

The narrator has had enough by this stage: she throws open the window and jumps out, taking the clock with her. She decides to go to the police-station to tell them about the open window, but when she looks back, the window has been closed. And we know that she locked the door behind her when she first entered the room containing the clock.

There are no answers. We don't know what it was that was coming up the stairs, or why it had to hop rather than walk. We don't know why it was scratching at the doors – or what it was scratching with. We don't know why it made sure the clock was fully wound. We don't know whether Mrs Caleb knew about this thing, whether that was why the servants left, or whether Mrs Caleb deliberately set a trap for the narrator. We don't know how whatever it was got through a locked door…or why it closed the window.

Again, there is that sense of an intruder in an empty house and the house itself resenting the intrusion, so that everything disturbed is put back where it was by unseen hands. And curiously, the details the narrator gives us in describing the mysterious sounds she can hear *ought* to disperse the tension, because the images used are almost homely – the big bird, the little fingernail against the wood – but this isn't the case. It makes it worse. The big bird hopping becomes in our mind's ear a misshapen monster that drags itself painfully from place to place; the fingernail scratching becomes a talon, or what's left of a finger. Once you start speculating, there's no limit to the number of images and alternative narratives your mind can conjure up. Leave it to the reader's imagination, and something as simple as a clock that is fully wound when it really shouldn't be can be absolutely terrifying.

Adapted from original texts posted to www.auntymuriel.com on 7 and 18 April 2013.

It could have been so good: Daphne du Maurier's *Rebecca*

Rebecca could have been a much better book *if Maxim really had loved Rebecca* and if she really had been everything we believe her to be until we learn the 'truth'*. As a study of jealousy, the first half of this novel is an absolute masterpiece. The second-best second wife, dowdy, timid and self-effacing, believes herself to be in the unenviable position of trying to take the place of a woman who will always be young and beautiful, who will never grow old, and who didn't live long enough for her husband to tire of her. Du Maurier's writing here is absolutely superb. The second wife becomes gradually more and more obsessed with Rebecca, recreating her image and bringing her to life again in many and various situations such as unpacking the valuable china cupid which is later broken. Aided by Mrs Danvers in particular, she constantly compares herself to the beautiful and much-beloved first wife and finds her own self wanting.

But the narrative goes downhill once Maxim spills the beans, and then the story turns into a thriller in which it becomes imperative to demonstrate to the court's satisfaction that Rebecca committed suicide rather than being murdered – which she did, in a way. How much better the book would have been if Rebecca *had* died in a freak boating accident after all, leaving Maxim alone and lovelorn, only to marry again quickly in an attempt to find happiness with another. The second wife would have been driven insane by the knowledge that she could never be another Rebecca, that her husband had been lost to her from the start. The only ending *that* book could have had would be the second not-good-enough wife chucking herself out of the window after all. Much better.

The trick, of course, is *never to show Rebecca*. Her myth mustn't be punctured. It has to be left to the reader/viewer to create their own mental image of the perfect wife for Maxim: tall, slim, elegant, staggeringly beautiful, the perfect hostess; someone who can ride a horse and who knows a lot about china. Rebecca needs to be left out of it entirely, so the reader/viewer can experience the same mental processes as the second Mrs de Winter and is given a free hand to invent an impeccable and irreplaceable Rebecca.

*In recent years, critics have leapt to Rebecca's defence, pointing out that Maxim's version of events must be weighed against his own background and personality; also, Rebecca is dead and cannot speak for herself. I don't know *how far I agree with these arguments because they are written and presented within a theoretical context that has its own agenda, but they do bear some scrutiny and are certainly worth further consideration.*

Adapted from the text originally posted to www.auntymuriel.com on 24 May 2013.

'My little stories like birds bred in cages': the letters and journals of Katherine Mansfield

I've recently written an essay on Katherine Mansfield's short story *The Man Without A Temperament*, and because the details of the story bear so close a resemblance to Mansfield's own illness and exile to warmer climes in order to escape the damp chill of an English winter, I felt I ought to look at some biographical material to see if I could work out what Mansfield really intended when she created the character of Robert Salesby. I couldn't, of course, and it was foolish to try, but if nothing else came of this, I'm glad I looked into Mansfield's journals and letters because they are a delight.

I've since invested in a nicer edition of the journal along with a copy of the notebooks edited by Margaret Scott. The latter is a big heavy book of about 700 pages, because Mansfield was a prolific writer in spite of her frequent comments about not being able to work. Her letters alone run to five volumes. But when I was composing my essay, the only biographical material I had to hand was a copy of the Penguin *Letters and Journals* edited by C K Stead. It's okay. Stead has picked out plenty of good bits and explained the procedure for doing so in the book's Introduction. The material is organised by location and date, so the Contents page provides at a glance a record of Mansfield's movements between frosty England and various warm riviera-type places before she underwent treatment for her tuberculosis in Switzerland and finally died of a pulmonary haemorrhage at the age of 34 in Fontainebleau. Given the extent of Mansfield's written output, Stead's volume is a slim one, and although the various sections are held together with biographical notes (printed *in italics*, which is unnecessary and annoying), it's sometimes quite hard to follow who's who and what's going on. A few more footnotes definitely wouldn't have gone amiss, or even a list of 'characters' at the front and their relation to Mansfield. In general, readers don't like having to stop every three minutes in order to flick back through the pages to find out who such-and-such is, or to verify that a particular passage comes from a journal entry and not a letter to John Middleton Murry. Nevertheless, it's a book worth having, especially when one considers that I only paid £1.99 for it in a charity shop.

Obviously one of the chief pleasures in reading a book like this is finding a tart description of another writer. It's like coming across a character you think you already know and then finding out that you don't after all. Virginia Woolf, for example, was jealous of Mansfield's writing - apparently the only writing

Woolf was ever jealous of - but although the two women were on very friendly terms, Mansfield didn't always return Woolf's admiration. She reviewed *Night and Day* in 1919, and wrote to Murry:

> ...I am reviewing Virginia to send tomorrow. It's devilish hard. Talk about intellectual snobbery - her book *reeks* of it. (But I can't say so.) You would dislike it. You'd never read it. It's so long and so tāhsōme...

Letter to J M Murry, 13 November 1919

Mansfield had travelled through wartime France early in 1918 and saw at first hand the devastation caused by years of conflict. She felt that Woolf's book was 'a lie in the soul...the novel can't just leave the war out'. In a letter to Murry dated 10 November 1919, she wrote that 'I feel in the *profoundest* sense that nothing can ever be the same - that, as artists, we are traitors if we feel otherwise: we have to take [the war] into account and find new expressions, new moulds for our new thoughts and feelings'.

Mansfield and Murry were also friends with D H Lawrence and his wife Frieda, although the relationship was not always harmonious. Mansfield did not like Frieda at all: 'F. is such a liar... To my face she is all sweetness. She used to bring me in flowers, tell me how "exquisite" I was'. Lawrence himself was extremely difficult owing to his volatile temper, and in a letter to S S Koteliansky written in May 1916, from which the quotation above is taken, Mansfield describes a physical fight between Lawrence and Frieda that left Mansfield feeling 'furiously angry'.

> [Lawrence] is so completely in her power and yet I am sure that in his heart he loathes his slavery. She is not even a good natured person really; she is evil hearted and her mind is simply riddled with what she calls 'sexual symbols'.

The friendship between the two couples broke down completely when Lawrence wrote to Mansfield in February 1920 as follows: 'I loathe you. You revolt me stewing in your consumption'. Mansfield's response was to write directly to Murry, beseeching him never again to defend Lawrence or to publish good reviews of Lawrence's work in Murry's paper, *The Athenaeum*.

Mansfield read everything she could get her hands on, and she offers a comment on Thomas Hardy's *The Well-Beloved*. I found it amusing, chiefly because I'm no fan of Hardy's work myself.

It really is *appallingly bad, simply rotten* - withered, bony and pretentious... The style is so PREPOSTEROUS, too. I've noticed that before in Hardy occasionally - a pretentious, snobbish, schoolmaster vein..., an 'all about Berkeley Squareishness,' too... I hope to God he's ashamed of it now at any rate.

Letter to J M Murry, 5 June 1918

But my favourite has to be Mansfield's judgement on poor old E M Forster, who, in her opinion,

> never gets any further than warming the teapot. He's a rare fine hand at that. Feel this teapot. Is it not beautifully warm? Yes, but there ain't going to be no tea.

Journal, May 1917

I'll leave it there for this post, which is a tad unfair to Mansfield because I realise I've made it look as if her journal and personal correspondence amounts to nothing more than a catalogue of catty comments about other authors, but there is so much more to her writing than that. She was living in 'interesting times' and fighting a losing battle with consumption. She faced death alone, separated from her husband and in exile from both her native land (New Zealand) and her adopted homeland (England). She battled every day with intense bodily suffering and died while still in her early thirties, but she left behind eighty-eight marvellous short stories as well as her journal and a voluminous output of letters and literary reviews. She had an enormous thirst for life and chastised herself for being afraid when her illness intervened to prevent her from embracing life as she felt she ought. Using a metaphor usually reserved for the journey into death, she wrote to Murry in October 1920:

> We resist, we are terribly frightened. The little boat enters the dark fearful gulf and our only cry is to escape - 'put me on land again'. But it's useless. Nobody listens. The shadowy figure rows on. One ought to sit still and uncover one's eyes.

Mansfield died a little over two years later, in January 1923, depriving the literary world of one of its most talented voices, and one which doubtless had much more to say...but her short time had run out.

Originally posted to www.auntymuriel.com on 7 February 2016.

The missing enactor in *Our Spoons Came From Woolworths*

There are quite a few reviews for *Our Spoons Came From Woolworths* online, all largely focused on the same points. To begin with, the book's reviewers claim that it is mostly autobiographical in spite of its disclaimer, and there is certainly more than a passing similarity between the life of the fictional Sophia and that of her creator. Both married a fellow artist, both suffered extreme poverty, both left their husbands and worked as part of the domestic staff in a country house. However, the disclaimer states that:

> The only things that are true in this story are the wedding and Chapters 10, 11 and 12 and the poverty.

My feeling is that it's probably best not to overdo the biographical reading, especially as the author Barbara Comyns has asked you not to. But – and this is another point on which all the reviews agree – Comyns is plain in her wish that special attention be paid to the three chapters mentioned. These chapters deal with the birth of her first child and the absolutely appalling treatment to which she was subjected. Her fictional counterpart, Sophia, is only 21 years old and extremely frightened. In fact, and in reference to the reviews again, Sophia seems initially to have a fairly hazy notion of how babies are created in the first place and certainly has no idea how to prevent conception:

> I had a kind of idea if you controlled your mind and said 'I won't have any babies' very hard, they most likely wouldn't come. I thought that was what was meant by birth-control.

The blame for her repeated pregnancies is laid very squarely at her door by her husband Charles and his awful mother, Eva:

> She didn't seem to think it was Charles' baby – only mine, because later on, when I was upstairs putting on my coat, she kissed me quite kindly, but spoilt it by saying 'I shall never forgive you, Sophia, for making my son a father at twenty-one.'

How dismal it must have been to be female in the 1930s. And this is before the NHS, of course, so to add insult to injury, Sophia had to find the money to pay for her wretched hospital birth. Once admitted, she is given an enema and a 'large dose of castor oil', which combine to render her helpless with sickness and diarrhoea. The nurses reprimand her every time she makes a mess and accuse her of having 'disgusting habits'. Sophia begins to feel that she has committed a criminal act in having a baby and is humiliated by the whole depressing experience:

> they made me put my legs in kind of slings that must have been attached to the ceiling; besides being very uncomfortable it made me feel dreadfully ashamed and exposed. People would not dream of doing such a thing to an animal.

Of course, the ghastly Charles can barely tolerate the child at all. Sophia tells us that: 'I felt I had most unreasonably brought some awful animal home, and that I was in disgrace for not taking it back to the shop where it came from.'

The story of Sophia's early life is a woeful one, but apart from the chapters discussed here so far, it is told with such lightness of touch and such humour that it is a very amusing book. I wondered how this could have been achieved and pondered the sense of temporal distance that characterises the novel. I had already noted the lack of direct speech which Sophia herself comments on at the beginning of chapter nine: there is indeed some direct speech, but mostly the reader is following Sophia's own account of events, and spoken utterances are generally rendered in indirect speech as they are filtered through Sophia's voice. Sophia relates her tale to us exactly as she does to her friend Helen, which gives us the framing device for the story. There is slightly more to it than this, however. My understanding of the novel is that the distance is created because there is no second Sophia, the Sophia-narrator of the past. There is only the Sophia of the present, which explains why everything can be told so simply, with emotional reactions boiled down to bald statements such as 'I felt very sad' or 'I was happy'. While the Sophia of the present day can remember that at such-and-such a period she was indeed very happy or very sad, she cannot describe her emotions as fully as she would have done at the time.

To clarify this further, let's consider another semi-autobiographical novel such as *David Copperfield*. There are at least two narrators: the David of the present day, the one who is telling the story, and the David of the past, the one who is living the story. These two Davids are the same character, but two different enactors, because they exist in different time periods, and one is older and knows much more than the other. But when the events of the novel are described, they are told from the younger David's point of view and presented to the reader as the events are being experienced. And this, it seems to me, is the difference between Comyns' novel and the conventions of biographical novels that one has come to expect. The tale is told by the present-day Sophia and there is no younger Sophia-enactor. This would account for the ever-present sense of distance.

The novel by no means suffers as a result of this device, however. On the contrary, it is refreshing – and no less emotionally charged for not giving way to lengthy lamentation. The reader is a human being after all and is perfectly well equipped to imagine how Sophia must have felt without having it carefully spelt out.

Adapted from the text originally posted to www.auntymuriel.com on 21 February 2016.

Acknowledgements

My thanks, as always, to Roy Booth for his enthusiasm for my writing and his unwavering support of this project. Thanks are also due to everyone whose financial contributions to the crowdfunder made this book possible, with a special mention for the first contributor, James Byrnes.

Given that two sections of the book comprise work done for two Master's Degrees, I would like to thank my tutors: Rose Lovell-Smith, Jim Miller, and Mark Amsler in Auckland, and all the many and various tutors who taught modules on the MA in Literary Linguistics at the University of Nottingham. In addition, I owe thanks to the staff and students at Cheviot Area School in New Zealand who participated in my tourist/traveller survey. The tables based on Paul Simpson's work have been reproduced or adapted with the publisher's permission, likewise Paul Kidby's symbol for the Summoning Dark. Finally, my heartfelt thanks are due to Rachael Ball and Stephen Collins, who very kindly allowed me to reproduce their work at no cost to myself, for which I am extremely grateful.

INDEX

H

- *The Pupil*	22fn
Jane Eyre (Charlotte Brontë)	241fn, 132
Jardine, Penelope	152
joke	32, 119-120, 340-341
Joyce, James	37, 320-321
- *Araby*	21fn, 37

K

Kafka, Franz (*The Trial*)	16fn, 110-114
Kesey, Ken (*One Flew Over the Cuckoo's Nest*)	63fn, 88fn
Keyes, Daniel (*Flowers for Algernon*)	34-35
Khayyam, Omar (*The Rubaiyat*)	120, 227, 234
Killers, The (Ernest Hemingway)	22
King Lear (William Shakespeare)	119fn
Kristeva, Julia	226, 228-229

L

Lawrence, D. H.	
- and Katherine Mansfield	349
- *Odour of Chrysanthemums*	22fn
Leech, Geoffrey	21
- and Mick Short, *Style in Fiction*	4, 22, 27fn, 30fn, 37, 40fn, 43-44, 52, 61-63, 67, 76fn, 85, 93, 99, 107, 110, 115-116, 263-264, 267, 290
legends	232
levels of narration	248, 320
lexical items, lexical choice (see also word meaning)	27fn, 32, 35, 43-44, 52, 104, 115fn, 124, 204, 265, 269
Lighter Than My Shadow (Katie Green)	250, 320-321
limitations of language	252
linearity of reading process	317
linguistic competence	117

U

Uncanny Valley	314
ungrammaticalities	231
unity of time	213
universal minds checklist (see also Alan Palmer)	201
unreliable narrator	169, 239, 342
Uspensky, Boris	82, 83fn, 87, 88fn

V

vampires	78-79, 172, 305, 339
vectors (focalization)	209-211, 214
verbalisation processes	131
verbo-visual narrative (see also comics)	214, 317-324
Verfremdungseffekt (Bertolt Brecht)	155, 159
Vikings	218-222
Visit, A (Shirley Jackson)	239-245
visual and verbal tracks	253
visual imagery	262
visual language	255
visual metaphor	271
visual modality	276
visual perspective	209, 280
visual storytelling	247
visual vocabulary	286
vocabulary choices (see also word meaning)	328
voice	15fn, 47, 51, 56, 61, 64, 66, 69-73, 75, 77-79, 82, 87, 93, 97, 100, 166-167, 170, 173, 177, 184, 186, 195, 203, 210, 212, 223-224, 228-229, 234, 236, 267, 279, 285, 302, 329-334, 336, 352
voice-over	262, 283, 302, 310, 321-322
Voices at Play (Muriel Spark)	165
Voyeur, Le (Alain Robbe-Grillet)	175

W

XYZ

Milton Keynes UK
Ingram Content Group UK Ltd.
UKHW050929180724
445734UK00010B/186